Tarnished Crown

Also by Carol Flake:

REDEMPTORAMA

TARNISHED CROWN

THE QUEST FOR A RACETRACK CHAMPION

Carol Flake

DOUBLEDAY & COMPANY, INC.
GARDEN CITY, NEW YORK
1987

Library of Congress Cataloging-in-Publication Data

Flake, Carol.
  Tarnished crown.

  Includes index.
  1. Chief's Crown (Racehorse) 2. Racehorses—United
States—Biography. 3. Horse racing—United States.
I. Title.
SF355.C45F54 1987   798.4'3'0973   86-19878
ISBN 0-385-19775-6

To John, always my hopeful, and
to Sir Quasar, my fallen knight

Tarnished Crown

"O! for a horse with wings!"
—William Shakespeare, *Cymbeline*

INTRODUCTION

The Hopeful

In the spring of 1984, I stopped worrying about culture and politics, about bombs and computers, and I began looking for a horse: not a horse to buy or even to ride, but a horse who would give me a quick getaway nonetheless. I was looking for a champion: a beast with a destiny, a horse who had been born in a year of biotech businesses and trivial pursuit, of space shuttles and designer jeans, who would somehow charge through all the clutter and emerge a hero.

The horse I was looking for was not an animal who could pull a plow or a carriage, who could prance in a show ring, who could cut cows from a herd. By birth and training, he would be able to do only one thing. He would be able, however, to do it better than any other kind of animal; he would be able to do it better than any other breed of horse; and better still than 99.9 percent of his own breed. He would be able to run very fast, carrying a human on his back.

Like nearly everybody involved with the business and sport of horse racing, I was looking for a thoroughbred who could win the Kentucky Derby.

This quest, however, had as much to do with Walter Farley, Robin Leach and Boethius as with Secretariat. It had something to do with the deep, mythic bond between human and horse; it had to do with America's morbid fascination with wealth and fame; and it also had to do with a dark, ironic element of fate that seems to set the world of horse racing apart from other endeavors.

Horse racing may have begun as the sport of kings and gentlemen, but it remains a humbling experience for most of those involved in it. Racing is a ride on the wheel of fortune, where money counts, but where neither wealth, hard work, nor social standing is any guarantee of success.

My quest for a Derby horse was a return, with a twist, to the dreams of my youth.

As a kid, I had never owned a real horse of my own, only an improvised hobby horse, a broomstick and stuffed sock, with a leather belt for reins and shreds of yarn sewed on for a mane. But that broomstick was my Bucephalus, on which I conquered the neighborhood; I was a centaur, both horse and rider, both beast and master. Sometimes I would run away with myself.

When I learned to read, I devoured anything that had to do with horses—my father's old collection of Will James books about the West, biographies of great racehorses like Exterminator and Black Gold, and of course Walter Farley's Black Stallion series. Farley's rogue stallion, an animal too fierce to be ridden by anyone except his young friend Alec, had little to do with the cute and cuddly creatures of the animal kingdom usually portrayed in children's books; he was something out of myth, more heroic than any human protagonist. And, it must be admitted, he was sexy: "His mane was like a crest, mounting, then falling low. His neck was long and slender, and arched to the small, savagely beautiful head. The head was that of the wildest of all wild creatures—a stallion born wild—and it was beautiful, savage, splendid." What's more, the Black could put his wildness to good use; he could win races.

All that wild splendor seemed too grand for the quiet little town where I grew up; it belonged to another world somewhere, another world I might find someday. A fast horse, I thought, could really take you places.

In the meantime I tried to get it all down on paper. Over and over, I tried to draw the ineffably regal and spirited creatures I dreamed about. Like the cave paintings at Lascaux, they were ritual beasts—magic animals that held the key to power and success.

Sometimes, when I was bored or lonely, I would conjure up an image of the perfect horse, the creature I could never get right on paper. When we would set out on long trips to my grandmother's farm in East Texas in the family station wagon, I would imagine myself riding alongside the car on my wild steed; sometimes I would become the horse rather than the rider, trying to imagine what it would be like to run that fast, so fast that the wind would bring tears to my eyes.

My grandmother had long since sold all her horses, so my only riding experiences had been on pony rides at various carnivals and fairs. The reins were always tied down, and the ponies were trained to plod calmly around a circle, so there wasn't much challenge involved. But a couple of times I managed to undo the restraints, and I had the ponies trotting snappily, their fat little bellies bouncing, before the irate managers could catch me.

One day, when I was nine years old or so, a horse magically appeared in my grandmother's cow pasture: a big, shaggy colt with a piece of rope tied around his neck. I suggested to my friend Andrea, who had come along for her first visit to a farm, that we hop on the horse and go for a ride. We searched in vain for a bridle in the cobwebbed tack room in the abandoned barn where my grandparents had once stabled their draft horses. That was enough to discourage Andrea, who was always a sensible sort. But I felt certain that the horse had somehow materialized on the farm as an answer to my nightly prayers, and I was destined to ride him. I convinced Andrea that I was a terrific rider, an Indian-style veteran who had no need of saddle, bridle, or bit. Lugging an old milk-stool up beside the horse, who was grazing peacefully, I clambered aboard. Andrea climbed up behind me, and with a whoop we were off.

The horse moved directly into a gallop without benefit of a walk or trot, and we headed directly toward the barbed wire fence at the far end of the pasture. I clung to his mane, and Andrea clung to my waist. The horse was running flat out, like a racehorse, and the going was remarkably smooth, despite clumps of tall grass and weeds that loomed up along the way. When we seemed certain to crash into the fence, I yanked the horse's mane to the left, and he spun around neatly, executing a hairpin about-face. I hung on, but Andrea let go of my waist and went flying into the fence.

The strange horse and I galloped around and around the pasture, until he wearied of the game and slowed to a walk. Andrea had extricated herself from the fence and gone for help. When my grandmother arrived, after daubing Andrea liberally with Mercurochrome, she told me that the horse I had commandeered was her neighbor's champion cutting horse, an extremely valuable quarter horse trained to herd cattle by running very fast and making very sharp turns.

And so it was that my dream horse proved to be as real as my friend's wounds. Unknowingly, I had encountered my first blood-and-money horse—a well-bred horse whose speed meant risk, whose ability meant gain. A horse who gave you the edge.

What was it that horses represented to me? Part of it undoubtedly was the kind of sublimated sexuality that makes men smile knowingly when you talk about girls and horses. A lot of young girls do "grow out" of their horse fever when they get interested in boys—hence the stereotyped notion, as poet Maxine Kumin has described it, that "girl children long to sit astride the muscular power and rhythmic motion of a horse out of deep sexual urges," a longing that eventually is redirected "toward its natural object of fulfillment, the adolescent boy." Horses, in a sense, suggest to a young girl the kind of sensual intimacy that might exist between living beings, a relationship based on body language—on touch and trust.

Horses, however, also represented another impulse as primal as sex—a desire to be linked to the natural world. To be linked with an element of wildness, and yet to retain a measure of control.

Farley's proud horses, forever wild, suggested the kind of primal power D. H. Lawrence had been so obsessed by: "Horses, always horses . . . You were a lord if you had a horse. Far back, far back in our dark soul the horse prances. He is a dominant symbol: he gives us lordship . . . And as a symbol he roams the dark underworld meadows of the soul." Without the horse, Lawrence felt, man had lost touch with something vital and became diminished: "Within the last fifty years man has lost the horse. Now man is lost. Man is lost to life and power—an underling and a wastrel."

I think horses meant the same thing to me that "horsepower" did to many boys and men—they meant freedom. Like the spotted horses that ran amok in Faulkner's *The Hamlet,* the horses that roamed my imagination challenged the boundaries between the "wild" and the "domestic."

Prancing and snorting on the edges of our consciousness, like vestiges of a myth, certain horses seem to suggest a means of venturing out into the world and conquering it. And racehorses, with their inordinate will to win, represent the ultimate symbol of worldly longing. With racehorses, whether you own them, watch them, or bet on them, you seem to be reverting to some older, darker way of looking at the world, a way of testing your fate, of finding your place in the scheme of things.

Horses can be great equalizers. Put a short man on a horse, and you have a king, a conqueror, or a jockey; Louis XIV, Napoleon, or Willie Shoemaker. According to a medieval bestiary dating from the twelfth century, *equus,* the Latin word for horse, is derived from a word meaning "level" or equal. But as the bestiary's anonymous monk goes on to explain, horses, like their masters, want to win: "The spiritedness of horses is great. They exult in battlefields; they sniff the combat; they are excited to fight by the sound of the trumpet . . . They are miserable when conquered and delighted when they have won." Consequently horses have also been a means and a symbol of lordship.

As Diana Vreeland put it in an explanatory note to her 1985 "Man and the Horse" exhibit at New York's Metropolitan Museum, "A man mounted on his horse is twice the man he is on the ground." Virtually the entire exhibit was given over to the engraved armor, the tricorne hats, the whips, the crops, the crested livery and the racing silks that have made the horse a mount of the ruling class.

The Arabian horse had given Muslims the means to conquer North Africa and to invade southern Europe, while the invention of the stirrup gave Charles Martel and his Franks a means to defeat them at the beginning of the age of chivalry—an age inspired by the horse. And eventually the fast, long-winded horses that the British bred by crossing their big, sturdy mares to the light, swift Arabians became the most aristocratic of all horses—the thoroughbred.

A good thoroughbred can still make a commoner a kind of king. Racing in America, which grew out of county fairs, tobacco-field challenges, and wild duels through colonial streets, continued to pay homage to the English stud book—the family Bible of the thoroughbred, in which the pedigree of every thoroughbred in England had been inscribed since 1793. Americans themselves might betray a mongrel pedigree, but their racehorses could trace their ancestry back to the same three foundation sires as their English counterparts. And America named its most famous race after an English peer—Lord Derby, for whom the English Derby had been named in 1771.

Nevertheless, winning the Triple Crown of racing—the Derby, the Preakness, and the Belmont—has become a very American sort of quest, a quest begun by sporting tycoons, the would-be lords of the American turf, and continued in recent years by men and women with new money and new ways of approaching the game. Long before the Super Bowl, the World Series, and the Indianapolis 500, winning the Derby meant reaching the pinnacle of the sports world. And yet, except for the Derby, racing has never attracted the kind of broad public interest that such all-American sports as baseball and football have amassed. Racing, which, after all, involves a form of gambling, has been considered a game of kings and touts, with very little social ground in between. There have always been more Puritans than cavaliers in America.

Racing, too, has had few stars of any longevity to attract a following the way baseball and football do. Every year, racing may have its prodigies—its Dwight Goodens and its Darryl Strawberrys—but its Reggie Jacksons have long since been retired. Except for the great geldings like Kelso, Forego, and John Henry, the best horses are rushed off the track to the breeding shed at age three or four, to "improve the breed," before they can progress from star to legend. Frequently, because they begin running at such a tender age, they retire with the ankles and the knees of disabled veterans.

There was a long, dry spell for equine horses between Native

Dancer, the gray ghost, in 1953, and Secretariat, the chestnut cover boy of three different news magazines when he won the Triple Crown in 1973. And there has been another dry spell since 1980, when the mighty Spectacular Bid went undefeated in his fourth year and the stalwart Genuine Risk became the first filly since Regret, in 1915, to win the Derby.

My own interest in racing, which survived puberty and survived college, had not, however, survived a terrible accident that occurred on the track in 1975. Like millions of other Americans, I had tuned in on a bright July afternoon to watch a match race between Derby winner Foolish Pleasure and Ruffian, the undefeated filly champion. Ruffian, who had won the New York Racing Association's Triple Crown for fillies by a combined total of 25 lengths, was perhaps the greatest filly in the history of American racing. The fillies of her generation had never been able to challenge her, and so it seemed a natural step for her to take on the fastest colt of her generation.

Ruffian had come along at the height of the feminist movement, and she had become a symbol of achievement to many women. And oddly enough, she aroused the kind of resentment among certain men on the track as feminists had in the business community. One trainer was heard to say, "No filly can run that fast; she must be a dyke." And so, in that match race, there were those who were rooting against her, just on principle.

And so, when Ruffian, who was leading the race by half a length near the half-mile pole, snapped her right front ankle in two but kept running, her body propelled, stumbling, in fear and pain, the late Moody Jolley, known on the backstretch as the meanest man in racing, was heard to say, "You throw a fast half-mile at the bitch, and she comes unbuckled." And so, at a subsequent press conference, Moody's son Leroy, the trainer of Foolish Pleasure, did not express his regrets, but said that racing was not for those who wear "short pants."

At the time, Ruffian seemed to symbolize, in the most tragic fashion, what might happen to talented females who tried to keep up with the boys. But in retrospect, I think her death had less to say about feminism than it had to say about racing: about human hubris, which had created a breed of horse so fast, so beautiful, and yet so fragile.

Eventually I learned that men, too, had been affected by Ruffian's death—sportswriters, in particular, who had come to think of her as some kind of super-horse, a vision of strength and grace. Jack Mann, who wrote Ruffian's obituary for the *Horseman's Journal*, and who had stayed up all night after the accident while the vets tried to save her, said that "she was as special as Willie Mays. There was an extra dimension to her." When she had gone out to the track before the race, he said, "she was like a young girl, so strong and fresh. And when they brought her back, she looked like an old lady." He prefaced her obituary with lines from Coleridge's "Epitaph on an Infant":

> Ere Sin could blight or Sorrow fade,
> Death came with friendly care.

Before Ruffian's death, I had ignored the dark side of racing—the toll it takes on horses, on those who love them, on those who depend on them for a living. I had finally learned what racetrackers learn from day one: the pain/payoff quotient. For every winner there are scores of losers; for every victory there is a heavy cost.

With Ruffian, the cost, I think, had been the momentum of the sport. Two years earlier, Secretariat's remarkable achievements had gotten people interested in racing again. But her death had told the public that racing wasn't for people in "short pants." It wasn't, in other words, for those who loved animals; it was for cool-headed gamblers, for professionals who could look at horses as numbers or chances in a lottery. Racing, always precariously balanced between sport and game of chance, seemed to belong now more completely to the world of casinos than to the world of ballparks and playing fields.

Sportswriters who had allowed themselves to get attached to certain horses found themselves backing away. One sportswriter told me that after Ruffian he never again allowed himself to care for a horse. Suddenly a huge audience had learned the hardest lessons racing can teach about the cruelty of fortune, the overreaching nature of man, the fleeting nature of success.

It was not a lesson that mainstream America was interested in learning in such a fashion.

I didn't get interested in horse racing again until the summer after I had lost a job in New York. I had been fired by an elderly bon vivant who scribbled his criticism of my work in purple Magic Marker memos and who would call for his assistant every day before lunch to bring in his raspberry yogurt and to tie a purple bib around his neck. This man and I had different priorities, beginning with our choice of favorite colors. At the time, I was interested in the farm crisis, country music, the political peccadillos of television preachers, while my mauve-mad boss was hot for the latest scandal behind the baffles at the New York City Ballet.

I had climbed my way up from my sleepy Texas hometown into a high-profile New York publishing job, only to find that my real roots and my priorities lay elsewhere.

I had grown uneasy in the trendy cafes and style emporiums of New York, and I dreaded the apotheosis of the upscale, gourmet-kitchen consumers who would later that year be labeled as Yuppies. I dreaded the possibility that I had become part of a poached-peaches-and-Gucci tide. I found myself longing for a world where men with purple Magic Markers had no power, where almond croissants had no cachet.

If I had been younger, and if I had lived in a different time, I might even have thought about running away to the circus. But this was an era when daredevils were dwarfed by their Super Dome arenas, and lion tamers made silly television commercials for American Express.

I had forgotten about the places where grown-ups could still run away, where men and women rode untamed animals, where fortunes could be made in a day.

And so it was that, twenty years after the magic cutting horse had made my fantasies come true, horses came to my rescue again. While recuperating from urban malaise in my rented shack in the Berkshires, I used to drive past a sign proclaiming that horse racing would be taking place for two weeks at the Great Barrington Fair. The setting was wonderful—a small bullring of a track, a rickety grandstand, and a mountain backdrop.

Out of curiosity, my boyfriend and I showed up for the races one afternoon. We didn't buy a *Racing Form*, figuring that the horses were so old and decrepit that knowledge of previous performances would be of little help. Gradually, though, we got hooked on the strange menagerie of animals that filled the backstretch of Great Barrington's fairgrounds, and we found ourselves returning every afternoon.

Some of the horses boasted excellent bloodlines, with sires even I could recognize. There was the gorgeous Zation, a strutting chestnut who looked as though he should be running at Saratoga instead of the fair circuit, but who lacked the lungs and the courage to win even a cheap claiming race; ancient Trumpeter Swan, of royal breeding, who had won some big races and more than a quarter of a million dollars earlier in his career, but who was now grinding it out week by week; the reliable Prince Jac O, who could never have won at a respectable track but who won five in a row at Great Barrington.

This bizarre collection of backyard pets, winded losers and aging veterans astonished me with their courage and willingness. They tore around the track as though their lives depended on it—which, in many cases, it did, since the fairs were the last stop before the glue factory or meat-packing plant for many worn-out horses. The previous year, I learned, a Connecticut plant had cleaned out the fairs to fill a huge demand for canned horsemeat in France.

Thoroughbreds, it seemed to me, had experienced, more than any other creature, the heights and depths of human stewardship. They had played the role of king, king-bearer, or sacrificial lamb, depending on the needs of those who owned them. The world they belonged to seemed an older, more primitive world than the one where I had made my way—a world of quests and exploitation, of great victories and unexpected tragedies. It was a feudal world of lords and serfs, of wealthy owners and track-bound grooms, where one's destiny was determined less by hard work or money than by bloodlines and the whims of fate.

Every day owners and horseplayers alike were trying to beat the odds, trying to make the payoff before the pain or the losses became too great. For every Secretariat, there were a million Zations, and there were a million long shots who never came in. Some horseplayers, however, claimed to have found the clue to all mysteries, the edge that would finally beat the game. And there were newcomers to the sport who were trying to minimize the fateful element of racing, to make it conform to rules of supply and demand, to the cost/benefit models they had learned in business school or in making their fortunes in shipbuilding, oil exploration, computer design. Others were applying the most practical strategy of all—using OPM, Other People's Money, to invest in horses. The sport of kings and tycoons was becoming a business of multiple partnerships and syndicates.

Eventually the horses that had drawn me away from Madison Avenue, to Kentucky and Saratoga, led me back to Wall Street and Seventh Avenue. The marketing of thoroughbreds, like the marketing of art, was a speculative business that depended on brokers who could sell their product to high rollers and investment-seekers on the basis of promise rather than substance. The thoroughbred breeding business depended on the buyer's willingness to gamble, balanced against his desire for a good investment or his desire for prestige.

And yet there was still one great quest, one great dream, that set racing apart from all other pursuits, that kept everything going, from grooms who scraped by on $225 a week to breeders who paid half a million dollars for one mating of a mare to the stallion Northern Dancer. It was the hope for a classic horse—for a fast, precocious two-year-old who would be able at age three to extend his speed for the grueling mile-and-a-quarter of the Derby, the mile-and-three-sixteenths speed trap of the Preakness, and the mile-and-a-half marathon of the Belmont.

I decided that I wanted to be part of such a quest, to hitch a vicarious ride on the wheel of fortune. And so, in the spring of 1984, I began looking for a young thoroughbred with the "look of eagles"; a contender.

My plan was to follow this "chosen" colt for the most crucial year in his life, from his debut as a two-year-old through his campaign for the Triple Crown. The odds of finding such a colt,

I knew, were very high. Out of the 38,483 registered thorough-breds born in 1982, only a dozen or so would make it to the Derby in 1985.

Even choosing a colt that became two-year-old champion would be no guarantee of success. After Spectacular Bid, the only top two-year-old to make it as far as the starting gate of the Derby had been a plucky gelding named Rockhill Native, who never managed to win a big race longer than a mile. And even as I was beginning my search, Devil's Bag, the most promising young horse in recent years, was showing signs of imminent failure; he never made it to the Derby.

I began calling my hypothetical colt the Hopeful, after the big race for two-year-olds at Saratoga that had been won by so many promising young horses who had gone on to prove them-selves: Man o' War, Native Dancer, Nashua, Secretariat, Affirmed.

I knew I was going to have to do a great deal of hoping once I chose my horse. I was going to have to hope that he would stay sound, that he would stay healthy, and that he would stay a contender—three wishes that seldom came true for the owners and trainers of young horses. The stressful, high-stakes road to the Derby tested horses and their handlers alike, and few proved equal to the test.

I was hoping, too, that my chosen horse could help me outdis-tance the deadening ambitions of the overly networked, overly analyzed, and overly jazzercised world from which I had grown so alienated, a world that had lost its connectedness not only to the earth but to the spirit. The Hopeful was to become my getaway horse, a flesh-and-blood hero who would lead me in a quest through the strange, self-enclosed world of the track, a quest for the sense of wildness and wonder I had lost so long ago.

CHAPTER 1

Sufferin' Downs

Beggars mounted run their horse to death.
—William Shakespeare, *King Henry VI*, Part III

THE SEARCH for a great two-year-old colt at the racetrack was
something like the search for a hot tip on the stock market.
Those who were in the know were not always willing to share
their information, and those who didn't know were always generous with their advice.

Possession of a good thing at the track inspired conflicting
impulses—toward secrecy and toward hype. On one hand, a hot
unraced colt could be the means of a major betting coup if his
prowess were kept secret. Trainers frequently went to great
lengths to disguise their young speedsters, including rigged
workouts in the morning to fool the clockers. When Ruffian, for
example, made her first start, against a well-bred filly named
Suzest, trained by the garrulous Woody Stephens, Stephens was
said to have bet on his filly and to have advised his friends to do
the same. Ruffian's laconic trainer, Frank Whiteley, however,
had kept mum. And so when Ruffian took the lead and romped

effortlessly to a 15-length victory in track-record time, she paid $10.40 for each two-dollar ticket that had been wagered on her to win.

On the other hand, it was hard for most people to keep a secret at the track; the urge to boast of a fast two-year-old was as great as the desire of the minister in the Greek fable to tell the world that King Midas had the ears of a donkey. The minister in question, bursting with his secret, had dug a hole into which he poured his knowledge, and the leaves of the tree which grew up in the same spot were soon whispering the secret to the breeze. At the track, one whisper to one horseplayer was sufficient, and the dark horse was suddenly the favorite. Few Woody Stephens first-time starters, in fact, went to post at odds greater than 2 to 1. The previous year, when eventual two-year-old champion Devil's Bag made his debut in August, he had been the worst-kept secret on the Saratoga backstretch.

And so, as I began to ask every owner and trainer and track veterinarian I met if they knew of any good two-year-olds, they would either go poker-faced or smile and nod smugly. I soon accumulated a list of long shots which, when I perused it a year later, turned out to be mostly a compendium of also-rans and broken dreams. Where was Moon Prospector, the fast colt who had almost equaled Belmont Park's track record for five furlongs in his first start in June? Where was Beat Me Daddy, the colt who won the Tremont Stakes at Belmont, the first major two-year-old race of the year?

I realized early on in my search that sure things were as rare at the track as reliable sources, and that I would have to find my own way of fighting the laws of probability.

The first thing I had learned about racing was to respect the odds. Whether the track was Great Barrington or Belmont, the odds were the barometer that you ignored at your peril. Although I had always been a sucker for the long shot, for the implausible plodder who might suddenly wake up to the talent lodged deep in genetic memory, the crowd favorites at Great Barrington came in at a rate of 40 percent; at other tracks, the average was around 33 percent. The lesson I learned was that there were few big surprises in racing, and few Cinderella stories, particularly out in the boondocks. Horses established their "class" early on in their careers, and they seldom ran above it. Racetracks, too, had their "class" system, reflecting the quality of horses stabled there; at the bottom were the fairs, and at the top were the big tracks of New York and California.

Although I harbored fantasies of discovering a Cinderella horse out in the hinterlands, a "low-born" horse like Black Gold or Carry Back, I realized that I was hardly in the position to act as a minor-league scout. If I was going to beat the odds against finding a Derby horse so early in the game, I would probably have to go to New York, where the talent had already been culled, to find my contender.

Like so many other pursuits, racing had polarized into two centers of power, East and West. Good horses and ambitious trainers, like hungry writers and ambitious actors, tended to wind up where the money and opportunities were—either New York or Los Angeles. And traditionally, the best horses had made their mark in New York before going to the Derby.

Although racing was a meritocracy, where every young thoroughbred had a chance to qualify for the Derby, both environment and breeding were part of the class system that ruled the sport. "You have a better chance of finding a Nobel Prize winner in Spanish Harlem than you do of finding a poorly bred Derby horse out in the sticks," one "society" trainer told me.

Chances were that my Hopeful would be unveiled at Saratoga, the great coming-out party for high-born two-year-olds. Chances were that he was being trained by one of a handful of trainers who consistently got the cream of the crop. And chances were that he had been born in Kentucky, near Lexington, on one of the twelve hundred or so breeding farms located within the twenty-five hundred square miles of bluegrass country, the great cradle and marketplace of the thoroughbred industry. Success breeds success in the horse business, and although only 20 percent of the foals produced annually come from Kentucky, horses bred in Kentucky win nearly 40 percent of the stakes races run in America every year; and of the top races—the graded stakes—Kentucky-breds account for an average of over 60 percent.

Mr. Tuckerman's track

Nevertheless, I began my racing apprenticeship at the lower middle of the sport rather than at the top, at a place where good horses were sent to wind down their careers rather than begin them. It was the equivalent of starting a search for a great young baseball player in Sun City. The track nearest my home happened to be Suffolk Downs, a fifty-year-old plant nestled amid the triple-deckered hills and industrial farms of East Boston, an oasis of concrete, glass and dirt just up the road from Logan Airport. Known by racetrackers around the country as Sufferin' Downs, Suffolk represented New England's compromise with the evils of gambling; its spartan white exterior and garish blue-and-orange interior seemed designed to afflict the gambler with guilt and ambivalence, but not enough to deprive the state of its regular percentage of his gambling dollars.

Suffolk had changed hands seven times since Bayard Tuckerman, a gentleman farmer and fox-hunting enthusiast from Boston's North Shore, had convinced the state legislature in 1934 to approve a bill legalizing horse racing and parimutuel betting in Massachusetts. It had taken Tuckerman, a Mayflower descendant, three all-out campaigns during three successive legislative sessions to get the bill passed, but during the Depression, legislators finally could not resist the temptation of a proposal that would create jobs and replenish the state's diminished tax base.

Harness racing had been popular in New England since colonial days, but flat racing and horseplaying in Massachusetts had fallen under persistent post-Puritan bans on all "racy" pursuits: dirty books, gambling parlors, houses of ill repute. Harness racing, it seemed, had been acceptable to city fathers because it represented an extension of the horse's utilitarian role as beast of burden; bound by traces and guided by a whip, the horse was restricted to a socially acceptable trot. Even preachers, who often had to drive their buggies around a far-flung circuit, could understand the virtues of a fast-going trotter. Flat racing, on the other hand, with riders astride wild-eyed, foam-flecked horses running pell-mell down a track, represented a loosing of constraints, an abandonment to disorder. In flat racing, horses and men seemed to bring out the wildness in each other.

Rejecting the idea of a country track, the Eastern Racing Association, led by Tuckerman, chose as their site a tidal marsh five miles from downtown Boston that spanned the edges of the towns of East Boston and Revere. Although the new grandstand and clubhouse were the largest of their day, Suffolk was immediately overshadowed by New Hampshire's Rockingham Park, a track originally built by a group of tycoons that included August Belmont 2nd and John "Bet a Million" Gates.

Rockingham, which had been reopened two years before Suffolk's debut, served as a way station for wealthy owners who were shipping their horses between Saratoga and Belmont Park. Rockingham's owner, Lou Smith, had introduced New England to both exotic betting—the daily double—and exotic racing. He sponsored an ostrich race (which the big birds survived, only to succumb two days later to the cold weather), a cowgirl race, and a series of plow-horse races, during which local farmers could galumph around the track on their Percherons.

Boston's most exciting era in racing had come in the late 1960s, when former White Sox owner Bill Veeck turned his considerable promotional talents to Suffolk, which had been purchased by Realty Equities Corp., a New York-based company interested in diversification. When Veeck first saw the Downs looming up beyond a field of storage tanks, he remarked that it reminded him of a concentration camp. Undaunted, he began to plan his first gimmick: the Lady Godiva Handicap, a race for eight three-year-old fillies, to be ridden by eight female jockeys. At the time, in 1968, women jockeys had just begun their assault on various jockey clubs throughout the country that had refused even to license women, much less permit them to get to the starting gate. Veeck was no feminist, however; he told the press, "Lady jockeys? Well, they do more for the silks than the boys do."

In the tradition of Lou Smith, Veeck tried other gimmicks and giveaways, including potted petunias on Mother's Day, a free racehorse, a chariot race called the Ben Hur Handicap, a reenactment of Custer's last stand, and a turkey chase. Veeck's antics, however, failed to bestir a city that had grown apathetic about racing, and Suffolk remained caught in a squeeze between two powerful forces in New England: the Puritan heritage, filtered through the pieties of Irish Catholicism, and a notoriously corrupt political system.

Subsequent owners fared better with the politicians than did Veeck. During the administration of Governor Ed King, a solid horse fan, the track's Turf Club would be more crowded at midday with politicians than the statehouse dining room. However, many of the concessions granted by the legislature over the years as short-term cures for Suffolk's ills turned out to be long-term problems. Suffolk was permitted to conduct racing all year long, which meant that there was no season for racing, as there was for other sports; no special time of the year that seemed to belong to the horses. Suffolk became the track of the endless meet, a monotonous grind from season to season. Every day before dawn, horsemen and horses roused themselves for the rigors of training, in soreness and in health, in sleet and snow, in swelter and in smog.

Fans, too, seemed to succumb to the grind. My first trip to Suffolk in mid-winter was a real shocker. Bleary eyes stared out from pale, unshaven faces as I walked through a smoky ward of canes and wheelchairs. Even Damon Runyon, I thought, would have had trouble rounding up a lively cast of characters at the Downs in February. The scenario fulfilled my worst fears about horseplaying as a form of preemptive misery, a form of engagement with fortune that temporarily blotted out other problems —unshoveled snow, unpaid bills, dead marriages.

Where were the young sharpies, the renegade academics, the refugees from Beacon Hill that I had expected? The population of horseplayers that had already begun to age when Bill Veeck took over the Downs had not replenished itself, had not passed on the tradition to sons and daughters, as baseball and football fans had done for generations. Suffolk seemed to be fulfilling Bill Veeck's dire prophecy about the future of racing: "Its fans are dying, and the sport is dying with them."

On the other hand, I realized that it had been such a startling experience to find myself in a setting entirely devoid of Yuppies that I had experienced a mild version of culture shock. The

Suffolk grandstand was one of the last ungentrified outposts in Boston, a haven where no one talked about condo conversions and country kitchens. Possibly, I had mistaken a worthy obliviousness to the benefits of the Beverly Hills Diet and the Jane Fonda Workout Book for signs of ill health and decrepitude.

Still, the term "handicapping" seemed particularly appropriate at Suffolk, when applied to the job of forecasting the outcome of a race. Handicapping, in fact, at a track like Suffolk took special skills, honed by frustration and nurtured over many seasons. One had to learn the foibles of the flawed but gallant horses that filled the backstretch, the bandaged veterans, the cheap youngsters, the handful of hard-hitting stars. And one had to learn the foibles of the track surface as well, which seemed to change its texture with the tides that ebbed and flowed beneath the landfill that underlay the track. And then there was the other set of variables—the trainers; the ambitious newcomers, the worn-out veterans, the consistent wise guys.

Above all, one had to learn the secrets of the claiming game, a form of gambling that involved more bluffing than poker, more sleight of hand than three-card monte. At Suffolk, as at most other tracks, the basic mode of competition was the claiming race, in which horses were as expendable as chess pieces. Designed to keep races competitive, the claiming race consisted of horses entered in a race for a set price, say $3,500, for which they could be "claimed" by another owner or trainer after the race. In order to claim a horse from such a race, any licensed owner or trainer could simply fill out a slip, sign it, and drop it into a claim box, like a valentine, half an hour before post time.

Claiming was the ultimate gamble, and a number of owners had gotten their start in the sport that way, including three men whose judgment about horses was about to be tested in a very big way in the coming year. One was the late Carl Rosen, the man responsible for America's designer jeans craze. Rosen, who ran a garment manufacturing company called Puritan Fashions in the suburb of Waltham, loved to play the horses, and he had run a few cheap claimers at Suffolk before getting more ambitious. During his first trip to the big summer auction held annually at Keeneland racetrack in Kentucky, Rosen had bought three yearlings, among which was a filly he named Chris Evert, after the tennis star who had endorsed a line of his sportswear. Chris Evert's namesake, purchased for $38,000, had proceeded to win the Triple Crown for fillies. A few years later, Rosen earned a different kind of fame when he asked Calvin Klein to sign his name on a line of denims for young women.

Another claims-to-glory story was that of Peter Fuller, the Boston car dealer who had sold Rosen his Cadillacs. Fuller had been even more fortunate than Rosen with the Suffolk claiming box, though his luck had run out in unexpected fashion. The son of former Governor Alvan Fuller and the man who was to become, in the words of one journalist, "the most famous Boston horseman since Paul Revere," Fuller had bred a claiming mare named Noor's Image to the great Native Dancer, and the result was Dancer's Image, the horse who won the Kentucky Derby in 1968, only to be disqualified on a dubious charge of illegal doping. It would take Fuller another fourteen years to breed another horse as good. This time, it was a filly named Mom's Command, who outgrew Suffolk Downs after one race.

Suffolk, in fact, had sometimes served as a kind of farm team as well as retirement village for big-time racing, and among the well-known trainers who had once tried their luck at Suffolk's claiming game was a precocious young French Canadian named Roger Laurin, who would become best known, until he took charge of a colt named Chief's Crown for Carl Rosen, as the man who gave away the job of training Secretariat to his father Lucien.

Sir Quasar's rescue

For those who didn't make it out of the marshes of Suffolk, it seemed harder to survive on the farm team than in the big time. Claiming a horse could be a risky business, with all the camouflage strategy going on; and with the low purses and limited pool of horses, there wasn't much room for error. What you saw was not always what you got. And it could be an equally risky business for horseplayers, who at a track like Suffolk were always trying to second-guess trainers who might or might not be trying to win—who might or might not be able to place their horses in spots where they could win. I had heard mutterings in the grandstand about nearly every trainer on the grounds, ascribing to them the darkest of motives or the heights of stupidity.

One trainer who seemed immune from such complaints was Bill Perry, a young, transplanted Southerner whose winning percentage over the winter had been 44 percent, hovering at 35 percent all spring. Horseplayers fell over themselves to bet on Perry's horses, seldom letting them go out at odds over 2 to 1.

For the past three years, Perry had been training exclusively for Scorpio Stable, a partnership consisting of a local liquor merchant named Paul Shahian and his associate Marge Ansara, an astrology devotee. The previous year, Perry and Scorpio had made a name for themselves with a horse named Let Burn, a huge, four-year-old gelding sired by Big Burn, a horse whose greatest distinction in his brief racing career had been bumping Secretariat out of contention during Big Red's maiden race at Belmont Park.

Every year Suffolk seemed to give rise to a "big" horse, like a cactus yielding up a single bloom. In 1984, it was Mom's Command, but in 1983, Let Burn had been Suffolk's local hero. He won the Massachusetts Handicap, Suffolk's biggest race, which had been won in previous years by the likes of Whirlaway and Riva Ridge, and then he had gone on to make a run at the Eclipse award for the nation's top sprinter. Unfortunately, however, a chronically bad ankle kept getting worse, and Let Burn was trying to beat the best horses in the country on a left front leg that looked like a giant Q-Tip.

Now most of Perry's string consisted of horses he had claimed or bought from other trainers who had given up on them. One of his horses in particular had caught my eye, a small, four-year-old chestnut gelding with a name suggesting the possibility of chivalry in the age of quantum physics: Sir Quasar. Quasar was the fastest horse out of the starting gate I had ever seen; he had the pure acceleration of a drag racer. However, before Perry bought him, he had not been capitalizing on his speed, and he had been running at the $15,000 claiming level. Under Perry's roof, he moved up in class, running every race as though his tail were on fire.

Quasar, who was a great-grandson of Count Fleet, but who

looked more like the great-grandson of Smoky the cowhorse, became my first equine hero since Ruffian. When he ran at Suffolk, I could forget the field of oil tanks, the ancient railbirds muttering obscenities, the crumpled tickets on the scuffed concrete floor.

Bill Perry's barn

If the society trainer were correct, the odds of my finding a Hopeful at Suffolk Downs were probably about the same as those of Sir Quasar winning the Whitney Handicap at Saratoga. But horse racing, I discovered, was actually a small world, where a good horse could take you from coast to coast, or at least from Suffolk to Saratoga. And I knew if I were going to reduce the enormous odds against picking a potential Derby contender out of a sea of untested two-year-olds, I was going to have to begin with the basics.

I wasn't even quite sure what racehorse trainers did on a day-to-day basis, other than saddle their horses before a race, mutter a few instructions and then give the jockeys a boost up. The notion of animal training called up images of lion tamers sending beasts through hoops, obedience experts teaching dogs to heel, behavioral scientists subjecting rats to electrical shocks. How much difference did a trainer make in a horse's performance? Would Secretariat have been Secretariat had he been trained by someone other than Lucien Laurin? How did one "train" a horse to achieve what one expected of a human athlete—to ration his speed, to give his utmost at the wire, to ignore pain?

All I knew about training horses came from Walter Farley, the *Racing Form,* and a quirky little book called *Training for Fun and Profit—Maybe!,* written in 1942 by one Keene Daingerfield, who was now a venerated racetrack steward in Kentucky.

Daingerfield's wry, succinct advice to prospective trainers was designed to replace illusions of money and success with practical notions about the ordinary, everyday grind of training horses. Said Daingerfield: "The primary thing for the neophyte to remember is that there is no legerdemain connected with training horses, no sleight of hand, no magic words to change a bad horse into a good one . . . Anyone with ordinary common sense can win races with good horses; no one can win them with bad ones."

A good trainer, according to Daingerfield, was the one who made the most of what he had: "There is . . . a proving ground: the great body of ordinary animals. The trainer who gets maximum results from average material is the good trainer."

If that were the case, then Bill Perry's barn would be a good place to start. He knew how to win with ordinary horses, and he knew about the pressures of training a "big" horse. And by coincidence Scorpio had bought the first two-year-old that had caught my attention that spring—a tall, gangly colt named Foxy Greene who had been entered in Saratoga's two-year-olds-in-training spring sale.

Foxy Greene, who was bred in the hunt country of Virginia, had a name and a pedigree that symbolized perfectly the schizoid extremes of a thoroughbred's world: the elegant pursuits of the landed gentry and the wiseacre toughness of the racetrack. His sire was the champion sprinter Shecky Greene, named for the comedian, and his dam was Lady Foxcroft, a daughter of leading broodmare sire Boldnesian.

Perry didn't seem surprised when I described my quest for a great two-year-old; trainers, I was to learn, never seem surprised at anything. But then, my quest wasn't really all that odd, since nearly everybody in racing is involved, one way or another, in a similar mission—a search for a "big" horse.

Perry didn't have a phone at the barn, but he had returned my call right away, early one June morning, after I had left a message at the stable gate. "I don't know if I can help you, but you're welcome to come on by," he said in a sharp, staccato voice that belied his boyish looks. His Southern drawl obviously had not survived Yankee ridicule and a dozen New England winters.

When I arrived, the horses had already finished their morning exertions, and Perry was seated behind a battered desk in his small, cluttered office, paying bills and looking through the condition book—two activities, I learned, that took up an inordinate amount of time in a trainer's schedule. Often, trainers' offices were the only heated or air-conditioned rooms on the backstretch, including the tack rooms and barracks that a number of racetrackers called home.

The condition book, which trainer Oscar Barrera once described as his "best friend," outlines the "conditions" of forthcoming races—age limits, weight allowances, maximum number of races won within a specified time period, entry fees, purses. The trainer's job is to decode the conditions and find races where his horses will fit.

"That won't take long," Perry snapped, then smiled sweetly, closing up his account books, when I mumbled something about wanting to pick his brain. He was a little defensive, it seemed, about the lack of a higher education. His parents in Aiken, South Carolina, had been strict fundamentalist Christians, and at seventeen he had run away from home. He finished high school in Aiken, living on his own, and he began to hang out with some migrant track workers who were employed at Aiken's big training track. Aiken was the traditional wintering ground for some of the country's biggest stables, which sent their horses and trainers south for R & R during the coldest months. Perry's father had run a gas station, where he filled tanks and wiped windshields for the likes of millionaire Paul Mellon and trainer Lucien Laurin.

Despite the fact that Perry was terrified of horses, his new friends talked him into heading farther south with them to Miami's Tropical Park racetrack the following winter. He managed to get a job as a hot-walker, the lowliest trade at the track, and he learned to disguise his fear, he said, when it was a choice of walking sweaty horses or starving. His big problem, as it turned out, was not the horses, but the people on the track. One of the friendly migrant workers stole his meager savings, hidden in a shoe in the tack room where he was sleeping. "I was green and countrified and didn't know what I was doing," said Perry. Eventually he followed veteran trainer Frank Calcagni north to Suffolk, where he was hired as a groom by top trainer Lynn Whiting. "Lynn wasn't like anybody else I had met on the track," said Perry. "Everybody was always trying to take advantage of you. But he was a real human being, someone I could relate to."

Few trainers start at the top of the business. Most had come up in the racing world the way Perry did, starting as hot-walkers or grooms. Even those who had followed their fathers into the business had mucked their share of stalls and carried their share of water buckets. Said Perry, "The only way to learn how to read horses is to start at the bottom."

The backstretch, I was learning, did have a lot in common with the circus. It was something you could run away to, a high-walled world always in bivouac. And training horses, like walking a tightrope or swallowing a sword, wasn't something you could go to school to learn; it was a trade passed on from person to person, along with a load of practical wisdom and a soupçon of balderdash.

Training racehorses, as I learned from Perry, actually involved three different functions: running the stable; keeping the horses fit; and placing horses in the right spots.

The first function, it seemed, was the most trying of all, since it meant dealing with owners, finding and holding on to good help, and keeping the books. But the second, since it involved soundness, was ultimately the most demanding. To keep a horse on his toes and to keep him sound required a very delicate balance between patience and rigor—a balance, I learned, that few trainers commanded.

Over the years, Perry, like other young trainers, had tried a number of the training "gimmicks" that swept the backstretch —"interval" training, which involved a daily series of sprints of increasing duration; acupuncture; laser therapy; and the "Blue Boot," a patented device that sent a mild electric current to injured tissues in a shin or ankle. On any given day, you could walk across the Suffolk backstretch and spot horses hooked up to strange contraptions that seemed to belong in the history-of-medicine exhibit in the Smithsonian.

Trainers tended to try a little bit of everything and then stick to the few techniques that actually seemed to work. But no "gimmick" had yet replaced rest as the best treatment for sore limbs, nor had any fancy exercise programs replaced the standard regimen of daily slow gallops and periodic fast workouts that trainers had been relying on for over a century to bring their horses up to a race.

Some trainers, I learned, were "leg" men, who specialized in coping with the multiple forms of lameness that racehorses were heir to—the inflammations, swellings, soreness, and strains that were routine for a thousand-pound animal expected to accelerate almost instantly from a standing start to speeds of 35 to 40 mph, whose full momentum was borne at mid-stride on a single foreleg, slimmer than a dancer's.

Perry's specialty, however, was not legs, but heart. The will to win, he felt, was something you could recognize in a horse, but which you couldn't teach. Like speed, it was either there or it wasn't. And so he liked to claim horses that tried hard. And he had an uncanny ability to judge when a horse was at its sharpest, ready to do battle. "Horses don't lie to you," he liked to say.

Later, Perry took me around the barn to meet his horses, a process that always lies somewhere between a tour of an art collection and an introduction to an extended family. First on the tour was Let Burn, who had not been able to race since his triumphs the previous fall in New York. Known around the barn as Ernie, the huge, powerful horse still showed enough promise that Perry was reluctant to retire him. His morning workouts at six furlongs would have beaten any horse on the grounds at that distance, as well as most of the sprinters in New York. He was so fast that Perry considered him a "freak." But Perry feared that, during a race, Ernie would push himself to the point of injury, and that no training regimen could guarantee his safety.

Lilian, Ernie's pretty, sharp-tongued groom, was sitting impatiently next to the stall, keeping the horse's front legs anchored in a tub full of ice. "With this ankle," she snapped, "it's like a person with cancer. It's never going to go away. He has some good days and some bad days."

Next were Ski Resort and Snowgun, two horses that Perry had claimed from an owner who had made a small fortune from a big ski resort in New Hampshire. Since Perry had claimed them, both horses had run up big winning streaks, Snowgun with eight straight victories, Ski Resort with six. And then, of course, there was Sir Quasar, who, Perry said, didn't "look like much," with his shins scarred like an African warrior, and his sore shoulders keeping him in restless motion, rocking back and forth in his stall. "I don't really know why I bought him," said Perry. "I guess I go for the underdog." He had taken a fancy to the little gelding when he had seen him trying hard in a claiming race, and he had bought him privately.

Perry had recognized in Quasar that most valuable of qualities to a horseman. As Keene Daingerfield had described it, "Class makes no difference in your fondness for a 'trier,' and a true-hearted plater is much more to be esteemed than a sulky stake horse. If you get one that is 'pure of heart,' you should be ready to fight, bleed and die for him."

Quasar popped his narrow, delicate head out of his stall and nodded aggressively when he saw the doughnut I had brought in tribute. Downing it in one gulp, he lowered his head and let me scratch behind his ears. Perry looked surprised, since Quasar didn't like to be touched. But Quasar, like any athlete worth his oats, knew hero worship when he saw it.

As we continued around the barn, the horses munching busily at their haynets, the grooms patiently wrapping bandages like Red Cross volunteers, I had an idea that I should start my apprenticeship the same way Perry had, to learn to "read" horses close up, rather than from the grandstand and the *Racing Form*. Mustering my courage, I asked Perry if I might try walking "hots" for him. "You'll have to learn how to cuss and spit," he said, looking amused. Unfortunately, he had a full crew, but he'd get me a license, he said, so I could come out in the mornings and try my hand at it.

"Watch out," said Jeff, one of his grooms, a slender, scholarly-looking man who had overheard us as he was bending over in a stall, brushing a foul-smelling salve onto the hooves of a colt named Irish Chips. "You're gonna get hooked, and you'll never be able to leave." Looking up at me over the stall webbing, he smiled wryly. "I started out as a writer too. I came here to earn some money between assignments, and here I am. Now I'm a little scared to go back out there," he said, pointing vaguely with the oily brush toward Boston, but meaning, I think, the world at large, outside the walls of the track.

A week later, with an official hot-walker's license in my pocket, I parked my car beside the field of oil tanks adjoining the Downs and walked through the gate to the backstretch, nervous as a greenhorn on the first day at the ranch. At dawn, the track was already humming, hooves clattering over the cement alleys between the barns, grooms muttering to their horses as they strained to tighten the buckles on saddle girths. There were a lot of women around, exercise girls with long hair tucked under metal caps, blue-jeaned grooms with strong arms lugging heavy water buckets. Everybody I passed looked tough and preoccupied, and I was wishing I had chosen something less conspicuous in the way of footwear than my purple running shoes.

The rows of barns stretching back from the edge of the track smelled of horses, of mucked straw and saddle soap, like any stable, but raised to an exponential level; to a horse lover, it smelled like heaven. As I gulped in the horsey morning air, though, I recognized another smell common in any athletic locker room: liniment. The backstretch not only smelled like a stable; it smelled like a horse hospital.

John Coll, Perry's tall, curly-haired young foreman, fresh from animal husbandry courses at a local college, was walking a small, unruly two-year-old bay named D.K.'s Pleasure, an unraced, bargain-basement colt Perry had bought recently for $1,500. "Here you go," he said, handing me the shank, a strap of leather attached by a chain to the colt's halter, and pointing me down the path that led around the stalls under the eaves of the barn. As I looked down the shedrow, there didn't seem to be much room for error between the outer walls of the barn and the teeth of the horses whose heads poked out over their stall webbing. "Just remember to stay on his left side," said John, reminding me of the first of several basic clauses in the *sub rosa* contract drawn up between humans and horses.

Training racehorses, I sensed, was a matter of priorities, and getting a horse to cooperate around the barn seemed far less important in the overall scheme of things than getting him to cooperate on the track. And so, while racehorses spent as much time in the company of humans as most horses, much of that time around the barn was spent in fear, anger, and frustration on both ends of the shank.

The idea, I supposed, was that a racehorse could never be "broken" to human control the way other young horses were, or he would lose the fire and heedlessness that he needed on the track; he merely agreed to relinquish a certain portion of his wildness in exchange for food and shelter and obedience to certain rules—such as staying on his left side when you were walking him or getting on his back. Horses who kept their end of the bargain were said to be "kind"—that is, easy to work with. It was that "kindness" that grooms and hot-walkers depended on for their safety.

In the coming year, I would find myself frequently depending on the kindness of strange horses, and not all of them would be as gallant as D.K. was that day. He looked at me curiously and started to trot away, but when I tugged on the shank he slowed down to my pace, and we managed to make our way around the shedrow for the required half-hour promenade. But already I feared that with thoroughbreds you could never take anything for granted; you could never let down your guard.

Thoroughbreds seem to produce their own natural amphetamines; even on the backstretch, they seem "wired." Nearsighted and color-blind, they often decide that flight is the better part of valor. And so anything can spook a nervous horse—a quick gesture toward the head, a sound outside the shedrow, the flutter of a pigeon zooming through the barn. A couple of times D.K. snorted and began to prance and toss his head, and Kathy, another hot-walker who was leading a horse behind me, told me that the day before, D.K. had knocked her off her feet and begun dragging her down the shedrow until Jeff had come to her rescue.

"Don't worry about it," said Red, another hot-walker who had been walking a horse a few paces in front of me. "I never met a horse I didn't like. And I only met about five horses in twenty years that were really mean." Red was a short, red-headed man of about fifty or so who worked as a hot-walker to supplement his income as a jockey's agent. His jockey, a young man named Diego who had just arrived in Boston from Puerto Rico, had not had much luck so far in getting mounts; New England, surprisingly, was replete with small men who were willing to risk their spinal cords every day on the racetrack.

Red himself had once worked as an exercise rider, and his passion for horses had not been quelled, even by a bizarre accident that had become something of a Suffolk legend. One morning, he had taken a young colt out on the track when the trainer's regular exercise rider was late, and the animal had bucked and thrown him. The colt then proceeded to run haphazardly around the track at full speed, until he crashed into a filly who was coming the other way. The filly, as it turned out, was the colt's sister, and both horses were killed in the collision.

That was something Walter Farley never told you about, the kamikaze element of the thoroughbred's wildness. Perpetually cooped up in a stall, except when sent out to the track for exercise or races, the thoroughbred that suddenly found himself free of rider, reins or shank tended to go crazy. A loose horse was like a Ferrari without a driver, with the pedal pushed to the floor. Even in his stall, a horse could find a dozen different ways to hurt himself. Perry had recently come to the barn one morning to find that one of his best young horses had managed to bow a tendon simply by getting his leg wedged in the stall door.

It was that addled disregard for self-preservation that caused some trainers to say that horses were dumb. Horses were always doing dumb things, destructive things, and they could hurt you without even knowing it. In some experiments, horses were shown to be even slower than cows in figuring out how to get through a maze.

Yet racehorses seemed to turn animal behaviorism on its head. All horses, I knew, learned by experience, and they possessed extraordinary memories about pleasure and pain. They could remember quite well the particulars of where, how, and by whom they had been hurt. Why, then, despite the punishment thoroughbreds got on the track—the clods of dirt in the face, the bumping and jostling from other horses, the welts from the jockey's stick—did they run so fervently? Why did they try so hard, for such elusive rewards? Perhaps that was the ultimate "dumbness"—that urge to run, at all costs, which had been reinforced in the thoroughbred by two centuries of selective breeding and which was sometimes called courage.

The sprinter Tarantara, whom I had once seen at Saratoga, was a case in point. The big chestnut had been injured badly in a race, and after a long layup he had been brought back to the track with a metal pin in his ankle. In his first comeback races, the horse seemed to be reserving himself, particularly on the stretch of track where he had been hurt, as though to avoid injury. But gradually the will to win asserted itself, and one day I read in the *Racing Form* that Tarantara, who had won several races in a row, had been put down on the track after shattering a leg in the final race before he was to be retired.

In the case of John Henry, the legendary gelding who could still win big races at the age of nine, the horse had apparently learned enough from his years of racing experience to plot his own strategy during a race. Faced with a wall of horses in front of him, he would look for his own holes to charge through, and in recent years he had begun to change leads (that is, change the foreleg that caught the brunt of his stride) just before the finish line to give himself an extra edge at the wire. On the track, John Henry was pure efficiency. Back in his stall, however, the horse was said to be a holy terror.

The fight-or-flight instincts that had served wild horses so well on the plains and that kept thoroughbreds so competitive on the track often proved dangerous and self-destructive, particularly when greedy or incompetent humans were involved. So many of the racehorse's prerogatives, I suspected, had been preempted by humans that he simply couldn't be counted on to look after himself; he hadn't had a chance to learn how.

As I led D.K. back into his stall, his groom Wolf, a stockily built black man in his early fifties, was in the next stall working on Foxy Greene, massaging his legs with alcohol to increase the circulation. He applied a sticky clay poultice on Foxy's front legs to draw out any heat, and wrapped layers of cotton and protective bandages around all four legs. Not only were a thoroughbred's legs thin and fragile; they were plagued by poor circulation, which prevented the quick healing of sore or damaged joints and tendons. Foxy, Bill told me, would not be ready for the races for several months.

Perry's ability to deduce the readiness of his horses seemed almost mystical to me. He would simply watch them run in the mornings, sometimes alone, sometimes in company with other horses, and then he would extrapolate from all those morning gallops and stopwatched workouts to actual races, deciding when his horses were ready to win, and in what company they belonged.

But trainers, I knew, couldn't always wait for their horses to show them they were ready. If you had cheap horses, you had to run them frequently just to cover training costs, and if you had "big" horses, you had to go for the "big" races.

The most important—and the hardest—task of a trainer, then, was to make the most of his horses by balancing soundness with racing opportunities. Horatio Luro, the Hall of Fame trainer, who had sent Northern Dancer to victory in the Derby and Preakness, had said that a trainer's job was to keep from squeezing the lemon dry.

Some trainers, however, seemed to want lemonade every day. At Suffolk, the notion of resting a sore horse seemed as alien as playing croquet with flamingoes. Before Perry knew any better, he said, he had claimed horses off certain trainers who had "tapped" their horses—that is, removed the fluid from inflamed knees or ankles and then injected cortisone into the joints. A tapped horse was capable of a good race or two, but eventually the cortisone ate away at the cartilage in the joints, and Perry had found himself in possession of horses who had knees like ninety-year-old arthritis victims.

During the next few days, as I got to know Perry's horses in the mornings, I learned that nearly every horse that went to the races was doing so in spite of some kind of conformation flaw, some athletic injury, some health problem. It would have been the same for any professional football team. But often a horse's life and not merely his limbs were at stake.

I began to have a difficult time reconciling the mornings and afternoons I spent with the horses—the mornings on the back-stretch getting to know them as flawed but endearing individuals, the afternoons at the races learning to look at them as running machines. I found it strange that when a horse went lame in a race, it was said that he had "broken down," as though he were a car or a vacuum cleaner.

The wonder was how close thoroughbreds did seem to athletic machines, running nearly every race at a consistent rate. From what I could see, when horses were treated well in the mornings, they gave you everything they had in the afternoons. When they ran worse than usual, there was frequently a reason: pain, weariness, or bad racing luck.

I realized that even the way I rooted for horses was different from that of most horseplayers. I would cheer my favorites when they ran, the way I cheered for my baseball heroes when they came to bat or my football heroes when they made a play. I would call the horses by name, shouting ballpark endearments: "Come on, Quasar, you're the one!" But all around me, I could hear the chanting and imprecating of numbers: "Come on with that four hoss! The four! The four! Hit that four!" And if my horse happened to win, I would get as carried away as if my ship had come in. I regularly broke the cardinal rule of handicapping, which sanctioned cheering, as one turfwriter put it, only if you had just won ten percent of your gross annual income.

One hot, muggy day after I left Perry's barn, I went over to the grandstand to watch a few races. I hadn't planned to bet, but before the third race, a route for $5,000 claimers, I put a token bet on a little three-year-old gelding named Terwick, a half-brother to Perry's current star, Snowgun. Terwick had never shown as much talent as his brother, but he was consistent; he always tried, and he usually managed to finish "in the money." Terwick had been claimed by a trainer named John Smith on April 16 and had been run seven times since then, with an average of only five days to recuperate between races. He was dropping down from the $10,000 claiming level, and the notation in the *Form* on his last race said "done after 1/2." The horse had stopped running after three furlongs, and chances were that he had a problem and Smith wanted to lose him.

As the race progressed, I had gotten distracted by a fight in the grandstand between two guys who had collaborated on one betting ticket, and I looked toward the finish line, surprised that Terwick was not in the top three. When I glanced back up the field, I finally saw him, lying on the track, his legs twitching in the air. He had snapped an ankle, and the horse ambulance was already proceeding up the track to pick up the carcass after the vet "humanely destroyed" the animal by injecting a lethal dose of barbiturates.

Suddenly, the romance of picking winners vanished. It was that moment when a sport goes beyond its limits and becomes something else, when the trapeze artist falls without a net, when the sportscar crashes into the wall, when the quarterback is carried unconscious off the field, when both bull and matador spit blood, that moment when spectators either experience pity and terror, taste blood, or . . . feel nothing.

I looked around, hoping for another sympathetic face, someone else who could share my horror. The crowd, however, was engaged in the usual recriminations and second-guessing and tearing up of tickets. Only those who had bet on Terwick seemed disturbed by the sad little heap of flesh and bone lying on the track. The background murmur became a buzz, however, when Jim Hannon, the track announcer, informed the crowd that Terwick had been claimed before the race. Claiming was a no-return business, and Terwick's unlucky new owner now possessed a corpse.

I could see that as far as most horseplayers were concerned, and indeed most trainers, my response was understandable, but it was out of proportion. For them, an occasional broken leg was simply part of the game, part of the adverse odds that they were trying to beat. I felt a bit like the character in the film *The Shooting Party* who becomes sickened at all the blood and flying feathers, as the pleasure-shooters blast away at ducks and pheasants. James Mason, the kind, courtly owner of the estate, explains the carnage as part of a kind of supply-and-demand cycle. The pheasants, he says, are merely fulfilling their destiny, the purpose for which they were raised. Were there no hunting, he says, there would be no pheasants to mourn for.

Thoroughbreds, however, were not raised to be killed for pleasure. When they died on the track, something had gone wrong. I knew that bad things happened at the track out of the blue, accidents that could not have been foreseen or prevented. Less than a week later, Swale, the winner of the Derby and the Belmont, would die mysteriously, during a routine bath after a routine morning gallop. Despite all the rumors about foul play, the horse's death was simply one of those times when the wheel of fortune took a sudden and inexplicable turn. But Terwick's death, I was certain, had nothing to do with fortune and everything to do with greed and irresponsibility. His death was no freak accident; it was the result of a long series of events, a chain of cause and effect.

First in the chain was drugs. With a year of racing cards to fill, Suffolk faced the problem of finding enough sound horses. Horses running all year long got sore, and they could seldom earn enough from the cheap purses at Suffolk for their trainers to consider a vacation for either themselves or their horses. The answer, as it had been at other tracks where references to the "sport of kings" seemed merely ironic, was drugs—legalized drugs, of course. In Massachusetts, you could keep a sore horse in the running by administering Butazolidin (Bute), an anti-inflammatory painkiller, and you could keep a horse with respiratory problems in training by using Furosemide (Lasix), a diuretic designed to reduce bleeding in the lungs.

And so who was at fault? One could blame John Smith, for not giving his horse a chance to rest, just as one could blame Suffolk Downs, for cheap purses that did not give trainers a chance to treat their horses right. And one could blame the state for an inordinate tax takeout that cut into purses and track improvements. (A year later, the state of Massachusetts did cut its takeout, allowing Suffolk to raise its purses and, consequently, the level of racing.) And one could blame all three—the trainer, the track, and the state—for permitting horses to race on Bute. Unable to feel the pain and weakness in his ankle, Terwick had run in the heedless way that hard-hitting horses do, and it had killed him. But ultimately, I realized, the chain of cause and effect that had killed Terwick had started elsewhere, and it had to do with problems inherent in the sport itself.

Suffolk had become a haven for flawed horses, horses who might have been born for better things, but who either couldn't make the grade at better tracks, or required drugs in order to race. Suffolk, in a sense, provided a safety net for the racing industry, a place for horses to fall, a way for those who had invested in thoroughbreds to keep getting their tax write-offs and to eke out a little purse money when their potential Secretariats turned out to be short-winded.

One thing was certain—cheap horses were being pushed too hard. And I suspected that even the good ones were often worked too hard as well. I began worrying about my Hopeful, knowing how hard a two-year-old had to be pushed in order to get to the Derby. There were so many things that could go wrong along the way—shin splints, that afflicted nearly every two-year-old at some point; bone chips, like those that had been discovered in X rays of superstar Devil's Bag's knee at the time of the 1984 Derby; colic, that had taken Timely Writer, Suffolk's greatest Triple Crown hope ever, out of contention in the spring of 1980; and fractures, which could come with one wrong step. Timely Writer had survived colic only to break a leg in the Jockey Club Gold Cup, a race in which he should never have been entered.

I thought about abandoning the quest before I had even found my Hopeful. I wondered if there could be any payoff, even winning the Derby, that was worth the heavy costs. But perhaps there were ways, after all, to beat the pain/payoff quotient, measures that could change the odds, making the sport less of a losing proposition, for horses as well as humans.

Clearly those answers weren't to be found at Suffolk; perhaps I could find them in Kentucky, where the saga of the thoroughbred in America had taken on epic proportions.

CHAPTER 2

Kentucky's Blood-and-Money Horses

King of racers and king of stallions
> —Epitaph on the grave of Longfellow

Here lies the fleetest of runners the American Turf has ever known, and one of the gamest and most generous of horses.
> —Epitaph on the gravestone of Domino

. . . she was of the best blood of Kentucky, the bluest Bluegrass aristocracy, very proud and acrimonious—or maybe it is ceremonious . . .
> —Samuel L. Clemens, "A Horse's Tale"

BEFORE you even leave tiny Blue Grass Airport in Lexington, Kentucky, the signs get you thinking about breeding. On the way to retrieve your baggage, you walk past displays touting the famous studs of Airdrie, past icons of the lush green pastures of Claiborne, and you start thinking about momentous matings, about all the spindly-legged potential Secretariats for sale, gamboling as babies behind white fences before they go out to do battle on the track. You think about human bloodlines, too, about bluegrass empires built on the potency of stallions and the salesmanship of their owners.

When you arrive at the Hertz counter, you might recall that the late John D. Hertz was responsible not only for your rental car, but also for the great Count Fleet, America's sixth Triple Crown winner. When you pick up your complimentary Hertz map, you see that you are located in the middle of a vast array of thoroughbred kingdoms and duchies, twenty miles east of Versailles and thirty miles south of Paris. Yet it seems, in some way, to be a very small world.

Next door to the airport is Nelson Bunker Hunt's Bluegrass Farm, where the Texas oil-and-silver baron, a 30-year veteran of the bluegrass game, applies his own peculiar theories of breeding and training. Hunt is said to cull out potential stars from each crop by means of foal races, in which a group of babies are separated from their dams and then turned loose en masse to discover those who can reach their mothers most quickly. Hunt has never won the Kentucky Derby with one of these culled homebreds, but he has done well in Europe, winning both the English and the French equivalent of the Kentucky Derby within four days of each other in 1976.

Across the highway is Keeneland, the fifty-year-old track and sales emporium where the most expensive yearlings in the world are auctioned off every July during a three-day marathon of bidding. If Kentucky is the great thoroughbred nursery of the world, Keeneland is the ultimate casbah, where the best bloodstock in the world changes hands, passing from old-time bluegrass barons to the new empire-builders in the game, the big spenders from oil-producing states: Dubai, Arabia, Texas.

Kentucky, with its limestone-rich soil, its Amish-imported grass, its legions of honorary colonels, its highfalutin Old-South glamor and its rock-bottom redneck toughness, was where the sporting tycoons of the Northeast had come after the Civil War to play at animal husbandry, hiring the local hardboots and joining the local surviving gentry in creating an equine aristocracy and the ruling class of the racing world.

As long as the sporting gentry controlled the bloodlines, they controlled the game. Now, however, although a few big farms still dominated the industry, fortunes and bloodlines had been dispersed, and the best genes were for sale to the highest bidder. With one good sire, like Seattle Slew or Northern Dancer, you could start your own dynasty.

I had arrived in Lexington a week before the Keeneland sale, a few days before the influx of custom choppers and Lears, as breeders were polishing their yearlings and buyers had just begun studying their sales catalogues. I had come to Kentucky, where the careers of so many great horses had begun and ended, not only to narrow the search for my Hopeful, but to learn how it all started, how thoroughbreds were bred and bought and sold, to learn how a sport that was a losing proposition for 90 percent of those involved in it had spawned a multi-billion-dollar industry.

I wanted to learn what sort of world my Hopeful had been born into. Even if my chosen colt had not been through the sales ring at Keeneland, he had probably been foaled at one of the nearby farms. And less than a year from now, if he should live up to his promise, he would be running in the Derby, less than a hundred miles from his birthplace. And if he demonstrated that he were made of the right stuff, he would earn the right to retire to bluegrass pastures to try to pass on his speed and stamina to future generations.

I had visions of my Hopeful becoming part of the great bluegrass saga, an organic cycle of birth, money and death with a kind of Whitmanesque sweep to it. One could concoct an equine epic called *Leaves of Bluegrass*, about a young colt who grows fast and strong as he grazes on the lush green fields that nourished his ancestors; who ventures out into the world and makes his fortune; who returns to those same ancestral fields as a stallion, to frolic and graze briefly in the mornings before he hies to the breeding shed to create still further generations; who will eventually lie beneath those fields, where his descendants will graze and return . . . and on and on.

As I drove into town, a thundershower had just broken the oppressive heat and humidity of the afternoon, and an arc of lightning lit up the perfect paddocks of Calumet Farm on the left. Fireflies had begun blinking in the fields, and I felt as though I were gazing on horse heaven, with broodmares grazing peacefully in the foreground, and red-trimmed white barns stretching out into the distance. It was not the first time I was to feel an envious longing for the enchanted horse world created by the rich—a world eons away from Suffolk Downs, a world from which cheap horses and hard-up humans, except those in servitude, had been exiled.

Calumet, whose name at the moment reminded me of Kismet, a kind of fantasy kingdom built on the winds of fate, had actually been named for the brand of baking powder that had made its founder wealthy; a kingdom built on biscuits. William Monroe Wright had dreamed of winning the Hambletonian with a great trotter, but his son Warren dreamed of the Derby and founded a dynasty of runners that would dominate racing for two decades, with eight Derby winners, two colt Triple Crown winners and three filly Triple Crown winners. "Calumet laid it over the competition like ice cream over spinach," Red Smith had said.

I found it difficult to believe, looking at Calumet's freshly painted white rails and sleek horses, that the farm was in decline as a racing power, that the more commercial farms had come to dominate the breeding business. Unfortunately, Calumet's greatest champions, Whirlaway and Citation, had never managed to produce anything nearly as good as themselves at stud; they had failed that ultimate test of an aristocratic sport—that of "improving the breed."

Federico Tesio, the master breeder, had said that equine dynasties must inevitably decline and new sources of genetic input be found—an observation that could apply to human racing dynasties and human ruling elites as well. Horses, according to Tesio, could sustain a dynasty for three generations before the power began to decline; one can only speculate that his estimate of human staying power over the generations would have been less generous. Many of the great families that had ruled both the racing and breeding of thoroughbreds were now into their third and fourth generations, and while some of them were holding their own, most had found it necessary either to cut back, seek new partners, or go public with their operations.

Cousin Leslie's sales pitch

The most commercial breeding enterprise of them all was Spendthrift, the forty-eight-year-old farm that had recently gone public, its shares currently selling at $7 on the over-the-counter market. Like so many racetracks and breeding farms, Spendthrift was founded during the heart of the Depression, at a time when land was cheap, jobs were scarce, and thrills were

Combs was particularly persuasive with the rich and famous, attracting such clients as MGM's Louis B. Mayer and cosmetics doyenne Elizabeth Arden. Riding the crest of a post–World War II boom in breeding and racing, Combs became known as "Master Salesman of the Century" and "Prince of the Thoroughbred Party Circuit." He sponsored lavish promotional parties and took out ads, heretofore a taboo for a gentleman's pastime. As one of Combs's rivals put it, "If you've got the money, he's got the time." But Combs's most important contribution to the breeding business came from his pioneering work in syndications—that is, the dividing of a stallion's reproductive potential into "shares." In 1947, Combs had syndicated Mayer's stallion Beau Père, who died before he could service any of the syndicate members' mares. Undaunted, in 1949, acting as Mayer's agent, he sold shares in the imported English champion Alibhai for $15,000, which rapidly escalated in value to $50,000. Most important, in 1957 he headed the syndication of Nashua, at that point the leading money winner of all time, for $1.25 million— the world's first million-dollar syndication.

Nashua was one of the great celebrities of the horse world; he had won the Preakness and the Belmont and defeated Derby winner Swaps in a legendary match race only two months before his owner, New York socialite William Woodward, Jr., was mistaken for a prowler and shot to death by his wife—a bizarre event that was to find its way into "Answered Prayers," Truman Capote's infamous fiction fragment. However, Nashua's record-breaking syndication price was due more to performance than to notoriety; the sum was directly in proportion to the horse's earnings on the track: at his retirement, Nashua had earned $1,288,565 in purse money.

It would take another ten years of upwardly spiraling stud fees and sales prices before Spendthrift and other farms would be able to inflate a horse's worth as a stallion to several times his earning power on the track. When Affirmed, the great Triple Crown winner and the first horse to earn $2 million on the track, arrived for stud duty at Spendthrift in 1979, a number of $16 million stallions were already standing at stud.

hard to come by. In 1936, Leslie Combs II, great-grandson o.
Gen. Leslie Combs, a law partner of Henry Clay, bought 127
acres of prime bluegrass land from the heirs of Elmendorf
Farm's Daniel Swigert, another of his great-grandfathers, at
$400 an acre, and named his farm Spendthrift. Initially, the
farm was to be named for Swigert's best-known colt, Hindoo,
but Combs's elegant wife Dorothy had not relished the notion
of presiding over Hindoo Hall. And so Combs had decided to
honor Swigert's other famous colt, the great-grandsire of Man o'
War, whom Swigert himself had named during a fit of pique
after one of his wife's legendary shopping trips.

Combs, a former football star who had played left end for
Centre College on Bo McMillan's famous Praying Colonels of
1922, had spent a couple of years in the coffee business in
Guatemala, then returned to America to get started in the
banking and insurance business in West Virginia. Combs did so
well that he was able, with the help of an inheritance from his
grandmother, to retire to Kentucky to buy an estate and play
the country gentleman. He had all the credentials: old Kentucky blueblood, old Kentucky charm, an heiress wife, and an
excellent polo game.

But Combs was a born salesman, and he found thoroughbreds
to be a most marketable product. Leslie Combs II became
"Cousin Leslie," a horse trader who could sell a one-eyed mule
to a sharp-eyed mogul. Said one writer, when Combs "releases
pronunciamentoes in his thick bourbon accent, hardly a prospective horse-buyer alive can resist the feeling that he is in the
presence of at least a domestic oracle . . . the Oracle of Kentucky." Combs once told a Louisville sportswriter: "It was like
taking candy from a baby. I'd been working my ass off up there
in Huntingdon; and I came down here and said, 'Well, this
thing's a joke. All these rich people who don't know a horse
from a petticoat coming in to spend their money.' "

As Combs and other breeders discovered, when you sold a
thoroughbred you weren't just selling a horse; you were selling
a symbol. You were selling chances in the winners' circle; you
were selling centuries of breeding; you were selling glamor,
excitement, a little bit of Charles II and his cavaliers, a little bit
of the Vanderbilts and the Whitneys. You were selling dreams.

"My father changed racing from a rich man's hobby to a modern-day business," said Brownell Combs, Leslie's son, a rock-jawed, six-foot-six bear of a man. "He commercialized it," he said proudly. We were sitting in his office at Spendthrift, the walls and desktop covered with trophies and mementoes of various sports: a boar's head, a sailfish, a bronze hot-air balloon, a framed copy of the famed photo finish in the 1979 Belmont, with Affirmed, who now stands at the farm, a nose ahead of Alydar.

Going public had been just another step in Spendthrift's progress toward complete commercialization. But according to Brownell, the step had been taken out of necessity—first of all, to avoid inheritance taxes when his father died and, secondly, to raise capital for the expansion and diversification of the business. "Even though longevity is a factor in our family," said Brownell, "none of us are immortal. My father is eighty-two. And we felt it would be a shame to have the whole thing carried off in an auction cart for the benefit of the government. And the way the market was going, with the Arabs and the big syndicates—if we were going to retain our position in the business, we needed an infusion of outside capital." Spendthrift's first major effort toward diversification had, in fact, been an unsuccessful effort to take over Churchill Downs.

Since 1980, Spendthrift had also been offering breeding and racing partnerships, starting at $75,000 a share, for investors who wanted to get their feet wet in the horse business by buying a piece of the hock. "They get the same depreciation, the same tax benefits as if they had bought a whole horse," said Brownell. "It's better for a new investor to get into a partnership with a top farm than to go on their own. They learn the business in a small way instead of getting fleeced by a trainer and getting out. And they have a chance to make some money. Our 1980 syndicate, for example, bought a yearling named A Phenomenon for $100,000, and we're going to syndicate him for $4 to $6 million this year."

Was there any loss of glamor or romance when you were a business partner rather than an owner? "The great American dream is that you're going to have a champion," said Brownell. "It doesn't matter if it's a limited partnership or not. This whole business is built on dreams, and the business aspect has not changed that. But no one is rich enough to afford horses as a hobby and stay in it. If you're not treated as a business by the IRS, you can't stay in. You've got to show a profit two years out of seven."

I wondered, however, what kind of decisions a group of business partners would make when the profit motive came up against the welfare of the horse—and against the good of the game. Once stallions had begun to be syndicated for millions of dollars, and yearlings had begun to bring millions of dollars in the sales ring, the priorities of the sport—of the business—had changed. A horse had to be hustled onto the track as early as possible to recoup the owners' investment, and it had to be hustled off the track once it proved itself in order to keep the investment safe. And if a horse were injured on the track, perhaps because of a flaw in conformation, it was sent to stud anyway, with the chance that its unsound limbs as well as its talent would be perpetuated. Brownell Combs disagreed: "It's like saying that I would pass on all my football injuries to my children."

To prove his point, Combs merely had to gesture toward the stud barn down the road, where the great stallion Raise a Native was housed in comfort. The big chestnut had demonstrated remarkable, precocious speed as a youngster, but had injured a tendon early in his career, after only four races. Yet he had sired a number of outstanding racehorses, including Exclusive Native and Majestic Prince, who had stood at Spendthrift, as well as Alydar and Mr. Prospector.

On the other hand, Raise a Native, as his groom had pointed out to me earlier in the day, seemed to have been destined for unsoundness, with a big, heavy frame hulking over his long, thin legs. And while he had passed on his brilliant speed and talent to many of his progeny, he had also passed on a certain fragility. Many of his gifted sons had suffered serious injuries on the track, some earlier than others—Exclusive Native after his two-year-old season and Majestic Prince during the running of the Belmont Stakes.

When the sporting tycoons ruled the game, the classic races, particularly the Derby and the Belmont, had served as the speeded-up human equivalent of the Darwinian process of natural selection; those horses that passed the test were allowed to breed. It seemed to me, however, that commercial breeders had less interest than their predecessors in the notion of "improving the breed," at least in terms of soundness. The notion of altering the breed to make it more durable was tantamount to suggesting that a truck axle be installed in a Ferrari. Yet ultimately commercial breeders, too, paid the price for the thoroughbred's fragility. Less than a month after my visit to Spendthrift, A Phenomenon broke down in the Forego Handicap at Saratoga, a race that was to be his last before retirement to stud; the horse's leg had shattered, and he could not be saved.

When we had concluded our conversation, Brownell excused himself to get ready for a ceremonial unveiling of a statue of Nashua that his father had commissioned the year before to commemorate the horse that had made Spendthrift famous. The sculptor, said Brownell, was Liza Todd, the daughter of Elizabeth Taylor and the late Michael Todd, and she would be present for the ceremony.

As a small crowd, including a local TV crew, gathered beside the canvas-shrouded statue in front of the stallion barn, I went up to the barn to view Spendthrift's current celebrity, Seattle Slew, who was lounging in his stall, his head aimed toward a portable fan that was keeping the heat of the afternoon at bay. He looked over at me with a casual glance of confident superiority, the kind of look that used to make me uncomfortable when I wore the wrong dress to a country-club dance. Some horses seem to know how valuable they are, and Slew clearly had no problems with an inferiority complex.

Unlike Nashua, however, Slew had not been to the manor born. He had been Keeneland's greatest bargain, purchased at auction for $17,000 by Karen and Mickey Taylor, a farmless young couple from Washington in the lumber business, in partnership with veterinarian Jim Hill and his wife Sally. Slew had not only won the Triple Crown, but had proved to be the kind of sire that breeders dream of, a sire who stamps his sons and daughters with his own greatness. In his first crop had been Slew o' Gold, the best horse of his generation, who was still in training that summer; and in his second had been two ill-fated champions, Swale and the filly Landaluce, who had died at two.

Despite their humble beginnings in the horse business, the Hills and the Taylors moved quickly to the top of the Kentucky heap; with two great Slews to their credit, they started their own farm, built their own racing stable, and even bought their own bank. And they became quite selective about the kind of mares that filled the senior Slew's dance card. When composer Burt Bacharach expressed a desire to breed his champion filly Heartlight No. 1 to Slew, he was turned down because the filly's breeding didn't measure up.

"We're gathered here to honor a great horse," Brownell was intoning.

Liza Todd, a quiet, diminutive woman with Liz Taylor's blue eyes and Michael Todd's square jaw and wide mouth, lifted the cover from the statue to reveal a lively bronze of Nashua's groom Clem Brooks leading the temperamental stallion—his destination, one assumed, the breeding shed. Standing to one side was Brooks, a sturdy, elderly black man cut in the classic mold of the great Kentucky grooms whose fates had become intertwined with those of their famous charges. "If I'd had any say about it, when it came time to put Nashua down," said Brooks, "they would have waited a day and given him another mare."

Refreshments were to be served in the breeding shed, announced Cousin Leslie: "That was his stomping grounds, so it's appropriate." The senior Combs did not linger, but got in his bright red Cadillac and drove back to the office, his horn blaring a tinny version of the call to post.

Kentuckians, I was learning, honored their favorite horses with a kind of idolatry that was usually reserved in the South for fallen Confederate generals—a kind of idolatry that fell short only of Cimon, the Greek horse fancier who had himself entombed with the two mares that won him three Olympic races. All across bluegrass territory are statues and memorials to departed heroes, to vanished dynasties: the statue of Bull Lea, Calumet's greatest sire, at the center of the farm's horseshoe-shaped cemetery; the likeness of Black Toney, Colonel E. R. Bradley's first great thoroughbred, erected on the portion of old Idle Hour Farm that now comprises John Galbreath's Darby Dan Farm; and the grandest of all, Herbert Haseltine's statue of Man o' War, moved in 1976, along with the horse's remains, to a place of honor next to the entrance of the Kentucky Horse Park.

After his death, Man o' War had been embalmed for open-casket viewing, and more than two thousand people attended his funeral. According to legend, the great champion died with an erection, and a horse blanket was placed discreetly over his loins.

There is both a glory and a melancholy to all these well-weathered memorials, to the great marble shafts inscribed with names of long-lived progenitors, to the simple gravestones honoring beloved steeds who died before their time. One is reminded of the inevitably bittersweet nature of a relationship with horses. As Lexington writer Maryjean Wall put it, "Involvement with horses is a tenuous, often fragile affair that is frequently carried on in spite of numerous misfortunes." After Swale's death, John Sosby, general manager of Claiborne Farm, had told her, "You celebrate one day and shed a tear the next."

Kentuckians, however, honored their stallions not only in death, but also in life. "A horse should be treated as a gentleman," California governor and horse breeder Leland Stanford had said. But Kentuckians hadn't been satisfied with that; "We look on them as patriarchs, as kings," said John Gaines, of Gainesway Farm and the Gaines pet-food fortune. Gaines had bought his farm in 1966 from C. V. Whitney, who was paring down the estate he had inherited from his father, Harry Payne Whitney—who in turn had bought the land from the estate of James B. Haggin, a native Kentuckian who had made his fortune in Western gold, silver, and copper mines.

Gaines had turned his farm into a showplace, constructing stallion barns reminiscent of the stables of the Gilded Age, when horses were housed in structures laden with Roman arches, cupolas and minarets. At Gainesway, practical design features were gussied up with such ostentatious luxuries as curved redwood beams and wrought-iron box doors that moved on solid copper wheels. Set high into sharply pointed gables were stained-glass windows that reproduced the red-and-green Gainesway crest.

Gaines, who had followed Cousin Leslie's lead in syndicating expensive stallions, had also become a promoter and defender of the tycoonish traditions that had ruled the sport. He had, in fact, become a kind of visionary of the sport—a founder of a new tradition that was to rival the Kentucky Derby in spectacle and importance. It was Gaines who had come up with the idea of the Breeders' Cup.

John Gaines's grail

"I thought it was manifestly unfair," Gaines was saying, as we sat in two deck chairs placed alongside the barn at Keeneland that had been assigned to his sales yearlings. Gaines, a deep-voiced, scholarly-looking man, was referring to a program aired in May 1979 by CBS's *Sixty Minutes* on the subject of drugs and racehorses. The CBS show had, in fact, been inspired by a series of newspaper and magazine articles exposing the high break-down rate of horses who ran on legal medication.

The show got Gaines to thinking about the bad image of racing and how it might be improved. "The program had a very serious impact," said Gaines, adjusting his thick, horn-rimmed spectacles. "It was an astonishingly stupid, one-sided portrait of the sport. And I wanted to share with the public the beauty and spirit and mystery of racing—the values we in the sport feel are important."

By the late 1970s, racing, in fact, had become an invisible sport for most of America, with only the Triple Crown races providing the kind of televised excitement the public had come to expect from a sport. Racetrack operators had resisted early efforts to televise their races, and, as other sports proved highly adaptable to the medium, racing came to be perceived by deci-sion-makers in the media as an arcane sport, with millionaires on the top, gamblers on the bottom, and no meat—no middle-class fans—in the middle. Although the stakes for the breeding end of the sport had risen dramatically, the stakes for the racing end were dropping fast.

Eventually Gaines came to the conclusion that "horse racing has only got one thing to sell, one thing to present to the public, and that is the suspense of finding out who has the best horse in the world." Merging the genetic imperatives of racing with the glamor and spectacle of the Super Bowl, Gaines hit upon the idea of an equine Olympics to be sponsored by breeders: a "definitive championship event that would show racing in all its glory." Such an event, he theorized, would attract national television coverage and keep the superstars of the track in training longer. What's more, such an event could also promote a central authority for racing equivalent to the power once held by New York's Jockey Club. Breeders could consolidate their power and save the sport as well.

Enlisting the support of rival bluegrass barons, in the spring of 1982 Gaines incorporated Breeders' Cup Limited, a nonprofit corporation headed by a directorship of leading breeders. Funded by annual stallion nomination fees and one-time nomination fees for the progeny of nominated stallions, the Breeders' Cup was designed as an extravaganza to celebrate the elite of the racing world, with any other benefits to be of the trickledown sort. As Gaines envisioned it, the Breeders' Cup would satisfy the urge of wealthy owners to determine "who has the best horse."

Only months after its formation, however, the tenuous new alliance of breeders began to dissolve in acrimony, as longstanding feuds and differences in philosophy began to surface. One young breeder characterized the proposed distribution of $13 million in purses on one day of racing as "undemocratic" and "bordering on the obscene." At the urging of a minority faction of breeders, the directors finally agreed on a more egalitarian approach, with a portion of the organization's funds to be allocated for various stakes races at tracks across the country. In keeping with Gaines's penchant for spectacle, however, the breeders bypassed the best tracks of the East and chose Hollywood Park, located in Los Angeles, California, for the first Breeders' Cup series, to be held in November of 1984.

Gaines, as he didn't mind admitting, was "never just a good ole boy," a run-of-the-mill hardboot. Like Cousin Leslie, he knew the value of showmanship. But unlike Cousin Leslie, he never promised his clients a rose garden for the price of a rare bulb. Thoroughbreds, according to Gaines, had never been and never would be a financially sensible proposition. In fact, he scoffed at the notion that racing could be approached as a business. "The key word in racing," he said, "is sport. When you try to analyze it according to standard economic indices, it doesn't make sense. Just as the Met doesn't make sense, and the great ballet companies don't make sense. They aren't meant to.

"Money is never the big thing in racing. That's why it was so fascinating to the Vanderbilts, the Whitneys, to the earlier age of owners. And it's the same thing that fascinates the new people in the game—the Robert Sangsters, the Stavros Niarchoses, the Allen Paulsons. With all of their wealth and power and ability to move into any world or any sphere—there are no doors that aren't open to them—there is one place that is not open to them automatically, and that's the winner's circle. It's something they can't control.

"A young couple living on an Indian reservation may own a horse called Seattle Slew. All men are equal on the turf and under the turf. The quest and the striving are for the same thing —the best horse."

In the twinkling of an eye, however, Gaines the philosopher became Gaines the horse trader. He had spotted a group of wealthy buyers doing some shopping around before the auction. "Here come the Arabs," he said to his barn manager. "Get 'em over here."

In a moment he spotted another important customer. "Here comes Lukas," he said to a groom. "Get that filly out."

D. Wayne Lukas, a former basketball coach and a leading trainer of quarter horses, had been training thoroughbreds for only six years, but in that time had risen quickly to the top of the game. He had an eye for potential athletes that had made him perhaps the most effective buyer in the world at the yearling auctions. He had once described his ability to spot a good horse in a crowd as the ability to pick the hidden rabbit out of one of those *trompe l'oeil* paintings. And, just as important, he had gained the complete confidence of a handful of high-rolling partners who were willing to back his judgment to the tune of millions of dollars. Chief among them was Eugene Klein, former owner of the San Diego Chargers. As one turf writer had told me, "Klein thinks that Lukas can walk on water."

A few barns away, another breeder/showman was getting wound up into a spiel. Tom Gentry, unlike John Gaines, looked to be just another hardboot, with his good-ole-boy belly and deep drawl. But Gentry, who was competing with bigger and more prestigious operations, had become a leading consigner at Keeneland every year. His secret, which was no secret at all, was promotion—promotions both grand and small.

It had all started, he said, with gimmicks. "I was the first to do anything with giveaways," he said. One year he had given away ballpoint pens to potential buyers, and he had met Sonny Werblin, the sports entrepreneur, that way. "I gave him a Tom Gentry pen, and he gave me a New York Jets pen." And they continued to do business. In subsequent years, he continued to ply wealthy clients with pins, buttons, cigarette lighters. "You've got to add or subtract or do something new every year," he said. One year, when he had owned a one-eyed Derby candidate named Casseleria, he had distributed stickers with the motto: "Thine eye has seen the glory."

"This year we have new shirts on the help," he said, pointing to a groom clad in a bright yellow shirt with the Gentry insignia. "And we've got new graphics," he said, pointing to a series of gold signs with purple lettering, promising "Nearly 10 to 1 return," proclaiming "Fantastic! Let the record speak for itself!"

That night, Gentry the carnival barker was planning to get his customers under the big top—literally. The theme for the 1984 installment of his annual bash for buyers was the circus. Donning a straw hat and red-striped carny-man jacket, Gentry welcomed his guests to a back pasture of his farm that had been transformed into a midway, with a menagerie, a Ferris wheel, fortune tellers, and real helicopter rides. While guest star and horse enthusiast Burt Bacharach crooned "What's New, Pussycat" under a striped tent, Nelson Bunker Hunt gamely lined up for an elephant ride, and men in turbans and cowboy hats lined up at the oyster bar. The cost for the extravaganza was approximately $100,000—an amount equal to four times the median income in America for a family of four. Three days later, at the conclusion of the Keeneland sale, Gentry was $7,855,000 richer, not counting the cost of the party.

Mr. Taylor's bubble

Since the dollar's decline in the early seventies, the Keeneland sale had become an international bazaar, during which rich Americans competed with even richer big spenders from Japan, Europe and the Middle East, driving the cost of well-bred yearlings into the rarefied realm of Revere teapots and Rembrandts. Thoroughbreds had become a kind of international currency, particularly for those with a strong currency and a competitive instinct. As Brownell Combs had told me, "There's always some currency that's really strong. From 1969 to 1973, the Japanese made the market at Keeneland. In 1973, they withdrew but were followed by the Greek shipping kings until the oil tanker market softened. The Greeks were followed by English gambling king Robert Sangster. If they blow up the Persian Gulf, somebody else will come along. We feel the next 'country,' in fact, will be Texas."

The thoroughbred market had, in fact, become something of a bluegrass bubble. John Finney, president of the auction firm Fasig-Tipton, which conducted major sales in Lexington preceding the Keeneland sale, and at Saratoga in August, had reassured breeders: "Well, if it is a bubble, it's cast iron; it's a pretty stout bubble. What's the record of this industry over the last twenty years? Have we beat inflation? Have we been valid international coin? Yes. Whoever has the money on the given day, whether it's the Arabs or the Japanese or (for those of us with long enough memories) the Americans, whoever has the money on that day wants to buy the best horses."

In recent years, however, those who had the money were creating a bubble within the bubble. Ever since Irish trainer Vincent O'Brien demonstrated with a son of Northern Dancer named The Minstrel that American horses could win big European races, the big spenders had gone after offspring of the Dancer, who turned twenty-three in 1984, as though the Canadian stallion were the golden goose. And he had proved them right more than not.

Bred by Canadian industrialist E. P. Taylor at his stud farm at Oshawa, near Toronto, the small bay horse, a grandson of Native Dancer and of Tesio's great Nearco, had sired more stakes winners than any other stallion in history. In 1984, perhaps his greatest year, two of his sons, Secreto and El Gran Señor (the latter named for the Dancer's trainer, Horatio Luro) battled neck-and-neck down the stretch to place first and second in the Epsom Derby, a race that Disraeli had once described as "The Blue Riband of the Turf." What's more, Northern Dancer had proved a sire of sires, a creator of dynasties; his sons The Minstrel, Nijinsky II, Lyphard, and Vice Regent had proved to be highly successful stallions. Another son, named Danzig, stabled at Claiborne Farm, whose first crop had just made it to the races, was rumored to be the Dancer's next great star at stud. I had seen Ziggy's Boy, a son of Danzig, win impressively at Belmont, and I had heard that another Danzig colt, Chief's Crown, was even better.

In the early 1980s, the bidding at Keeneland for Dancer blood had become so intense that certain Europeans began to band together to bid against the Arabs. During the sales of 1981 and 1982, Robert Sangster, heir to the Liverpool-based Vernons' soccer-pool fortune, had joined with associates like Stavros Niarchos, the Greek shipping magnate, to claim the highest-priced yearlings, setting an auction record of $4.25 million in 1982 for a colt by Nijinsky II. The man who had lost in the bidding wars was Sheikh Mohammed bin Rashid al Maktoum, the young defense minister of the oil-rich kingdom of Dubai.

In 1983, however, the Sheikh was not to be outdone, and he went to the wall for a colt by Northern Dancer out of a mare named My Bupers. By the time the dust had cleared, and Sangster had folded, the colt had cost the Sheikh $10.2 million, more than double the previous record. As the final hammer went down, the silence in the Keeneland auditorium was followed by thunderous applause, and some breeders even rose in standing ovation to the Sheikh's gesture of grand munificence.

Sportswriter Mark Kram, who had attended the event, found

himself turning to the theories of anthropologist Marvin Harris to explain the display of one-upmanship he had witnessed: "The puzzling thing is not that people hunger for approval, but that occasionally their craving becomes so powerful that they begin to compete with each other for prestige as others compete for land, protein, or sex. Sometimes this competition grows so fierce that it appears to become an end in itself. It then takes on the appearance of an obsession, wholly divorced from, and even directly opposed to, rational calculations of material costs."

Don Johnson, a tall, lanky coal magnate from eastern Kentucky, whose Crescent Farm had bred the record-breaking colt, had hit the jackpot after only five years in the business. The Sheikh, however, had not. His prize colt, named Snaafi Dancer, had not yet made it to the starting gate.

And now, in 1984, yet another bidding war for a top Northern Dancer colt was to take place in the decorous Keeneland auction hall. Robert Sangster, bidding against Allen Paulson, the custom-jet magnate from Georgia, paid $8.25 million for a half-brother to Devil's Bag, sired by Northern Dancer out of the mare Ballade. Sangster had bid vigorously for the colt even though his request to X-ray the legs and feet of his prospective purchase had been turned down. Two days after the sale, Sangster's team of veterinarians informed Keeneland officials that they had discovered a problem with the colt's right front foot.

Ordinarily, Sangster would have had to bite the bullet. The operative principle at the sales, enforced by years of custom and by the cumulative power of the breeders, is "Buyer beware." However, because Sangster was a valued customer, Windfields Farm agreed to buy back half an interest in the colt, and the matter was then hushed up by both parties to the transaction.

The high-roller intrigue of such events might have made good headlines, but the real loser in the Keeneland bidding wars was the game of racing itself. The high prices paid for top yearlings was part of an upward spiral of costs that made it difficult to make a profit in any aspect of horse racing and prevented the expansion of the sport to a larger public.

The Breeders' Cup was a brilliant idea, given America's taste for spectacle and Super Bowls. An annual day of rich races might keep a few good horses in training longer, and it might generate some new fans. But as any preacher knows, after the revival you've got to keep them in the church. You've got to keep them in the grandstand at Suffolk Downs as well as at Belmont and Saratoga and Hollywood Park. Racing's problems on a day-to-day level had become a self-perpetuating chain of cause and effect that would take more than a day of bread and circuses to break.

This is how the spiral worked: As the prices for select yearlings escalated, more horses were bred, and the market became saturated; the bottom and the middle of the market had softened and even begun to drop out. Owners who had paid exorbitant prices for their horses had little hope of recouping their costs on the track, so they tended to syndicate their horses as early as possible, for the highest possible prices, thus ensuring the trend of high stud fees, which in turn kept the costs of breeding a quality yearling artificially high.

The early retirement of good horses from the track and the exportation of America's best young horses to Europe lowered the quality of racing in America and frustrated fans and bettors, depriving them of potential stars and heroes, preventing the influx of new fans and bettors needed to keep the sport alive. Decreased attendance at the track and a lower betting handle meant less revenue for racetrack operators, who in turn cut the purses paid out to owners, making it increasingly difficult for the latter to cover their expenses. Declining revenues from the track also influenced state legislatures that had grown dependent on those revenues to extend the number of racing days each year and to permit medication needed to keep sore and tired horses on the track. The result was a continued dearth of good horses and a perpetual glut of unsound and mediocre animals whose ultimate fate was not a happy one.

The Prophet's war horses

The Arabs were hardly to blame for this complex chain of cause and effect, but the seemingly boundless supply of their money had driven the stakes for breeders into the stratosphere; their money fueled the spiral. And yet there was a certain ironic justice in their dark-eyed, bearded presence at Keeneland, and at Ascot and Epsom and Newmarket, the British race courses where they preferred to take their Kentucky purchases. In a sense, it had all begun with the Arabs, or at least with their horses. With a prophecy in the Koran.

God, as the legend goes, had told the wind, "I will form thee into an essence and create a creature like thyself." And when God made the horse, he said to it: "Thou shalt fly without wings and be unlike any other, and thou shalt be favored by the love of the master of the earth. Men shall follow thee wherever thou goest . . . upon thy back shall great riches repose."

The origins of the Arabian horse trace back from North African conquests and Indo-European migrations to desert sand and then to myth. In all probability, the Bedouins of Arabia began importing horses from Egypt sometime after the birth of Christ. But legend has it that the small, fleet-footed creatures once roamed wild in Arabia and that it was Baz, the great-great-grandson of Noah, who captured the first wild horse. In Saharan legend, the first horse breeder was Ishmael, who owned a prize mare who gave birth to a filly too weak to keep up with the caravan. Ishmael did not abandon the foal, but ordered that she be wrapped in goatskin and carried. And so it was that the filly survived, but because of her stunted legs became known as the Crippled One. Her daughters, known as the Benat el-A'waj, Daughters of the Crooked One, were to bring her great honor, and it was they who became known as the *kehila*, meaning the purely or thoroughly bred.

In another legend, the prophet Mohammed was said to have deprived a large band of mares of water during three days of desert travel. Finally, he released them within sight of a river, and the frantic horses ran for the water. Just before they reached the bank, the Prophet had the horn of battle blown, and five mares of the hundred responded, turning away from the water toward the call of battle. These five became known as the "mares of the Prophet," from whom the *asil*, or animals of pure blood, were descended.

From the Arabian horse, then, came the cult of noble blood. So obsessed were the Bedouins with bloodlines and selective breeding that stallions were only allowed to breed after they passed harsh tests of speed and stamina, being ridden over hot desert sand at distances of up to fifty miles. Before battle, Bedouins were known to sew up the vaginas of their "war mares" to prevent unwanted matings. Once a mare mated to a stallion of impure blood, she was considered forever contaminated.

Over the centuries, two basic types of the North African horse, known as the Arab and the Barb (the latter named for the Barbary Coast), were inbred to preserve a purity of pedigree, to maintain the prepotency of the breed—the ability of parents to transmit their essence and quality to their offspring. So special was the horse to the Bedouin world that prized stallions and mares were treated like honored members of the family, brought into the tent at night. Pedigrees were handed down orally from father to son, and the finest horses were offered as prizes to valued allies or confiscated by enemies as spoils of war.

Because the Arabian was so prepotent, the horse was coveted by European breeders as well, who desired to "lighten" their stock, to cross the "warm" blood of their heavy, armor-bearing, plow-pulling beasts with the "cool" blood and light frame of the desert-bred horse. It was all in the blood, thought breeders, the ability of certain horses to "stamp their get" with their own characteristics.

And so it was that three unraced Arabian stallions, brought to England during the years between the Restoration and the Age of Reason and bred to a motley group of English mares, became the source of all thoroughbred horses. The first, known as the Byerly Turk, had been captured from a Turkish officer at the siege of Vienna in 1688 by one Captain Byerly of York. The second, the Darley Arabian, foaled in 1700, had been purchased from Syrian friends in Aleppo by a British merchant named Thomas Darley and sent home to the Darley family seat in East Yorkshire. The last, the Godolphin Arabian, about whom so many legends have been spun, was said to have been discovered drawing a water cart in Paris, although it is more likely that the stallion was one of four presented by the Bey of Tunis to the King of France; three of the four were set loose in the forests of Brittany to edify the wild herds that roamed there, and the fourth was sold to Edward Coke of Derbyshire, who resold the stallion to Lord Godolphin.

From the descendants of these three imported stallions came the three great foundation lines of the modern-day thoroughbred: the Matchem line, descended from the bay grandson of the Godolphin Arabian; the Herod branch, named for the great-grandson of the Byerly Turk; and the Eclipse line, begun by the fabled grandson of the Darley Arabian, who had been undefeated in his racing career and considered so valuable that he was taken to stud in a cart. Of these three foundation sires, Eclipse, who was born in 1764, the year of the great eclipse of the sun, was the most influential, and it was his line that predominated in subsequent generations of racehorses.

Although the matings that produced the three great thoroughbred sires had been a matter of serendipity rather than calculated eugenics, the thoroughbred family tree had acquired the sanctified aura of biblical genealogy by the time the first national studbook was published, more than a century after the Byerly Turk had been captured in battle. The "blood" horse, as the thoroughbred was then known, had acquired a royal pedigree, and solemn portraits of favorite horses took their place with ancestral oils above the mantelpieces of the wealthy and titled.

The very word "thoroughbred," which first appeared in the *Stud Book* in 1821, was used to imply the opposite of half-bred, and it became a common term of approbation used to designate a person or a creature of ascertainable pedigree. My favorite antique postcard, in fact, which dates from 1908, depicts a pink-cheeked young woman in a fancy bonnet clasping a bewildered-looking horse around the neck; beneath the picture is the caption "Two Thoroughbreds."

Although no official definition of the term had actually appeared prior to 1911, when experts declared the word to be a literal translation of the Arabic word *kehilan*, meaning pure-bred, the capitalized form of the word became accepted as a proper noun that applied specifically to the breed of horse descended from Matchem, Herod, and Eclipse.

The royal blood of the thoroughbred was indeed distinctive; it was hot and thick, the dense-celled hemoglobin of an athlete, with more red cells to transport oxygen than that of other breeds. But the secret of thoroughbred genetics was not, as breeders had once thought, carried in the blood. Nor could such characteristics as speed and stamina be reduced, like hair color, to a Mendelian formula, as Federico Tesio had once theorized. A good horse was a composite—strong shoulders, straight legs, perfect pasterns—of hundreds of characteristics, each of which was transmitted independently from sire and dam to offspring.

Modern-day breeders had not done much refining of the oldest principle in animal husbandry—breed the best to the best and hope for the best. Although all thoroughbreds, if you looked back far enough in their pedigree, carried the genetic code of champions, some horses, breeders learned, were better able to transmit their strength than others, and these were the blood-and-money horses. And some "nicks"—crossings of bloodlines—were more successful than others. Working inductively, looking back at generations upon generations, breeders could narrow their odds a bit.

In the early twentieth century, one Colonel Vuillier of France, in tracing the ancestry of the great horses of his time, noticed the recurrence of certain key sires and dams, and he developed a system by which one could calculate the "dosage" of various family lines in the pedigree of an individual horse, thus predicting his chances of success. The Colonel believed that mating a stallion and a broodmare with opposite and complementary ancestries, determined according to his system, would actually produce a foal closer to the ideal mixture of qualities than either parent.

In 1925, Vuillier got the chance of a theorist's lifetime when the immensely wealthy Aga Khan, leader of the Ismaili Muslims, asked him to take over his stud farms. The Aga, who had grown up in Bombay and Poona, had developed an early passion for racing that had long gone unrequited. During a visit to London he was a guest at a dinner party, where he was seated next to the sister-in-law of trainer George Lambton, who suggested to her dinner partner that he talk to Lambton about starting his own stable. "What was pent up from childhood and would never have come out, suddenly became an irresistible mental storm," wrote the Aga in his memoir, and the result was a flood of money and determination expended in the direction of thoroughbred breeding. Vuillier, however, died shortly thereafter, and his wife, Madame Vuillier, was persuaded by the Aga to continue her husband's work.

Within a decade, the Aga had become one of Britain's leading breeders, and four of his stallions would become leading sires in America. Eventually the Colonel's dosage system would be revised and updated in the 1950s by an Italian scholar of breeding named Franco Varola, and again by an American expert named Leon Rasmussen of the *Daily Racing Form*, whose system would become the most uncannily accurate predictor of Derby and Belmont winners in America.

The Aga's legacy

In 1949, when Arthur B. "Bull" Hancock, Jr., of Claiborne Farm imported the Aga's seven-year-old stallion Nasrullah, a son of Tesio's Nearco, the course of racing in America took one of those wheel-of-fortune turns.

Kentucky had dominated thoroughbred breeding in America since before the Civil War, and little fresh blood had been brought into the genetic mix since a flurry of stallion importations between 1830 and mid-century. The Kentucky equestrian tradition, though, seemed to have been imported, intact, from England, with ladies and gentlemen riding to hounds on English saddles in English pink coats and caps, quaffing mint juleps from silver-plate goblets patterned on the English Pimm's Cup. As equine historian Charles E. Trevathan put it, "the American turf is only the English turf transplanted, with some alterations to a new soil. Our whole instinct for racing comes from our English and Irish ancestry."

Bull Hancock, however, was more practical hardboot than country gentleman, and his decision to import Nasrullah came from need rather than fashion. He had inherited Claiborne and an instinct for successful nicks from his father, Arthur, Sr., who had transformed the lush green expanse of the former tobacco farm near Paris, Kentucky, into the General Motors of American breeding. In 1926, the senior Hancock had formed a syndicate to import the French stallion Sir Gallahad, who proved his mettle by siring Gallant Fox, America's second Triple Crown winner. And in 1936 he formed another syndicate to import the Aga Khan's stallion Blenheim II, in whose first American crop was Whirlaway, another Triple Crown winner.

Nasrullah, however, who had been contrary and unpredictable on the track, was to become the most influential of these syndicated European imports, bringing an infusion of fresh blood not only to Claiborne, but to a number of breeding farms and racing families. Nasrullah was one of the great blood-and-money horses, a sire of ninety-nine stakes winners and a sire of sires. His breeding record over several generations was so impressive that one was tempted to lapse into the biblical "begat" when speaking of his descendants. Among his sons were Never Bend, who begat the great European champions Mill Reef and Riverman; Nashua, the mainstay of Spendthrift Farm; and Bold Ruler, the font of the Phipps racing dynasty and the begetter of Secretariat.

With Secretariat, in fact, the fates of three thoroughbred powers—the Hancocks, the Phippses, and the Chenerys—had come together in a twisted sort of genetic nexus.

The Phippses, like so many families who had made great industrial fortunes during the late 1800s, had found in horses a common interest with the land-rich, English-descended Southern gentry. Racing had social cachet, and it also had a competitive edge that never seemed to wear thin.

Mrs. Gladys Mills Phipps of Wheatley Stable, a diminutive dowager who had inherited the Gold Rush fortune of her father, Ogden Mills, and the steel-making fortune of her husband, Henry Carnegie Phipps, had sent her favorite filly, Miss Disco, to Nasrullah in 1953, and the Phippses found themselves the sole owners of Bold Ruler, a horse plagued from the beginning by injuries and illness, but who was to prove the fastest as well as the most prepotent of Nasrullah's sons. Two years earlier, Chris Chenery of Meadow Stable, a self-made utilities magnate from Virginia, had sent his mare Imperatrice to another of Hancock's stallions, Princequillo, a horse known for his stamina, and in 1951 the filly Somethingroyal was born.

The Phippses did not sell Bold Ruler's services, but parceled them out in a foal-sharing system. A mare owned by a chosen breeder would be sent to Bold Ruler for two seasons in succession, and the first choice of foals would be determined by the toss of a coin. However, Chris Chenery, a friend of Mrs. Phipps's son Ogden, had instituted a slightly different arrangement, whereby he would send two mares to Bold Ruler each season, with the coin toss to determine ownership of the resulting foals.

In 1968, Chenery's health had begun to fail, and his forty-six-year-old daughter, Penny Tweedy, had begun to make the decisions for her father's Meadow Stable. Accordingly, in 1968, Tweedy shipped the mares Somethingroyal and Hasty Matelda down to Claiborne from Chenery's farm near Richmond, Virginia.

In 1969, Tweedy sent Chenery's mare Cicada to Bold Ruler along with Somethingroyal, who had given birth in the spring to a filly. Somethingroyal had "taken" again, but Cicada had proved to be barren, and the annual coin toss took a fateful turn. Under the rules of the arrangement, the winner of the toss would automatically get first choice of the 1969 foals, either the Somethingroyal filly or a colt by Hasty Matelda, while the loser would get the second choice of the first pair as well as the first choice of the next pair of foals. However, since Cicada had proved barren, the winner of the toss would actually be the loser; the loser of the toss would not only get the second choice of the first pair but also the only foal born in 1970—the foal that Somethingroyal was carrying.

At Saratoga, in the summer of 1969, Penny Tweedy met Ogden Phipps—who had begun to take over Wheatley for his mother—for the fateful flip, to be carried out at the offices of the New York Racing Association. The luck of the Chenerys proved to be stronger than that of the Phippses that day, and Ogden Phipps, who was accompanied by his trainer Eddie Neloy, became the owner of the first foal by Somethingroyal, a filly named, ironically, The Bride, who was never to lose her maiden —to win a race—as a runner. And in March of 1970, Somethingroyal, who had been sent back to The Meadow, gave birth to a strapping chestnut colt with three white socks and an irregular blaze across his face: Secretariat.

Secretariat's life was to be full of bittersweet ironies, including the fact that those most responsible for his birth never lived to see him win the Triple Crown. Gladys Phipps had died in 1970, at age eighty-seven, before seeing the chestnut foal, and Bold Ruler, debilitated by cancer, was put down the following spring at the untimely age of seventeen. Another year, and Bull Hancock was gone; yet another, and so was the ailing Chris Chenery.

And now, in the summer of 1984, the gravestones of Blenheim, Bold Ruler and Nasrullah lay in the small cemetery plot behind the unassuming brick office at Claiborne, and Secretariat grazed and romped in a nearby paddock, the number one equine tourist attraction in Kentucky.

Claiborne's sales yearlings had already been sent off to auction, and I was waiting in the cemetery for Mike Griffin, the yearling manager, who was to give me a tour of the farm. I had a feeling that Claiborne, with its tangled web of bloodlines and racing dynasties, would also be entangled in the fate of my Hopeful. It was a place, one felt, where racing sagas had often begun and ended.

I had stopped in front of the still-fresh grave of Swale, who had been buried there only a month before, after his unexpected death on a bright Sunday morning after the Belmont. Swale, a son of Seattle Slew, who had carried Claiborne's yellow silks to its first Derby victory, was to have returned there at stud, to perpetuate the cycle, to generate more winners. Instead, he had died inexplicably, like the victim in a cheap thriller, and his particular ripple in the thoroughbred gene pool had been lost forever.

"They can find a hundred ways to break your heart," said Griffin, coming up beside me and looking down at Swale's gravestone. Griffin, a stocky, ruddy-faced man with the rough, strong-looking hands of a cowboy, had taken over Swale's training for the Triple Crown events when the colt's regular trainer, Woody Stephens, ailing with pneumonia and a set of broken ribs from a fall in the bathtub, had fallen apart.

I had heard the saying about heartbreak a dozen times, but like so many racetrack saws, it wore well. The first time you heard a racetrack gem, you assumed the speaker was a poet-in-the-rough, but when you heard it again and again you recognized it for a platitude, a stock phrase that seemed to offer a certain comfort, a way of confining the damage.

Griffin seemed eager to get away from the sad little grave; as though in search of an antidote, we walked over to see Secretariat, who was very much alive, grazing at the far end of his two-acre paddock, located just across the way from the breeding shed. Breeding season, which lasted from February to June, was over for the year, and Big Red's only duties now were to entertain visitors. As if on cue, the horse raced toward us so furiously that I backed away from the fence. Griffin caught Secretariat's halter as the stallion lunged his head toward him, eyes rolling. Suddenly I felt as though I were back in the world of Walter Farley, a world where wild stallions ruled and humans paid obeisance. Big Red, however, has always appreciated admirers, and he posed regally for a moment with his neck arched, letting me pat him on the nose. I regressed back even further, to Greek myths, to Pegasus, the symbol of pure aesthetics, flying toward Olympus, to Poseidon changing himself into a stallion to pursue the goddess Ceres.

Secretariat was probably the closest thing I would ever see to a pagan god, and I felt as though I should have brought an offering to place on the altar. "If you had a camera," said Griffin, "he'd really strike a pose for you. He loves to have his picture taken. One day a guy came out here with a towel folded in the shape of a camera, and he made some clicking noises, like a shutter, and the horse stood like a statue for him."

Even Secretariat, though, who could still take your breath away when he thundered across the grass, had found one of those fabled ways to break an owner's heart. I had seen evidence of it at Suffolk Downs, where a flashy but faint-hearted chestnut gelding named Debrett was winding down his career in $5,000 claiming races. Debrett, named for the human equivalent of the British studbook, would never become a member of the equine peerage, though he was a son of Secretariat—from that expensive first crop of Big Red's babies that were to have set the track on fire.

When Chris Chenery died in January of 1973, Penny Tweedy, who had already abandoned her role of conventional suburban housewife to take charge of Meadow Stable operations, was faced with huge inheritance taxes. Rather than disperse Meadow's bloodstock or the racing stable, she had decided to syndicate Secretariat, a month before his first start at age three. To handle the syndication she chose Bull Hancock's son Seth, a tall, phlegmatic young man who, according to the terms of his father's will, shared the ownership of Claiborne with his mother and his sisters, Nancy and Dell, and was to share the management of the farm until the age of thirty-five, with an advisory committee comprised of his father's colleagues Ogden Phipps, Charles Kenney, and William Haggin Perry.

Seth's job was to sell twenty-eight shares at $190,000 each, which would make Secretariat, who had not yet proven his mettle at the classic distances, the most expensive stallion in history, and which would accelerate the trend of early and expensive syndication of promising colts. In yet another of those bittersweet ironies, the first share was bought by Ogden Phipps, who, but for that unlucky toss of the coin, would have owned the colt outright. Other shares were purchased by the rich and elite of the racing world, including Zenya Yoshida, leading breeder of thoroughbreds in Japan and a big spender at Keeneland; William McKnight of the 3M Company (Minnesota Mining and Manufacturing) and owner of the breeding and racing operation known as Tartan Farms; Alfred Gwynne Vanderbilt, of the railroad Vanderbilts, and breeder and owner of the great Native Dancer; E. P. Taylor, the Canadian industrialist who had introduced his own Nearco strain into American breeding with Northern Dancer; and Paul Mellon, of Rokeby Farm, philanthropist, connoisseur, and heir to the immense Mellon banking and oil fortune.

It was Mellon who had bred Debrett, sending his regally pedigreed mare All Beautiful, dam of Arts and Letters, 1969's Horse of the Year, to Secretariat in March of 1974. Mellon, a cultured man who seemed to hew to the ancient Muslim view of horses as a great aesthetic gift to mankind, approached the matters of racing and breeding thoroughbreds with an atavistic reverence. He had selected All Beautiful as a potential mate for

Secretariat with the greatest of care, and when the resulting foal, Debrett, proved too unruly as a two-year-old to handle on the racetrack, he had the colt gelded—a gesture that shocked a racing world accustomed to making the most of the breeding potential of their horses. Mellon, however, did not believe in breeding untested horses, and he wanted Debrett to take his chances at the track. A gentleman's gamble.

Like most of Secretariat's first crop, Debrett was merely an ordinary horse. And like many ordinary horses with no breeding potential, he was doomed to the downward spiral that wound up at tracks like Suffolk or, worse, the county fairs.

By the time Secretariat had begun to work on his second crop of foals, Seth Hancock was heard by a reporter to say that he hoped the second crop would prove better than the first: "There's no doubt about it," he said in the summer of 1975, "Secretariat has not reproduced himself with anything like the consistency we hoped for." Word was sent to the forthright Seth by angry breeders to cool it, but unlike Cousin Leslie, Seth didn't believe in the principle of gilding the gelding.

Secretariat's second crop did fare somewhat better, as both the filly Terlingua, trained by Wayne Lukas, and the colt General Assembly, trained by Leroy Jolley, showed flashes of brilliance. But as the years passed and championships came and went, it became clear that Secretariat had been one of those genetic freaks, a sport, as they are called, who had loomed above the others of his species but who would not reproduce in his sons and daughters the particular genetic combination that made him so extraordinary. As with so many other Triple Crown winners—Whirlaway, Assault and Citation before him, and Affirmed after him—it seemed that a genetic experiment had culminated in a single individual and had been exhausted in the process.

Tesio had said that it all depended on energy—on how energy was conserved or expended, within the life of the individual horse and between the generations. Horses, he said, were born with a certain store of energy, by which he meant something like life force, and if too much were expended they would not have enough left to transmit to their offspring. Good race mares, he observed, often made the poorest broodmares: an observation Bull Hancock had also made; it was the daughters and sisters of good race mares, Bull used to say, that made the best broodmares. And given the various drugs and steroids regularly injected into fillies on the racetrack, Bull's observation was not mere mystical speculation.

Tesio felt, however, that both sires and dams could become burned out by too much racing or too much expenditure of effort without time to "recharge." If that were the case, then perhaps the Triple Crown had failed in its Darwinian purpose of selection. Perhaps the stress of competing in those races not only weeded out the lesser horses but exhausted the best ones.

Yet those three races, particularly the Derby and the Belmont, still provided the strongest correlation breeders could find between a horse's potential as a racehorse and as a sire. Horses with brilliant speed who could win the classic races, they believed, tended to become classic sires. And as for stallions like Raise a Native, who sired the great Alydar, Exclusive Native (himself the sire of Affirmed and Genuine Risk), and Majestic Prince, but who had never been proven as a three-year-old— well, that was just one of those unexpected genetic bonuses.

Perhaps the problem lay in another of Tesio's more far-fetched theories. Perhaps it was the "arranged marriages" themselves, the quick, antiseptic couplings in creosote breeding sheds, that were the problem for some horses. For Tesio, wildness was all, and the best breedings were those that involved the most passion. Said Tesio, "The atmosphere of intense sexual urge . . . was intended by nature to accumulate a powerful charge of nervous energy which alone, when released through the sexual act, can result in an animal richer in will-power than his fellows, winner of all his battles and a successful producer."

In his gnomic little tome, *Breeding the Racehorse,* based on a mixture of impromptu experiments, practical experience and mystical mumbo jumbo, Tesio recalled the real-life fable of the beautiful mare Signorina and the cheap stallion Chaleureux. Signorina had not been able to produce an outstanding foal, and as a last resort her owner, a Neapolitan named Cavaliere Ginistrelli who had moved to Newmarket, England, to "defeat the English on their own ground," had arranged to mate Signorina with the renowned stallion Isinglass for the fee of three hundred guineas. As Signorina was being led down High Street for the expensive rendezvous, she passed by Chaleureux, one of the lesser stallions of the area, who was being paraded around in order to drum up business, as was the custom at the time.

Chaleureux, who lived up to the heat implied in his name, became intoxicated with the mare, and Signorina responded in kind. When the two of them would not budge, Ginistrelli, who was, like Tesio, "a 'character' with original ideas," accepted the inevitable. "They love!" he said. "A love match it will be." Eleven months later, Signorina gave birth to a filly named Signorinetta, who grew up to be one of the greatest fillies of all time, winning the Epsom Derby and, two days later, the Oaks, a feat which only two fillies since 1780 had been able to accomplish. Two years later, Signorina was sent to Chaleureux for an arranged rather than a spontaneous rendezvous, and the resulting foal, Star of Naples, never won a race.

In Kentucky, of course, all matings were "arranged," and the proceedings were designed to maximize efficiency and minimize injury. And so, when a mare was thought to be in heat, it was not the valuable stallion who began the courtship, but a surrogate stud, a "teaser," a Sisyphean creature doomed forever to frustration who was used to determine the degree of the mare's receptivity. If the mare didn't kick the poor teaser or resist his advances, she was ready for the real stud, and the teaser was led away. The mare was then taken to the breeding shed, where she was hobbled and twitched into submission— her upper lip roped into a twitch and one foreleg tied up. Only then could the valuable stud approach her, he having been soaped up and swabbed with antiseptic. Lest there be any clumsiness on the part of the stud, attendants stood by to choreograph the action, to guide the stallion into the mare, to pull him away after he had ejaculated. Northern Dancer, the Alan Ladd of horses, was shorter than many of his mares, and he used his own custom-made mounting ramp to gain proper entry.

Perhaps Secretariat, in some perverse way, was withholding his essence during his twice-a-day mounting sessions, while Northern Dancer was able to imprint his essence on an inordi-

nate number of his offspring. Northern Dancer sons and grand-
sons all had a certain, immediately recognizable look to them,
while Secretariat's offspring came in all shapes and sizes.

There was hope, however, every time Big Red entered the
breeding shed, and over the years it became apparent that
Secretariat fared better as a sire with small, fast mares than with
the big, strapping mares who had been sent to him his first
season. One daughter, Lady's Secret, was to become his first
champion, in 1986. And as Secretariat's older offspring began to
breed, it appeared that his daughters, who had always fared
better on the track than his sons, might also make good broodmares—that his genes might benefit from the dilution of a generation or two. One of the most promising of these daughters
was Carl Rosen's Six Crowns, a winner of a small stakes race at
Aqueduct and over $100,000 in two seasons of racing.

In July of 1974, after Rosen's filly Chris Evert won the Coaching Club American Oaks at Belmont to secure the filly Triple
Crown, Penny Tweedy jokingly told Rosen that the two of them
should mate their Triple Crown winners. It would be like one of
those European royal marriages, an intertwining of crowns. A
sure thing.

However, although Rosen might have expected that the mating of champions like Secretariat and Chris Evert would produce a genetic equation in which two plus two would equal at
least three, Six Crowns was maybe a one. Tall and rangy like her
mother, she lacked both her mother's brilliant speed and her
sire's tremendous closing kick. But she was a steady, consistent
horse who would run well when not overmatched. When she
was retired at the end of her third year, Rosen sent her down to
Claiborne, where Chris Evert was still boarded.

That first spring at Claiborne, Six Crowns was bred to the
Argentine stallion Forli, and the following spring Rosen told
Seth Hancock to breed her to Claiborne's new young stallion
Danzig, a son of Northern Dancer who had been trained by
Woody Stephens. Rosen had seen Danzig run at Belmont, and
though the colt had been retired with bone chips in his knee
after only three races, Rosen had liked what he had seen. What's
more, the stud fee was a bargain $20,000—a fraction of the cost
of the services of the farm's top stallions. The result of the

mating was a colt named Chief's Crown, Rosen's first homebred colt, who had made his first start in June of 1984. Rosen, however, in yet another one of those sad ironies, had not lived to see the debut of his promising little bay colt. He had died in August of 1983, leaving control of both his horses and his business to his young son Andrew.

Chief's Crown was now being trained by Roger Laurin, and therein lay yet another of those Nasrullah-line ironies. Laurin had been hired by Penny Tweedy, on the advice of Bull Hancock, to train Meadow Stable's horses. However, a month before Riva Ridge made his debut and a year before Secretariat's first start, Laurin had given up the Meadow job to work for Ogden Phipps and his son Ogden Mills Phipps, known as Dinny. It was the hottest job in racing, and Laurin couldn't refuse. Bold Ruler's remarkable success as a sire had given the Phippses one big horse after another, and they were looking to their champion Buckpasser to succeed him as a leading sire. It was the equivalent of being offered a job to train the New York Yankees or the Boston Celtics—a sure road to the Hall of Fame.

Roger recommended to Tweedy that she hire his father Lucien to replace him. Unfortunately, however, Buckpasser did not prove the ideal mate for the Phippses' Bold Ruler–line mares, and Wheatley began a slow decline, even as Meadow was on the rise. Roger had sent his father on the way to glory and the Hall of Fame, but his own new job was to prove a shattering disappointment.

Although he produced a two-year-old filly champion, Numbered Account, the same year that Riva Ridge won the two-year-old championship, that accomplishment did not seem to suffice, either for Roger or for the Phippses. During that fall of 1971, in fact, Roger, as well as much of the racing world, was convinced that his filly could beat Riva Ridge. She finally got her chance in the Garden State Stakes, which came only eight days after she had won the mile-and-a-sixteenth Gardenia Stakes and only two weeks after she had won the Frizette. She was a tired filly, and Riva Ridge won decisively.

Eddie Sweat, who was Riva Ridge's groom at the time, later told me, "I don't think the filly had a shot to beat Riva Ridge, but I think Roger wanted to prove something." And in following years, when people asked him to compare himself with his father, Roger would say, "Well, I'm taller."

As Mike Griffin and I walked through the creosote-fenced fields to reach Danzig's paddock at the near end of the farm, beside the road to Paris, I realized yet again how much of the history of racing was a saga of generations. Until recently, it had been mostly a story of families, primarily of fathers and sons, of attempts to accumulate fortunes or bloodlines and pass them on.

Danzig, unlike Secretariat, didn't feel like putting on a show. Grazing quietly in a far corner of the pasture, he looked up at us, his small, savage head, powerful neck and chest strongly reminiscent of Northern Dancer.

Griffin didn't have much to say about the six Danzig yearlings that had been raised and broken at Claiborne the previous year. They had been sensible youngsters, he said, in a noncommittal way. "But they could turn out to be flash-in-the-pans. Danzig had soft bones—he had those bad knees." Nevertheless, I had a feeling that there was something special about them, particularly Chief's Crown, who seemed to embody so many odd nicks and whose pedigree was so full of ironies.

In Chief's Crown, two Triple Crown winners crossed genetic paths with Northern Dancer; Suffolk Downs met Churchill Downs; and Seventh Avenue converged on Paris, Kentucky. There had to be some significance in all that. But I wouldn't know for sure until Saratoga, where I would see Chief's Crown run for the first time.

CHAPTER 3

Saratoga's Hot Springs of Hope

We—are August . . . Where there's only one month of a calendar, all life is in it.

—Hortense Calisher

The good times of Saratoga, I believe, as of the world in general, are rapidly passing away.

—Henry James

"SARATOGA AND SUFFOLK both begin with S," Peter Fuller once told me, "but that's where the resemblance ends." Every year, when racing in New York moves north, Saratoga's brief season inspires railbirds to rise to the occasion with plaid pants and boaters, and stirs turf writers to flights of rapture. There is a special intensity to Saratoga, as James Agee observed, due to both the shortness of the season and the history and location of the town. Saratoga, said Agee, "grants none of that leisure for the gentle build-up and the dying fall which is the typical rhythm of more typical seasons but is brutally shear-lopped fore and aft." When fans "come to a small town thirty miles north of Albany in the foothills of the Adirondacks for thirty days' racing," he said, they "come to sit down and stay the time out, night and day."

For four weeks in August, Saratoga becomes the town of "Health, History, and Horses"—a place of pilgrimage, thronging with believers, swells, and touts who come to revive their spirits and renew their faith in racing. The cycle of racing that culminates in the spring with the classic races begins again, as the best young two-year-olds in the country make their debut, and the survivors of the previous generation battle it out for the three-year-old championship.

Paradoxically, because so many great horses have lost at Saratoga, the track is known both as the cradle and as the graveyard of champions.

For some, even the idea of Saratoga is enough to keep the cycle going. Said Joe Palmer, the most bookish of sportswriters, "As a man sweltering through the lone and level sands of the Sahara draws new strength from an inward vision of green palm trees and cool water in some verdant oasis, so it is possible to struggle through Jamaica-in-July in the hope of Saratoga."

Like any fashionable destination, Saratoga has had its ups and downs, but it has always been a place with mythic restorative powers. Before one came to Saratoga for the horses, one came for the waters, for the saline springs that bubble up from layers of limestone and shale through the cracks of the Saratoga Fault. Long before Gentleman Johnny Burgoyne and his hired Hessians lost the battle of Saratoga to the legions of Benedict Arnold, the famed waters of the swampy, pine-forested valley in the foothills of the Adirondacks had brought wounded Iroquois warriors to drink and bathe. Jacques Cartier had heard of Saratoga's springs in 1535. However, the first white man known to have sampled the curative powers of the springs was William Johnson, an Irish baronet who had come to America in 1738 to tend his uncle's New York estate and to set up a trading post.

Commissioned by the British as Commissary of New York for Indian Affairs, Johnson discovered a strong affinity for the Mohawk Indians, frequently joining them in their festivals and powwows, daubing himself with paint and dressing himself in animal skins and feathers. The Mohawks were so grateful for his efforts on their behalf that they named him Chief Warraghiyagey (He Who Does Much) and awarded him more than a hundred thousand acres of land, making him one of the greatest landowners of the colonial era. During his visits to local villages, he fathered over a hundred children by various Iroquois women. One of them, Molly Brant, sister to Joseph Brant, the great Mohawk chief, he made mistress of Johnson Hall, his baronial mansion, where he entertained social and political leaders of the day.

In late middle age, Johnson began to pay the price for an impulsive life, and he suffered from gout and dysentery. His thigh throbbed continually from a musket wound he had received in a battle at Lake George. When Molly's ministrations of drugs and herbs failed to alleviate his troubles, an escort of Iroquois braves took him by boat down the Mohawk River to Schenectady and from there bore him on a litter to High Rock Springs, a cone-shaped rock from whence bubbled the magical waters whose location the Iroquois had kept secret for so long. For four days Johnson lay inside a birch-bark hut on a couch fashioned by the Iroquois from forest leaves, drinking and bathing himself in the salty water that had been dipped from the spring with dried gourd shells. When he was called back by a crisis at home, he found that his health had improved so much that he was able to walk part of the way. Writing to his friend Philip Schuyler, scion of the region's most powerful family, Johnson confided, "I have just returned from a visit to a most amazing spring, which almost effected my cure."

Mr. Baruch's baths

On a Tuesday, the last day of July, I had gone in search of those same magic waters, which were bubbling more slowly now, after two centuries of therapeutic baths and commercial bottling ventures. You can still find echoes of Saratoga's mythic powers in the inscriptions atop the colonnade at the old Hall of Springs, where an anonymous poet shamelessly cast aside all restraint in a series of apostrophes to the spirit of the spa: "Thy glory lies within thy vales that inexhaustible hold forth the cup of health and joy to all that come . . . Worn Indian warriors and huntsmen exhausted renewed their vigor at these enlivening springs . . . Renowned art thou and to the joyous scene health and pleasures drawest the thronging multitude."

Inspired by the vast, high-ceilinged halls and quiet green

expanses of the great European spas, the Hall of Springs was built by the state in the 1930s for the purpose of conserving the rapidly dwindling underground springs and promulgating the virtues of mineral baths. Inspired by his father's, Dr. Simon Baruch's, belief in the therapeutic powers of mineral springs, statesman and Wall Street wizard Bernard Baruch had convinced Franklin Roosevelt to fund the project. Said Baruch at the time: "I am interested in physical medicine because my father was. I am interested in rehabilitation because I believe in it. I am interested in arthritis because I have it."

Nowadays, the Hall is no Baden Baden, despite its WPA-era columns and porticoes; gone are the days when a *kur* meant chandeliers and orchestras, spouting fountains and strolling neurasthenics. The Washington bathhouse, long abandoned, is being converted into the National Museum of Dance, and patrons of the Roosevelt and the Lincoln go mainly for the cheap rubdowns rather than the fickle waters, whose color varies daily from reddish to gray and whose bubble-power may range from champagne to flat.

On this warm, lazy day, twenty-four hours before the start of Saratoga's racing and social season, the grounds were preternaturally calm. I could hear the distant thunks of a tennis game from the courts near the Gideon Putnam Hotel, and I could almost hear the ghost of ailing tycoons splashing in the stained porcelain tubs. There was a metallic, medicinal smell in the air, but it seemed to promote languor rather than vigor.

It occurred to me that the real elixir at Saratoga now is the horses; the track is where the pulses quicken with hope. And the ultimate elixir, it seemed, is a good two-year-old. "No one with a good two-year-old has ever committed suicide," goes the old track saying.

Mr. Morrissey's track

The theme of Saratoga, Joe Palmer had said, is young horses and old friends. Until recently, however, the dominant historical theme of the spa had been young horses and old tycoons. Without tycoons willing to take a gamble, Saratoga might be better known as a brand of bottled water than as the most fabled racetrack in America.

After Johnson's discovery of the springs, a succession of famous and powerful men coveted the waters, including George Washington, who considered buying the whole works. It was a lumberjack named Gideon Putnam, however, who foresaw how the waters might be turned into gold. Putnam built a comfortable guest house alongside a newly discovered spring known as Congress Spring, and the resulting influx of visitors enabled him to begin building a village.

By the 1830s, Saratoga, which came to be called simply The Springs, enjoyed a reputation as America's most fashionable resort, a summer retreat with a slightly racy reputation, enhanced by the attacks of James Gordon Bennett, owner of the sensation-blaring New York *Herald:* "Beautiful Saratoga! Cradle of fashion and intrigue! Rendezvous of lacqueys and jockeys! Seraglio of the prurient aristocracy!" Before the arrival in town of John Morrissey, however, Saratoga's reputation for raciness had not yet been earned. The primary pastimes for the belles and *grandes dames* who flocked to Saratoga were promenades, ballroom dancing and matchmaking.

Morrissey, a tall, heavy-browed Irishman, had turned a talent for street-brawling, bullying, and gang-leading into a successful career in politics and the boxing ring. While friendly policemen looked the other way, Morrissey opened a series of gaming parlors around New York City, maintaining a reputation in private poker sessions as a fair and honest player.

In 1861, Morrissey came to Saratoga with his roulette wheels and faro tables and an entourage of dealers and bouncers. Setting up shop on Matilda Street, near the posh hotels on Broadway, he soon monopolized the town's gambling trade. However, when he decided to open a racetrack in 1863 for the further amusement of his patrons, he needed assistance. The war was on, and horses were in such demand that in Kentucky, it was rumored, the great sire Lexington, blind and fifteen years old, had to be hidden away in order to avoid conscription. Blueblooded horses were in as short supply as able-bodied men.

For his fledgling racing association, Morrissey called on William R. Travers, the Wall Street broker, clubman and society wit; John R. Hunter, a Westchester sportsman; and Leonard W. Jerome, the lawyer and yachtsman whose daughter Jennie would become Lady Churchill, mother of Sir Winston Churchill. Citing the ideals of progress and genetic purity that aristocrats commonly used as their rationale for racing horses, the group called themselves the Saratoga Association for the Improvement of the Breed of Horses.

Morrissey's first meet was held on a roughly hewn track in the pine woods called Horse Haven. It lasted for four days, featuring two races a day. With victories at Gettysburg and Vicksburg to celebrate, thousands of notables showed up for the races, even though the grandstand was small and the land was covered by piny growths. The following year, the meet was moved to a new track built across the way on a 125-acre tract of land purchased by the racing association. In tribute to Travers, the association's president, the first Travers Stakes was held, even as the Union armies were marching on Atlanta. Appropriately, the race was won by Travers's own Kentucky, son of Lexington, bred in Ashland, Kentucky, by John Clay, a son of Southern statesman and onetime Saratoga patron Henry Clay.

Now, one hundred and fifteen years later, Saratoga was the oldest racetrack still in use in America, and the Travers was still one of the three big races at the Saratoga meet; it was considered a postscript to the Triple Crown, a further test of the best three-year-olds, indicating those that might go on to compete against older horses in the fall. My wildest dream was that the horse I chose as my protagonist would begin and end the championship cycle at Saratoga: that he would win the Hopeful and return to Saratoga the following year to win the one-hundred-and-sixteenth running of the Travers.

Madame Jumel's parade

I had rented the ground floor of a turn-of-the-century cottage on Circular Street, just three blocks from Union Street, the grand promenade that sweeps from Canfield Casino and the fountains of Congress Park to the racetrack. My landlord, like many nonwagering Saratogians, vacates his house every August and retreats to Vermont. I couldn't imagine anyone voluntarily

leaving a proximity to the best racing in America, but my landlord's heart lay in another sport. He had lined his walls with
autographed baseball bats and gloves and collages of faded
cards and clippings. I felt as though I were inhabiting a shrine
dedicated to the memory of the Brooklyn Dodgers. There were
so many calls for him at odd hours and from odd places that I
feared he might be a drug dealer, until one of the importunate
callers explained that he was seeking baseball mementoes.

Saratoga, like so many resorts whom the wealthy have pa-
tronized and abandoned, is full of ghosts. Two houses down
from my cottage was a small, well-pillared white mansion said
to be haunted by the spirit of Madame Jumel, the most notorious in a series of fancy women who have attempted to rule
Saratoga society. Madame Jumel, born Elizabeth Bowen, the
illegitimate offspring of a sailor and a prostitute from Provi-
dence, Rhode Island, had beguiled her way into polite society
with a series of advantageous affairs and marriages, among
which was a brief liaison with former Vice-President Aaron
Burr. Nevertheless, she had never succeeded in impressing the
stately dowagers who guarded the portals of the social order in
New York, and she focused her energy on Saratoga Springs,
where *grandes dames* from Boston and Philadelphia as well as
New York vied for the lead in the daily procession of carriages
that paraded down Broadway to Lake Saratoga. Madame Jumel,
who could have taught Ben Hur a few lessons in ruthless chariot
racing, seldom failed to attain the lead in her big, gold-colored
carriage, from whence she would graciously reign as queen of
this wheeled elite.

One day, however, after she had found her way with unusual
ease to the front of the procession, she noticed that the sidewalk
spectators, instead of looking on in awe as she waved her os-
trich-plumed fan, were laughing and pointing. Looking back,
she saw only a single coach following her in the procession, a
rattletrap painted the same gold color as her own carriage,
pulled by four bony nags. Inside the carriage was a former slave
named Thomas Camel, dressed in a low-necked gown, lan-
guidly waving an ostrich fan in parody of her grand manner-
isms. The following day, her carriage again retained the lead in

the procession without opposition. In Madame Jumel's lap was a
pistol.

Mrs. Whitney's ball

On Wednesday, August 1, the first day of the meet, as I was
exploring the grounds of the racetrack, admiring the effect of
the potted pansies and geraniums set against the brightly
striped awnings and gleaming white cupolas of the clubhouse, I
saw an apparition worthy of Madame Jumel. A pale, pretty
blond woman of fifty or so, dressed in a pale pastel swirl of silk
and chiffon, had arrived in a horse-drawn carriage, accompanied by TV cameras and reporters. It was Marylou Whitney,
wife of Cornelius Vanderbilt "Sonny" Whitney, the sportsman,
tycoon, and scion of one of racing's greatest dynasties. Asked a
young woman reporter, somewhat nonplussed by the atavistic
splendor, "Do you ever get tired of all this?" Tipping the floppy
brim of her hat toward the proffered microphone, Mrs. Whitney replied: "Never. Sometimes I think I was born in the wrong
century."

Mrs. Whitney had, in fact, been born in Kansas, to a middle-
class family in the country-club set, as I learned when I was
invited to lunch a few days later at Cady Hill, an old stagecoach
inn that the Whitneys had converted into a comfortable, unpre-
tentious country house. Mrs. Whitney greeted me in one of her
timeless, white satin-and-lace creations, the kind of dress that
always made me think of modern-day Cinderellas. Her voice
combined the broad A's of upper-class polish with an impulsive,
almost dizzy warmth. A divorcee with four children when she
met Whitney at a dinner party in Arizona, she had worked as
host of a TV cooking show. Whitney cast her in *Missouri Trav-
eler*, a Western he was producing, and in 1958 she became his
fourth wife.

When he first brought her to Saratoga, however, the spa had
become a little démodé, as had most of the former millionaires'
meccas in the East. Cleveland Amory, in his history of great
American resorts, had observed that by the early fifties all the
money and energy seemed to be flowing West: "Riding high,
wide and handsome on oil wells and expense accounts—two

forms of wealth which because of current tax structures are really the last remaining 'money' in the old sense of the word—the West's great resorts, Palm Springs and Sun Valley, Reno and Las Vegas, Tucson and Phoenix, Prescott and Santa Fe, Colorado Springs and Aspen, are, in contrast to the East's ghost towns, all social boom towns."

Undaunted, Mrs. Whitney set out to revitalize the spa's social scene. Recalled Mrs. Whitney, as we sipped tea in Cady Hill's bright, cushion-strewn morning room: "When Sonny first brought me here, I had read about the old traditions of my husband's family, and I couldn't believe there was no social life. It was deader than a doornail. All the social life revolved around the golf and polo clubs, and it was a little stuffy. I thought somebody should perk it up."

She began giving dinner parties every year on the Tuesday night before the season began, and a big bash on Whitney eve, the Friday before the Whitney Stakes, named for William Collins Whitney, Sonny's grandfather. This year, the theme was to be winter carnival, complete with mock-ice rink, and the guest of honor was to be Kirk Douglas.

"Nobody goes to Marylou's ball," a Saratoga socialite from the old days had told me. "She has a following of new people coming into the business and people who need to go to her parties to meet people. You have to realize she has only been on the scene fifteen or twenty years, and people are not sure where she came from."

Nevertheless, whether by talent or by default, Mrs. Whitney had become the de facto *grande dame* of Saratoga. Her parties were so popular that police had to be hired to turn away gate-crashers. Said another socialite, a Marylou supporter, "She deserves credit for hanging in there, for keeping the social thing going when everybody had lost interest." Over the years, her enthusiasm began to catch on, and every hostess now had to stake out her own special night each season.

What's more, Mrs. Whitney not only tolerated journalists; she even went so far as to court them. "One year," she said, "attendance at the races was going down, and my husband and I had not done much commercially with the press. This is a very private time and place for us; that was the attitude of my husband. So I started asking how we could get Saratoga on the map. I had been part of the media—I was an anchor girl on the radio and I did TV. I know what it's like. They can help you if you're nice to them. I began to invite the press. I said, certainly come, this will help Saratoga.

"I talked to Sonny's friends. I asked how the media would picture us—they'll just say we're a bunch of rich, stuffy people unless you open up to them. People want to know about the social life. You can't have an exciting summer place without knowing that there is a social life too. You have to let people look at you and see you and be nice to the general public."

One year, Ciro's, a popular hangout near the racetrack, sponsored a Marylou Whitney Look Alike contest, and instead of responding like Madame Jumel to the implied mockery, Mrs. Whitney upped the prize from a trip for two to a trip for four to Los Angeles.

Said Mrs. Whitney: "A lot of people were shocked with me, going to the track for the past ten years with TV cameras. I heard a lot of whispers. But we have the same box at the track as Sonny's grandfather, who saved the track. And Commodore Vanderbilt was here all the time. I like to think I can carry on some of that tradition."

Mrs. Whitney, it seemed to me, had indeed carried on the Whitney tradition of sportsmanship: an American-style noblesse oblige that is both self-serving and generous. Nearly a century earlier, when racing at the spa was falling apart, it was William Collins Whitney, a descendant of Revolutionary War General Josiah Whitney and cotton-gin inventor Elias Whitney, who came to the rescue. Toward the end of the 1890s, when politicians, preachers and newspaper editors across America began to crusade against the more conspicuous excesses of *fin-de-siècle* frivolity, one of the first casualties of the newly righteous was Saratoga. Always the least stuffy of the watering holes of the wealthy, Saratoga had thrived on the sporting activities that tempted millionaires and hustlers alike: the racetrack and the casino.

In the old days of the grand hotels, one could rub elbows at the roulette wheel with the Vanderbilts or fraternize with bookies named Joe "The Orator" Cleason and "Tiffany" Wolfgang (the latter so named because he guaranteed his prices to be as good as anything in the Grand Union branch store of the famous New York jeweler). The People's Party as well as the Democrats and the Republicans had regularly held their state conventions at the spa. However, as the statewide campaign against gambling heated up, fashionable people with pretensions to respectability began to stay away from Saratoga. As Joe Palmer once described it, Saratoga "fell flat on its face."

One might say that the spa had developed an image problem. In August of 1894, Joseph Pulitzer, publisher of the New York *World,* sent his star reporter Elizabeth Cochrane, who wrote under the pseudonym Nellie Bly, to expose the decadence of life amid the upstate springs. Pulitzer touted Bly's indignant tirade with such headlines as "Reputable and Disreputable Women, Solid Merchants, Bankers, Sports, Touts, Criminals and Race-Track Riff-Raff Crazed by the Mania for Gold." As a writer for *Harper's* observed at the time, "Mr. Whitney . . . took control of a race-track that had fallen upon a sporting name as bad as that of Guttenberg" (a track in New Jersey where horses were said to be prodded by electrical shock devices).

Whitney, a stock speculator and Tammany Hall power broker who had originally gotten involved in racing to outdo James R. Keene, a Wall Street rival and founder of the Jockey Club, mustered his considerable influence among New York financial circles and put together a syndicate of wealthy sportsmen to buy the track and set it on a more honorable course. In 1901, Whitney and his colleagues instituted two important races for two-year-olds, the Saratoga Special and the Hopeful, the latter a futurity, whose first nominees would not run until 1903. The Hopeful, in a sense, became a symbol both of racehorse owners' faith in their young horses and of their faith in the sport's capacity to renew and perpetuate itself.

Although a Keene horse won the first Hopeful, the first Saratoga Special was won by Goldsmith, a Whitney horse, and the following year the winner was Irish Lad, a one-horse stable owned by Whitney's son Harry, who was to win the race four more times, once with a filly, the legendary Regret. Whitney's grandson, Sonny, was to win it thrice. The Whitneys had less luck with the Hopeful, however, Harry winning it once and Sonny thrice.

The renaissance of racing at Saratoga that followed Will Whitney's rescue effort, reported the writer for *Harper's*, was a "frank return to the old life of pleasure," bringing together the kind of motley crowd that only a combination of horses and high society seemed to draw: "Cubans released from thraldom, Southerners whose fathers and mothers gave up coming North, Catholic priests and Espiscopal ministers, negroes on a holiday, smart-looking brokers, horse-trainers, merchants of middle Broadway of the type celebrated by Puck, Tammany politicians pursy and red-necked, sweet old-fashioned white-haired ladies in black, vague superannuated gentlemen eager for a few more years of life." Saratoga's revitalized social elixir blended the regimen of the mineral baths with the rigors of social climbing and the daily stimuli of the track.

The secret of Saratoga, when Saratoga worked, was a precarious balance between elegance and vulgarity. And in 1984, it was a balance that still existed, thanks to Mrs. Whitney. From lower Broadway, where fast-food franchises adjoined the last of the gilded-age hotels, to mansion-lined upper Broadway, where hostesses competed for the best nights, you could still find that combination of social pretensions and lower depths that kept society at the old spa so lively.

As for the larger problems that plagued racing outside the magical oasis of Saratoga, it was clear that no single tycoon, nor a claque of tycoons, nor a cluster of limited partners could rescue the sport. Not even John Gaines's holy breeders' grail alone could keep the "round table" of racing together.

Twilight of the tycoons

Sonny himself, who joined us for a luncheon of salmon mousse and roast beef, decorated with radishes done up to look like tiny red mice, took a less exalted view than his wife of his role in perpetuating the blue-and-brown Whitney silks. A tall, slender man with a patrician nose and bright blue eyes, he spoke slowly and deliberately, but nonetheless I felt he liked to be considered a bit of a wag. His father, Harry Payne Whitney, and his mother, Gertrude Vanderbilt Whitney, great-granddaughter of the "Commodore," who was to gain more fame as little Gloria Vanderbilt's aunt than as founder of the Whitney Museum of Modern Art, had always expected him to start from the bottom of a business and work his way up, to build on his fortune before he could inherit it. He had worked in the mines before founding the Hudson Bay Mining Company, and he had flown planes in the Army before founding Pan American Airways.

He had played polo, he said, only because it had been his father's great passion—a passion undeterred by an incident in which the elder Whitney put out his best friend's eye—and because of his rivalry with his cousin Jock Whitney. After he won world polo championships in 1936 and 1937 against his cousin, he felt as though he had proved himself sufficiently and got out of the sport entirely.

As for racing, it was not an obligation he could put away so easily, although he had tried it once or twice. When Harry Payne Whitney died in 1930, a week before he was to run Equipoise in the Pimlico Futurity, Sonny considered withdrawing the horse. But Equipoise, who was known as "the Chocolate Soldier," appeared to be the best young horse in the country, and friends of the elder Whitney convinced Sonny to keep the horse in the race. As it turned out, Equipoise won with a rousing finish, after stumbling in the mud and trailing the field by twenty lengths. Whitney found himself leaping to his feet and shouting with excitement, thinking the sport was easy. The Chocolate Soldier was to remain Sonny's best horse, winning the Whitney in 1932, although during the next decades Whitney raced more stakes winners than any other American.

When Whitney was once asked if there were a single horse that could fulfill every dream of an owner—for speed, endurance, courage—he had replied: "I happen to have owned the horse. His name was Equipoise. Equipoise had that ineffable something that no computer will ever be able to discern: the competitive spirit. Horses have it just as humans do. Equipoise couldn't bear the thought of another horse passing him in a race." Equipoise had been the ideal competitor, the fighter who would bite a rival rather than be passed.

When I asked Whitney about his current stable, however,

inquiring whether he had any good colts who would be making their debut at the meet, his eyes did not light up in the dreamy way I had come to expect from owners of unraced two-year-olds. He owned one promising two-year-old, he said, a full brother to his good three-year-old Hail Bold King named Inca King. But he no longer visited the stables regularly, he said, nor attended the races except when his own horses were running. And soon, he said, he would be phasing himself out of racing. He seemed more interested in talking about his other endeavors, particularly Marine World, the world's first oceanarium, that he had built in Florida during the 1930s. "I think we came from fish, not from monkeys, you see."

Because the racetrack seemed such a complete and self-sufficient cosmos, I kept forgetting that it did not circumscribe the lives of wealthy owners, most of whom had made their fortunes and their marks elsewhere. I was always overestimating the importance of horses in the lives of the "horsey" set, and Mr. Whitney was careful to place his horses in perspective for me. "All my businesses were exciting," he said. "The horses were just part of it." For Whitney, as for most old-guard owners, horses had been the third proving ground—after business and society.

One of the best things about horses, though, said Whitney, was that they had given him a chance to meet ordinary people. He liked to wander around his farm in Kentucky, he said, and talk to the hill folk. Which led to his oft-repeated story about the day his father's horse Whiskery won the Kentucky Derby.

On a casual evening walk around his father's farm after the race, as his father and his cronies were playing poker in a private railroad car, Whitney saw a group of stablehands gathered around a bonfire, celebrating the victory with drink and song. "In the shadows a few yards away I saw a horse tethered, so I went up to one of the men, who didn't have any idea who I was, and I asked him who the horse was." It was the mare Regret, the only other Whitney horse to have won the Derby, thirteen years earlier. The men had brought her up on the hill to join the celebration. Whitney sat around until the wee hours of the morning, listening to the singing, and for the first time, he said, he "had some appreciation of the real emotions that go with horse racing."

Whitney was no ordinary plutocrat, but I was reminded nevertheless of Ortega y Gasset's theory about why rich men and aristocrats in the Western world have tended to get involved with the breeding and racing of horses. By engaging in hunting, said Gasset, men could recreate an earlier, archaic form in life when humans still lived within the orbit of animal existence. And in racing, he said, men could cloak their primitive drives for pleasure and domination with the veneer of gentility and sophistication. If Sonny Whitney, for example, couldn't openly savage a competitor, his horse Equipoise could.

Horse racing, as John Gaines had theorized, gave rich men another frontier, another proving ground—a goal that money couldn't buy. And so the basic motivation in a rich man's sport, according to the Gaines/Gasset theory, was not only to defeat your rivals vicariously, but to ride the wheel of fortune—to experience the very dangers and risks that your money has sheltered you from. And thus racing gave you something in common with the less fortunate.

"If you talk to people in the hills, to working people, you find that they like the same things we do," said Whitney, "that they have a great sense of humor." He had stolen his best jokes from those people, he said, and began to recount a few. Learning that I lived in Boston, he obliged with the old chestnut about the schoolteacher and the scrod.

Less than two weeks later, on the Friday before the Travers Stakes, in which his colt Hail Bold King was entered, Whitney announced that he was retiring from horse racing, and that most of his racing and breeding stock would be sent to auction. Summoning reporters to the small press box atop the clubhouse, Whitney said that when he took the stable over from his father in 1930 it was a "small business compared to what it is today. What I am saying is that to be in the top echelon of the sport today is a full-time job. I have reached an age when I prefer not to attempt this, because when I undertake a job I aim to be the best in the business." Racing, he was implying, was no longer a rich man's hobby, but big business.

As he finished his announcement, I felt that the track bugler should have played taps for the end of a racing dynasty—and for the end of the gilded era of an American sport.

Whitney was one of the last monied aristocrats who had once dominated the upper echelons of horse racing in America. These alfresco aristocrats, for whom many of the great stakes races have been named, had been a versatile sort, as accustomed to deference at presidential cabinet meetings as at the Jockey Club or in their own board rooms. It was said of William Du Pont, Jr., one of Whitney's contemporaries, that he was a man who could "roll a bandage, exercise a horse, ride a race, design a stable, breed a top class runner, build a racetrack and write a perfect piece of legislation."

Nowadays the sporting tycoons, like the towering elms that shade the paddock at Saratoga, were dying off. The Saratoga elms have been replaced by maples as they wither, one by one, and the elder statesmen of horse racing were being supplanted by a variety of new species. Many of these hardy new owners seemed to know more about tax shelters than they did about horses, and they approached racing as a business rather than a sport.

When Whitney's horses were sold at auction, two of the most ambitious of these newcomers bought Hail Bold King and Inca King as part of their bids to build new dynasties out of the shreds of the old. Robert Brennan, who had beaten Cousin Leslie to the punch by founding ITB, the first big public-owned racing and breeding venture, had bought Hail Bold King. Inca King had gone to Barry Schwartz, of Calvin Klein fashions, the Bronx-born businessman who had bought out Puritan Fashions from Carl Rosen's heirs after Rosen's death. So far, however, both Brennan and Schwartz had been seen far more often in the paddock, amid the pre-race promenade of owners, than in the winner's circle.

Hail to the Chief

On the afternoon of Whitney eve, August 3, Marylou Whitney and a smattering of the old dynasties fanned themselves in clubhouse boxes, but the eighty-second running of the first big two-year-old race of the meet, the Saratoga Special, once run as a winner-take-all event, lacked even a token old-guard entry. Sky Command, the big gray colt from Churchill Downs who had won the Belmont Juvenile so easily in his second start, was the handicappers' favorite, and Nickel Back, owned by Eugene Klein and trained by D. Wayne Lukas, was second pick. Third choice, but the bettors' favorite, was Chief's Crown, the Danzig colt I had been so eager to see.

I'd like to say that my first glimpse of Chief's Crown had the impact of a trumpet blare, the fanfare of a curtain being opened on a five-act drama. Secretariat, according to his biographer Bill Nack, had that sort of impact on people as a two-year-old. Veteran turf writer Charlie Hatton, said Nack, had risen to his feet in awe when he first saw Big Red: "Hatton had seen thousands of horses in his life, thousands of two-year-olds, and suddenly on this July afternoon of 1972 he found the 106-carat diamond: 'It was like seeing a bunch of gravel and there was the Kohinoor lying in there. It was so unexpected.' Hatton thought, 'Jesus Christ, I never saw a horse that looked like that before.' "

Secretariat had not yet been able to produce a son or grandson that could command such instant respect, and Chief's Crown was not likely to improve his grandsire's reputation for stamping his get. The Chief, as I took to calling him almost immediately, was closer in appearance to his other grandsire, Northern Dancer, although he did not yet have the bulldog stockiness of the Nearctic line. He was a small colt, just over fifteen hands, with a delicate, sculpted head and sleek, well-balanced body. He was a common bay color, a plain, used-penny brown that edged into black at his mane and tail. His eyes were ringed with black, giving his narrow face the bruised look of a coddled prince who had gotten into a fight. A suggestion of floppiness to one of his ears added the only touch of commonness to his appearance. There was an air of tough composure about him, though, as José Mena, his young Cuban groom, led him around the cluster of maple trees designated as the saddling area for the horse who had drawn the No. 4 post position.

Compared to the flashy, excitable Ziggy's Boy, the other Danzig colt I had seen in July, he didn't radiate charisma, but he

did exude a calm, don't-mess-with-me air that bespoke a colt who had taken the demands of the track in stride. Nothing seemed to surprise or alarm him; it was as though his manners in the paddock were as genetically ingrained as his proclivity to run.

The Chief's personality seemed remarkably well suited to his jockey, Don MacBeth, a quiet, pale, intense man of thirty-four, a Canadian whose forte was icy composure rather than macho histrionics. Roger Laurin had made a habit of using young, hungry riders on his most promising horses, and although Mac-Beth was not young, he was still in the stage of proving himself. He had ridden Deputy Minister, the champion two-year-old in 1981, but since then his record had been spotty; he had scored enough upsets in big races to keep himself near the top of the game, but he did not get the best mounts on a regular basis.

During the parade to post, MacBeth and the Chief both looked like pros who were accustomed to keeping their emotions to themselves. There was none of the prancing or display I had come to expect from good, fit young horses; the Chief walked like an old veteran who didn't waste any energy on nonessentials. His ears perked up when he neared the starting gate, but I still saw no evidence of the pre-race dancing that often precedes a winning effort.

When the buzzer sounded, both Do It Again Dan and Nickel Back beat the Chief out of the gate. After a quarter of a mile, Sky Command surged to the lead, followed by Don't Fool With Me. The Chief was third, three lengths back. He did not run with the easy grace of a natural athlete, but reached out from the shoulders with an awkward, pounding stride. He could really cover the ground, though, with that big reach, like an Olympic swimmer, and after a half mile he passed Don't Fool With Me easily and loomed up outside Sky Command. At the top of the stretch, he stuck his neck in front, and Sky Command tried to hang on, but the Chief swept by him, scoring by nearly three lengths.

There is my Hopeful, I thought, as I looked at the time on the scoreboard: a minute, ten and one fifth seconds, the fourth fastest Saratoga Special ever, nearly three seconds faster than his great-grandsire Nearctic had run the race, more than two

seconds faster than last year's winner, Swale. The track was fast, but not exceptionally so; the Chief was either a precocious speedster or a horse of real quality. I would know for sure three weeks later, in the Hopeful; with its extra half-furlong, the race traditionally had weeded out the speedballs from the stayers, pointing up the colts that had a future.

My decision to choose the Chief did not come from a blinding flash of handicapping insight, but from a combination of factors that tend to influence the amateur gambler rather than the pro; I was going not only by the Chief's performance and pedigree, but by a feeling I had about him, about the convergence of influences and coincidences I had felt in Kentucky, and which I felt again in Saratoga.

Perhaps I would get as lucky as staffers for *Sports Illustrated* did thirty years earlier when they, too, were looking for a special horse. When I had described my quest for a Hopeful to Whitney Tower, Sonny Whitney's cousin, the venerable former correspondent for *Sports Illustrated* who was now serving as head of the Museum of Racing, Tower reminded me of the incredible good fortune of the *S.I.* photojournalism team that had set out in 1954 to follow the life of a racehorse from birth through his three-year-old year. Calumet Farm was still at the peak of its glory, and they had narrowed their odds by choosing a Calumet foal. Yet who would have thought that the little gray colt, named Iron Liege, would go on to win the Derby? For one thing, it was Calumet's General Duke who had shown promise as a two-year-old. What's more, Iron Liege had been born the same year as three other great horses: Gallant Man, Bold Ruler and Round Table. And yet Iron Liege seemed to have been born under a lucky star.

General Duke never made it to the Derby. And during the course of the race, in the spring of 1957, the great Willie Shoemaker, aboard Gallant Man, made the riding error of the century. Gallant Man had taken the lead briefly a sixteenth of a mile from the finish line, and Shoemaker, thinking he had crossed the wire, stood up in the irons. Meanwhile Iron Liege, with Bill Hartack aboard, retook the lead and won the race. It had been a bizarre mistake, considering, as one steward observed, that

"you can't miss the finish line at Churchill Downs—it looks like the Taj Mahal."

I didn't know yet whether the Chief would be as lucky, but I felt that he at least had a head start. So far, he had done everything asked of him, and he had yet to do anything wrong.

After watching him for a few mornings on the track and back at the barn, I became convinced that he was a special colt, unlike any other I had been around. There was an eagerness and intensity to him that set him apart—a sense of energy held in reserve that Tesio would have approved of. In his stall, he was always at the door, watching intently everything that was going on, and when he was outside he seemed to be drinking in the environment, sizing it up, through his eyes, ears, even his skin.

Sometimes there was a sweet, vulnerable coltishness to him, especially when you fed him a carrot. He would quiver with eagerness. But he was never really playful, like most other young horses. The Chief seemed to know that he was carrying a heavy responsibility on his shoulders, as the dutiful grandson of two Triple Crown winners. When he walked to the track in his grave, serious way, I was reminded of certain child prodigies who bypass the frivolities of childhood in order to go on stage.

But the Chief was also carrying another kind of legacy. He had been bred not by a bluegrass baron but by the man who had made a fortune from Calvin Klein jeans—the clothing manufacturer who got his start in racing at Suffolk Downs, the gambler's gambler whose luck had carried until he got sick. The Chief, in a sense, was a belated gift from an absentee father to his children, who at first had little notion of the value of the bequest. And he was trained by a man who had been involved in a different kind of legacy—a man who had relinquished the greatest horse since Man o' War to his own father, but who also, at first, had little notion of the value of the gift.

On the more pragmatic side of things, I figured that at this stage of the game the Chief had the best odds of any horse in the country of winning the Derby. He had not been born with the prodigious talent of a Secretariat, but he had been born with an extraordinary aptitude for racing. He seemed remarkably sound and track-smart, and he had improved with each race. And with each step in his career, he had narrowed his odds.

When he was born, the odds of the Chief winning the Derby were at their highest—technically, some 38,500 to 1, the size of the foal crop of 1982. Already, his odds were greater than those of Secretariat, who was born amid a smaller foal crop.

In reality, though, the Chief's odds were not as great as they seemed. When the average foal is born, he faces less than a fifty-fifty chance of ever making it to the races, and the odds of his ever winning a race are approximately one in forty. For the sons and daughters of leading sires, however—those whose successful offspring merit them a ranking on the average-earnings index—the odds are somewhat better for becoming winners: one in seven. The odds of such a horse winning a stakes race are one in eighteen, and the odds of being nominated to the Derby are about one in a hundred; of actually winning the Derby, one in fifteen hundred.

Although the Chief's sire, Danzig, was still a novice, he was already ranked second on the list for new sires of two-year-olds. And by winning a stakes race at Saratoga, the Chief had narrowed his odds still further. Based on previous winners of the Saratoga Special who had competed in the Derby, the odds that the Chief would run in the Derby were 5 to 1; and that he would win it, 16 to 1. However, since more and more colts in recent years had bypassed Saratoga, I figured that the odds for the Chief in my own private advance summer-book wagering on the Derby were about 10 to 1.

The odds, however, of the Chief becoming a truly great horse, of towering above his generation as Secretariat had, were vastly higher. And the odds of his "improving the breed," as Secretariat thus far had failed to do, as a sire, were incalculable.

When you looked at the statistics, the very existence of a Secretariat, who seemed to set new track records with every race, seemed a fluke. As British equine researcher Brian Singleton once said, "You take Secretariat and put him into a biomechanical model on a computer and smoke comes out of the back of the machine . . . He shouldn't be."

The genetic history of the thoroughbred, in fact, seemed to follow, in speeded-up form, the pattern that occurs naturally in many biological systems: early experimentation and later standardization. According to paleontologist Stephen Jay Gould, when a "new body plan arises, evolution seems to try out all manner of twists, turns, and variations upon it . . . When systems first arise, they probe all the limits of possibility. Many variations don't work; the best solutions are found, and variation diminishes. As systems regularize, their variation decreases."

Over two centuries of selective breeding, the average height of the thoroughbred was increased by eight inches, and the average speed by twelve seconds a mile. During the nineteenth century, when a number of stallions were imported to America, and breeders even tried breeding their "blood" horses to other breeds, like Chickasaws, Narragansetts and Morgans, thoroughbreds kept getting taller and faster.

As the average length of races decreased, the emphasis in breeding shifted from endurance to speed, and the overall conformation of the thoroughbred changed accordingly. As French equine expert Colonel H. Cousté noted in his little book on mechanics, *Une Foulée de Galop de Course*, printed in 1906, the long, straight back of the thoroughbred had been shortened, and the croup (lower back) had begun to slope, allowing for shorter and faster strides.

With the strictures, however, brought by trying to hew to the British *Stud Book*, the genetic options narrowed, and by the time of Man o' War, who competed in 1918 and 1919, a genetic plateau had been reached. Track records began to stabilize or be whittled down by mere fifths of a second. In England, the times posted for the great Epsom Derby haven't changed much in seventy-five years. And as for the Kentucky Derby, the great Citation's time in 1948 was two seconds slower than the track record set in 1914 by Old Rosebud. In 1964, Northern Dancer set a new track record of two minutes, which stood until Secretariat whittled it down by three fifths of a second.

It seemed that thoroughbreds, selectively bred as a kind of equine "master race," chosen for speed-related characteristics such as strong heart and large lung capacity, had come as far as their thin, fragile legs would take them. Already, their speed, stamina and desire were often far greater than their knees and ankles could support.

By contrast, human athletes, who obviously were not "selectively bred" for speed but who were drawing on a much vaster genetic pool, had succeeded in whittling down speed records at a much faster rate. In 1896, Edwin Flack of Great Britain won the first Olympic 1,500-meter race in 4:33.2, equivalent to a mile in 4:53.87. Within forty years, Roger Bannister had run a four-minute mile, and by 1981, Steve Ovett of Great Britain had run a mile in 3:47.33, an improvement of nearly 22 percent. If Kentucky Derby performances had improved at the same rate, Secretariat should have run the mile-and-a-quarter in 1:38.

That night, I came home from the races to watch the Olympics on television, surrounded on every wall by mementoes of baseball heroes, and I started wondering again about what trainers were talking about when they claimed that thoroughbreds were "athletes," about what that notion meant in comparison to humans who competed and raced. With humans, some athletes obviously began with either a physical or a mental edge—like Ted Williams's legendary eyesight or Muhammad Ali's mythic reflexes. Some humans, like gymnast Mary Lou Retton, with her compressed frame and "Dick Butkus thighs," clearly had the ideal build for their chosen sport. Some, like Mary Decker Slaney, had even been discovered, like thoroughbreds, to have a higher supply of red blood cells than their competitors. Some, like hurdler Edwin Moses, had developed a technological edge, using biofeedback and computer analysis of performance. Yet none of these advantages would have mattered without physical and mental discipline and some evanescent quality that could only be called the will to win.

In one sense, you couldn't account for equine winners the way you could human achievers, for whom psychological factors were often the key. When a horse literally ran itself to death, struggling to the finish line on three legs, he was obviously not obeying the complex motives of, say, a war hero who risks his life in battle. Yet trainers often talked about "courage" in horses in the way coaches talked about courage in human athletes. When it came down to questions of aggressiveness and will and physical tests of speed and stamina, the correlation between humans and horses was closer. Even though, in the case of horses, their vocations had been thrust upon them rather than chosen, many of the same criteria for winning seemed to prevail.

Some horses, like Secretariat, had been gifted with perfect conformation and a magic way of going. Using a computerized analysis of gait efficiency, MIT professor George Pratt had concluded that Secretariat's gait had been close to perfect, with "as near to a continuous flow of thrust as four legs can manage." Similarly, a complete physical analysis of the great gelding John Henry by *Equus* magazine revealed that although the old boy was small, his conformation was perfectly balanced—the length of his back in perfect proportion to the length of his legs. Like Secretariat, his legs came down on the track like the spokes of a wheel, providing for maximum thrust and power. In addition, he was discovered to have abnormally strong bones and an unusually large heart. And as for that intangible quality—the will to win—he seemed to have more of it than any horse around. "You can see it in his eyes," Bill Perry had told me after he had seen John Henry one morning at Belmont Park. "The look of eagles," the old-timers used to call it.

Sir Quasar meets the Whitneys

Winners, I was to learn, come in all shapes and sizes, and sometimes they come when you least expect it. The day of the Whitney, Bill Perry was shipping in two horses, Sir Quasar and a sulky three-year-old colt named Oakward. Oakward was scheduled for the second race, a $75,000 claiming race, and Quasar was entered in the last race, for $50,000 claimers. Quasar's race, however, offered the additional incentive of a trophy named in honor of the Eurythmics, the British New Wave group, who were in town to perform that night at the Performing Arts Center near the Hall of Springs. The group's big hit, "Sweet Dreams," which came on at first like a sweet, electronic lullaby about visions of happiness, was actually a twisted anthem about love and pain, with an undercurrent of cruel irony. Not an inappropriate song for the track, I thought.

An hour before post time, I went over to visit Quasar at the receiving barn, located next to the training track, across the road from the main track. He was already working himself up, shifting his weight and swinging his head back and forth like a pendulum. "He been like this all day," said Felipe, his groom, worriedly. When Quasar saw me, he eagerly poked his head out of the stall for a scratch and a pat, but then retreated to the back of his stall for more fretting. He was already glistening with sweat, and I wondered if Perry would even be able to saddle him.

It was Perry's first time at Saratoga, and I spotted him wandering around the grounds. "Where do you saddle up?" he asked. He seemed astonished at the idea of horses being saddled under the trees with spectators milling about, within hoof-reach.

Undeterred by Perry's country-boy guise, I went off to bet an all-Suffolk daily double, combining Fast Lane Gal, a talented three-year-old filly trained by Suffolk veteran Vinnie Blengs, with both Oakward and another Blengs horse, Majestic Wine, in the second race. Fast Lane Gal was listed as 8 to 1 in the morning line, while both Oakward and Majestic Wine were listed as 5 to 1. I was hoping for even longer odds when horseplayers looked at the form with the usual prejudice against Suffolk.

The local sharpies, however, appeared to be wise to the Suffolk horses. Fast Lane Gal, who opened up a five-length lead within the first quarter, and who was never headed, went off at 2 to 1. In the second race, Majestic Wine went off at 4 to 1, while Oakward went up to 6 to 1. When Oakward blasted out of the gate, I thought I would make a small killing, but by mid-stretch Majestic Wine had turned on his strong closing kick, and he appeared to catch Oakward just at the wire. The stewards took more time than usual to examine the photo of the finish, and I was puzzled when the numbers of both horses appeared on the board, flashing, until I realized that it had been a dead heat. Both my daily double tickets were good: Fast Lane Gal with Oakward paid thirty-six dollars, and Fast Lane Gal with Majestic Wine paid thirty-two. Clearly, it was going to be one of those days when wishes were horses, and even beggars could ride.

Later, I went down to the paddock before the Whitney,

which had essentially become a match race between the promising three-year-old colt Track Barron, trained by Leroy "No Short Pants" Jolley, and the four-year-old Slew o' Gold, the late-blooming son of Seattle Slew who last year had been fourth in the Derby and second in the Belmont, and who then had come on later in the year to beat older horses in the big autumn races at Belmont. Slew had won the Woodward and the Jockey Club Gold Cup, and he had lost the Marlboro by a nose after a rash attempt by his jockey Angel Cordero to push Bates Motel, his main competitor, wide in the stretch. The third horse in the field was a fair-to-middling five-year-old named Thumbsucker, who was probably in it just for the third-place purse money.

I took one look at Slew o' Gold, and I knew that the three-year-old Track Barron didn't have a chance. Nor would any other horse in the country that day against Slew. If there were any doubt in my mind about what a good horse looked like, Slew was a one-horse course. His coat a burnished brown that gleamed gold in the sun, his head and neck sculpted as though in bronze, he resembled the four prancing gilt horses that grace the basilica of San Marco in Venice. I had seen one of the San Marco horses exhibited on a huge pedestal at the Metropolitan Museum in New York, and Slew, if he had been dipped in a vat and gilded, could have substituted. If Secretariat had suggested the quintessence of nature, Slew suggested the perfection of art.

Perry told me later that he, too, had stationed himself at the paddock early so he could get a good look at Slew. "To the average person," said Perry, "he's a beautiful horse. But as a trainer, I know how good he is. It's like only a connoisseur of wine knows how good a certain wine really is."

I combined Slew with Quasar in the last race for the late daily double, and I thought what a wonderful sport it was, to be combining on one ticket the best horse in the country with my nervous hero from Suffolk Downs.

Slew had little trouble living up to his looks, shadowing Track Barron around the track until midstretch, then galloping past him with as much ease as though he were out for an afternoon stroll. Angel Cordero was still holding him in check as he swept by the finish line, and you knew the winning margin of a length could as easily have been ten.

Fans had already begun to leave the stands when Felipe led Quasar out under the trees to be saddled for the last race, and I wondered if the little gelding would even make it to the starting gate. I had never seen a horse so lathered before a race. He was sopping wet, as though he had just emerged from a dip in Lake Saratoga, and he was shaking from head to toe. He kept stamping his feet, as though he were tying to intimidate his competitors. Bill had to enlist a third person to hold Quasar's ear while he put the saddle pad over the number-cloth and strapped on the tiny saddle. After he gave jockey Gregg McCarron a boost up on Quasar's back, the horse finally stopped quaking and began to prance proudly, a small, dripping facsimile of the show Slew had put on in the paddock earlier. It was the look of a very small, very wet eagle.

After the horses were loaded into the starting gate, it was Quasar who leaped out first, his teeth bared, but he was quickly overtaken by Flying Pocket, a four-year-old gelding who was running for a tag for the first time. Furious at being passed, Quasar regained the lead midway along the backstretch, and after a half mile in a suicidal forty-four seconds, he began to open up two and then three lengths on the field. Incredibly, he was still two lengths ahead at the top of the stretch, and he hardly slackened, sweeping under the wire in 1:094/5, the second best time of the meet for six furlongs.

I could almost hear Annie Lennox singing "Sweet Dreams" as Bill Perry made his way briskly down to the winner's circle with heavy Paul Shahian hurrying to keep up. Lennox, the androgynous lead singer of the Eurythmics, smiled coolly at Perry as she handed him the trophy, but Perry, still stunned by Quasar's victory, hardly registered Lennox's white jumpsuit and bright orange, butch-cut hair. He had never heard of the Eurythmics, he said, but he was saving the trophy for his daughter. After one day at Saratoga, he was the spa's leading trainer in race-won percentages, with a two-for-two record.

Mrs. Penna's dogs

During the following week, as the Fasig-Tipton yearling auctions got underway, the social season also heated up, and the different social and geographical factions of America's horsey set commingled in annual luncheons, balls, and an amateur dog show.

On Monday night, venturing through the turnstiles of the National Museum of Racing for the annual Museum Ball were New York blueblood owner/breeders, bluegrass barons, Palm Beach polo people, and the odd British luminary, like Ian Balding, who trains horses for Queen Elizabeth II. When ninety-three-year-old John A. Morris, owner of the nation's oldest racing silks, came in, sinking down immediately onto a tufted Victorian sofa near the entrance, Neal Smith's trio, imported from Palm Beach, launched into "Fugue for Tinhorns" (also known as "I Got the Horse Right Here"), from *Guys and Dolls*.

It was Morris's wife Anita who had once told Cleveland Amory that raising thoroughbreds was "very expensive," but that this was "all the better from the point of view of 'Society.' " Explained Mrs. Morris, "You see, it's so expensive that it takes more than one generation of money." Appropriately, Sonny Whitney was seen posing in front of solemn portraits of his father Harry and his grandfather Will Whitney.

"Saratoga in August is the most important place to be in the United States," Whitney was telling a reporter, and I thought about Saratoga's new Chamber of Commerce motto, "the August place to be," which could be seen on bumper stickers and lapel buttons all around town. And I also thought about an older sobriquet that a nineteenth-century writer had once applied to Saratoga: the "Augustan Age of American Clownery."

That phrase, however, was perhaps more apropos for the annual Saratoga Dog Show held the following week on Tuesday, the track's day of rest, for the benefit of the Thoroughbred Retirement Foundation, a new charity established to benefit old claimers who didn't die, but just faded away. The TRF provided the funding for a small program in upstate New York that trained prisoners to care for retired track veterans.

The chairman of the show was Eleanor Penna, née Kane, former sportswriter and wife of Angel Penna, who then trained for Ogden Phipps's Wheatley Stable. She had commandeered August Belmont IV, a descendant of the founder of Belmont Park, to serve as judge. Among the contestants in the "Dogs Who Least/Most Show Their Breeding" category was Fluff the pekinese, owned by glamorous Palm Beach heiress Mollie Wilmot, who herself suggested the look of a lean, blond-haired borzoi. Entered in the Dog/Owner Look-Alike contest was a showy dalmatian named Aly Khan, lent for the day to Marylou Whitney, who had worn a spotted dress to match. Her main competition was provided by actor Albert Finney, a longtime horse fan who had brought his huge mastiff puppy Winston and a chauffeur who followed him with a silver ice bucket containing a bottle of champagne.

Concluding the entries was a rather elderly German shepherd led by Salvador Dali look-alike Horatio Luro, "El Gran Señor," trainer of Northern Dancer, who had just announced his retirement from the track. Outside the paddock, trainer José Martin, a very thin, wiry man who was leaning on the paddock rail next to his father, Pancho Martin, said: "We have some dogs, but they're over there in the barn. If they had a pig show, we might win that."

It seemed a strange if festive way to raise money for a handful of animals to escape the unhappy fate of the masses of thoroughbreds who had worn out their usefulness on the track and who were useless for breeding purposes. In fact, it seemed a mere drop in the silver ice bucket. So far, only a dozen horses had been chosen for the program, while there were hundreds of horses at Suffolk Downs alone who would not wind up in green pastures. What would happen to them? What would happen to Quasar when his infirmities overpowered his desire to win?

Saratoga, however, is a place for hope, sweet dreams and happy endings, however illusory. During the remaining days of the meet, I set about to discover the Chief's most likely rivals for the Hopeful, and possibly for the Derby.

On August 15, another potential Danzig star, a colt named Nordance, was to make his debut. Nordance, whose dam was a full sister to the great champion Shuvee, was trained by Hall of Fame trainer Allen Jerkins, and he was owned by Centennial Farms, a multiple partnership headed by Boston investment banker Don Little.

Little, a tall, robust man, was a proper Bostonian, a polo player well connected in business and social circles who had developed a passion for the racetrack uncharacteristic for his social class. Lacking the stratospheric wealth required to get involved in racing in a big way, Little got his feet wet by enlisting a few business acquaintances as partners in a handful of claiming horses at Suffolk Downs. The partners didn't make much money, but they didn't lose much, either. Little realized that the only real investment potential at the track lay in the top end of the business, and he began to offer partnerships in well-bred yearlings that he picked out at auction with the help of a couple of advisors, including Kentucky breeder Robert Clay.

For $50,000, a partner would own one out of twenty-five or so shares in a million-dollar group of yearlings. Nordance, purchased for one of these partnerships, had cost $210,000 at the 1983 Keeneland auction, and he was part of a package that included three well-bred fillies. Already, the success of the Chief had increased the value of every Danzig son and daughter, and that auction price seemed a bargain. It was a bit like investing in a wildcat oil venture. Except, as Little liked to say, "It's not any fun to watch your oil well in Midland, Texas. And you can't pet your tax shelter."

Part of what Little was offering his investors was the aura of Saratoga, the glamor of the clubhouse and the walking ring. As his fellow partnership-promoter Cot Campbell, a Georgia insurance broker, put it, "What I package is the pageantry of racing." Centennial owned a house near the track, and investors could come up for a race and become a Whitney for a day. For $50,000, in other words, an investor could buy part of an illusion —an illusion to appreciate for a few days a year and then depreciate for the entire fiscal year.

Today, not all of Nordance's two dozen owners had showed up, but there were enough to make a small, well-hatted crowd in the paddock before the race. Across the way from the Centennial crowd was another crowd of partners, this one under the aegis of Cot Campbell, whose colt Brookfield had been a late scratch from the race. And in the center of the paddock was Barry Schwartz, whose colt Keepayourmouthshut, trained by Steve Jerkins, Allen's son, was the morning-line favorite. Standing to one side, like the last of the old-line sporting crowd, was the Paul Mellon contingent, for whom the colt Danger's Hour was to make his debut.

It was an apotheosis of new ownership, of the investment collectives and ambitious individuals that had come to rub elbows with the Whitneys and the Vanderbilts and the Mellons and ultimately to supplant them.

Nordance, unlike the Chief, did not display good paddock manners, and his groom had wrapped the metal chain of the shank under his upper lip to keep him under control. He did look like the Chief, however—the same bay color, the same delicate head. There was no doubt that Danzig was stamping his get, seeming to overwhelm the genetic influence of his mates.

Nordance's workouts, while respectable, had not demonstrated either the speed or the precocity of the Chief, and he went off at 4 to 1, while Paul Mellon's well-bred colt was the longest shot in the field. Bettors knew that neither Allen Jerkins nor Mackenzie Miller, Mellon's trainer, liked to push their two-year-olds.

Both colts ran according to expectation, with Nordance running an easy, even third all the way around the track, crossing the finish line some eight lengths behind the leader, and Danger's Hour loping along in eighth the whole way. Both were likely to improve considerably in their next starts, but neither, clearly, would be a threat to the Chief for quite a while.

Miller and Mellon, however, had other colts up their sleeves. Although Paul Mellon hadn't entered a horse in the Derby in a dozen years, there were rumors in the Saratoga press box that his Rokeby Farm had produced a bumper crop of homebreds in 1982, and one of them in particular, a colt named Desert War, seemed to be improving dramatically. In his first race at Belmont in July, the chestnut colt by Damascus had been second by five lengths to Chief's Crown, when the Chief broke his maiden, and then he had run very poorly two weeks later. But on the day of the Whitney, Desert War had run away from a very well-bred group of maidens, including a colt named Herat by Northern Dancer, owned by Bull Hancock's widow, Waddell.

Mack Miller, however, who had been training for Mellon since 1977, seemed remarkably casual about his colt's immediate prospects. A tall, genteel man with shrewd blue eyes, Miller tilted back the chair in his tidy office near the training track. "I thought Desert War wasn't even eligible for the Hopeful. But the jockey's agent, who was trying to get the mount for his boy, came running back and told me he was. You see, old man Mellon doesn't believe in running his young horses too soon. When I said to Mr. Mellon last month, 'I'm going to run a two-year-old,' he said, 'Isn't that premature?' But this colt never made a bobble in his training. When that bugger ran like a dog in his second race, it was because he got his tongue over the bit."

Miller, a native Kentuckian with a reputation as the most "gentlemanly" trainer in New York, was also known as a fanatic about all-natural food and fabrics. Scorning the showy, white plastic bridles used by Wayne Lukas and the synthetic-fibered blankets favored by some stables, he allowed only the best leather and wool to be placed against his horses' skin.

Miller's first prominent owner had been Charlie Engelhard, a high-rolling millionaire, who, said Miller, "changed my life. He was a great sportsman who did everything first-class. And to go from him to Mellon was a million-to-one shot. Great owners are hard to come by."

The great owners, according to Miller, were the patient ones. "The longer you wait with a young horse, the better chance you have of a sound horse. But a lot of people don't let you be patient with a horse. It's because of the economics of the thing —the tremendous worth of the animals. The Arabs set the thing on fire, and there's a new gimmick all the time to propel this thing to new heights. I don't know what the answer is, but we've got to be recycled—we need something to bring us back to our senses. We've gotten so greedy and selfish and big that we've got to topple. It seems that we need a depression to bring things down, to start all over again.

"That need to get the fast return on a big investment—that's why we have so few older handicap horses around. The most killing time for a horse comes when you are preparing him for the Derby, from January to May, because you have a series of steep steps to climb. A lot of horses don't make it, and they turn into bums."

And what if Desert War turned out to be a good horse? Would he run in the Derby? "Mr. Mellon doesn't have anything to prove; he isn't looking for prestige. He'd probably run the horse in a couple of races in New York in the spring and then go for the Belmont and the Travers."

Said Miller, who hadn't been particularly impressed by the Chief: "We just haven't seen any great two-year-olds yet this year. Everybody thought that other Danzig colt, Ziggy's Boy, was the Second Coming, but he's already been beat by a fifteen-hundred-dollar horse."

Mrs. Bujnicki's bargain

That fifteen-hundred-dollar horse was my next stop on the backstretch that morning. Doubly Clear, the Cinderella horse, was stabled at the old Horse Haven receiving barn, scheduled for demolition the next year.

The previous October, a large, dark-bay colt sired by a no-name stallion called Two a Day, was entered at the yearling sale at the Timonium racetrack in Maryland. Two a Day's stud fee at Carlo's Equestrian Center in Albuquerque, New Mexico, was $500, and so far he had not produced a single stakes winner. The colt's dam was a sixteen-year-old mare named Clear Mistery, who had produced only four other foals, none of them winners. Consequently, the ill-bred colt was hardly noticed by anyone at Timonium except a young woman named Judy Bujnicki, who had come to the sale to look for a horse she could use in the show ring. Bujnicki had been breaking yearlings at a farm in Orefield, Pennsylvania, to supplement her husband's income as a self-employed truck driver, and she had a little extra money to burn when her $5,000 claiming horse had won a race. She hadn't brought her checkbook to the sale, however, and she convinced the farm's owners, Tom and Ann Brede, to sign the sales receipt for her and advance her the money for the tall, sleek-looking yearling.

Bujnicki had the colt gelded in February and proceeded to break him in as a show horse, teaching him to change leads and do figure eights. But the horse had matured so fast and appeared so well coordinated that Bujnicki had thoughts about trying him on the track. She sent the gelding for a ninety-day trial period to her old friend Steve Rowan, a sixty-one-year-old trainer at tiny Penn National racetrack in Pennsylvania, some seventy-five miles away from her home in Bethlehem. During his first weeks in training he didn't impress Rowan much, so the horse was entered for a maiden claiming tag of $18,500 in his first start. After Doubly Clear finished second, beaten only by a length, Rowan upped the ante to a $28,000 claiming race, and the gelding won easily. His next start was an allowance race, in which he finished second.

What came next was a string of stakes races that had made Doubly Clear the richest two-year-old in the country. On July 21, the gelding had been vanned up to Suffolk Downs for the Mayflower Stakes, Boston's biggest race for two-year-olds. Doubly Clear's regular rider, Joe Garcia, had been suspended temporarily for careless riding, and the mount was given to thirty-six-year-old Robert Fitzgerald, who had never won a major stakes race in twenty years of riding and who planned to retire at the end of the year. Fitzgerald began to lay on the whip at the quarter pole, and the big gelding managed to edge out the local favorite, Medieval Secret, as well as a couple of fancy imports from New Jersey.

In his next race, the Tyro Stakes at New Jersey's Monmouth Park, Doubly Clear had little trouble with Ziggy's Boy, who in his only previous start had run five furlongs in 57 3/5, a mere fifth of a second off the Belmont track record. Ziggy had looked so fast in that race that his seventy-seven-year-old trainer Walter Kelley declared that the colt was the fastest he had ever seen. Eleven days later, Doubly Clear beat Ziggy's Boy again, in the Sapling Stakes at Monmouth, for which the gelding had to be supplemented for $10,000. And then Judy Bujnicki started thinking about Saratoga.

On this cool, sunny morning, Bujnicki was still marveling,

albeit wearily, about the fairy-tale quality of it all, despite the
decision by Saratoga's stall manager to assign her gelding to the
wrong side of the track (stakes horses are usually stabled next to
the main track). "I've always dreamed of Saratoga," she said.
"When I told my mother we were coming here, she said, 'Great!
We can pretend to be the Whitneys.' " A stocky woman with a
short, no-nonsense haircut, dressed in non-designer jeans,
Bujnicki, however, would probably never be mistaken for a
Whitney, or even a young Liz Taylor. Nevertheless, the evidence of a charmed life was there. "I've read *National Velvet,*"
she said, "and this is a story just like that one—a young girl
buying a horse, turning it over to an older trainer and then
having success with the horse."

When dreams come true on the racetrack, however, they
sometimes bring as much stress as they do happiness. A good
horse, I was to learn, can change your life forever, before you
even know what's happening. "You could set a bomb off under
this horse, and it wouldn't bother him," said Bujnicki. "His
nickname is Wimpy because he's so laid-back and lazy. But I'm
just the opposite. I can't eat—I can't keep anything down on the
day before he races. I can't sleep.

"The media haven't left me alone for a minute since this
whole thing started. And all kinds of people keep calling me and
pestering me with offers to buy him. I've had offers in excess of a
million dollars. But they don't understand that the reason I got
him in the first place was to have fun. I'd rather have him to look
at than a fat checkbook."

She walked over to the gelding's stall and patted him fondly
on the nose. The horse looked at her calmly with large, bright
eyes. "If he doesn't run well in the Hopeful," she said, "it won't
destroy me. He's my friend, my pet."

A friend came by on her way to the track kitchen and asked
Judy if she wanted anything from there. "Something I won't
throw up," she said wanly.

A few moments later, Rowan returned from the track kitchen
to take Doubly Clear out of his stall to graze under the oaks for a
while. A small, compact, white-haired man with a reluctant
smile, he was wearing a bright red baseball jacket, and he
seemed to be having the time of his life. Rowan had once gal-

loped horses for the legendary Sunny Jim Fitzsimmons, and he claimed to have worked as a rider during the filming of *National Velvet*. However, as Rowan saw it, this story wasn't *National Velvet*, but another fable. "Me and him," he said, pointing to the gelding, "it's called *Tobacco Road*, tryin' to get lucky.

"This isn't my piece of cake, Saratoga," he said. "I would have picked an easier spot. But I'm doing it for Judy. You know, my father used to bring me here as a boy, for the waters. I was born with a defect in my breathing—I never had a whole lotta air."

And now, he said, Woody Stephens had just sent word that he thought Doubly Clear was the best two-year-old in the country. "But I didn't bring him here to humiliate anybody," said Rowan. "I been looking up an awful lot, hoping the Lord's in my corner. The other day a pigeon almost hit me in the eye."

The following morning at Roger Laurin's barn, after the Chief had come in from his morning gallop, Laurin wasn't doing much gazing at the heavens. As we headed back out toward the track, Laurin kept his gaze carefully on the ground as he walked in a fast, rolling gait, like a sailor who has yet to adjust to land. It was a cloudy morning with an occasional drizzle, and the track was soupy. In the second set of the morning, he had just sent out Bear Hunt, a moody colt who had injured a tendon during last year's Derby and finished third to last, and a beautiful two-year-old filly named Faquer, a daughter of the champion mare Producer. "She's a proud filly," Roger said admiringly, as Faquer strutted and played on her way to the track.

A stocky, well-tanned man of medium height whose tinted aviator glasses hid his eyes effectively, Laurin was not yet entertaining any sweet dreams about the Chief—at least not in public. "Isn't it a little early?" he had asked when I told him that I had chosen the Chief as my Hopeful. "Maybe you should wait and call your book *The Champagne*," he said, referring to the autumn stakes race at Belmont that traditionally has drawn the best two-year-olds in the East. "You'd have better odds if you waited to pick your horse. But Andrew will love it," he said, referring to the Chief's owner, Andrew Rosen.

Laurin, I was to learn, was something of a pessimist, who could always envision the worst. "He's like Eeyore, in *Winnie the Pooh,"* Jack Mann of the Baltimore *Sun* had told me. "He can find the dark side of everything. He's a real worry-wart." It was a trait, apparently, that had existed long before his ill-fated choice of jobs in 1972, when he picked the Phippses over the Chenerys. "He was always like that," Mann had said. "I can remember back in 1964, when Roger had his first good horse, a filly named Miss Cavandish that he had bought for $1,500. She was going to run in the Kentucky Oaks the next day, and we were out the night before, and he spent the whole time talking about the ways she could get beat. And sure enough, he was right. The favorite was a filly named Blue Norther, who was ridden by Willie Shoemaker, and Miss C. went out at 9 to 2. Well, they get to the quarter pole, and Miss C. is coming up on the outside, and she's going to go right around. But she's being ridden by Manuel Icaza, Mr. Aggressive, and he sees room on the rail, and he jerks her over, gets her out of stride, and she gets beat half a length." The following day Laurin consoled himself by attending his first Kentucky Derby, and he watched Northern Dancer defeat the favored Hill Rise.

At least I knew Roger wasn't a master of hype, like some trainers; he wouldn't get carried away, as Woody Stephens had the year before with Devil's Bag, inflating hopes and syndication prices beyond all reason. What's more, I liked his wry, bleak sense of humor that could take you by surprise. When he smiled, he looked much younger than his forty-nine years.

Thinking about Judy Bujnicki and her uneasy stomach, I asked Roger if he felt any pressure yet with the Chief. "There's a lot more pressure in *not* having horses that peak," he said. "You've got to win one once in a while. It's a long time between dreams."

When I told Roger about my apprenticeship at Suffolk Downs, he said, "Yeah, Sufferin' Downs. I was there thirty years ago. It hasn't changed—they've still got the same tickets on the ground." Roger, in fact, had gotten his start in New England when his father sent him north with five horses to Scarborough Downs in Maine. Lucien Laurin, who had been born in Saint Paul, Quebec, some fifty miles north of Quebec, had been training since the early 1940s after a spotty record as a jockey that included a suspension from Narragansett Park in Rhode Island for alleged possession of a battery-charged device (Laurin still contends that he was framed; and the suspension was later lifted, in 1941). Laurin Senior had worked his way up the leaky-roof circuit on the East Coast, going from Charlestown to Rockingham and finally New York, where he trained his first champion, the two-year-old filly Quill, in 1958.

Roger had been walking hots for his father, and by lying about his age he had gotten his trainer's license at age seventeen. "I won my share of races in New England," he said, "but I didn't win anybody else's share." He went back to school, at Sir George Williams College in Montreal, for a couple of years, but couldn't resist returning to the horses. By the time his father had conditioned his next outstanding horse, Amberoid, who won the 1966 Belmont, Roger had become an equal.

In the fall of 1965, when Captain Harry Guggenheim and his regular trainer Woody Stephens came to a parting of the ways, Guggenheim asked Stephens to look for a replacement: "I don't want an old man or a fat man," he had told Stephens. A great-grandson of the original American Guggenheim and heir to a share of the family's copper-mining fortune, Guggenheim had earned his title by joining the flying navy in World War I and by serving in World War II aboard the aircraft carrier *Nebenta Bay* during the invasion of Okinawa.

Before Stephens could suggest a replacement, however, Guggenheim had called Laurin at Belmont and offered him the job. But first, said Guggenheim, he wanted Laurin to come to his estate, Falasie, on Long Island, to look at his horses. Laurin rushed to the parking lot and asked a valet to get his car, but one of Laurin's cronies had driven off with it. Desperate, Laurin borrowed the valet's car, which was, in his words, "a real clunker." As he later told a reporter, "I mean, it must have been a '47 Packard. But I had no choice, so here I came, sputtering up to Captain Guggenheim's estate in this awful-looking thing. I thought, 'Uh-oh, you've blown it now.' " Guggenheim did give him the job, but after a couple of years the Captain went shopping again, and in 1970, Laurin was hired by Chris Chenery, only to resign within a year.

When he had recommended his father for the Meadow Stable job, Penny Tweedy actually had some doubts about Roger's replacement. She had seen Lucien at work the previous winter in Miami, when Roger's horses, including the Meadow horses, had been stabled near his father's barn at Hialeah. She had noticed that Roger was in fact running his father's stable much of the time, and Lucien seemed eager to retire. And in fact, until she offered him the job of training the Meadow horses, he had been planning to do just that. After Secretariat's triumph in the Triple Crown, Lucien would continue his threat to retire, periodically divesting himself of his horses, and he always seemed halfway in, halfway out the door.

Roger himself had taken some time off after parting ways with the Phippses, and over the years he had managed to improve his golf handicap considerably; there were some sportswriters who claimed that, in fact, Laurin's problems with the Phippses had stemmed from his long hours on the golf course. One of Roger's co-workers at the time recalled that Roger had gotten to the point of jumping at the sound of the telephone, fearful of yet another demanding call from Ogden Phipps.

More likely, the problem had been one of subtle but constant pressure. Bill Winfrey, who had trained for the Phippses at the height of the Wheatley empire, when Buckpassser had just won the two-year-old championship, had suddenly quit his post, telling a reporter: "I just didn't have a feeling of freedom there . . . They simply took a strong interest in everything, and . . . I never liked to have someone looking over my shoulder . . . After a while it kind of got to me a little bit. Another thing, I could see that you didn't achieve any goal there. It was always 'look for the next one,' instead of enjoying the one we'd just had."

Perhaps Roger could have taken a tip from the unflappable Eddie Neloy, who had succeeded Winfrey at Wheatley and who was said to get along quite well with the Phippses. Neloy had once encouraged one of his less charming stable hands to take a Dale Carnegie course—a course that should have been titled "How to Win Races and Influence Owners."

Neloy himself had frequently played golf with Ogden Phipps, although it cost him a few dollars. According to one story, a reporter named David Alexander had once congratulated Phipps on his golf prowess: "You know, Eddie tells me that you are quite a whiz on the links. He tells me that every time he plays with you he loses ten bucks. But Eddie says he'd rather lose ten bucks than lose Buckpasser." According to the story, Phipps frowned, then replied: "If Eddie is throwing all those games to me, I'll fire him. I'm very proud of beating Eddie." Four years later, the diplomatic Neloy had died on the job of a heart attack while still in apparently hale and hearty middle age.

Since his job with Wheatley, Roger had tended to train for owners outside the racing establishment—for those who, like Andrew Rosen, tended not to interfere in the day-to-day affairs of their horses. Rosen, with his one horse stable of Chief's Crown, his love of golf, and his relative inexperience seemed the ideal owner. At this stage of the game, he was content to let Roger make all the decisions. Rosen, however, was no longer the Chief's official owner. After the Saratoga Special, the rest of the Rosen family realized what a good horse they had on their hands, and now it was the "Rosen estate," whose *nom de course* was Star Crown Stable, that was to be listed in the racing program as proprietor of the Chief. The estate consisted of Carl Rosen's widow Shirley, his daughters Lisa and Michelle, his sons Andrew and Douglas, and his nephew David. The Chief had become a family horse.

It was still Andrew, however, who showed up at the track in the mornings to talk to Roger, who was trying to learn the ropes in the horse business. And when I met him on Saturday, the day before the Hopeful, he seemed to be making an effort to follow in his father's footsteps at the betting windows as well. Advising Andrew on his bets and relaying his money to the windows was Freddie Bond, a tall, boisterous man who had played the same role for Carl Rosen.

Andrew, the youngest of Rosen's four children, had grown up with his brother and sisters in the Boston suburb of Newton, and then, as Puritan Fashions began to thrive, the family moved to a big house on Job's Island, in the Dedham headwaters of the Charles River. The brothers were sent to private schools, Douglas to Brown and Nichols in Cambridge, and Andrew to the Fessenden School in Newton and then to Lawrenceville in New

Jersey. In the early seventies, Carl Rosen moved Puritan's head-quarters to New York and began the first of several innovations in the fashion business when he asked promising young tennis star Chris Evert to endorse a line of sportswear. The following year, he bought the filly who was to bear the same name, with equal athleticism.

In 1977, Rosen persuaded designer Calvin Klein and his business partner Barry Schwartz to endorse a new line of chic but affordable jeans, and Puritan Fashions suddenly became big business. Andrew Rosen, who had been whiling away his time on the golf course in California and Florida while taking classes at the University of Miami—"I enrolled at Spyglass and Pebble Beach, then transferred to Doral"—was brought in to handle the Calvin Klein deal, despite his lack of experience. Doug Rosen, Andrew's older brother, had already struck out on his own in the advertising and film production business, and had shown no inclination to work in the cutthroat garment business. Five years later, when Carl Rosen discovered he had cancer, he designated his still unseasoned son Andrew as his successor at Puritan. Fifteen months later, Rosen died, and Andrew found himself at the helm of a huge business, and at the helm of a small breeding operation and racing stable.

Such a legacy might have furrowed the brow and deepened the ambitions of a number of men, but Andrew seemed to have bobbed along like a cork over the sudden onrush of responsibilities. A tall, genial, good-looking man, he seemed even younger than his twenty-eight years—just a kid, I thought, who inherited a good horse out of the blue, while other men in the business had spent a goodly portion of their time and fortunes just to get an animal half as good. At the moment, the Chief was simply a hobby that had suddenly become lucrative. "I still play a lot of golf," said Andrew. "I play at a course about ten minutes from Belmont, so I can stop by the barn in the mornings on my way."

On August 26, the day of the Hopeful, and the next-to-final day of the Saratoga meet, all things seemed possible—for young horses and old, for Cinderellas and bluebloods alike. The best young colts of the East were going to battle it out at the spa, while the old veteran John Henry was going to meet a tough

international crowd in the world's then-richest race, the Budweiser-Arlington Million at Chicago's Arlington Park, which was to be televised at Saratoga after the Hopeful.

The first seven races went by in a kind of fog, and all I could remember of them later was a New England man who went into loud raptures after the fifth race had been won by Roving Minstrel, a colt who had run previously in a small stakes race at Rockingham Park. "The Rock is the best!" the man shouted to all the swells in the clubhouse. "Suffolk stinks, but Rockingham lives!"

Thirty minutes before the eighth race, Roger chose to saddle the Chief in the covered stalls inside the paddock instead of under the trees, while the other trainers had decided to brave the crowds. I walked over to the tree designated for horse No. 8, where Judy Bujnicki, still in jeans, was holding Doubly Clear's reins while Steve Rowan straightened the saddle. Just across the walking path was Rowan's newly assembled claque—a group of weathered-looking codgers who had known him in the old days at Saratoga. "They have the biggest cheerin' squad," said one tout, putting a series of hieroglyphs on his racing program.

"Put him back with the claimers," shouted a disagreeable young man in a bright yellow shirt, puncturing the buoyant mood. "This horse doesn't belong in this race." Quickly, before I realized I had even opened my mouth, I yelled at the man, "Why don't *you* join the claimers, you bum!" and the crowd that had gathered around the tree applauded. "You tell 'em," said one of Rowan's codgers. It hadn't taken long for me to go from observer to participant in this drama. I realized that, although I wanted the Chief to win, I didn't want Doubly Clear's dream to die. "He's given everybody on the track hope that they can do it too," Bujnicki had told me—"all the grooms and hot-walkers making twenty bucks a day."

Back in the paddock, the Chief was circling with his usual grave aplomb, and Don MacBeth was looking similarly grave in Star Crown Stable's conspicuous, neon-pink and green silks. The Chief was to break from the third post position, just outside a big gray colt named Tiffany Ice, who was second choice behind the Chief on the morning line, probably on the strength of his victory in the Sanford Stakes two weeks earlier. Sky Com-

mand, the Chief's principal rival in the Special, had broken down in that race, the first casualty among the early Derby contenders.

When the gates buzzed open, Doubly Clear broke into the lead, but within a few strides he had dropped back, and a speedy Leroy Jolley colt named Vindaloo took the lead, with Tiffany Ice on his heels and the Chief a length back. After half a mile, the Chief had edged up beside Tiffany Ice, and Doubly Clear was two lengths behind him. The early fractions were very fast—the half mile in 444/5 seconds—and Vindaloo began to tire. As they came around the turn, Vindaloo dropped back to third and the Chief swept by Tiffany Ice. Doubly Clear, still in fourth, was less than four lengths behind the Chief, but at the top of the stretch he began to lug in, and he brushed a small colt named Do It Again Dan, whom he had beaten easily in his two Monmouth races. The Chief began to draw away from Tiffany Ice with that heavy, pounding stride that seemed to dig into the track like the sowing attachment on a tractor, and Doubly Clear dropped back to sixth. As the Chief swept under the wire, nearly four lengths in front of the field, Doubly Clear was struggling along, nine lengths behind him.

At the finish of the race, I spotted Steve Rowan in the clubhouse, leaning on a rail, his face pale and strained. He was clutching his chest, and he was obviously having a difficult time breathing. *Tobacco Road* or no, this had hit him hard. Rowan knew, perhaps even better than Roger Laurin, that it was a long wait between dreams.

The Chief had made the cut, but Doubly Clear hadn't. That extra half furlong, that mere sixteenth of a mile, added to the six furlongs that these two-year-olds had already been asked to run, had made the difference between a precocious, early-blooming horse who would probably never run a distance, and a potential classic horse—a genuine Derby contender.

The Chief's time of 1 minute, 16 seconds was a mere three fifths of a second slower than the stakes record set by Bold Lad in 1964, and he had finished the race two fifths of a second faster than Secretariat had done in 1972 on a slow, tiring track.

As I surveyed the previous winners of the Hopeful, however, I realized that the Chief had not actually diminished the odds

against his winning the Derby. The previous winners of the Hopeful seemed to be divided between great horses who hadn't won the Derby—Native Dancer, Nashua, Buckpasser—and promising two-year-olds who had faded or been injured before they made it to the Derby—including Bold Lad. Ominously, the previous five winners of the race before 1984 fit into the latter category. But for the moment the Chief was indeed my Hopeful, and I had no reason to think anything would stop him.

Moments after Andrew had picked up his trophy, the Chief's victory was swallowed up in another, larger victory—a victory for old age, underdogs, and racing itself.

Turf writers in the press box were crowded around a television set to watch the Arlington Million, to see yet another chapter in the track's greatest Cinderella story ever, a story that had continued to come true, year after year. Foaled in the same crop as Affirmed and Alydar, who dueled their way to greatness in the classic races, John Henry was first sold as a bargain-basement weanling for $1,100, then entered as a yearling in the Keeneland sale, where he brought $2,200—a mere $700 more than Doubly Clear had brought at Timonium. Changing hands three more times because of his terrible temper, John Henry was finally sold to bicycle importer and longtime horseplayer Sam Rubin for $25,000. And now, six years later, John Henry led the list of all-time money-winners at the track with $4,882,797.

The squib by handicapper "Sweep" beside John Henry's name in the *Racing Form* said "classy warrior"; beside Robert Sangster's Royal Heroine, he had written "hard-hitting filly." And it was Royal Heroine, as it turned out, who gave John Henry a run for his money, streaking to the lead, then dueling with the late-running Nijinsky's Secret. As those two were running head and head at the top of the stretch, Nijinsky's Secret began to drift out a bit, and John Henry, who had been laying low just behind them, surged through the hole. Later, John Henry's jockey Chris McCarron would say that John Henry had seen the opening even before he had, and he had charged through on his own accord. As John Henry swept under the wire, the press box erupted into cheers such as I had never heard before; I could have sworn I saw a few turf writers make hasty swipes at the corners of their eyes.

A few minutes later, as the race was replayed in the club-house, a well-dressed, middle-aged man began to chant, as John Henry began his run at the top of the stretch, "Come on, old man, come on, old man," over and over, his voice crescendoing until the old gelding had passed the wire. And for a moment, I felt as though I were a part of a world where no horse ever broke down, where age did not mean decrepitude, where no heart was ever broken, and I knew a different kind of hope altogether—a hope that was as close to faith as you could get on the racetrack.

CHAPTER 4

Jockeying for Position at Belmont

> He was well born, as the saying is, and that's worth as much in a man as it is in a horse . . . and pap he always said it, too, though he warn't no more quality than a mud-cat . . .
>
> —Mark Twain, *Huckleberry Finn*

A T SARATOGA, the entire racing world is compressed into a few square miles, with globe-trotting owners partying in their mansions on Broadway, only minutes away from the stable-hands who are calling out their choices to the short-order cook at the track kitchen. In September, however, after the horse vans have rolled into Belmont Park, located between suburbs twenty miles east of Manhattan, the racing cosmos splits up again. The owners retreat to their non-horsey pursuits and their apartments on Sutton Place, the limited partners to their offices on Wall Street and the World Trade Center, the trainers to the daily grind and their cottages in Garden City, the grooms to the perpetual smell of horses and their barracks on the backstretch.

Summer camp is over, but the games are not. During the next two months of the Belmont fall meeting, Saratoga's flashy two-year-olds are obliged to stretch out to prove their precocity, while the best three-year-olds of the spring and summer face the sterner competition of the top veterans. And as for the rest of the horses, it's all-out warfare.

After the diversions of Saratoga, the ongoing battle of the trainers resumes. Belmont is perhaps the most difficult place in the world to win races on a regular basis, and trainers are constantly looking for an edge. Things are so tough, according to one backside legend, that when a young girl came to Belmont to look for a job, her mother accompanied her to check out the situation. The mother asked Leroy Jolley what kind of atmosphere the track would be for her daughter to work in. "You know Buddy Jacobs?" Jolley asked the mother. Jacobs at the time was on trial for murder. "Well, around here, he's just a regular guy."

Once the domain of private trainers who trained for the old sporting families, Belmont's deceptively bucolic backstretch is now ruled by trainers like Woody Stephens with multiple owners and large public stables. Occasionally, trainers team up successfully with single backers, as Frank "Pancho" Martin did with Sigmund Sommer during the 1970s, and as John Parisella has done recently with computer magnate Ted Sabarese.

One of the richest landlords in New York, Sommer had built three office towers in Manhattan and some forty-five shopping centers around the region, and he collected rent from twenty-seven apartment buildings on Manhattan's East Side. Sommer and Martin acquired their horses not from auctions or breeding farms, but from the claiming ranks. "I got the best breeding farm in the world right here. Belmont Park!" Sommer once bragged.

Sabarese and Parisella, however, had come up with a different technique. They bought "made" horses—horses who were already in stakes-winning form. At one point, they had considered buying Let Burn from Paul Shahian and Bill Perry. That approach, however, had gotten too expensive; they began to go to auction, and Sabarese now bought some two dozen yearlings each summer.

Said Parisella, a heavy-browed, demonstrative Brooklynite who could have played a character role in *Mean Streets:* "A trainer has to offer an owner some glamor and some romance these days. He has to put on a show. When I first met Sabarese, he was only going to buy one or two horses, but he got hooked. When you introduce somebody into racing, it's like a drug dealer and a junkie."

This year, however, the star of the Belmont backside was Cuban trainer Oscar Barrera, who had become famous for his magical powers of reconditioning. Barrera would claim a horse and within days have the horse ready to win. Said Oscar to a reporter: "No matter what the condition of a horse's ankles or knees may be when I get him, I work on him and try to send him into a race groomed to fit a king. Close attention to detail and individual care help a lot." Not everyone, however, felt that good grooming was Oscar's only secret, and track officials, as well as, reportedly, a government agency, had taken a strong interest in Oscar's training techniques. So far, however, no one had been able to solve such puzzles as Barrera's miraculous turnaround of a horse named Shifty Sheik, whom he claimed for $35,000 and turned into a top stakes contender, a horse who would come close to upsetting Slew o' Gold in the Woodward Stakes.

Mr. Belmont's club

Things had changed considerably at Belmont since the days when August Belmont himself ruled the horsey set. Like Saratoga, Belmont Park owed its existence to a group of sporting financiers who wanted to formalize their favorite pastime. During the 1890s, the tycoons who were building racing dynasties with the wealth accrued from oil, steel and railroads were discovering that the principles of laissez faire that had abetted their own rise to wealth and power simply did not work when it came to racing. Without regulation, there was no way to ensure the identity of racehorses, and the running of "ringers" was common practice. Without a central authority, the naming of horses, too, was a haphazard process that resulted in frequent duplication. In the first two volumes of the American *Stud Book,* for example, one could find 102 fillies named Fanny and 139 horses named John. Moreover, tracks often established racing dates that conflicted with their competitors in the same city.

In 1894, a group of distinguished owners met in New York

City, led by W. C. Whitney, socialite August Belmont II, and Whitney's old Wall Street rival James R. Keene, and the result was the founding of the Jockey Club, modeled after England's society of the same name. Leadership of the Jockey Club was virtually identical with that of the Westchester Racing Association, formed the next year, under whose auspices the new track called Belmont Park was built on Long Island, on land purchased by Belmont and Whitney, in 1903.

The Jockey Club in England had been formed by chance, during the 1730s, when the nobly born, horse-owning habitués of the Star and Garter, a fashionable coffeehouse at Newmarket, decided to expand their unofficial camaraderie into a club that would become arbiter of sporting pastimes, and of racing in particular. The hundred or so charter members included twelve dukes, some forty earls and baronets, and one "Jimmy" Boswell, Dr. Johnson's biographer. The official club uniform consisted of a brown cutaway coat with gold buttons, to be worn with white doeskin breeches, boots, and spurs. On the wall of the Jockey Club at Newmarket still hangs a well-preserved hoof of the great Eclipse, shod with gold and stapled upon a gold salver bearing the coat of arms of his breeder, the Duke of Cumberland, a son of George II.

Like their English role models, the members of the American Jockey Club established themselves by *fiat*. The Jockey Club simply took upon itself the power of assigning dates for race meetings, of licensing owners, jockeys and trainers, of appointing officials and of disciplining those who disobeyed the rules. Also like their English counterpart, the Jockey Club became a very exclusive fraternity, from which those who actually made their money from horses appeared to be barred. The notion, for example, of a real jockey belonging to the Jockey Club was as absurd as that of a real elk joining the Elks. For decades, the Club also barred Jews, blacks and women, even though the father of August Belmont II was himself a Jew. As writer Bernard Livingston once put it, the Jockey Club became America's equine House of Lords.

Born August Balmain in the Rhenish town of Alzei in 1816, Belmont's father had moved up quickly in the Rothschild banking world, then moved to the United States during the financial

panic of 1837. After changing his name and setting up a successful financial operation on Wall Street, Belmont Senior married
the daughter of Commodore Matthew C. Perry and became a
force to contend with in New York society.

The younger Belmont came into his own during the height of
robber baron excess, and he had little trouble finding his own
niche in the rush of empire-building, presiding over the digging
of the Cape Cod waterway and the building of the IRT branch
of New York's subway system. Adding his own shade of purple
to the Mauve Decade, he caused the requisite number of scan-
dals, including running off with his friend Will Vanderbilt's wife.
Yet he continued to preside, as augustly as his name demanded,
over the Jockey Club until his death in 1926.

For the next quarter of a century, the Jockey Club continued
to rule the racing world, virtually unchallenged, frequently denying licenses to individuals considered undesirable by Club
standards. According to reporter Toney Betts of the New York
Mirror, those standards sometimes included ethnic origins.
Jockey Bobby Merritt, according to Betts, was denied a license
after Pinkerton agents reported that Merritt was seen con-
sorting with "Jews and Italians." In 1951, however, the monop-
olistic power of the Jockey Club was challenged by gambler Jule
Fink, racehorse owner and developer of a highly successful
system of speed handicapping. According to legend, when Fink
was twenty years old he had taken ten cents in carfare from his
mother and parlayed it into $30,000 within a span of ten days,
betting with pool-parlor bookies in his home town of Cincinnati.
When he teamed up with trainer Woody Stephens during the
1940s to put together a claiming stable, the duo became known
as the "Speed Boys."

Fink took the Club to court after his application to renew the
license of his racing stable was denied on the grounds that he
was "associating with gambling groups to the detriment of the
best interests of racing." Although Fink was defeated in the
lower courts on the basis of a 1934 New York State law delegat-
ing the power of licensing to the Club, the Appeals Court ruled
that "the licensing power given by the legislature to a social and

exclusive group of sportsmen is an unconstitutional delegation of legislative authority."

Consequently, as state governments authorized expansion of the sport during the postwar racing boom, they created their own racing commissions that bore ultimate responsibility for licensing, racing dates, and the enforcement of regulations. Officially, the power of the Jockey Club was limited to control over the *Stud Book*, still a function of considerable importance. And so the Club continued to preside over registration, identification, and naming of horses, as well as approval of racing silks. In other words, if one wanted to race a nag of dubious origins, name it something obscene, or deck a jockey out in silly colors, the Club still had veto power.

The Club, moreover, continued to wield considerable ad hoc power. During the early 1950s, when racing in New York began to stagnate, even as attendance across the country had increased by nearly a third, the chairman of New York's racing commission turned to the Jockey Club to recommend ways to revive the sport. It was the Jockey Club that recommended the integration of New York's four independent tracks into one single entity, the New York Racing Association, which would purchase the property belonging to the existing private associations. Under the new NYRA, the track at Jamaica, Queens, was closed down and sold as a housing development, and the old Aqueduct track was demolished to make way for a new, weatherized plant, where racing could continue through the winter months.

The Jockey Club managed to unify racing in New York. But racing officials in other states were reluctant to leave the regulation of the sport in the hands of an elite, New York–based organization, and the resulting decentralization of the sport presaged some of the chaos of the breakup of AT&T. Nowadays, one could get lost among the acronyms that represent the various factions and racing interests in America: the NASRC (National Association of State Racing Commissions), the TOBA (Thoroughbred Owners and Breeders Association), the HBPA (Horsemen's Benevolent Protection Association), and so forth.

It was that sense of fragmentation that John Gaines had hoped to remedy with the Breeders' Cup—to establish its board

of directors as a central force in place of the attenuated Jockey
Club.

After the court decision in 1951, the Club itself, which had
seemed frozen in time somewhere between the Restoration
and the Gilded Age, began to thaw at the rate of a melting
glacier. Sometimes a good horse could get you in, particularly if
he managed to upset a champion belonging to one of the inner
circle. During the 1950s, the Club admitted its first Jew, Captain Harry Guggenheim, whose horse Dark Star had defeated
Alfred Gwynne Vanderbilt's Native Dancer in the Kentucky
Derby; and in the 1960s the Club admitted two more Jewish
members, including Jack Dreyfus, of mutual funds fame, whose
Beau Purple had beaten the legendary Kelso three times. Ironically, four years later, Dreyfus was to achieve his great dream of
beating Secretariat. He did it twice, with the unlikely Onion
and the uneven Prove Out.

In 1983, the Club lifted the sex barrier by admitting three
women of impeccable pedigree and fortune, who had owned
three of the greatest horses in the history of racing: Penny
Chenery (she had dropped the Tweedy after divorce), Martha
Gerry, and Allaire Du Pont. Allaire Du Pont's Kelso had won
the Horse-of-the-Year title five times in a row, while Martha
Gerry's Forego had won it three times, and Chenery's Secretariat twice. Du Pont and Gerry probably ensured their election to
the Club by sending their champion geldings to Belmont in the
fall of 1983 to go on parade before the running of the Jockey
Club Gold Cup, in which another grand old gelding, John
Henry, was to compete. Mrs. Du Pont's generous, sporting gesture cost her dearly when the aging Kelso, who had strutted
proudly down the stretch before the cheering crowd, was
stricken with colic and died the very next day.

Carl Rosen's climb

When Carl Rosen first got interested in horses, he was as far
from the inner circle of the Jockey Club as Jule Fink. His garment manufacturing business, Puritan Fashions, connoted
tastefulness and tradition, with its unadorned labels, its respect-

able New England name, and its respectable dresses designed for respectable, upper-middle-class matrons. But Rosen himself was a flashy, larger-than-life high roller, a gambler in business as well as on the track. As one Suffolk trainer described him, "He was Asa Buchanan—that guy in the soap opera *One Life to Live* who has his own little empire."

Horses were just one part of it. Rosen parlayed his money and charm into a number of spheres. He played golf with pro Ken Harrelson and traded stories with Yankee outfielder Bobby Murcer. He also handled a number of business matters for Murcer, and once negotiated for his friend the largest contract in Yankee history. At one point, in the pre-Steinbrenner era, Rosen had even considered buying the Yankees. And he had once made a bid, along with Sammy Davis, Jr., and several other partners, for a football franchise in Orlando. He had come a long way from Puritan Boston.

Puritan Fashions had been founded by Rosen's father Arthur in 1907, and Carl himself had started at Puritan in 1936 as packer, shipping clerk and sweeper. Within fifteen years he had taken over as chief executive officer. He worked long hours at the plant in the Boston suburb of Waltham, with golf his primary form of relaxation.

Charlie O'Connell, a starter at the Pine Brook golf course, where Rosen was a member, remembers Rosen from those years as a wheeler-dealer who tended to arouse a bit of resentment from some of the other members of the club. Said O'Connell: "Some of the members were jealous of him. He was smart, he was lucky, and he had his father's money—the three things you need to succeed in life. And I think he liked to irritate people a little. He was always dropping in by helicopter, and he threw his money around. All the kids wanted to caddy for him because he threw around $50 bills." At one point, Rosen told O'Connell that he would like to run for governor of Massachusetts.

During the mid-1960s, Rosen started getting interested in horses. His daughter Lisa had become a crack performer in the show ring, and a number of acquaintances were involved in the hunting-and-show set. But Rosen's interest lay at the track, particularly at the betting windows, and O'Connell, a longtime habitué of Suffolk Downs, acted as his personal handicapper, becoming the first of a series of such "advisors." On days that Rosen couldn't get to the track, he would call O'Connell with wagers to relay to the windows at Suffolk.

Rosen also began to get into the claiming game, starting with a horse named Front Pew that had been running on the New England circuit. His son Andrew would sit on the backstretch rail, since he was too young to get into the clubhouse, watching Front Pew labor vainly down the track. The Rosen children, in fact, had a nickname for the horse that characterized his lack of winning ways: Back Seat.

O'Connell remembers kidding Carl about his cheap horses. "I would say to him, how come you go first class with everything else, and you dabble with cheap horses?"

In the early seventies, after Rosen had made Puritan a public company, moved its headquarters to New York, and persuaded Chris Evert to endorse his new sportswear line, he also decided to upgrade his racing stable. On the advice of a mutual friend, he acquired the services of a thirty-six-year-old trainer from Brooklyn named Joe Trovato. A tall, hefty, genial man who was known among other trainers for his fear of horses, Trovato had set out his shingle just the year before, after working for thirteen years as a jockey's agent. Among his clients had been the ever-aggressive Manuel Icaza.

Trovato had made his headquarters at Aqueduct, the New York Racing Association's winter track just down the road from John F. Kennedy International Airport. Aqueduct was known as the workingman's track, where trainers and railbirds who couldn't afford to fly South continued to conduct their business during the endless rigors of a Long Island winter.

I went to see Trovato on a gray, rainy day, when Aqueduct seemed as grim as Suffolk in the middle of a cold wave. Sitting behind his desk in his overheated, windowless office, Trovato was eager to reminisce about Chris Evert and Carl Rosen; but like so many of Rosen's racetrack associates, he prefaced his remarks by warning that he was in litigation with Rosen's estate.

"Before he asked me to work for him, I was probably the only guy at the track who didn't know Carl Rosen," said Trovato. "He loved the races, and he loved the challenge of picking winners. He was the kind of guy who was very busy at the track. He had all kinds of friends—different people for different occasions. He loved to sneak off from the clubhouse over to the grandstand and get hot dogs with the working people. He would socialize with everyone, and he got a lot of advice. His feeling was that you never knew where a winner will come from. He always had a chance to win some money that way because he didn't go much for favorites. He was always looking for a tip on a long shot."

Trovato and Rosen claimed a few horses, but Rosen had something better in mind. "One day he brought me to his office," said Trovato, "and he showed me the trophies his daughter had won in the show ring, and he said, 'The only thing I want is to develop a champion.' "

Rosen decided that he would begin his campaign for a champion in Kentucky, and so in the summer of '72 he set out with Trovato for the Keeneland yearling sales.

It was Rosen's first horse auction, but he was to demonstrate there the kind of luck that had inspired Charlie O'Connell to call him "the luckiest man God put on the face of the earth." When the filly whom he was to name Chris Evert was brought out into the ring, the bidding was slow. "That was before fillies were bringing the kind of money they do today," said Trovato. "And her sire, Swoon's Son, was a well-kept secret on the East Coast. His best races had been on the West Coast." Rosen paid $32,000 for Chris Evert, and $48,000 for a colt by Indian Chief II that he was to dub Bobby Murcer, after the Yankee star.

Neither Rosen nor Trovato had any experience in getting young horses broken and readied for the track, so Trovato asked a friend, trainer Phil Johnson, for advice. Johnson advised that Chris Evert, Bobby Murcer, and another colt Rosen had bought be sent for the winter to a farm run by Oren Stround at Landrum, South Carolina. Trovato got the filly back in May. "By the time we got to Saratoga, I could tell she was something special," he said. "There was constant improvement from each work; she just got better and better each time. When she got herself together, she knew she was an athlete, and she'd do what she had to do to beat other horses." The filly didn't make her first start, however, until mid-September at Belmont, when she beat the highly regarded Maud Muller by almost two lengths.

From then on, through New York's Triple Crown series for fillies, she was virtually unbeatable, although her winning margin hardly ever exceeded a length or two. That is, until her famous match race in California with the West Coast star Miss Musket, when she had won by fifty lengths. She had two quirks: the tendency to relax once she got the lead and to swish her tail angrily while she was running.

Some horses, once they got in front, would chase the ghost horse—they would keep increasing their lead, as though competing against the clock itself—against the vanished horse who had set the track record. But other horses were content merely to beat the horses on the field that day. The great Buckpasser had been one of those, keeping his backers on edge when he would squeak by the finish line, ahead only by a head, a nose, or a neck. Chris Evert, too, was one of those, content merely to beat the fillies who challenged her. Said Trovato, "She would seldom destroy the competition, but she would always beat them by just far enough."

During Chris Evert's Triple Crown campaign in the spring of 1974, Rosen struck up a friendship with Penny Chenery, and the two would have drinks together at the clubhouse. "We had a relationship of kidding encouragement," Mrs. Chenery recalls. "He admired my horse, and I admired his." It was during the course of that jocular clubhouse relationship that Chenery had told Rosen that the filly would make a perfect mate for Secretariat: a matching pair of Triple Crown winners. "The resulting foal," she told him, "would be one of the most celebrated in years."

Rosen, as it turned out, took Mrs. Chenery's advice after Chris Evert was retired with ankle problems early in her fourth year. Trovato called Seth Hancock, who told them the fee for a mating to Secretariat would be $80,000, with no guarantee of a live foal.

Rosen must have felt a bit like the father of Cinderella, with his tiny racing stable of cheap claimers and so-so allowance horses and his nonexistent breeding program. Chris Evert had raised him to the rank of blood-broker, and he had visions of his own racing dynasty. Even as he was pushing money through the betting windows every weekend, his dream had always been for the highest stakes of them all—the Derby. And although Chris Evert had not been able to win the Derby, she had given him the wherewithal to breed a Derby winner.

And so, in the spring of 1975, Rosen and Trovato flew down to Claiborne for the mating of the champions, the Northeastern Jew from the garment business and his demonstrative Italian trainer making a conspicuous intrusion into the hushed decorum of the bluegrass world.

Rosen told Seth Hancock that he wanted to be present for the birth of the foal the following year. "His attitude was like it was a party that could be scheduled," recalls Hancock. But by the time Chris Evert started labor early one Sunday morning, in the spring of 1976, it was too late for Rosen to get there. Although the resulting foal, disappointingly, was a filly, Rosen named her Six Crowns, in honor of the *hieros gamos*—the sacred marriage —that had taken place in the creosote breeding shed at Claiborne. "Naming a horse Six Crowns is presumptuous," says Penny Chenery now. "But with Chris Evert he had already broken that jinx of naming a horse after a person. He was such an optimist."

With Chris Evert's subsequent offspring, all fillies, Rosen reverted to the tennis connection, with Tournament Star, Wimbledon Star, and Center Court Star. And when Six Crowns gave birth to her first foal, a filly by the Claiborne stallion Forli, he named her Chosen Crown. He had named one colt he bought at auction Prince Andrew, and the horse had run a close third to Seattle Slew in his debut. But when Rosen picked a name for Chris Evert's first grandson and the first colt of the filly-laden Chris Evert line, he was perhaps even more presumptuous— and even more optimistic than he had been over that first royal mating. He named the colt after himself.

One of Rosen's employees, who had been a fan of *Get Smart*, the spoofy TV detective show, began calling Rosen "Chief," using star Don Adams's nasal inflection, and the nickname stuck. Says Penny Chenery, "The name was appropriate for Carl—it was always his way or nothing." And so it was that the little bay colt, born in April of 1982, was called Chief's Crown. But before that summer was over, Rosen knew that he was mortally ill.

"When Carl got sick, he was going to beat it," said Trovato. "It was a project, like everything else he did. He offered the doctors an incentive by offering a sliding scale of donations to the hospital, depending on their success." Rosen also started worrying about his family, about all those hours he had been away, at work, on the golf course, at the track. "Carl was married to his work," said Trovato. "The kids didn't want for anything, but maybe he didn't give them enough of himself."

In the meantime Rosen and Trovato had parted ways, leaving Trovato with bittersweet memories and, according to Trovato, some unfulfilled promises. "Carl was a good-hearted man," said Trovato. "I can remember times when he would get his private jet, and we'd just go—to the Derby, the Preakness, whatever. He was generous to my wife and kids. He helped me buy my house, sent us to Europe. But he made some promises that he didn't keep.

"At the time you promise something, it's just a dream. But now those dreams have turned out to be worth a lot of money. He used to say to me, 'I'm going to make you a millionaire, you schmuck,' and he may finally do that."

Suddenly, in the midst of his recollections, Trovato began to weep, and he pulled out a handkerchief from a pocket. "It's not that we were geniuses," he said, recovering his composure, "but together we achieved the dreams we both had." Folding up the handkerchief and putting it away, he stood up to leave. "If you didn't know Carl, you really missed something."

A few moments later, as I walked from the barbwire-fenced backstretch, across the empty parking lot toward the graffiti-laden subway platform where I would catch the A train back to Manhattan, I thought about the way people and horses could pass through your life, about the way Carl Rosen, with his crazy luck, his fast filly, and his generous bankroll had passed through Trovato's life like a comet, setting it afire and leaving it somewhat diminished once he had gone.

Rosen's legacy to his son Andrew, I realized, had been an extraordinarily taxing one, in more ways than one, and perhaps Andrew's seemingly carefree demeanor was one way of dealing with it. So far, Chief's Crown had been merely an unexpected bonus, a gift out of the blue, the icing on the cake. But Puritan Fashions, which had made him a multimillionaire, had also been left to him with a price.

Early one morning in 1977, when thirty-four-year-old Calvin Klein, who had recently designed his way to the top of New York's disco-celebrity set, was dancing at Studio 54, an emissary from Carl Rosen approached him with a very attractive proposition. If Klein would put his name on a moderately priced line of jeans, to be manufactured by Puritan, Rosen would pay him a million dollars, and he would guarantee him at least a million dollars a year. Klein had designed an expensive line of jeans for Bloomingdale's the year before, but they hadn't sold, and the idea of marketing a more affordable line of jeans appealed to him.

Klein's best friend and business partner, Barry Schwartz, with whom Klein had grown up in a tough neighborhood in the Bronx and who handled Klein's financial affairs, negotiated a deal with Rosen that specified a generous royalty of one dollar to be paid to Klein for each pair of jeans that sold, with a provision for a cost-of-living increase. And so it was that a new form of Calvinism was allied with a new form of Puritanism: the alliance of slick image-making with super-salesmanship. The resulting product, designer jeans, were to transform the fashion and the advertising industry and to bring Puritan Fashions a gross income of $246 million a year. When nothing came between Brooke Shields and her Calvins, nothing stood between Carl Rosen and success.

Rosen even managed to hire his chief competitor, Warren Hirsh, an innovator in the fashion business who had done for Gloria Vanderbilt and Murjani jeans what Rosen had done with Klein and Puritan. Murjani's Vanderbilt line had been launched almost simultaneously with the Klein line, and Murjani's heiress-in-aspic ads had actually preceded the famous Brooke Shields come-hithers. Rosen signed one of those million-down, millions-to-come deals with Hirsh to bring him aboard Puritan.

But eight weeks later Hirsh was released, with a substantial settlement, and the repercussions were felt from Seventh Avenue to *People* magazine.

Hirsh, who left the fashion business and eventually started an office-supply venture, now remembers Carl Rosen with surprising detachment. Says Hirsh: "Carl was an excellent businessman, and he had a great business mind. In the garment business, you have to be an entrepreneur—you can't be stiff or straight-laced in your decision-making. It's like the entertainment business—you're only as good as your last hit. And Carl had that entrepreneurial talent. He was very flamboyant. He was a risk-taker. But he hurt a lot of people over the years."

One of the issues Hirsh and Rosen had disagreed on was diversification. Rosen had dispatched Hirsh to close all the other Puritan divisions in order to focus on the jeans, and Hirsh had disagreed. "It surprised me that he relinquished so much power to them," said Hirsh of Rosen's decision to go exclusively with Klein and Schwartz. Said another observer, "The whole structure of the business changed. They had been dealing with a lot of different designers, and now it was all Calvin Klein."

Inevitably, Rosen and Schwartz clashed. Both were prone to bouts of temper and yelling. As Joe Trovato put it, "Carl and Barry were both millionaires, they were both dictators. But Carl was sixty years old. He was old money, so to speak, and Barry was new money. Carl used to say, 'This punk is trying to tell me what to do.'" But Rosen and Schwartz also found each other to be kindred spirits, particularly when it came to the horses. Rosen had even found in Schwartz a kind of racetrack stepson who shared both his financial acumen and his love of the horses.

It was Rosen, in fact, who got Schwartz interested in the track. When I asked Schwartz about Rosen, his voice took on the warmth and the get-a-load-of-this tone that I was coming to expect when people spoke about Rosen's antics at the track. It was as though Carl Rosen still had people shaking their heads, whether in admiration, incredulity or anger. Said Schwartz, "Carl got me started. I went to him for names and advice." When Schwartz decided to begin claiming horses, he employed Rosen's trainer, Trovato, and they had moderate success. In

1981, Schwartz's claiming horses made him the nation's twelfth leading money-winner.

Schwartz remembers fondly his trips with Rosen to the track. "The racetrack lost a great patron when Carl died," Schwartz says with a certain formality, as though in eulogy. "Carl was a very colorful person. He really moved; he had a lot of energy. He'd fly to the racetrack at the drop of a hat. We'd fly down and back to the Derby. He'd have the whole thing arranged. Before the 'official' sign was up on the tote board at the end of the race, we'd be heading for the exits, and we were the first plane off the runway. At eight o'clock, we'd be home.

"One day I had a horse running at Hollywood Park, and he said, 'Let's go.' He hadn't been to California in years, since that big match race, but all the ushers knew him, the $50 ticket sellers knew him.

"He was a great handicapper. I was with him a half dozen times when he won over $100,000. He once won $207,000 at OTB, and they were saying it was the largest amount of money ever paid out at one time. They wanted Carl to make a commercial."

Calvin Klein's coup

When Rosen became ill, however, the tensions that had been accumulating in the Puritan/Klein partnership began to heat up. There had been bickering all along about everything from advertising to distribution, and each camp claimed credit for the success of the jeans. But it was Rosen's appointment of his son Andrew as his successor that brought things to a boil. As Trovato put it, "Andrew had to win Barry's and Calvin's confidence, and he couldn't. He didn't have Carl's killer instinct." Andrew, as Warren Hirsh observed, "was at a terrible disadvantage. Without Calvin Klein, he didn't have a company. If he was God himself, I don't think he could have come out on top."

Carl Rosen died on August 9, 1983, and as though his passing had shaken the very cosmos of the garment industry, there were heavy rains and flooding that day. A series of power outages caused much of the garment district to shut down for the afternoon.

Three months later, Schwartz and Klein made a bid for control of Puritan that Andrew Rosen couldn't refuse. Citing Andrew's inexperience and a plunge in third-quarter profits from the previous year, the two partners offered to buy Puritan for $16.50 a share—or a total of $60 million for the controlling share of company stock owned by the Rosens. According to *Women's Wear Daily*, Schwartz indicated that if Rosen didn't accept the offer he would pursue "alternate" means to take over the company—that is, he would make a hostile tender offer to shareholders. Said Klein later: "If Carl thought I would stand for his putting a young kid in to run the company, then he was a fool. By doing that, he forced me to buy the company."

And so it was that Klein and Schwartz swallowed Puritan into their empire, giving Andrew a job as titular head of Klein's jeans division, but retaining the real power themselves. Carl had made his heirs rich, but he had not been able, after all, to pass on his empire, intact, to his children. He did, however, leave them something whose value Barry Schwartz could appreciate far better than they—something that Schwartz, with all his financial acumen, had not yet been able to buy: a true Derby contender.

Like Rosen, Schwartz had ambitions that accelerated quickly from claiming races at Belmont to thoughts of Kentucky and Churchill Downs. Like Rosen, Schwartz started looking at bloodlines and attending the yearling auctions. He bought a seven-hundred-acre farm in northern Westchester County, where he built, from scratch, a major breeding program that put him on a footing, at least investment-wise, with some of the Kentucky breeders and ahead of all the individual breeders in New York. Schwartz had gotten hooked.

Unlike Carl Rosen, however, whose good fortune with horses had reached beyond the factors of money and work, Schwartz was stuck with the same odds that people with ordinary luck and ordinary advisors face every day at the track and every year beside the auction ring. In 1980 he entered a long shot in the Derby, a colt with the ignoble name of Degenerate Jon, who finished eighth, twelve lengths behind Genuine Risk, at odds of 61 to 1. And by the fall of 1984 his $20 million investment had not yet brought him a young horse in the same league with Chief's Crown.

Even after his death, Carl Rosen's lucky touch seemed to linger over his only homebred colt. The very timing of his death, in fact, had kept the colt in the family. His widow and his children, who had never shared his passion for the track, considered selling all of Rosen's horses, including Chris Evert and the little Danzig colt. Tournament Star had been sold at a Fasig-Tipton sale in Maryland for $1.9 million, and Chris Evert herself had been entered in a Fasig-Tipton fall catalogue. The champion mare had recently slipped a foal, however, and she was withdrawn from the sale. Chief's Crown was not put on the auction block because the big yearling sales at Keeneland and at Saratoga had already taken place.

The threads of both of Carl Rosen's empires had begun to unravel. "Dispersing the stable was always a possibility," Andrew had told me at Saratoga. "The executor of my father's estate, Miles Rubin, sat down with me, and he said that as executor he didn't think it was the most prudent thing to keep it going. There was a lot of pressure to sell." Andrew, however, began to consider the idea of keeping the stable together. He had become intrigued by the world of the track, where his father had been as much at home as he had been on Seventh Avenue, and he undertook to educate himself in the horse business. Miles Rubin told Andrew that if he were willing to spend the time on the horses, he and the rest of the family would be willing to take a wait-and-see attitude. They could always sell if things didn't work out.

A month after his father's death, Andrew and his sister Lisa made a trip down to Claiborne with Roger Laurin to take a look at the Danzig colt his father had been so excited about, and Laurin liked what he saw. Seth Hancock, too, was encouraging. He had liked the looks of Chief's Crown enough to urge Rosen to send Six Crowns back to Danzig the following season, although Rosen did not take his advice, and the mare was sent instead to Mr. Prospector, currently one of Claiborne's hottest sires.

Carl Rosen had engaged Laurin as his trainer a few months

before his death, in one of those impulsive gestures that turned out, in retrospect, to be so canny. The ailing Rosen had dissolved his association with Joe Trovato, and he had been dissatisfied with the progress of his current trainer, a spiffy dresser named Jimmy Picou. At that point, according to a trainer at Suffolk Downs named Dennis Manning, Rosen had begun to look around for another trainer, and Manning himself had been approached by a friend of Rosen's, asking if he were interested in coming to New York to train Rosen's horses. Manning had trained a few of Rosen's claimers, and at one point he had taken charge of Tournament Star and Wimbledon Star, when Rosen had shipped them up to Suffolk.

In the meantime, however, Rosen had run into Laurin in the clubhouse at the Meadowlands racetrack. Spying Laurin at an adjacent table, Rosen, who was accompanied that night by his doctor and by his handicapper Freddie Bond, had approached the laconic trainer with the idea of his training two of Rosen's Evert-line fillies. He also had a terrific colt, he told Laurin, waiting in the wings, who would be ready to race the following year. He had known Laurin from their early years in New England, and the two had maintained a jocular acquaintanceship over the years. Laurin agreed to take the horses, and although the fillies had never shown much promise on the track, Laurin was still interested in training the Danzig colt. In December of 1983 he had the colt shipped down to his father's training farm in Holly Hills, South Carolina, where the Chief was said to have given the farmhands a hard time. He was a tough, headstrong colt, who learned fast but who needed a firm hand.

Chief's Crown was sent to Laurin's barn at Belmont in April, when Laurin was still in Kentucky with his Derby contender Bear Hunt. The stable crew, however, were more impressed with another recent arrival, a strapping chestnut colt named Damascus Sam, with a huge, noble head and a playful personality. Karen Thomas, Laurin's regular exercise girl, chose Sam as her personal favorite after riding both colts, and Chief's Crown was assigned to Laurin's other exercise rider—a slender, quiet black man known as Cigar. The first time the two colts worked together in the morning, Sam outran the little bay. But to

Thomas's surprise, that was the last time it happened. The Chief didn't like having dirt kicked in his face, and he quickly learned to keep his head in front. Laurin, however, urged Cigar to teach the Chief to relax, to reserve his speed. He didn't want a sprinter, a speed wastrel; he wanted a classic horse. The colt ran with his head low to the ground, and Laurin began to use a shadow roll—a layer of sheepskin—over the colt's nose to protect his eyes from the dirt kicked up from the track.

Before the Chief's first official, timed workout, Roger Laurin called Andrew Rosen and told him if the colt could do three furlongs in thirty-five seconds and change, they would know they had a good colt. The Chief complied easily, telling Laurin that he was ready for the real thing.

Laurin had decided on Don MacBeth as the regular jockey for the Chief, but MacBeth was out of town on the day of the Chief's Belmont debut, so Laurin chose as his temporary replacement Angel Cordero, whose temperament was as hot and excitable as MacBeth's was cool and collected. The question of riders became moot, however, when the starting gate sprang open on that warm, breezy June afternoon. One of the frightened young colts tossed his rider and decided to run alongside Chief's Crown, who had broken slowly. With his panicky shadow running beside him, the Chief rushed up from last place to fourth, fell back to sixth, then was swept wide at the top of the stretch as he made another rush, winding up fourth, a total of eleven lengths behind a colt named Don't Fool With Me. A green but promising effort.

In his next start, eight days later, with Don MacBeth aboard, the Chief broke quickly, but he was immediately overtaken by two speedsters—Tiffany Ice and Secretary General. The Chief dropped back to fourth, and was lagging seven lengths behind the leaders at the three eighths pole—that is, three furlongs from the finish line. Around the turn, he moved up to third, and at the top of the stretch he went after Tiffany Ice, who was running two lengths behind the leader, Secretary General. The Chief swept by Tiffany Ice in mid-stretch, and by the time Secretary General hit the finish line the Chief was only a length behind him. It was four lengths back to Tiffany Ice and the rest of the field.

Thirteen days later, the Chief finally entered a race as the betting favorite—as he was to do subsequently in every race in his career, until the Woodward Stakes on August 31, 1985. Already, the Chief was a pro who inspired confidence in those who had seen him run. This time the Chief broke quickly, lunging from the gate, and he led at every pole, beating his closest competitor, Paul Mellon's Desert War, by five lengths.

And now, with the fall season about to begin, the Chief was the great bay hope of the East. He was, in fact, practically the only hope of the East. Carl Rosen's lucky touch had continued, it seemed. Judging by the quality of two-year-old races at Saratoga, and by the maiden races run thus far at Belmont, the best of the East did not offer the Chief much competition. According to Steven Crist of the New York *Times*, the Chief's generation would "have to be judged the weakest two-year-old division in several years."

It appeared that the Chief's toughest competition would come from elsewhere in the country. This had become a year when horses from the provinces actually had a shot. A son of Alydar named Saratoga Six, trained by Wayne Lukas, was winning races easily in California, and his chief competitor in the West, Spectacular Love, also showed a great deal of promise. In Florida, the top two colts, the undefeated Smile and the speedy Spend a Buck, looked very tough, and in the Southwest and Midwest, a colt named Bionic Light was running very fast times.

Bionic Light, who was owned by an Oklahoma rancher named Loy Dickson, was the hard-luck horse of the bunch. One morning during a workout the colt had managed to slip and fall under the rail and skin his back. Nevertheless, before the cut had even healed, the colt managed to win the Juvenile Stakes at Nebraska's palindrome, Ak-Sar-Ben, by an easy six lengths. After the race, Dickson loaded the colt into a small, one-horse trailer hitched to his pickup truck and headed back to his stable in New Mexico. Along the way, Dickson noticed in his rearview mirror that the trailer was whipping back and forth suspiciously, and then he took a second look. Incredibly, there was a horse running the opposite way down the highway. It was

Bionic Light, who had somehow managed to break his halter, kick open the trailer gate, jump backward out of the trailer and land on his feet, while the truck had been tooling along at 45 mph. After chasing the colt for a quarter mile or so down the road, Dickson finally caught him with the help of a friendly farmer, and Bionic Light seemed none the worse for his adventure.

Finally, on Saturday, September 15, the Chief would get the chance to test Bionic Light and another of the regional favorites, Spectacular Love, in the $100,000 Belmont Juvenile, at seven furlongs, while Slew o' Gold took on Paul Mellon's Fit to Fight and Oscar Barrera's Shifty Sheik in the Woodward Stakes.

The Chief had been training well, and he had gotten a new groom. José Mena had never rubbed a horse like the Chief before, and he had become obsessed with the colt, hanging around his stall all day, even when the horse was supposed to be resting. In Laurin's opinion, the young Cuban was getting on the Chief's nerves, and he gave the colt to a more experienced groom, Eddie Sweat, a heavily muscled black man of forty-six with the physique of a body builder. When I was first introduced to Eddie, all I saw was a huge bale of hay coming toward me down the shedrow, supported by a pair of short, bandy, very sturdy legs. Known as "Shorty," Eddie was a horseman's treasure, a truly great groom, who had rubbed both Riva Ridge and Secretariat for Laurin's father.

Eddie had grown up on a farm in Holly Hills, near Lucien Laurin's training farm, not far from the coast of South Carolina. He was the sixth of nine children born to David and Mary Sweat, who tilled the land as tenant farmers. Eddie, who worked at a number of jobs after school, picking cotton, corn and watermelon and digging sweet potatoes, used to admire the horses frolicking in Laurin's fields, and he began to think about asking Laurin for a job. "The horses looked so beautiful when I walked by Mr. Laurin's farm," said Eddie. "I started out to work with them when I was sixteen, but I only worked a couple of weeks and quit. They scared me. But I came back when I was a little older and a little more patient."

By 1955, Eddie was rubbing horses at the farm, and he proved so good at it that Laurin took him to the racetrack.

Within three months there, he had become the most trusted groom in the stable, and he was given the best of Laurin's horses. In 1966, he rubbed Laurin's first classic winner, Amberoid, who took the Belmont. In 1975, when Lucien Laurin had gone into one of his temporary retirements, Eddie had gone to work for Roger, and he had become the anchor of the stable. And now he had the Chief, whom he had quickly grown fond of. "Just about every horse I rub, I fall in love with," said Eddie. And even though the Chief gave him a hard time, sometimes guarding his stall with his teeth and hooves, Eddie's calm, easy strength was more than a match for the Chief's territorial imperatives.

September 15 came up rainy, and the Belmont track was a mile-and-a-half ring of slop. In the race prior to the Futurity, Roger had entered a big, good-natured chestnut filly, Crumpets, who had won a modicum of fame by breaking her maiden at Belmont in July at the longest odds of any winner that season: 70 to 1. Crumpets had run poorly in her next three starts, but she was still considered the sweetheart of the stable. When I had visited the barn earlier that morning, Crumpets had stolen the drawstring of my hooded jacket while I was standing next to her stall talking to Steve Jordan, Laurin's foreman. She had handed it back, however, dangling from her mouth like a worm, when I asked. This afternoon she was going off again at long odds, this time at 18 to 1. Crumpets broke well, in the middle of the field, and she moved up to third after a quarter of a mile. Hugging the rail, she loped to the front of the field at the top of the stretch, and swept under the wire a length ahead of her nearest competitor.

It looked as though things were going to go Laurin's way all day—that is, until the gates opened for the fifth race. The Chief, who never seemed to forget a lesson he learned on the track, had broken well again, but he was soon at sea on the sloppy track. Bionic Light and Spectacular Love went to the lead, and the Chief had dropped back to sixth after a quarter of a mile. He couldn't seem to get his footing, and he seemed to be running in slow motion, as in a dream, when the monster is gaining on you and you can't seem to get going. Finally, coming around the turn, he seemed to get the hang of it, and he began to move. He passed three horses, including Ziggy's Boy, in short order, and at the top of the stretch he was within a half length of Bionic Light, but four lengths behind Spectacular Love, who was still going strong. Swinging very wide to get around Bionic Light, who was drifting out, he changed leads and seemed to shift into another gear, his front legs cutting smoothly through the slop. He was flying now, gaining inexorably on Spectacular Love, but the wire was too close, and he finished a length behind the California horse.

Although the Chief had lost, he had made some converts in the press box. "This race impressed me more than his others," said Russ Harris of the New York *Daily News,* the man considered the steadiest handicapper in the New York press. "He was going like a freight train at the end."

At this stage of the career of a two-year-old, that flourish was what everyone was looking for—how a horse finished the race, not how he began it. What they were looking for was evidence that he could handle each increment of distance. And so far, it seemed, each half furlong had helped the Chief. Just now, at seven furlongs, he had run well at the longest distance his sore-legged sire had ever attempted. And so each furlong after this one would be an answer to a question.

The selling of the Chief

Nevertheless, although the Chief still had questions to answer and things to prove, the Rosens began thinking again about selling. Devil's Bag, last year's flashy two-year-old, had been syndicated the previous fall, after the colt had won his first five starts in awesome fashion but before he had completed a race around two full turns of the oval. Seth Hancock had called the owners, Dr. and Mrs. James Mills, with an offer in October, and by December the colt was syndicated for $1 million a share, with twenty-six shares sold and ten retained by the Millses.

Although the dutiful Chief had not stirred turf writers to the kind of dreams the brilliant Devil's Bag had inspired, he had become a valuable commodity in the bloodstock market. Shortly after the Futurity, at a sale in Newmarket, England,

Miles Rubin ran into Kentucky bloodstock agent John Stuart and his partner, Peter Bance. Bance, an insurance agent, had handled the policy on Chris Evert for Carl Rosen during a time of financial difficulties, when Rosen had leased the mare for a year to help resolve an IRS debt. Rubin told the partners then that he was in the market for syndication possibilities for the Chief.

The Rosens seemed undaunted by what had happened to Devil's Bag after all the buildup. Steven Crist had chronicled the colt's rise and fall in a poignant series of articles in the *Times*, and the saga had bestirred many observers to an even greater cynicism about both the backstretch and the breeding business. The horse had failed to win a single important race as a three-year-old, and Seth Hancock had been predicting that never again would a horse be syndicated so early in his career. Nevertheless, Miles Rubin gave Stuart and Bance a letter granting them power of attorney to negotiate a syndication deal, and Claiborne was their first stop. Not surprisingly, Hancock told them that he thought it was too early to syndicate the horse, and he advised them to wait until after the colt's campaign as a three-year-old.

Meanwhile, on October 6, the Chief had avenged his loss to Spectacular Love with an easy victory in the mile-long Cowdin Stakes, notching another furlong on his stamina record. The horseplayers had made him the favorite again, and he had justified their faith. Bionic Light had battled for the lead with Don't Fool With Me, while the Chief and Spectacular Love held their own duel in third and fourth place. The Chief put Spectacular Love away after half a mile, then took over the lead from Bionic Light at the middle of the turn and drew away to win by six lengths. Bionic Light had held on for second, and a horse with the peculiar name of Script Ohio was third. Script Ohio, who belonged to Dan Galbreath, son of Pittsburgh Pirates owner and Darby Dan Farm owner John Galbreath, had been named for a half-time marching maneuver performed by the Ohio State Buckeye Band.

The next morning at the barn I encountered for the first time the "Eeyore" side of Roger Laurin, who seemed to take little joy

in the Chief's victory. In answer to my question, he replied that
he hadn't done much celebrating. "He was supposed to win,"
said Roger. "When you're a one-to-two shot, you're supposed to
win." The Chief's victory, he said, hadn't really affected the
barn. Looking around at Eddie Sweat, he said, "These people
are used to good horses." This was hardly a time to rest on a bed
of laurels, then, and sip champagne. "This is a one-step-at-a-
time thing," said Roger. "He has to keep improving, or he can't
be great." Relaxing a bit, however, he said that the Chief at this
stage of the game was like the Mets' pitcher Dwight Gooden—
"a freshman who shows a lot of promise."

The following day, Roger began to get caught up in the spirit
of things. The Chief, after all, was about to be syndicated, and
his market value depended not only on performance, but on
hype. Roger found himself proclaiming, with uncharacteristic
bravado, that the Chief was the best horse in the East, and that
he was ready to meet Saratoga Six in a battle of the coasts.

The search for a syndication deal continued apace, as the
Chief was shipped to California for the Norfolk Stakes at Santa
Anita and the Breeders' Cup at Hollywood Park, where he
would meet Saratoga Six as well as Smile and Spend a Buck to
decide the two-year-old championship. On October 26, however, the Chief won a preliminary victory by default. Smile was
discovered to have a bone chip in one of his knees, and Saratoga
Six broke down badly in a morning workout.

Wayne Lukas had accompanied Saratoga Six to the workout
on a pony, and as the colt broke off at a fast gallop in front of
him, Lukas heard a sharp, terrible sound, like the snapping of a
tree limb. It was Saratoga Six's ankle shattering.

And so, while the Chief was testing the hard, baked surface of
a California track, his two principal opponents were lying on an
operating table.

As training intensified and race distances increased, the attri-
tion of good two-year-olds had begun to accelerate. With their
soft, still-growing bones, their ill-controlled eagerness, their
foolhardy speed, they were like fourteen-year-old boys that had
been sent out to play on the bone-wracking fields of the National Football League. Sometimes, as I read the casualty re-

ports, I thought of young soldiers sent out to fight an old men's war.

In some ways, it seemed, the late bloomers, the big, clumsy horses who took time to grow into runners, might be the most fortunate. Precocious young horses were either sent out to race early and often, to take advantage of their speed before other young horses caught up to them in ability, or they were put on the classic-distance regimen, in which their survival depended on both soundness and luck. In the first case, the idea was to make money quickly. And in the second case, the idea was to prolong the big payoff, which would come with syndication, usually after the big races at age three.

In the Chief's case, however, the big payoff was to come even before the Breeders' Cup. After Seth Hancock had turned him down, John Stuart had begun negotiations with Johnny Jones of Walmac International, a stud farm near Lexington with European connections and a respectable roster that did not yet boast any breeding-shed superstars. The Chief was to be syndicated for a total value of $20 million, with the Rosens to retain twenty shares and Jones to sell twenty shares for $500,000 apiece. However, when Jones asked to have the colt vetted, the deal hit a snag. Roger Laurin refused to allow a complete veterinary exam, on the grounds that the procedure would require the administering of a tranquilizer. The Norfolk was coming up in a matter of days, and Laurin declared that he didn't want to disturb the Chief's daily routine with a lengthy physical exam or unaccustomed drugs. Jones would simply have to take it on faith that the colt was sound.

When Jones failed to confirm the deal, Miles Rubin and the Rosens began to get restless. One evening, John Stuart ran into Robert Clay, of Three Chimneys Farm, at a local club in Lexington, and the two men discussed Chief's Crown. Stuart was aware that Clay, who was new to the syndication business, had been following an ambitious plan for his farm. Clay had set out to acquire one champion a year for the next six years, and his first acquisition had been Slew o' Gold, whom he had syndicated the previous year, just before Slew won the Jockey Club Gold Cup. Clay had written to the colt's owners, the Taylors and the Hills, after the colt ran in the Derby, stating his admiration for the horse and the kind of deal he would like to work out with them. Four months later, after another deal had fallen through, Jim Hill called Clay, who was traveling in Spain, at three in the morning, with a very tough deal. They wanted $16 million, and they wanted to keep fourteen shares, Hill told Clay.

At that stage of Slew's career, before he had beaten John Henry in the Jockey Club Gold Cup, Clay was taking a considerable risk. For one thing, Slew was a rig—that is, only one of his testicles had descended—and his fertility was thus in question. However, within a weekend Clay was able to find buyers for each $400,000 share. Clay, who could trace his ancestry back to Henry Clay, came from one of the leading families in Kentucky, and although his own interest in stallions was recent, he had already built a powerful international network of connections that included some of the best-known Arab and European high rollers. The list of shareholders in Slew o' Gold included Allaire Du Pont, Stavros Niarchos, Will Farish, and Sheikh Maktoum al Maktoum. A later round of syndications included Barry Schwartz.

Ironically, it was Schwartz who became an intermediary of sorts between Clay and the Rosens. Clay had told Stuart that he would probably be able to line up most of the Slew shareholders for shares in Chief's Crown, and Andrew Rosen acquired from Schwartz a list of the Slew syndicate, as well as an assurance that Clay was a good man to do business with. In the meantime, the Chief had won the Norfolk on October 27, beating a mediocre field of California horses in his first race around two turns, and Stuart called Clay to set up an appointment. Clay came to Stuart's office on a Wednesday afternoon to work out the terms of the deal, and then made a trip to his bank to secure a loan for $10 million. On Friday afternoon, the two men flew to Wilmington, Delaware, to meet Miles Rubin and close the deal.

Clay spent the weekend on the telephone, and by the following Monday, when the press corps began to arrive in Los Angeles for the Breeders' Cup, he was ready to announce the syndication of Chief's Crown. He had sold eighteen shares, at $500,000 apiece, to many of the Slew o' Gold group, including Bert Firestone (owner of Derby winners Foolish Pleasure and Genuine Risk), Stavros Niarchos, Sheikh Maktoum, and Greentree Stable (the heirs of Jock Whitney). He had warned them that they were taking a risk, that if the Chief lost the Breeders' Cup their investment would probably decline in value by as much as $200,000. On the other hand, if he won, they would be getting in early on a two-year-old champion.

For the most part, Clay had avoided commercial breeders and had picked shareholders who were interested in breeding horses to fill their own racing stables rather than to sell at auction, so that in forthcoming years there would be only a handful of sons and daughters of the Chief for sale, and his offspring would be in even greater demand. Clay had not been able to sell the final two shares to the breeders he preferred, however, so he kept those two shares in his pocket, to sell after the Breeders' Cup.

Already, the Chief had become part of the international blood-and-money set, as the intersection of Kentucky and Seventh Avenue reached out to the far reaches of the rich—to Paris, Dubai, the Greek isles. His sperm had been apportioned out for the rest of his lifetime, his loins dedicated to providing future winners for a fabulously wealthy group of horse fanciers and gene merchants.

CHAPTER 5

The Hollywood Spectacle

When I bestride him, I soar, I am a hawk, he trots the air; the earth sings when he touches it; the basest horn of his hoof is more musical than the pipe of Hermes . . . He is indeed a horse.

—William Shakespeare, *Henry V*

HORSES AND MOVIES have been intertwined in California since 1872, when a vagabond British photographer named Eadweard Muybridge was hired by Leland Stanford, the governor of California, to help win a $25,000 wager. Stanford, an avid breeder and owner of racehorses, was convinced that at some point in the thoroughbred's racing stride all four hooves left the ground. After five years and $100,000 worth of unsuccessful research, Muybridge finally hit on the idea of setting up a series of cameras along the track, attaching a trip wire to each camera shutter and stretching it across the track. On a board behind the track he marked lines and numerals to measure the horse's progress. On a sunny spring day in 1877, Stanford's horse galloped down the track, tripping the wires and becoming the star of the nation's first series of "motion" pictures.

Muybridge had frozen the horse's motion into a sequence of still frames; in one of them, he had caught the animal in midair, with all four legs outstretched like a carousel horse. Stanford had won his bet. And, a decade later, the movie business was born when Thomas Edison learned how to reverse Muybridge's process, to turn a series of frozen frames back into the illusion of motion. Edison had discovered that the mind's eye will transform the brief, discontinuous bits of action captured on film into a semblance of actual motion.

Edison's successors in the business had discovered that the viewer's credibility was greater still; that the mind's eye would transform fragments of plot and dialogue into the stuff of dreams.

Marje Everett's glitter

In choosing a California track for the site of the first Breeders' Cup series, the board of directors were going for sunshine and glamor, and they were acknowledging the success of California racing as well as the continental drift of money and power toward the Sunbelt. Although the overall quality of horses had remained higher in the East, due to its vast reservoir of Kentucky bloodstock as well as to the traditional lure of Saratoga and Belmont, California could boast of champion jockeys like Laffit Pincay, Hall of Fame trainers like Charlie Whittingham, and equine stars like John Henry. California racing, like California baseball and California football, might have suffered initially in comparison to the East, but the power of the sun and celebrities seemed to be prevailing.

While Eastern racing was struggling to maintain the status quo at its aging plants, southern California tracks were booming. Fans seemed to thrive on the thin, fast, sun-baked surfaces of Western racing, where track records were broken as easily as studio contracts. Hollywood Park and Santa Anita traded national daily attendance records back and forth, and Hollywood Park regularly ranked first in tax and purse payouts. Hollywood annually distributed over $36 million in purse money and paid out another $36 million in local and state taxes.

If Eastern racing was still Damon Runyon and Henry James, California racing was *Dynasty* and *Lifestyles of the Rich and Famous.* Los Angeles was a perfect locale for a set of races designed as media events and as a lure for the wealthy horse owner with aspirations of grandeur.

Although Hollywood Park was actually a good half-hour drive from the mythical corner of Hollywood and Vine and from the fossilized footprints sunk in the pavement before Grauman's Chinese Theater, it had always managed to soak up a bit of showbiz aura. When the track opened in 1938, the first chairman of the Hollywood Turf Club had been Jack L. Warner, the most adventurous of the Warner Brothers, and the six hundred original shareholders in the park included Al Jolson, Raoul Walsh, Bing Crosby and Walt Disney.

At the time of the first Breeders' Cup, Cary Grant was a member of the track's board of directors, and Mervyn LeRoy, director of *Little Caesar* and producer of *The Wizard of Oz*, was president of the track.

The person who really ran the show, however, was Marje Everett, who had promised the Breeders' Cup folks a glittering backdrop for the races: everything but Charlton Heston in Roman togs driving a chariot. The only problem was that Hollywood Park, when you came down to it, was quite an ordinary track, lacking the spectacular natural setting of Santa Anita or the venerable clubhouse and verdant grounds of Saratoga.

Few racetrack operators, however, are as resourceful as Everett, a tall, broad-shouldered woman of then-sixty-two who bears a slight resemblance to Dame Margaret Rutherford as Miss Marple in *Murder Ahoy*. An adopted daughter of Chicago racetrack owner and power broker Ben Lindheimer, Everett, who had worked in various capacities at her father's tracks since dropping out of Northwestern University, bought out her siblings' racetrack stock after her father died in 1969. She survived a stock manipulation scandal involving a number of her father's friends in 1971 and moved west, where her husband, Webb Everett, a former jockey's valet whom she had married in 1958, had interests in both Hollywood Park and Golden Gate Fields. Thirteen years later, she was largest stockholder as well as chief operating officer of the track of the stars, where Cary Grant led the cast of thousands.

When Everett first submitted her proposal for Breeders' Cup day, along with a pledge for a sizeable charitable donation, to

Bunker Hunt and the Cup selection committee, she included as an added enticement the plans for a new $30 million Pavilion of the Stars, with the interior to be furbished by Walter Scott, the Academy-Award-winning set designer for such glitz-laden spectacles as *The Robe, Cleopatra,* and *Hello Dolly!*

Scott's design included a five-story atrium entrance with obligatory waterfall and a series of forty luxury suites equipped with wet bar, refrigerator, and TV sets. Out front, patrons were greeted by a large bronze sculpture that featured six horses appearing to leap out of a huge bowl.

Turf writers responded by christening the new clubhouse "Marje's Mausoleum" and pointing out that patrons who had paid $50,000 for their luxury suites could not see the finish line any better than if they had paid two dollars for a grandstand seat. Said one local columnist of the project, "They should call it 'Illinois Everett and the Pavilion of Doom.'" Nevertheless, although the bulldozers were still on the grounds when horses, handlers and turf writers began to arrive the week before Super Saturday, November 10, Everett, with her ever-present walkie-talkie and obsession with detail, had managed to pull the scenery together and start sprinkling the glitter before the TV cameras arrived.

Racing has never pretended to be a classless society, and Breeders' Cup visitors observed the customary stratifications in hotel accommodations. The turf writers, supported by the largesse of their publications, were staying at the Airport Hilton, while the better-heeled owners and trainers chose the Beverly or Beverly Wilshire. Marje Everett herself resided in a suite at the Beverly Wilshire. Grooms and hot-walkers found dormitory bunks on the track. I had chosen a tiny hotel in Beverly Hills that somehow managed to survive on flophouse rates. The catch was that there was no TV and no parking lot, and one had to outwit a two-hour parking limit on the streets as well as a complete ban on overnight street parking.

The desk clerk recommended that I park "after hours" in an adjacent lot reserved for fans of a theater that had been refurbished as a venue for rock concerts. Every night I would doze off in my hotel room around eleven, trying to listen for the last throbbing encore, usually around midnight or so, then venture out and find my car and move it into the lot after the carloads of bottle-smashing punkers had departed.

Every morning I would get up before dawn to beat the freeway traffic, arriving at Hollywood Park in that perpetual daze that afflicts racetrackers who try to live in the dual time zones of the racetrack and the fast track.

One huge barn had been set aside for the Breeders' Cup competitors, and as reporters gathered at the gate of the wire security fence in search of interviews, the feeling was more like that of the summer Olympics, with its pack of polyglot journalists and its dozens of athletes, than of the Derby or other big races, with a handful of contenders and a favorite or two. With seven races and a total of seventy or so horses to choose from, reporters could shop around for a story, trying to catch trainers' attention when they came close enough to the gate.

The Chief was being touted early on as one of the clear favorites of the series, and Roger Laurin was in great demand for interviews. Making an effort to be quotable, he would say of the Chief, "He acted like a champion, and we wanted to give him a chance to be a champ." However, the hype did not flow easily, and Roger's already legendary reticence frequently left reporters with only a sentence fragment or two after a fifteen-minute session. Although he had trained good horses before, this was Roger's first experience with the rudiments of star-making machinery, and he was not comfortable with it.

With only the Chief and another colt, the four-year-old Thalassocrat, to look after, it was difficult to keep occupied, and he took to walking the horses around the shedrow himself to avoid the attentions of reporters.

The Chief was to face ten rivals in the mile-long Juvenile race, four of whom he had already met: Secretary General, who had beaten him in his second start; Spectacular Love, owned by the daughter of the founder of Beverly Hills; Bionic Light, the Southwestern speedball whom he had beaten in the Cowdin; and Dan Galbreath's Script Ohio, whom he had beaten in the Cowdin but who had gone on to beat two other Breeders' Cup contenders, Spend a Buck and Tank's Prospect, in the Young America at the Meadowlands. Script Ohio's trainer John Veitch, however, claimed that he had an even better contender in his barn, a colt named Proud Truth, who had not yet made his debut.

Tank's Prospect, like Script Ohio, had been named by a sports magnate with a passion for football. Purchased for $625,000 at the Keeneland Summer Sales by trainer Wayne Lukas on behalf of Eugene Klein, Tank's Prospect had been named for Tank Younger, the former fullback for the Los Angeles Rams. The name was not inappropriate, since the colt, a son of speedster Mr. Prospector, who was also the sire of Eillo, the favorite for Saturday's sprint race, was a big, hulking sort—something of a bruiser, once he got moving.

Lukas, however, not only had an uncanny eye at the sales ring for horses that he referred to as "athletes"; he also had an eye for other men's horses who showed potential. If he couldn't beat them, he'd buy them. And one of the horses he had an eye on was the local favorite for the race, a strapping son of Secretariat who had been named with typical afflatus by yet another sports magnate, George Steinbrenner. Image of Greatness had broken his maiden in a brilliant race at Santa Anita on the same day that Chief's Crown won the Norfolk Stakes there. "It's the fastest maiden race run anywhere in the world," said the colt's trainer John Fulton, no doubt coached by his boss, a collector of superlatives.

Fulton, a quiet, auburn-haired man who had been with Steinbrenner for fifteen years, had once trapped rattlesnakes in the Everglades for a living. "I didn't always have the funds I needed in life, and you could get two dollars a foot for catching a poisonous snake," said Fulton. He was frequently asked by reporters what he knew about getting along with Steinbrenner that Billy Martin didn't know, particularly since Fulton's last big success for Steinbrenner had come in 1977 with the stakes-winning Steve's Friend. "Mr. Steinbrenner is different with horses than he is with ballplayers," said Fulton; "he has more patience." Within a month, however, Fulton was to get a taste of the Martin treatment. Lukas had become the trainer for Image of Greatness after buying a substantial share of the colt.

Spend a Buck was the Cinderella horse in the race; his owner, Dennis Diaz, a Tampa businessman who had retired, burned out, from the insurance and real estate business at age thirty-eight, had bought the colt as a yearling for $12,000 as part of his first foray into the horse business. On the recommendation of a mutual friend, he had given the colt in June of '84 to a young trainer named Cam Gambolati, who had taken out his trainer's license just six months earlier. Gambolati, thirty-five, the son of a wealthy Connecticut businessman who had moved to Florida, initially tried working with his father in the citrus industry and going to college, but his real passions were football and the track. After working as a statistician for the Tampa Bay Buccaneers during a five-year dry spell for the team, he signed on as assistant trainer to Norman St. Leon and had begun the difficult process of forming his own public stable when Diaz came along.

Gambolati was a slight, dark-eyed, olive-skinned man whose instinctive shrewdness, you felt, would probably have gone to waste had he tried to succeed in pinstripes. He had frequently considered going into a less risky line of work—"Nothing can make you consider running a laundermat more than training a barn full of slow horses," he told one writer. But fate had dealt him a good horse, and he had risen to the occasion. Although "Smile by a mile" had become the slogan at the steamy summer meeting at Calder, Spend a Buck had run a good second to the Florida star, and his luck proved to be even better. Bone chips in his knees had taken Smile out of action at a crucial time, and Spend a Buck had gone on to win over $500,000, acquiring the services of Angel Cordero. Said Gambolati, his hands jammed in the pockets of his faded baseball jacket: "The morning Saratoga Six broke down, we were going to run Spend a Buck in the Remson in New York, and Smile went down the same day. Angel Cordero had been riding Saratoga Six, and when his agent called that morning to say that he wanted to ride Spend a Buck, we decided to give our colt a shot here instead."

Diaz had to supplement the colt for $120,000, however, since he had not been nominated to the Breeders' Cup as a foal. Gambolati didn't much like the gamble—"It looks like the race is going to be set up for a closing horse, and Spend a Buck is very competitive; he drags Angel to the lead." He figured that Spend a Buck would not be able to hold on against Chief's Crown, so that the best he could hope for was second. The purse for second place was $225,000. "So we're betting $120,000 at even money; would you take those kinds of odds?"

My main occupation in the mornings was horse-watching. For someone who had apprenticed at Suffolk Downs, the presence of so much high-quality horseflesh under one roof and on one track was overwhelming. As the horses walked out of the shedrow toward the track, identified with their special gold Breeders' Cup saddle cloths, I would get the giddy feeling of a movie fan with a prime seat at the Academy Awards.

Although the most famous American star of all, John Henry, had come up with an ankle filling that would prevent him from competing in the Cup turf race, and the Europeans had not sent their top horses, there were plenty of good horses to watch. There was Slew o' Gold, prancing like the Platonic ideal of a horse; tiny Persian Tiara, whom I had seen win gamely at Saratoga; burly Strawberry Road, the Australian hope, who kept trying to toss his exercise rider over the inner turf course rail. And there was Lear Fan, who, for all his continental chic, was a son of Roberto, John Galbreath's stallion, named for baseball star Roberto Clemente and a favorite of Queen Elizabeth II.

Thoroughbreds, I was coming to realize, had indeed become international currency. Leon Rasmussen, the bloodlines specialist for the *Daily Racing Form,* estimated that the total value of the horses participating in the seven races, including syndication rights, was $250,000,000—a modest amount, perhaps, when compared to the net worth of Nelson Bunker Hunt before the silver crash, or to the total amount of money spent over the years on yearlings at Keeneland by Robert Sangster and the Arab brothers from Dubai, or even to the total ticket sales grossed by director Steven Spielberg's greatest hits. But it was an amount that put horse racing into the category of funny money, of the kind of wealth unimaginable to ordinary people, except as in voyeuristic interivews by Robin Leach or lurid vignettes in the *National Inquirer.* It was wealth in a realm so unreal in its values that a single spurt of a stallion's semen could be worth the entire take-home pay of a workingman's life.

Among the horses in the Breeders' Cup turf race, All Along had already won more than $3 million, and as a broodmare would be worth even more. Majesty's Prince had won more than $2 million, and his syndication value would be more than twice that much. In the classic race, Desert Wine had already been syndicated for $14,000,000 and Slew o' Gold, like his sire, Seattle Slew, would generate the income of a small industry. If he won, his syndication value would increase from $40 to $50 million. The Chief, whose paper value was $20,000,000, had become part of a world of fabulous wealth, a world so removed from ordinary life that he might as well have been a unicorn.

Yet these were horses, after all, creatures like those I had worked with at Suffolk Downs. They were part of the same world where 90 percent of owners lost money on their horses. They munched on oats and produced manure like any other beast of burden. What was the critical difference, for example, between Chief's Crown and Sir Quasar, who also had heart, who also was fast, and who also carried the genes of Nearco, the champion bred by Federico Tesio?

For months I had been trying to learn how to recognize a good horse when I saw one, and the Breeders' Cup horses confused rather than narrowed my criteria. "Even Ray Charles could see that Slew o' Gold is a good horse," Bill Perry had once quipped. But not all good horses looked like Slew o' Gold or Secretariat. Thoroughbreds might be a "master race," but even among the Breeders' Cup horses, who represented the best of their breed at this point in time, I could see as much variation in horseflesh as at Suffolk Downs.

They were beautiful, of course; but then, even a cheap horse can be beautiful. They were glistening with health and energy, their eyes bright and their coats shiny; but even a Great Barrington horse could be fed and groomed like a champion. Most had good breeding; but there were cheap claiming horses with pedigrees almost as impressive. Many of them had near-perfect conformation: straight legs, long necks, powerful, sloping shoulders. Many, however, had problems common to cheap horses. They had swollen ankles, bad knees, or the kind of conformation flaws that would slow the bidding in the sales ring.

Eillo, the best sprinter in the bunch, waddled like Charlie

Chaplin. Both Wild Again, a candidate in the classic race, and the turf horse Star Choice had been operated on to remove bone chips from their knees. Even Slew o' Gold wasn't perfect; he was a "rig," and his foot problems that had developed before the Whitney had become chronic.

Wild Again, who was to prove the true dark horse in the bunch, had been so neglected by the media that trainer Vincent Timphony's wife had undertaken a P.R. campaign for the horse. Timphony himself, a short, plump man who looked like a character actor specializing in good-hearted-gangster roles, preferred to play it low key.

On Thursday night, in the clubhouse elevator on the way to a party for visiting sportswriters, Mrs. Timphony introduced herself, with shy determination, to a well-known writer and proceeded to list Wild Again's accomplishments. "Vincent thinks he's going to win," she concluded. "He has no shot," said the writer after Mrs. Timphony left.

As the party got into full swing, Bill Allen, one of the horse's owners, stood out in the gathering like Mark Twain at a cattlemen's convention. He was dressed in a shiny gray tux jacket and black bow tie, with the dashing silver pompadour and moustache of a riverboat gambler. Bill Allen was one of the "new owners" that John Gaines had been talking about as the saviors of the sport, a man with Sunbelt money and a sporting instinct.

An insurance man from San Antonio and Miami, he had bought Wild Again for $35,000 with two partners, Californian Terry Beal and Ron Volkman, a real estate magnate from Dallas, with whom he liked to party, gamble and do business. They had named their partnership Black Chip Stable, for the color of hundred-dollar chips at the gaming tables of Las Vegas; but when they realized that associations with other sorts of gambling were considered unseemly in most clubhouses, they began to tell reporters that the stable was named for the black dots in their racing silks. Wild Again, Allen admitted, had been named during a party in New Orleans, when one of the partners said, "Let's go out and get wild again." Allen's girl friend Nina Martin had said, "That's a good name for a horse. Wild Again."

Wild Again's record so far had been uneven. The horse had missed nearly his entire three-year-old season because of the bone chips, and Timphony himself had been out of action with open-heart surgery. In April, however, Wild Again had set a track record at Oaklawn Park, and after going winless in six races he won the Meadowlands Cup Handicap by six lengths. Allen loved his flawed horse, and he believed in him: enough to supplement him for the Breeders' Cup for $360,000. Said Allen, "You have to be a little crazy to be in this business anyway."

As the week progressed I knew I would never again feel the same about cheap horses at Suffolk Downs. Every morning I was looking at the kind of horses those valiant but flawed claimers were meant to be, the kind of horses they should have been, had the genetic distribution system been an equalized subsidy and not a lottery. I had once watched a grotesquely swaybacked young filly break down during a $5,000 claiming race at Suffolk; a granddaughter of Northern Dancer, she had been sired by the same stallion as Gate Dancer, winner of the 1984 Preakness and one of the favorites to win the classic race on Saturday. Gate Dancer had never quite lived up to his potential, yet he had a far better chance than that sad little filly to beat the pain/payoff quotient. If he won on Saturday, his owners would beat the odds for good.

Two qualities, in particular, began to stand out as I watched seventy good horses in such close proximity, standing in their stalls, walking around the shedrow, galloping around the track. The best horses, it seemed to me, radiated either an air of confidence or an aura of aggressiveness—qualities that were also associated with certain of the human stars and assorted tycoons I was watching that week along with the animals. Like human stars, equine stars have "presence," I decided, whether the rowdy arrogance of a bully or the regal air of an aristocrat; they seem to own the very air they breathe, the ground on which they tread.

Aggressiveness was easy to identify—and to understand as a trait common to human and equine winners. All animals, including the human, have established an array of signals to assert dominance, to establish a pecking order. Even a "domesticated" animal like the horse has retained his own means of assertiveness within captivity, and the thoroughbred, who has kept more of his wildness than other breeds, has maintained an impressive arsenal of warning signals, including eye-rolling and head-tossing. When a thoroughbred is fit and at the top of his form, he is ready to fight for his territory, and his body language broadcasts a challenge. Fillies and mares, too, habitually establish dominance in the field, and they can transpose that assertiveness to the track.

Sometimes, though, a good horse's aggressiveness caused difficulties on the track as well as in the barn. Gate Dancer, for example, was a bully who preferred bumping into other horses to passing them, and his trainer, Jack Van Berg, had devised a series of ingenious devices, including a pronged bit, to keep the horse running in his own lane. In the wild, Gate Dancer would probably have been king of the road, but on the track he was an outlaw.

Confidence, the second important trait that I perceived in the course of my horse-watching, was harder to discern and define, without venturing beyond zoological constraints into poetic license. It was manifested by a certain "look"—a proudly arched neck, a controlled prancing on the way to the track; in a sense, it was the look of a leader who has already defeated his or her challengers. When I had occasionally seen that look before in horses in the paddock or in the post parade on the way to the starting gate, those horses had run well, unless racing luck went against them.

Confidence in a horse was an evanescent quality; it had to do not only with intelligence and ability, but with conditioning and past experience. A horse could develop confidence if his trainer placed him in races suited to his abilities; he could lose it if he were placed in races above his abilities or if he were forced to run with painful injuries or inadequate conditioning. I was convinced that Bill Perry's horses did so well because he built up their confidence; he knew when they were ready to run, and he placed them in races that he knew they could win.

Although trainers talked about their horses as though they were professional athletes rather than animals, they did not always treat them accordingly. A horse might be in top condition, at the top of his game, for one race and not another. Some horses were too sore or too ornery to follow a strict regimen, and the races themselves became their main conditioning program. Other horses were in the hands of trainers who behaved like drill sergeants, putting horses through their paces at a rate determined by the trainer's schedule rather than the horse's needs. And when stakes were as high as those for the Breeders' Cup, even the most flexible of trainers had to get tough and arbitrary with their conditioning programs. The races had wreaked havoc with ordinary training schedules.

Under ordinary circumstances, most top two-year-olds would have begun a slight letdown period before getting geared up for the big classic prep races scheduled in late winter and early spring. And under ordinary circumstances Slew o' Gold would not have had to race on a bad foot. Some of his competitors, however, were in worse condition. Canadian Factor, who was entered in the Classic race, looked as thin and worn out as one of the cart horses in *Black Beauty* who had fallen from prosperity into the daily grind.

I was having a hard time placing the Chief in this pantheon of equine presence; he didn't fit any of the generalities I was drawing from watching other horses. "He just doesn't look like a classic horse," said a Kentucky turf writer who knew his horseflesh. "Look at that short neck. He's just too small." I had never seen the Chief prance or strut on the way to the track; he never preened or "acted up" in the paddock.

The Chief's specialness, I thought, showed up in his composure during his public outings, when he seemed all business; as Roger said, he was a pro. The Chief seemed to know when it was important to expend energy and when it wasn't. But he was far from being a placid horse. In the privacy of his own home, he reverted to bad manners. In his stall, he continued to act irritable and territorial. On Friday morning, the day before the Breeders' Cup, he grabbed Eddie Sweat's cap to keep him from going into the stall to bandage his legs. "When he don't want you to do anything with him, you have to leave him alone until he makes up his mind it's all right," said Eddie, rubbing the top of his head where the teeth had almost penetrated.

Mr. Reagan's odds

Tuesday morning was election day, and I felt I might as well have been on a remote island, if there could be such an island anymore, where Reagan and Mondale were no more than pictures in a foreign newspaper. Gary Hart had run aground after the brief high tide of Yuppie ambition had subsided, leaving racetrackers none the wiser, while Ronald Reagan sailed along on an older, stronger current of selfishness. "That trainer looks like a Yuppie," I had observed to Bill Perry one day while we stood at the paddock fence comparing notes on the entries for the third race. "What's a Yuppie?" he had asked.

Politics, like social trends headlined in weekly news magazines, was part of the world "out there" that racetrackers were busy eluding. Even while third-graders in Ronald Reagan's mythical West Succotash were lathering Sassoon mousse into their punk hairdos, and young adults in East Podunk were sprinkling their radicchio with raspberry vinegar, racetrackers were eating grits and gravy, warning the barber to go easy on the sideburns. Elections might affect the tax brackets of wealthy owners, but political battles seemed to affect the track no more directly than the passing of a cloud, a sea change, the hint of a breeze. They had long since slipped through the cracks of the get-ahead, make-a-difference system that made the rest of America work. Racetrackers never settle down long enough in a place to register to vote, much less to notice who's running for county assessor; many of them prefer not to be questioned about the status of their citizenship.

In recent years, only a paragon like Secretariat had managed to link the track with politics and the world at large, and some of his impact undoubtedly had to do with timing. When he galloped onto the scene in 1973, public morale was at a low ebb. Revelations about Nixon's dirty talk and dirty tricksters had soiled the American dream, and the nation needed a hero. No ordinary mortal would do; the disillusionment with human heroes was too thorough. And so the big chestnut horse became a chivalric redeemer whose heroic feats were achieved the old-fashioned way—with sweat and muscle.

It was said by some at the time that Secretariat was the embodiment of God's will at work in the world, a messenger sent to divert America from its shame. A woman interviewed after the Belmont Stakes told a reporter that after Vietnam and Watergate, Secretariat had "restored her faith in mankind."

Who, then, could save America's soul in the 1980s? Certainly not Chief's Crown. Roger would have snorted at the notion that he was training the second equine messiah, after having relinquished the first one to his father twelve years earlier. But then, not even all the Breeders' Cup horses, plus all the Breeders' Cup men, could put America together again. Their mission was more specialized—to put racing together again.

At the track on Tuesday, only the Great Handicapper, whom I had met that morning amid the crowd of reporters at the Cup barn, seemed concerned about the results of the election; he was an avid Republican, an advocate of law-and-order and low taxes. "He'll win by 18 percent," he had said of Reagan, looking around for takers.

The Great Handicapper, a tall, intense, bespectacled man whose appearance was once described by writer Bill Barich as that of "a computer with a side interest in recreational drugs," was a gambling genius who had been diverted by the track from a career as a literary scholar; two weeks before graduation, he had skipped his Chaucer final in order to place a bet on Amberoid in the Belmont Stakes. He had complained at the time that "society confers its blessings on traditional academic pursuits but views the study of horse racing as utter frivolity." However, as a professional handicapper he had become more wealthy and famous than most tenured professors, and at the track, where he was as readily recognized as Mickey Rooney, fans would hand him their racing programs to autograph, launching into testimonials on how his betting advice had changed their lives.

The Handicapper was unimpressed by my view of the Breeders' Cup as a Reagan epiphany, a kind of dramatization of social Darwinism, with horses acting as surrogates for their wealthy owners, battling it out for greater wealth and power, while the middle class looked on and the poor groped for a piece of the action.

Although I considered the Handicapper an advocate of self-interest when it came to ideology, he was supportive of other handicappers and always generous with his expertise, handing out his opinions like gifts or tossing them out like grenades. "Gate Dancer cannot lose on Saturday," he said flatly, with the kind of certainty one ordinarily would associate at the track with fools or fixers.

He relied heavily on his speed charts, devised to account for every possible track variable, from speed bias near the rail to wind velocity, and horses had to earn big speed figures in order to earn his respect. Of Secretariat's legendary career, he had once written: "Romanticists could appreciate Secretariat for his strength, his grace, his exciting style of running. But for me the most awesome moment of his career came two days after the Belmont Stakes, when I sat down with paper, pencil, and the Belmont charts, calculated my track variant and wrote down the number 148 for the eighth race that day." The previous highest figure any horse had attained by his reckoning was 129.

"This is the weakest crop of two-year-olds I can remember," he said, when I asked him about the Chief and his competitors. "Rockhill Native would have been the champion of this bunch," he added, referring to the unremarkable two-year-old champion in 1979 who had faded before the spring Classics. Of Spend a Buck, he said: "I think his future is behind him. They tend to be limited, these kinds of speed horses. With each sixteenth of a mile they get weaker. It's great when you have these horses with poor breeding and the underdog trainers, but when the smoke clears, it's always Woody Stephens or Wayne Lukas. They have the pedigrees and they know how to prepare horses for the big races."

The Handicapper had decided to allow himself a day off from the races, and we headed for Rodeo Drive to window-shop for something extravagant to buy when he won the Pick 6, a bet that required one to pick the winners of the third through eighth races. The Pick 6, like the exacta, had been one of Hollywood Park's great contributions to the world of exotic wagering, and the Great Handicapper had become a master of it.

The Pick 6 had changed the pain/payoff quotient for handicappers forever. You only had to hit it once or twice a season, depending on how great the accumulated jackpot, in order to cover a year of hard luck. Winning the Pick 6 would allow one to try on shoes at Gucci's with the stars, to shop at Giorgio's with other overnight success stories. It would allow one the luxuries of Reaganomics without guilt, since track money was funny money, taken not from the pockets of the downtrodden but from the grasp of other handicappers, who wagered out of free will.

"My secret is resilience," said the Handicapper, as we walked through a cloud of perfume wafted from the door of Giorgio's and peered through a pet-shop window at an elaborate brass bed designed for small dogs. "Handicapping information is available to a lot of people. But what I have is resilience. Usually it takes only twenty-four hours to bounce back from a bad day. In extreme cases, a little more." When I knew him a little better, he told me about the time his resilience had been tested most strongly. When he had broken up with a longtime girl friend, he called his boss to say that he was feeling low and that he needed some time off. The boss had said, "Take a couple of weeks, as much time as you need." But the Handicapper had asked for forty-eight hours. "I'm capable of putting everything behind me when I have to," he said.

Wednesday, opening day of the season, was also the day of Ancients, as a group of remarkable old men gathered for the dedication of Hollywood Park's very own Hall of Fame, located on the ground floor of the Pavilion of the Stars. The group of honorees was a peculiar Hollywood mix of men and beasts, and even a woman: three horses, two jockeys, two trainers, two moguls, and four all-purpose celebrities.

Yeats's lament, "That is no country for old men," might apply to California as a whole, but not to the racetrack, where one is never too old to win nor too young to lose. As Fred Astaire, former owner of the Blue Valley Racing Stable, entered the still unfinished hall where portraits of the new honorees were to be hung, he was accompanied by his wife, Robyn Smith, the former MGM starlet turned jockey who had caused such a stir in the early 1970s by dating Alfred Gwynne Vanderbilt and by winning races on his horses. In 1972, Smith told the *Washington Post:* "I don't think I'm very good with young horses. Young horses like to play around with me. I get along best with old class horses, the old pros."

Astaire greeted a fellow octogenarian, Leslie Combs, the lord of Spendthrift Farm, and the two of them joined Cary Grant, better preserved than either of them, while Johnny Longden, the seventy-year-old jockey turned trainer, compared notes with fifty-five-year-old Willie Shoemaker, who would be riding three mounts in the Breeders' Cup races. Towering over them was seventy-one-year-old Charlie Whittingham, known as the Bald Eagle, Hollywood Park's all-time leading trainer, with 587 races and 144 stakes races to his credit at last count.

Astaire, along with Longden, Grant, Shoemaker and Whittingham, were to be honored with other living legends—Greer Garson (owner of Ack Ack), John Forsythe, and Mervyn LeRoy, as well as the late Citation, Swaps, Seabiscuit, and trainer William Molter. Swaps, whose most poignant defeat came in the famous match race with Nashua, the savior of Spendthrift Farm, had already been commemorated with a statue at the entrance of the grandstand. Also to be honored was Spendthrift's faithful customer Louis B. Mayer, who had ruled like a puritanical sultan over MGM's stable of stars, which included Greta Garbo, Jean Harlow, Clark Gable, Spencer Tracy and Katharine Hepburn. Mayer had been a champion of clean, wholesome family entertainment, grooming his errant stars into respectability, and taming the Marx Brothers, whose first film for MGM was *A Day at the Races.*

The script for Saturday's races also had its wild, madcap moments, improvised by jockeys and horses, with Marje Everett standing in for Margaret Dumont as the society matron at the center of the storm. Although NBC, with its eighteen-man camera crew and assorted hosts and color commentators, was prepared for an equine version of the Super Bowl, and John Gaines had been envisioning an ennobling spectacle, a *Chariots of Fire* on hooves, the result was closer to *The Good, the Bad and the Ugly.*

Post time for the first race was moved up to 11:14 A.M. so that the nationwide, four-hour telecast could terminate before the six o'clock news in the East. Gates opened at 9 A.M., and at 10 A.M. the flashy local Locke High School Band and drill team marched across the infield, where the drum major demonstrated a baton-bouncing version of break-dancing. Shortly thereafter, the Fifteenth Air Force Band of the Golden West marched out onto the track to play the national anthem, their bootheels digging deeply into the dirt in front of the finish line as they marked time. A greeting from newly reelected President Reagan flashed on the giant matrix board in the infield, and the grandstand resounded with boos.

At 10:45, a time when they were usually munching alfalfa from their haynets or lying down to rest after their morning exertions, the colts for the Juvenile race were led to the paddock, and the owners gathered in scattered bunches. John Galbreath, who was still pale and thin after convalescence from a heart attack, was surrounded by a large entourage of family members. He had come to root for Script Ohio, even as his beloved Buckeyes were kicking off against Northwestern in a game that would decide the Big Ten championship and a trip to the Rose Bowl.

The Rosen clan had also gathered in full force. Douglas Rosen, who had worked as head of finances for Gary Hart's presidential campaign and who had begun work on a video featuring fatbuster Richard Simmons, had flown in from Santa Monica. Hart, he said, had faded in the stretch, but he expected the Chief to finish with a flourish. Shirley Rosen had flown in from Palm Springs, exuding as much calculated California glamor as one of the well-preserved names of yesteryear seated in the Pavilion of the Stars. Her Boston roots had long since been transplanted to exclusive desert soil.

Adrian Rosen, Andrew's wife, was still excited about Marje Everett's party the night before, thrown at the home in Beverly Hills that Everett had bought for entertaining. Neil Diamond and other stars had been there. "Carl would have loved it," she said. Adrian had just found out on Thursday that she was pregnant, and Don MacBeth, ever the gentleman, turned to her just before Roger boosted him onto the Chief's back, waving with his whip: "This one is for the baby." The Chief, as usual, was the calmest horse in the paddock, walking with his head drooping toward the ground, as though checking out the soil content, while Script Ohio pranced and Secretary General foamed at the mouth.

Andrew was remembering another party and another race at Hollywood Park ten and a half years previously, when the Chief's grandam, Chris Evert, had been the star of the show, and his father had been the master of ceremonies. After Chris Evert had won the filly Triple Crown with an easy victory in the Coaching Club American Oaks, Jimmy Kilroe, then president of Hollywood Park, had discussed with Rosen a winner-take-all match race between his filly and the star of the West, Miss Musket, owned by Aaron Jones. Rosen would put up $100,000, while Aaron Jones and the track itself would each put up an equivalent amount. It was the sort of proposition that appealed to Rosen, and he began to orchestrate a party that would make him a legend at the California track.

In mid-July, he brought a hundred people to Hollywood Park, including his four children and Chris Evert, the tennis star herself, along with her then-boyfriend Jimmy Connors. At the time, Rosen had told Joe Hirsch of the *Racing Form*, "I've been to heavyweight championship fights, super bowls, world series and all-star games, but I've never gotten the kick out of anything that I've gotten out of this match." Always the businessman, however, he said: "I worry about the name of Chris Evert. I want it to be associated with victory, and not only because she endorses a line of my sportswear." He needn't have worried, however; the tennis star's namesake dug into the fast California surface, setting fractions of 214/5, 443/5, and 1:084/5 for six furlongs. She humiliated Miss Musket, chasing the ghost horse and winning by fifty lengths.

Her grandson would not have such an easy romp, however, though the crowd had made him an overwhelming 4-to-5 favorite. He had been listed as even money in the program, and he had been the consensus choice in the *Racing Form*. "Won prep smartly," said the pithy Sweep. Spectacular Love, the second favorite, who had been listed as 4 to 1 in the program, went off at 5 to 1, while Spend a Buck, who had been bet equally with the Chief by early-bird bettors, had gone up to 6 to 1 by post time.

The Chief continued to keep his cool as the horses were led to the starting gate, which for the mile race was located at the end of a chute feeding into the backstretch of the track oval. The gate was separated from busy Century Boulevard, at the east end of the plant, by only a chain link fence and a mere fifteen yards of dirt. The horses were loaded into the gate smoothly, however, and when the starting bell went off, Spend a Buck tore out in front of the field, just on the outside of Proudest Hour, with Secretary General bunched up tightly behind them.

When Proudest Hour weakened, Secretary General and then Bionic Light made a run for the lead, but Spend a Buck kept his head in front and opened up a two-and-a-half-length lead after three quarters of a mile, maintaining a faster pace than the subsequent winner of the sprint championship. Spend a Buck was proving to be that most deadly of combinations: a very fast horse with a will to fight back.

The Chief had broken slowly, and he trailed by six lengths after a quarter of a mile. MacBeth said later that the surface of the track was balling up under the colt's hooves, but it looked as though the Chief had lost his powers of concentration, and MacBeth had to tap him with the whip to keep his mind on the race. In any case, the Chief began to rally, and in the middle of the turn he swept by Spectacular Love and the rapidly tiring speed horses that Spend a Buck had vanquished. Moving to the outside at the top of the stretch, he trailed Spend a Buck by a length. Tank's Prospect had also begun moving up along the rail, and he trailed the Chief by a length and a half.

The Chief had begun to run with his best stride, reaching out with his shoulders, his head pumping in choppy, piston-like inexorability. Spend a Buck hung on stubbornly until the middle of the stretch, but the Chief had the momentum, and he gradually wore him down. As he passed Spend a Buck he seemed to let up just a bit, and Tank's Prospect began to loom up on the inside. The Chief's ears perked up, and he seemed to relish the challenge, hanging on by three quarters of a length when they swept under the wire.

Said Penny Chenery to a companion, "He didn't win convincingly." The Chief had not chased the ghost horse. But again, he had won by "enough." Said Roger, "I hope he never wins by more than a length."

In one of the photos taken of the finish, the Chief was poised to cross the wire, with his ears perked forward, as horses do when they are galloping easily. Don MacBeth's mouth was wide open, a big O of triumph. The Chief was completely in the air, flying, like the hero of Muybridge's bet-winning photos. Flying, even as the dawn horse, Eohippus, had fled from its enemies, all four feet off the ground. I thought about that prophecy in the Koran, when Allah told the horse, "Thou shalt fly without wings . . . upon thy back shall riches repose."

In the winner's circle, Roger let go for a moment of the endless scenarios of dread that kept marching through his head. His face glowed as brightly as his cream-colored sports jacket. Before the cameras clicked, he reached over to the Chief and patted him. "You're the champ," he told the horse, engraving the title in his mind. Now he had something that couldn't be taken away, no matter how the wheel turned from now on. "That horse's name will be on the first Breeders' Cup plaque, and that's going to mean something," he said. "Forty or fifty years down the line they'll remember the first winner of this race."

This had been a new race, a clean slate, a chance to make history, a chance to do something his father had never done. But NBC's Dick Engberg wouldn't let it be. Taking Roger by the elbow, he introduced him to the nationwide viewing audience as "Roger Laurin, son of Lucien Laurin." Said Engberg brightly, "He must have taught you well." Without a wince, Roger replied, "Yeah, I got a good start." Said Engberg, "Now you're really your father's son."

As the Rosens gathered for a celebratory drink, Roger's wife, Nina, suggested, "Let's go find Lucien." Turning to Roger, she said, "He should be in on this." One of the Rosens chimed in, "Good breeding." Roger's face was impassive again.

I thought about another scriptural passage, this one from the Old Testament, which seemed to envelop that lyrical prophecy from the Koran with a fatalism that was closer to the way of the world at the track: "A horse is a vain thing for safety: neither shall he deliver any by his great strength."

Earl Scheib's long shot

Andrew Rosen's good fortune continued. At Roger's suggestion, he had placed a two-hundred-dollar daily-double bet, combining the Chief in the first race with Outstandingly, a 30-to-1 long shot in the second race, the Juvenile race for fillies. Outstandingly had finished a head behind Fran's Valentine, a delicate, dark-bay filly who had only recently graduated from county-fair racing. Owned by Earl Scheib, the man who brought inexpensive paint jobs to the cars of New York and Southern California, Fran had won two races at Pomona's half-mile bullring before her trainer, Joe Manzi, decided to let her run in more distinguished company. Sired by Scheib's stallion Saros, who had suffered two bowed tendons while racing under Scheib's colors, Fran's Valentine had been named for her dam, Izza Valentine; for Scheib's late wife Fran; and for her birthdate —she had been born on Valentine's Day.

Earl Scheib, whose commercials appeared throughout the day on local TV during the broadcast, was as familiar to Southern California viewing audiences as Mr. Whipple. In a culture that valued slick, exotic cars that cost more than a second home, Scheib's forte was giving second life to heaps. I knew, in fact, a number of people with limited budgets who had taken him up on his promise to "paint any car for $99." When we were living in New York, my boyfriend once drove a rusting wreck up to a Scheib emporium in the Bronx and returned with a respectably shiny vehicle.

The seventy-year-old Scheib, who had persisted in breeding mares to his unfashionable, broken-down stallion, was an unlikely star in John Gaines's tycoon-laden script. But Scheib, who had been dabbling in the horse business for twenty years, had gotten one of the fastest rides ever from the wheel of fortune, swept up to unimaginable heights and then dashed to the bottom with one lash of a whip.

Sent off at odds of 70 to 1, it seemed that Fran's Valentine would live up to the serendipity and sentiment attached to her name. But as she was rounding the turn, her jockey, Pat Valenzuela, had yanked Fran into the path of Pirate's Glow, and the force of the collision had sent Pirate's Glow to her knees and into the path of Bessarabian, the favorite, who in turn impeded Weekend Delight. The four fillies were stumbling and reeling across the track as though they had entered a hidden force field, and only Fran, the perpetrator, recovered to make a run for the wire. Before Valenzuela had tossed his whip to his valet, the INQUIRY sign was up: within moments, Fran had been disqualified, and Outstandingly was declared the winner. Andrew Rosen, who had already earned a goodly share of the Chief's purse, found himself yet another $14,000 richer.

The rest of the afternoon was divided between favorites and long shots, between old money and new, between jet-setters and one-shot wonders. It was a day of diamonds and beer, of cars and stars, with the fifth race being sponsored by Mobil, the sixth by DeBeers Consolidated Mines, Ltd., and the seventh by Chrysler Corporation. It was not all as upscale as John Gaines would have wished, but there was little doubt that the image of racing was being gilded.

The Chief's race had been sponsored by First Jersey Securities, and the face of that other would-be savior of racing, Robert Brennan, was everywhere, on TV commercials and in the racing program. Like Gaines, Brennan, who was founder and president of International Thoroughbred Breeders as well as founder and president of First Jersey, was regarded by a number of horsemen as a kind of visionary of the sport—a man of new ideas and considerable capital-raising capabilities. In just ten years he had built up First Jersey, a tiny securities-trading firm, into a major brokerage house whose assets had been estimated at $250 million; and in just four years he had built ITB, one of the nation's first publicly owned companies involved in the breeding and selling of thoroughbreds, into an influential force in racing.

Brennan's ads for First Jersey, which had also appeared during the Super Bowl and other sporting events, featured Brennan, with his golden-boy good looks, inviting customers in a sharp New Jersey accent to "Come grow with us" as he piloted a helicopter over Grand Coulee Dam or strolled along the Erie Canal. As one financial reporter had earlier observed of Brennan's ad campaigns, the message was "Free enterprise, free spirit, unfettered imagination—these are the things that made America and First Jersey great."

If Gaines's plans for racing had to do with promoting the top end of the sport, Brennan claimed to be serving the interests of the common man. When Brennan founded ITB in 1980, he put up $1 million himself for 40 percent of the shares, while the First Jersey sales force peddled the balance to some forty thousand shareholders for over $100 million. His idea, he said, was to offer "the two-dollar bettor a chance to participate in the fun— the way Crest toothpaste users can own Colgate-Palmolive shares." (Crest is a Procter & Gamble product.) And when ITB purchased the ruins of the old Garden State Race Track in southern New Jersey, Brennan announced that his new facility, which would feature an atrium-enclosed paddock and casino-inspired interiors, would change the public perception of racing by making the sport more appealing to the middle class.

According to press packets for the new Garden State track that Brennan's publicity director was passing out during the Breeders' Cup day, Brennan proposed to lure the middle class "by erecting glittering new facilities with a personality and management style that make people feel welcome and interested in coming back." Said Brennan: "The average perception is that a racetrack is just some place where a bunch of seedy old unemployed men hang out because they have nothing better to do with their time. Either that, or they think it is a place that you can go if you are a rich fat cat—because you have second-, third-, or fourth-generation wealth and you belong there . . ." Racing, he was implying, was either Suffolk Downs or Saratoga, with no middle ground for the Yuppies and other upwardly mobile groups who had not been to the stables born.

Brennan was proposing, then, to replace the old class structure of the racetrack, articulated in the traditional tiers of club-and-grandstand architecture, with the more "wholesome" open grid of the marketplace. His aim was to sweep away in one great architectural flourish both the top-end exclusivity and the lower-depths vulgarity that have kept the demographics of the racing world so skewed.

Theoretically, one would not have to be the Aga Khan or a Whitney to be a part of Brennan's racing world. Yet Brennan seemed drawn as much to the old-money mystique of racing as to its profit potential. Two days after the Breeders' Cup races, he would buy C. V. Whitney's best horse, Hail Bold King, for $3 million, as though he were buying part of the Whitney aura.

Liz Taylor's choice

Between races and Brennan ads, NBC showed bits of famous movies that had featured horse racing, from a time when the sport was at once more glamorous and more raffish. Introducing a clip from *National Velvet*, Elizabeth Taylor, also a survivor from an era that was at once more glamorous and more raffish, reached back to the glowing innocence of her appearance as Velvet Brown, and for a moment one could forget the years of squabbles with Burton, the fat farms and detox centers, the Joan Rivers jokes. Asked by Engberg which horse she liked for the fifth race, she replied in a little-girl voice, the same voice that had made immortal that link between horses and girls: "I can't help it, Father, I'd rather have that horse happy than go to heaven." Elizabeth Taylor liked Princess Rooney for the Distaff race, she said: "It makes me think of Mickey. And I like Life's Magic, so I'll play them both."

Princess Rooney won by seven lengths, the biggest margin of the day, and Life's Magic came in second. The pros, however, weren't doing nearly as well as Liz Taylor in their picks. Torn tickets littered the floor of the press box, and the Great Handicapper was in despair.

Europeans, using American bloodstock descended from European sires, dominated the turf races: Robert Sangster's Royal Heroine beat a field of colts in the mile turf race, and the Aga Khan's Lashkari, a son of Mill Reef, sent off at odds of 50 to 1, defeated All Along in the regular turf race. In a sense, though, the latter race was all in the family, since All Along was to be retired after the race and sent to Mill Reef to be bred.

The Aga Khan IV was also, in a sense, linked to the outcome of the Classic race. His grandfather, the third Aga Khan, had bred three stallions whose names had become intertwined in the pedigrees of countless good horses in America: Blenheim, sire of Triple Crown winner Whirlaway; Nasrullah, sire of Bold Ruler and Mill Reef, both of whom had been imported by Bull Hancock; and Khaled, sire of Swaps, who had been imported to California by Rex Ellsworth. Khaled was also the sire of Bushel 'n' Peck, Wild Again's dam. Wild Again's second dam, Dama II, had also been purchased by Ellsworth from the Aga Khan.

When the starting gates opened for the $3 million Classic, and the silks flashed, it was Wild Again and the black dots of the Black Chip Stable that drew the eye. Sent off at 30 to 1, the small black colt had been lathered with excitement in the paddock, his eyes rolling and his ears pinned back. When he charged for the lead, his jockey, Pat Day, decided not to fight him, and Wild Again, like Spend a Buck, held off a series of charges by the other speed horses in the race. At the top of the stretch, Slew o' Gold made his run at the leader, but he did not get by. The horses bumped slightly, and Slew hung, as Wild Again fought back.

Slew's foot problems had finally taken their toll. The cracks in his right front hoof had been patched earlier in the week, but when the horse developed an abscess the patch had to be removed and the hoof repatched. Two hours before the race, his vet, Judd Butler, had felt heat in the horse's ankle. But this was Hollywood and the Breeders' Cup, and the show had to go on. Said Timphony later of Slew, "If he was 100 percent coming down the stretch, there'd have been no way we could have beat him."

But Slew was not 100 percent, and Wild Again was racing over his head. When Gate Dancer, who had been dallying a dozen lengths behind the field, made his charge outside Slew, he reverted to his bullying habits and crushed Slew against Wild Again's rump, causing Wild Again to lurch crazily, then regain stride. The three horses continued, bumping, down the stretch, with Slew the chopped liver in the sandwich. As they barreled past the wire, Wild Again stuck his nose in front of Gate Dancer, with Slew a half-length behind, only his rump visible behind the two halves of the sandwich. The INQUIRY sign lit up immediately.

At this point Terry Beal, Allen's partner, had to be given oxygen; he had been watching the race on TV from his hospital bed, only a day after open-heart surgery. Allen himself, who had bet $3,000 on his horse across the board when he noticed those incredibly long odds on the tote board, was floating in that rarefied realm where bubbles never burst, where horses are the stuff that dreams are made on. Gate Dancer was disqualified to third and Slew o' Gold placed second, while Wild Again remained the winner.

Tesio's energy

The following day at the track, while Slew o' Gold was loaded into the van to head for his bright new seraglio at Three Chimneys Farm, Marje Everett was toting up the take and NBC was checking its ratings. The Great Handicapper was regrouping for another assault on the Pick 6, and I was looking for some sort of pattern in yesterday's races. The Great Handicapper could explain the results in terms of speed charts and "trips," but his system had no way of accounting for Wild Again's tenacity or Gate Dancer's roguishness; and I could get no further than Tesio's vision—a vision of serendipitous matings, the inevitable rise and fall of dynasties, the dispersal of precious genetic resources across the earth.

Tesio's own stallion Nearco was the common denominator in the pedigree of every winner, appearing once, sometimes twice in each horse's family tree. Chief's Crown traced his pedigree back to Nearco through his grandsire Northern Dancer, and to Nearco's son Nasrullah through his grandsire Secretariat. Outstandingly's link to Nearco came through her grandam, Finance, a daughter of Nasrullah. The sprinter Fillo, a grandson of Northern Dancer, also traced back to Nasrullah through his great-grandsire Nashua. Royal Heroine, sired by Lypheor, a grandson of Northern Dancer, also traced back to Nasrullah through her dam, My Sierra Leone. Princess Rooney, whose victory had been the most decisive of the day, traced back to Nasrullah both through her sire, Verbatim, and her dam, Parrish Princess. Lashkari, of course, was a great-grandson of Nasrullah, while Wild Again, a grandson of Nearctic, was the closest of all to Nearco—only three generations away. On his dam's side, he was four generations away.

It was little wonder that Sangster and the Maktoum brothers were trying to corner the market on Northern Dancer blood. Like his grandsire, the little Canadian stallion and his prepotent offspring seemed to be able to reproduce themselves in perpetuity without a diminishment of speed or strength. Yet those bloodlines had been for sale long enough that no individual could ever dominate racing the way Sonny Whitney or the Aga Khan's grandfather had done. Distribution of talent was random and unpredictable enough that surprises like Wild Again and Spend a Buck were as bound to occur as the victories of Royal Heroine and Chief's Crown, with their "royal" pedigrees.

At the end of the day, the ever-resilient Handicapper had avenged his losses from the previous day by winning the Pick 6. Instead of moping around after Gate Dancer's defeat, he had skipped the big post-race celebration at the Pavilion of the Stars and gone home to study his racing form. He had woken up early the next morning, his optimism replenished. The pot was only $25,000—not the kind of jackpot Bill Allen and his cronies were still celebrating—but it represented a profitable victory of order over chaos, a vindication of the Handicapper's ultra-rational approach to racing. When Leonita, a three-year-old chestnut filly making only her third start, made a big move in the stretch to win the seventh race, she was doing what the Handicapper had predicted she would do, based on her "figs"—her speed ratings from the previous two races.

I had thought she would win, too, but my opinion was based on her attitude in the paddock; she had strutted and pranced, bouncing with energy. Almost unwittingly, I had begun developing my own set of visual clues for picking winners. But I knew I would never be able to look at horses "objectively," the way the Handicapper did, to reduce them to a set of figures and probabilities.

For one thing, I didn't have the discipline; I couldn't reconcile the euphoric sense of escape I felt so often at the track with the kind of fanatic attention to detail it took to make a betting system work. But more important, sentiment was still getting in the way. Horses were still my heroes, and I couldn't avoid a certain amount of blind faith in them. As for the Chief, I was starting to use that old track utterance that betrayed too much hope: "He could be any kind of horse."

CHAPTER 6

Lost in Paradise

*Inconstancy is my very essence; it is the game I never
cease to play as I turn my wheel in its ever changing
circle, filled with joy as I bring the top to the bottom
and the bottom to the top. Yes, rise up on my wheel if
you like, but don't count it an injury when by the same
token you begin to fall, as the rules of the game will
require . . .*

—Boethius, *The Consolation of Philosophy*

AFTER their Western detour to the Breeders' Cup, Roger
Laurin and other Eastern trainers who could afford a season in
the sun headed south for Florida, to Gulfstream and Hialeah, an
annual migration that had become *de rigueur* for big stables,
particularly those with Derby contenders, since the 1930s. The
top of the Eastern racing world moved south along with them—
the big-name jockeys, the big-time turf writers, and the big-
barn grooms who were rubbing a star.

It was the leaf-and-parasol circuit, where horses were always
saddled in the shade—from the elms of Saratoga to the oaks of
Belmont, and on to the palms of Hialeah. And if all went well,
the Derby contenders would go on to Kentucky just as the pin
oaks were budding and the dogwoods had begun to bloom.

The Chief had been "let down"—taken out of rigorous training—after his victory at Hollywood Park, and he was to resume
his stamina-building regimen at Gulfstream Park, where he had

arrived shortly after Thanksgiving. However, two weeks following his arrival in Miami, the barns of both Gulfstream and Hialeah were swept by a highly contagious equine virus that affected the pulmonary system of stricken horses, leading to a
buildup of fluid in the lungs and, in some cases, pneumonia. It
was the same virus that had spread through the Florida barns
the previous year, knocking two leading Derby hopefuls, Dr.
Carter and Time for a Change, out of contention for the Triple
Crown.

Already, a number of horses in Woody Stephens's barn had
begun coughing, and other trainers began inoculating their
horses.

Roger was hoping his barn had been spared, but it was his two
most valuable horses, the Chief and the graceful filly Faquer,
quartered two stalls down from the colt, who were stricken. On
Christmas Day, Faquer began coughing and running a fever.
Her temperature went up to 103 degrees, and she began to
weaken. Two days later, after Eddie Sweat had departed to visit
his family for Christmas, Cigar reported to Roger that the Chief
had coughed on the way to the track, and the colt was discovered to be running a mild fever. The nightmare scenarios had
come back, and this time they were real.

The following day the Chief's temperature had returned to
normal, but he was still coughing. Roger, with an attempt at
optimism, told Joe Hirsch of the *Racing Form* that the Chief
would probably be out of training for a maximum of ten days.
Said Roger: "If you have to miss any training, now is the time to
do it. I'm in no hurry to crank him up. My one concern is to have
him at tops on that first Saturday in May for the Kentucky
Derby. Everything else is preparation."

Faquer seemed to be recovering as well, but on New Year's
Eve she developed a severe case of colic, and she was losing
fluids at a frightening rate. On New Year's Day, Steve Jordan
loaded her into a van to be transported to the University of
Florida veterinary school in Gainesville for emergency surgery.
He also loaded several jugs of fluid, which were to be fed to her
intravenously during the trip to keep her from going into shock.
At Ocala, Jordan and the Gulfstream vet, Robert Shelton,
thought they had lost her. She fell, and her heart seemed to stop

temporarily. But the two men worked frantically to revive her, and the filly struggled to her feet. As the van pulled up to the gate at the Gainesville medical center, she was down to the last jug of fluid, and she was rushed to the operating room. Shortly before midnight, Jordan learned that the operating team, who had been recalled to the center from vacation, had not been able to save her.

The Chief, however, had survived. He had stopped coughing, and his lungs had begun to clear. He had lost weight and he had weakened, but he was very much alive.

And that was how the year had started that would come to seem both cursed and blessed for Chief's Crown and Roger Laurin. By the time turf writers had arrived to cover the opening of the Gulfstream season on January 8, the crisis was over. But the Chief did not return to the track for another week, and he was three weeks behind in his training schedule at a time when the countdown to the Derby made every workout important. Still, although the virus had caused a serious setback, the Chief had recovered early enough to bounce back into contention. The previous year, Time for a Change had almost died, and Dr. Carter had still been coughing in April. Their recoveries had been slow, and neither horse had been the same since the illness.

Bolles's boondoggle

Most of the itinerant turf writers and handicappers who could afford the journey South had rented houses for the season in Miami Lakes, a planned subdivision of artificial lakes and bungalows that gave its emigrants a little taste of home—if home, that is, were suburbia. Miami Lakes, one of the few unlatinized communities near Miami proper, was equidistant from the Gulfstream and Hialeah racetracks, but it was as far in spirit from the backstretch as it was from Little Havana five miles away. It even sported its own swingles bar/restaurant with a different theme every night of the week—fifties nostalgia, fraternity-party togas and beer. One could subsist in Miami Lakes forever without ever knowing José Cuervo from José Martí.

Despite the warnings of the Great Handicapper and other

friends who claimed to know the terrain, I had rented a cheap condo, sight unseen, in a complex called Westland Manor on the edge of Hialeah, a separate city that extended south and west of Miami. The condo's close proximity to the Hialeah racetrack did not impress the Handicapper. "If you're ten minutes from the track," he said, "you're probably two minutes from a gun shop."

Hialeah had become a Cuban diaspora, and as I drove in from the airport I found a modest, bustling city of single-story stucco and concrete-block homes, dotted with palms and malls and mini–shopping plazas. The closest gun shop did prove, however, to be only five minutes away—an emporium called Lou's Hardware Gun Shop, located next to Dalton's Photo and Bridal Shop and the Tiki Hair Design on Palm Avenue.

As I walked past Westland Manor's instant-stucco facade, graced with a layer of red tiles that paid token homage to the Hialeah mission style, the warm, late afternoon air was redolent with the heavy smell of stewing beans and the sound of salsa music. Propped up next to my door, adjacent to a mini-patio decorated with a dry, frog-shaped fountain and blue floodlights, was a Spanish-language *Yellow Pages*.

Things are never as they seem in Florida, the land of realtors' mirages, and in Miami, wherever you are, you are probably feeling as though you were somewhere else. All the ordinary landmarks and signposts add to the confusion. Was I entering an Anglo developer's cut-rate vision of a Cuban dream of the American version of a disinherited European peer's notion of home? To further confuse things, over the next few days I answered my doorbell to find a succession of Spanish-speaking Jehovah's Witnesses, Spanish-speaking cosmetics reps from Avon and Mary Kay, and Spanish-speaking teachers of English who promised *cultura, mejor empleo, superación económica, mejor condición social.*

I wondered, however, if I were feeling any more disoriented than the horseplayers perusing their racing forms on rented divans in Miami Lakes, or the Miami Beach sunbathers from the Frost Belt who were snickering at Shecky Greene's golf jokes in hotels that resembled lesser Las Vegas takeoffs of the Taj Mahal. Surely I couldn't have felt more estranged than the exiled Nicaraguan general who was said to travel faithfully from his mobile home in Sweetwater to his night watchman's job on a construction site in South Dade. Escape and exile was what Florida was all about.

Hialeah, built on land taken from the Seminoles and named with a trumped-up Indian word said to mean "top of the heap," has always been something of a never-never land. Like so many Florida communities, Hialeah began as a boondoggle—a tract of undeveloped swampland whose high water table was no more a sales deterrent than the swarms of mosquitoes to a series of land developers and lot boosters. In 1910, a promoter named Richard Bolles bought from the state 500,000 acres near Miami at two dollars an acre and began distributing brochures up North promoting his land as the ultimate easy-till garden, promising bumper crops of corn and tomatoes for a minimum of labor. When buyers arrived to inspect their prospective Edens, they were taken up the Caloosahatchee River by a paddle steamer named *Queen of the Everglades,* from whence they debarked onto an observation platform to view their submerged acreage.

As they swatted mosquitoes and mopped their brows, the buyers looked out onto what appeared to be a vast pond, but Bolles's hucksters transformed the panorama into an imaginary vista of drained and seeded land, into field after field of giant vegetables. Unfortunately, though, the power of positive thinking did not build dams or dig drainage ditches, and Bolles was subsequently indicted in a Kansas City court, despite supportive testimony from Florida officials, including ex-Governor Alvert W. Gilchrest, who demanded of the angry Midwesterners, "You have floods in Kansas City, don't you?"

The icy virtues of the Protestant work ethic, however, were no match for visions of endless sunshine and easy money. Bolles, who died before he could be extradited for trial, was followed by a wave of developers and hucksters the like of which America had never seen. Up North, books with titles like *Florida for Tourists, Invalids, and Settlers* and promotional pamphlets with titles like *Lure of the Southland* promulgated in purple subtropical prose the myth of Florida as perpetual paradise.

Once railroad tycoon Henry Flagler, the empire-builder of

north Florida, had been convinced to extend his Florida East Coast Railway southward—as the legend goes, he had been inspired by a fresh orange blossom sent from Miami during the 1894 freeze that devastated the St. Augustine citrus industry—trainloads of tourists, retirees, con artists, mobsters, and salesmen debarked on the mandrake-rooted spits and tidal marshes of south Florida in unprecedented droves. Adopting a uniform of white knickers and bow ties, armies of real estate men known as "knickerbocker boys" employed "bird dogs" who frequented the streets to lure prospective buyers into their offices. Successful salesmen became known as "Lord High He-Buzzards," who could "whack the bucks into a pile."

However, it was a daring Hoosier named Carl Fisher, the father of Miami Beach, and a New England transplant named George Merrick, the builder of Coral Gables, who would prove the full potential of the publicity stunt and the promotional advertisement. As a teenager, Fisher had boosted bicycle sales by riding across a tightwire suspended between the two tallest buildings in Indianapolis, and a few years later he had attracted buyers to his automobile showroom by floating over the city in the latest model suspended from a hot-air balloon. A devotee of speed, he raced every possible vehicle, from bicycles to balloons, and built the first shrine to mechanized horsepower, the Indianapolis Speedway.

When Fisher arrived in Miami on Henry Flagler's railroad, he did not dally like the oil and steel and cereal and department-store heirs who settled in at hotels like the Royal Poinciana in Palm Beach for a season of cards and polo and daily rides in so-called Afromobiles, the wheeled wicker chairs propelled by black cyclists. Looking across Biscayne Bay at a sandbar where a Quaker named Collins was trying to start an avocado plantation, Fisher had a vision of eclectic splendor. Going into partnership with Collins, he dredged and bulldozed the narrow sandbar into a subdivided tabula rasa, upon which he built a Spanish-Moorish hotel which he named the Flamingo, in honor of the Alice-in-Wonderland bird that had become extinct in Florida, and assembled a collection of exotic fauna and flora, including an elephant named Rosie. When a flock of flamingoes imported by poachers from Bimini died out, more birds were shipped in from Africa.

Meanwhile, preacher's son George Merrick, who had built his father's citrus groves into a 1,600-acre tourist attraction, began drawing up blueprints to convert the family plantation into Coral Gables, a Spanish/Mediterranean-style development that was to be part suburbia, part theme park, featuring grand entryways inspired by the Alhambra and the ruins of Tuscany. To promote his development, Merrick hired William Jennings Bryan, the orotund presidential candidate, who delivered his sales pitches from a floating platform in the Venetian Pool, a stony quarry that had been transformed into a tropical wonder of cascades, islands and caves.

Widener's retreat

As Bryan was hawking lots, two other developers, Glenn Curtiss and James Bright, were turning the land that Richard Bolles had abandoned into their own subdivided boomlet. Curtiss, a famous New York aviator and engineer who had made a fortune from his Curtiss Jenny during World War I, had come to Miami to open a flying school, and Bright, a Missourian, had come to south Florida to raise cattle. Like everyone else, however, the two men got caught up in the land rush, and in 1921 the partners announced the creation of the town of Hialeah. Ten-acre lots were snapped up, and the men had made a million dollars within ten days.

Curtiss was said to be a sober sort of man who preferred such genteel pursuits as fox-hunting, but before long, Hialeah was transformed from low-rent suburbia into a mecca for gamblers and bootleggers. An organization called Miami Studios chose Hialeah as the location for a motion picture studio, and a developer named Joseph Smoot, who later started the Santa Anita and Gulfstream racetracks, constructed a sports facility on land owned by Bright that included a greyhound racetrack, a horse track, a jai alai fronton and an amusement park.

Gambling, however, was illegal in Florida, and it was the founder of an Eastern racing dynasty—Joseph Widener—who came to the rescue of Hialeah, much as William Collins Whitney had "rescued" Saratoga. Widener's father Peter, a Philadelphia butcher, had in fact been a contemporary and a colleague of Whitney's who had built his fortune, like Whitney, by cornering the local transit market. The elder Widener, however, had gotten his start by selling horsemeat to the Union troops during the Civil War.

The younger Widener, raised on his father's money and dreams of social advancement, had begun racing a stable of thoroughbreds at the age of eighteen, despite his father's disapproval. But unlike the Whitneys, who were also new to the silks, he was considered a social interloper until he made a fortunate marriage into an old-line Philadelphia family.

When Widener began to winter in Palm Beach with the other Northern aristocrats and super-rich who had begun to travel south for seasonal recreation and repose, he discovered a need among the restless plutocrats for a diversion other than golf, tennis and surf: racing. However, it was customary for big stables to send their best horses to winter at farms in Kentucky or Virginia or at the big training center at Aiken. Winter racing had been limited to second-string horses who were sent to New Orleans. Moreover, the Hialeah track was overrun by bookies and lowlifes; patrons circumvented the ban on betting by buying postcards of the horses they favored or by purchasing "stock" in their choices.

Widener resolved to turn Hialeah Park into a Belmont of the South, a haven for winter racing, where the best thoroughbreds would compete and the best families would spectate. In Florida, such transformations can take place faster than the snap of a closing checkbook, and in 1931 the bookies were ousted and pari-mutuel betting was legalized, with the state to get a percentage of the take.

Horse racing was on its way to becoming a year-round operation that followed the horsey set in their seasonal migrations, and it was also on its way to becoming a highly commercial enterprise from which state governments could benefit.

Under Widener's reign, Hialeah Park was transformed into a setting as grand and exotic as Fisher's follies and the moguls' palaces that were being built in Palm Beach and along Brickell Avenue in Miami. The fountains, walking ring and saddling stalls were modeled after Longchamps, the most elegant course in France, and the clubhouse and grandstand partook of Miami's own evolving Mediterranean Revival style that blended ersatz Spanish, Italian, Moorish and Byzantine elements into gorgeous conglomerates of arches, balconies, loggias and colonnades. In the track infield was a squawking flock of flamingoes, Fisher's favorite birds, their wings clipped to keep them from heading back to their native Cuba.

As an additional exotic attraction, a small group of Seminole Indians, descended from the few hardy tribes who had survived the Trail of Tears and Seminole Wars of the last century, would join the flamingoes, before post time, in the infield. Like the brightly colored, long-legged birds, the brightly blanketed Seminoles had to be imported to the land where they had once lived; like the flamingoes, they had almost been wiped out by the white man who now found their rites so colorful and amusing.

Widener had inaugurated Hialeah's Golden Age, during which droves of splendidly dressed socialites, politicians, sports heroes and celebrities arrived at the track by train from their homes and hotels in Palm Beach and by limo from their mansions on Biscayne Bay. The Flamingo Stakes became one of the country's most important winter preps for the Kentucky Derby, and it was won by such immortals as Citation and Nashua, as well as two of the Chief's ancestors, Bold Ruler and Northern Dancer.

In recent years, however, as Widener's masterpiece came to be surrounded by the bodegas and gun shops of Hialeah's transplanted Cuban population, the town and country set, as well as the shuffleboard and beach-blanket sets, no longer flocked to the landlocked track. The state takeout on betting, which had proven so appealing to legislators in the 1930s, now appeared excessive, as the track's attendance and income began to decline. Turf writers began referring to the track in the same terms that novelists were using for the city of New Orleans—a faded *grande dame,* a bit tattered at the edges. Joseph Brunetti, a New Jersey developer who had secured a thirty-year lease on the track from the city of Hialeah in 1977, had made improvements, but he had not yet been able to reverse the downward spiral.

Developer Joseph Smoot's other original track, Gulfstream Park, located near the oceanside cliffs of condo high-rises between Ft. Lauderdale and Miami Beach, had been renovated in the 1960s, and track president James Donn, Jr., began to capitalize on his track's location and demographics. Gulfstream's own Derby-trial races, the Fountain of Youth and the Florida Derby, began to rival the Flamingo in prestige. And so began the war of the tracks, with each big track vying for the prime winter dates, between January and March, and feisty little Calder Race Course, built in 1970, settling for the long, hot grind between May and December. This year, Gulfstream had the prime dates, and the state Pari-Mutuel Commission had awarded it the winter dates for 1986 as well.

Horsemen seemed evenly divided on the merits of the two tracks. Although Roger Laurin had chosen Gulfstream as his home base for the Chief's Florida campaign, Woody Stephens and John Veitch had chosen Hialeah. Bill Perry, too, had stabled his horses at Hialeah; he had shipped down from Suffolk after Thanksgiving to try his hand at the big time.

After a sleepless first night in Westland Manor, I came upon Hialeah Park early the next morning with the same disoriented longing of the Kansas hicks who gazed upon Bolles's sodden acres, or the New York paleskins facing the sun on Fisher's newly flamingoed beaches. Driving up an avenue of royal palms, I parked at the clubhouse gate and walked through the cool, deserted halls to the track, where I could see two horses coming round the bend through the morning mist, their riders standing up in the stirrups. The first shafts of sunlight on the horizon pierced the row of tall Australian pines on the eastern boundary, illumining the dawn-pink feathers of nesting flamingoes in the infield. It was the rarest of Florida sights, a mirage that felt like the real thing, and for the first time since I had arrived in Miami I felt at home. I had found my very own never-never land.

I made my way down the pine-lined dirt avenue leading to the backstretch and got directions from an exercise rider to

Barn V, where Bill Perry's horses were stabled. When I arrived, Sir Quasar was being saddled to go to the track for a gallop, and there was the usual bustle around the barn. But the entire operation had taken on a different mood in this new setting, relaxed if not festive, with everyone but Perry wearing Hawaiian shirts and complaining about the spiciness of the food they had eaten the night before.

So far, however, Perry had not fared well since coming south. This year, more trainers than ever had decided to bring their stock to Florida, and Perry frequently found himself shut out of races that had already been filled. Sir Quasar and Foxy Greene were both a couple of weeks away from the starting gate. Quasar had injured his back and had not been the same since, and Foxy had come down with a skin rash, common in this warm, moist climate. He was also having some serious breathing problems—he sounded like a freight train when he galloped.

Although Bill Perry's problems had reminded me that no racetrack, not even Hialeah, was a fantasy-land, later that day I went in search of two other of Miami's attempts at paradise.

Crossing the bay to the southern tip of Miami Beach, where Fisher had envisioned his flamingoed retreat, I arrived at the famous Art Deco section, where hundreds of well-tanned elderly people were sunning themselves amid partially restored architectural odes to the machine age. Inside the Plymouth Hotel, with its bright turquoise movie-matinee tower, was a lobby cluttered with Naugahyde couches, arrayed before a slightly faded mural depicting some sort of classical bacchanal. Two old women and an old man were sitting there quietly, listening while a white-haired woman wearing a housecoat and tattered hairnet quavered out hits of yesteryear on a small, badly tuned piano.

It was one of those *ubi sunt* scenarios guaranteed to inspire poetic melancholy, and my whither-has-it-fled mood deepened when I traveled back across the bay to yet an older attempt at folly, an estate called Vizcaya that had been built between 1914 and 1916 by James Deering, the heir to the International Harvester fortune. A frail and eccentric bachelor who seemed to care more about statuary than about tractors, Deering had employed a thousand workers to build his villa and plant his gardens at a time when the entire population of Miami had not yet reached ten thousand. Inspired by the vague, gossamer idea of a Renaissance villa rather than any specific building, Vizcaya became one of those preposterously grand American conglomerations of styles, including an Italian rococo reception room, a Roman banquet hall, an old-Cathay bedroom and a Venetian salon.

The gardens, however, were what interested me, because I sensed a strange sort of continuity between Vizcaya's hedged vista of terraces, fountains and shrubs and the palm-laden grounds at Hialeah.

At Vizcaya, seated on a bench in a hidden nook I shared with a stone nymph, I felt an overwhelming sense of order and well-being—the kind of sentiment, undoubtedly, that Deering had intended his estate to evoke. That was something you were meant to feel in royal gardens or the retreats of the wealthy— the peace of mind that comes from the formal ordering of nature, from the confidence that the natural world can be shaped, like art, to suit one's dreams and desires.

Vizcaya, I realized, was Deering's version of the *hortus conclusus*—the enclosed garden that has symbolized the notion of earthly paradise since classical times. From Eden and Homer's Elysium to Spenser's Bower of Bliss, the place of perfect repose and inner harmony has been described as a garden, or park. The word paradise itself, in fact, derives from the Old Persian word meaning royal park.

Vizcaya, however, and gardens like it were closer, I thought, to the images of the enchanted gardens and false paradises used by poets to evoke the disparities between desire and fulfillment. Dante's Valley of the Princes, for example, was a paradise in the most ancient sense: a setting for princes and rulers preoccupied with earthly glories.

That was the image, it seemed to me, that linked the gardens at Vizcaya with Hialeah and Saratoga and other pastoral tracks, where wealthy and powerful men had built their own kind of princely parks. Racetracks, even more than ballparks, suggested not only a haven from care, but the desire of the wealthy and powerful to control fortune itself, as they had controlled nature in breeding the fast and fragile thoroughbred.

Ultimately, however, it was the very elusiveness of fortune that kept the sport alive. And it was not the millionaires, but the ordinary two-dollar bettors who had kept the tracks in business, just as the ordinary visitors with their five-dollar entrance fees were now paying the bills at Vizcaya. The royal palms at Hialeah, the fountains and the flamingoes were all part of a grand illusion.

As one of my Florida friends had described Hialeah, "You have this sylvan glade with these beautiful animals running around, and then you have all these slobs at the betting windows." But those slobs, of course, were the foundation of the illusion.

Gulfstream's gusto

Fortunately, this form of Florida melancholy is usually temporary, and I headed off for the races at Gulfstream the next afternoon with typical opening-day optimism. If Hialeah was the track of grand illusions, Gulfstream was the track of what's-happening-now.

I opened my *Racing Form* to the announcement of the Eclipse Awards of 1984, the racing equivalent of the Oscars, which are voted on every year by representatives of the *Daily Racing Form*, the Thoroughbred Racing Associations and the National Turf Writers Association. Seasons pass quickly in racing, and the awards now seemed belated kudos for long-ago bravery in battle. Two of the awards, in fact, were posthumous —for Swale, voted top three-year-old colt, who had died in June, and for Eillo, voted top sprinter, who had died of colic in December.

After the definitive showdowns in the different divisions of the Breeders' Cup, there were few surprises in the balloting. The Chief was voted top two-year-old colt, with a total of thirty points in the voting. Saratoga Six received fifteen points, and Spend a Buck three. Of the winners, only John Henry, voted top male turf horse, and Swale had not competed in the Breeders' Cup races.

The crowds, meanwhile, were streaming from the palm-lined parking lots to the orchid-tinted Gulfstream grandstand, hurrying with the excitement of kids arriving at Disney World. On the first day of a meet, they knew, anything can happen. All one's profits and losses from the past are wiped out, and the lights on the tote board glitter in promise of endless payoffs. Everyone gets a new program, a fresh start.

I was surrounded by tanned retirees arriving by the busload from subdivisions in Fort Lauderdale and points north. Horses, it seemed, were a diversion from shuffleboard, Mah-Jongg and shopping. I was reminded of the kind of tourists who will resolutely ride camels in Egypt or try dancing the merengue with their guides in Jamaica. Said one elderly woman, dressed in a rose-colored pants suit, "This is Florida; you've got to try everything."

A few fans lingered in the sun among the flowers in the Garden of Champions, where the fallen achievers Eillo and Swale were being inducted into a pantheon of horses whose careers had bloomed in Florida—Carry Back, Forego, Genuine Risk, Kelso, Northern Dancer, Spectacular Bid. TV monitors in the stands replayed the previous year's races in slow motion, and Swale's strong run down the stretch in the Florida Derby seemed to take on the heroic inevitability of myth.

Nevertheless, the first day of a meet was not a time for brooding on the past. In the infield pond, sailboats were tacking and miniature paddle wheels were churning. Gulfstream is a fun and upbeat track, known for its gimmicks and giveaways, and today's freebie was a free autographed picture of Joe Namath. Namath, whose recent career in show business had ranged from a dinner-theater revival of *Damn Yankees* to guest spots on *Love Boat* and *Fantasy Island*, had been named "Official Spokesperson" for Gulfstream's 1985 advertising campaign. He was to present the trophy for the feature race, and he was currently sitting in the press box giving interviews.

Why Namath? I asked a veteran turf writer. "He's a winner; he's associated with victory," said the *Racing Form* veteran, referring to Namath's superhuman performance in Super Bowl III, held at the Orange Bowl, in which he made good his boast that the upstart Jets would beat the Colts.

Today, however, Namath was to be upstaged by twenty cos-
tumed members of the Rio by Nite troop, who were currently
starring in a Vegas-style revue at the Deauville Hotel in Miami
Beach. The troop appeared to be dressed in a parody of the
Ascot scene in *My Fair Lady*, the women in feathered head-
dresses and orchid gowns slit up the side, the men in white tails
and top hats. Gathering in the clubhouse, they had their picture
taken with Gene Stevens, the publisher of the gossipy new track
tabloid *Post Time USA.*

Gushed Stevens in his subsequent *Post Time* gossip column,
accompanied by the photo: "Gulfstream proved once again
. . . that there's more to a day at the races than just trying to
pick winning horses. Racetracks must resign themselves to the
fact that in addition to gambling emporiums, they must also be
first-class entertainment centers. The pressures of competition
faced by modern racing suggest it must become as much a part
of show business as Frank Sinatra, Barbra Streisand, and *Dynasty.*"

It was the kind of day when even the handicappers felt
caught up in the holiday spirit. The Great Handicapper, always
optimistic, was even more so on the opening day of a meet. He
was planning a season-long assault on Gulfstream's Pick 6 wagering, and he very generously offered me a one-percent interest in the action. He was to be joined in his quest by a friend,
whom I'll call Luke, a tall, attractive, bookish-looking man who
had sold his family business in order to play the horses. The
arrival of yet a third partner, Hacker, was expected some time
during the meet, although the state of his finances as well as his
emotions was in question. The previous year, Hacker, who had
owned a promising two-year-old colt, had become convinced
that his horse was a Derby contender, and he had wagered as
though there were no tomorrow. Consequently, the horse had
to be sold, and it was currently running for a claiming tag at
Suffolk Downs.

Racing, I was learning, was not so much a great equalizer as it
was a great magnifier. The main hazard in playing the horses,
the Great Handicapper had told me, was the way the track
sought out your weaknesses. "Whatever character flaws you
have, racing will exaggerate them: egomania, paranoia, lack of

patience, lack of discipline, lack of confidence." It was as though he sensed that his own nerves, patience and confidence were about to be tested during this unpredictable season.

The track likewise seemed to bring out a trainer's weaknesses, or at least his vulnerabilities, particularly when he was under pressure. Since the Chief had gotten sick, a number of turf writers had begun to complain about Roger Laurin's secretiveness. "He's like the Richard Nixon of trainers," one veteran had carped.

When I paid an early morning visit to Roger's barn, I found the Chief still looking peaked and Roger looking worried. Roger's patience, it seemed, was in short supply. "Everybody wants to know how the horse is doing," he snapped. "The media, the insurance company that insured him for $20 million, the people who bought shares in him, people I don't even know. I have to make dozens of phone calls every day. If I had a sick child, they wouldn't be so concerned."

He had no definite plan, he said, for getting the horse back to the track. "I just have to take it day by day," he said. "It's not a game of numbers, where you can say he's going to do this or that in so many number of days. It all depends on the horse. He's doing all right, but he's not ready yet."

Roger felt that his handling of the horse would finally be judged by how well the Chief performed. "This is a black and white game. If you win, you were right. If you don't win, you were wrong."

I suggested, however, that the media attention was only going to get worse as the horse got closer to making his comeback. "No it won't," he said. "I'll just stop answering my phone."

Marino mania

Roger had reason, I thought, to be wary of the fickleness of the media spotlight. In recent weeks, Dan Marino, the Dolphin quarterback, had become the darling of the local media, and he could hardly take a breath in private. I thought of him as the subject of Police surveillance—that is, the rock band Police, with Sting's sinister promise of scrutiny in "Every Breath You

Take." When Marino and his teammates headed for the Super Bowl in San Francisco, Marino was commissioned to write a daily diary for the Miami *Herald*.

Fans seemed to have forgotten the bad times a year ago, when sports had seemed a symbol of dissension rather than unity. In 1984, during the week preceding the Orange Bowl, the city had been a powder keg, and while guests were waltzing at the Orange Bowl queen's ball, police had shot a young black man in the primarily black neighborhood of Overtown, and a band of protesters had raged through the streets. That riot had served as a reminder that Miami was a divided city, with whole populations feeling excluded from power.

This year, however, the disparate populations of the city seemed united in a common cause. Dol-fan mania had been sweeping the neighborhoods, and bumper stickers were everywhere. Nearly every bar was festooned with banners and stuffed cetaceans. Chuckles, the Miami Lakes swingles bar, sponsored a Dol-fan costume contest that was broadcast live on a local TV channel.

After Super Sunday, however, the invisible boundaries in the city went up again, and one fan was seen angrily scraping off the bumper sticker from his car. Dan Marino, loser, returned to a cool welcome.

Almost emblematic of the chill to the city's spirit were the cold winds that started blowing into south Florida even as the Dolphin front line was fading in San Francisco. At halftime the temperature had dropped to 44 degrees, and by the time the game was over it had reached 40 degrees. By midnight it was 28 degrees, the temperature at which citrus fruit freezes, and farmers across the state had lit the burners. By the next day, icicles hung from frozen oranges and grapefruits, and experts who inspected the dead groves were saying that an entire industry and way of life was doomed.

This was one of those seasons when fate could turn quickly, and nature could fight back—blindly, it seemed.

Fickleness in fans was to be expected. But such unpredictability in nature was referred to as "freakish"—an inexplicable abnormality, a capricious variation of the normal course of events.

On the track, however, one came to expect the "freakish" in nature—horses who were called freaks because of their speed, and events that were called freak accidents because of their seeming lack of cause. Trainers like Roger Laurin knew to expect a storm on the day of the parade, knew that hurricanes could hit on the day you took your new sailboat out for a spin.

Only a day before the freeze, one of those senseless, freak accidents had occurred at the track. Gulfstream was sponsoring yet another giveaway—this time, a thoroughbred. Before the eighth race, the Coca-Cola Bottlers' Sweepstakes, a ticket was to be plucked from a huge revolving drum, with the owner of the ticket to win the horse that won the Sweepstakes.

While the Sweepstakes horses were being led to the paddock, however, a horse from the previous race managed to get loose, and he spooked one of the waiting horses—a seven-year-old gelding named Umaticca, whom I had seen run at Suffolk Downs. He was a fast but inconsistent horse, and he had always seemed temperamental. I remembered seeing him rear up once in the starting gate, losing any chance to win the race. This time he reared up in fright and frustration, and he fell backward, out of control. He managed to break his back in the fall, and he was dead within seconds. Later that day, Umaticca's corpse was trucked to a processing plant, from whence it would be sent, as food, to an alligator farm. (In Florida, when a horse died on the track, the body automatically belonged to the state, which controlled the disposal of the remains.)

Although the track announcer informed the crowd merely that Umaticca had been scratched from the race, the stands were abuzz with the bad news, and the prospective racehorse owners in the crowd got an unexpected lesson in the workings of the pain/payoff principle.

Nevertheless, the Woody Stephens principle of racetrack recovery also applied. As Woody was wont to say, the sun does come up again the next day, no matter how badly you lose. And after the freeze the sun did return, inevitably, and as farmers began making juice of their salvaged crop, things at the track seemed to brighten. The Chief had returned to the track for easy morning gallops, and Foxy Greene had been entered in his first race.

Foxy's main competition, as it happened, appeared to be a Woody Stephens colt named Take Control, a son of Alydar, and a colt named General Buck, trained by Leroy Jolley. According to the morning line, Foxy should have been the third choice. However, by post time, his odds had gone up to 13 to 1.

Foxy, who had ambled to the paddock and to the starting gate as though he hadn't a care in the world, broke slowly. It seemed to take an eternity for his huge frame and long legs to get in motion. Around the turn, he was blocked behind a wall of horses, but his momentum had begun to build. His jockey, Vernon Bush, edged him closer to the rail, and he squeezed through a hole that had opened up in front of him. You could almost see the smoke as Foxy bounced against the rail and Bush's ankle scraped agonizingly against it for several yards. Later, Bush looked down to find that the friction had burned a hole in his boot. Now, he concentrated on keeping Foxy in motion. Suddenly finding his nose, then his head in front, Foxy accelerated and began to pull away from the field.

Ignoring my jubilant scream and the winning ticket I was waving, the Great Handicapper leaned over, as though to offer a dipper of cold water. "When a race is that slow, a horse has a lot of time to get out of trouble," he said. At that point, I didn't care. Foxy had shown both speed and persistence, and I felt vindicated for the feeling of hope he had aroused in me when I first saw him almost a year ago at the Saratoga sale.

Dr. Roman's dosage of doom

Two days later the Chief, who was still galloping slowly in the mornings, accrued another honor and another victory of sorts: he had been awarded top weight on the Jockey Club's Experimental Handicap for juveniles of 1984. That is, if a handicap race were designed for all the two-year-old colts and fillies of 1984, with top weight assigned to the best horse, the Chief would have to carry the highest impost—126 pounds, only two pounds less than the number assigned the previous year to the champion Devil's Bag. (Secretariat had been assigned the all-time high of 129 pounds at the same stage in his career.) Saratoga Six was rated just a pound below the Chief, at 125 pounds, and Spend a Buck at 123.

The annual Experimental Handicaps were considered a more objective measure of ability than the Eclipse awards. And, even more important, they were considered a strong predictor of a colt's Derby prospects. According to the Great Handicapper, the three most important indicators of a colt's chances in the Derby were his ranking on the Experimental Handicap, his performance in stakes races as a two-year-old, and his dosage index.

The Chief, with his 126-pound handicap ranking and his victories in four Grade I stakes, had passed the first two tests easily. But the third, which was a measure of heredity rather than merit, would prove his first failure.

In 1981, Dr. Steven Roman, an expert on thoroughbred bloodlines, published a treatise on his "dosage" theories in the *Daily Racing Form*. Roman had modified and updated Dr. Franco Varola's dosage system, which had assigned numeric value to certain important sires which appeared in a horse's pedigree. Roman came up with five aptitude classes—brilliant, intermediate, classic, solid and professional—which he felt indicated, according to previous statistics, the kind of racing style a sire would transmit to his offspring. A "brilliant" sire appearing in a horse's pedigree, for example, would indicate a propensity for speed rather than stamina, while a "solid" sire would indicate stamina rather than speed. A "classic" horse would indicate a balance of speed and stamina.

Using the point system that he assigned to certain important horses that he termed *chef de race* sires, he looked up the pedigrees and calculated the dosage index for Derby and Belmont Stakes winners since 1942. Roman then determined that no Derby winner had exceeded a dosage index of 4, and only two Belmont winners had done so. In subsequent years, Leon Rasmussen, who wrote a "Bloodlines" column for the *Form*, had used Roman's theory and figures to determine the dosage index of various Derby contenders, and Roman's figures, remarkably, had continued to hold true. Swale, for example, had shown a dosage index well within the four-point guideline, while his beaten opponent, the filly Althea, who had gone off as the Derby favorite, had shown a figure well in excess of the four-point limit.

As for the Chief, Rasmussen was predicting that the little colt's dosage index would prevent his winning both the Derby and the Belmont. Said Rasmussen of the Chief's pedigree, "the staying *chef de race* 'presences' in Six Crowns's family tree are not sufficient to overcome the brilliance inherent in the pedigree of Danzig." The Chief, then, was afflicted with an abundance of speed and a dearth of stamina in his family tree.

Ironically, Rasmussen was predicting that it would be another son of Danzig who would win the big races. Said Rasmussen, "It is 'Bloodlines'' opinion, based on the Roman Numerals of the two colts, that Stephan's Odyssey is 1985's colt of destiny." Stephan's Odyssey, who, like the Chief, had been foaled and raised at Claiborne, had occupied the stall next to the Chief's at the Claiborne yearling barn. Unlike the Chief, however, he had been something of a late bloomer. Owned by airplane broker Henryk de Kwiatkowski and trained by Woody Stephens, the colt had raced only four times, and he appeared to have taken Stephens and the bettors by surprise when he won the million-dollar Hollywood Futurity in December. Following the race, Stephens had said that the colt had been something of a mystery to him, and he was just getting to know him. Rising to the occasion, however, he quipped, "Maybe he'll be my Belmont horse."

I wanted to dismiss the whole dosage system as glorified statistical hocus-pocus. But Roman and Rasmussen had been right far more often than statisticians trying to predict the fluctuations of the national economy, and I felt that the Chief was now carrying far more on his back than the theoretical 126 pounds. He was carrying some very heavy odds.

I seemed to keep bumping into the odds, and into people whose mission it was to juggle them. Everything in racing, it seemed, was a matter of beating the statistics, beating the odds —the odds against breeding a good horse, against keeping a good horse in training, against betting on the best horse.

Of everyone I met, however, it was the Great Handicapper, I felt, whose need to beat the odds was the most intense. He didn't miss a day or a race, and he had always done his homework. He had, in fact, redefined and glamorized the very act of playing the horses, making of gambling at the races not only a vocation but a quest.

In the late 1960's, when the Great Handicapper had abandoned his academic career for the horses, a handicapper writing under the nom de plume of Tom Ainslee had just published *Ainslee's Complete Guide to Thoroughbred Racing*, the first major comprehensive guide to betting at the races. Ainslee's premise was that playing the horses had become a socially acceptable form of behavior—for working people as well as aristocrats—and that the odds could be beaten through hard work and knowledge of the fundamentals. Said Ainslee: "The skills of the expert handicapper are . . . closely comparable to those of the good bridge, poker or chess player. In any such competition, the player who depends on instinct, trial and error, inexpert advice, superstition or reckless guesses is at a disadvantage. He cannot hope to hold his own against persons who have acquired an understanding of the game as a whole."

Ainslee broke the art of handicapping down into several major factors, including the trainer, the jockey, the distance of the race, the current age and condition of the competitors, and their respective "class" and speed ratings. He listed so many possible—and plausible—betting systems, however, that you felt that an Ainslee devotee might be like the fox who lost the race for survival to the hedgehog. The two animals were being chased by a wolf, and the hedgehog resorted to his one trick— rolling up into a prickly ball—while the fox was busy figuring out which of his assorted tricks to use. The wolf seized the Renaissance fox instead of the single-skill hedgehog.

For Ainslee and other serious horseplayers, however, certain tricks were better than others. In Ainslee's system, a horse's "class" was considered perhaps the most important key to predicting his performance. Class, though, was tricky, because although every horse established its class over a period of time, some horses were "classier" than others. A horse who won consistently at a certain level of claiming race, for example, might have trouble moving up in "class" to allowance races. But a "classy" allowance horse, even one with problems, who was dropping down to a lower level of competition should be able to defeat his less talented rivals, whatever the speed rating of their previous races. Said Ainslee: "Go the class horse. Every time. The class horse does not care about the early pace figures or final times of lesser horses. Class rises to the occasion."

The Great Handicapper, however, was looking for a more objective, statistically reliable means of predicting performance. Serious handicappers, he observed, were divided into two camps—the empirical, who depended on individual, intuitive analysis of numerous factors in each race, and the rational, who believed that horses could be rated primarily by how fast they ran. The Great Handicapper was a born rationalist, who preferred super-realism to impressionism in art, and thus he became something of a speed freak who believed that time was all. Over the years, with the help of a computer-whiz friend, he had developed a sophisticated system of speed handicapping that depended on painstakingly calculated speed charts for each season at each racetrack. His charts were a marvel of relativism, allowing him to compare different horses who had run at different tracks for different prices on different surfaces and at different distances. There were variants for weather, wind velocity and hardness of track surface.

The Handicapper's manic search for the perfect speed chart resembled the quest of George Eliot's Mr. Casaubon for the key to all mythologies. Unlike the gloomy Casaubon, however, he reveled in his work, and his charts had brought him both fame and fortune. Success, however, was always fleeting, and his system was only as good as his last bet. He soon learned one of the basic lessons in professional handicapping: loose tips sink betting systems. When he published his theories, a better-educated betting public began to make use of his techniques, and it became harder and harder to beat the odds. It was a lesson that pioneer handicapper Robert Saunders Dowst had learned during the late 1930s, when he published his betting tips in *Esquire* magazine. Dowst had boasted that any idiot could make money by betting on highly consistent horses. But once his fellow gamblers got wise to the system, it no longer worked.

The Handicapper realized that no system worked forever and that the secret of beating the races was that there was no single secret. There was no philosopher's stone of handicapping that could perpetually transform raw data into cash.

The secret of handicapping, as he perceived it, lay in being able to discern the order in the madness, the pattern in the chaos of everyday racing. That was the main article of his gambling faith—that the results of a race were not random chance. Everything that happened in a race, he believed, could be explained. Horses ran a certain way because they had run a certain way in previous races or because the track was biased toward speed or because a certain trainer favored a certain method of training. In his view, Foxy Greene had won not because fate willed it or because he was a courageous and determined horse, but because the slow pace of the race had allowed him a big margin of error.

And when the Handicapper's speed charts, his analyses of track biases, his perceptions of trainers' tactics were not producing winners, he reexamined the results to find the pattern that he had missed. When he had a bad season, he managed to move his game up a notch for the next track or the next season. Such was the power of rationalism over fatalism. If the universe were a machine, one need only tinker with the motor in order to improve the results.

For all his rationality, however, the Handicapper had found himself resorting to some of the tricks of the empiricists to augment his speed charts. The most recent addition to his system was the technique he called "trip" handicapping, in which he observed each race carefully in order to discern which horses enjoyed relatively easy trips and which ones had to struggle, either by going wide or getting caught behind horses. His observations had taught him, for example, to mistrust the common wisdom about horses who dueled for the lead in a race. Common wisdom had it that a horse who was challenged for the lead would run faster than a horse who took the lead by himself. The Handicapper discovered, however, that a horse who got "loose on the lead"—that is, who was unchallenged for the lead—regularly ran faster times. The stress of being challenged, in fact, caused horses to run slower times.

On January 24, the Handicapper came to the track prepared to back his theories in a big way. He had called Las Vegas to parlay a bet on the second race with a bet on the fourth race; that is, if his horse won the second race, the winnings would automatically be rolled over into a bet on the fourth race. And by making the bet in Las Vegas, he wouldn't be affecting the odds at Gulfstream.

His logic was impeccable. In the second race, his choice was an 11-to-1 shot named Neoclassical who had had very subtle trouble in his previous race. The Handicapper had pointed it out to me at the time; Neoclassical had been trapped for nearly a quarter of a mile behind a front runner who was slowing down, and the horse had not been able to make his move until the top of the stretch, when it was too late. And, as the Handicapper predicted, in this race Neoclassical, with a chance to run, made a big move around the turn and won easily.

His choice in the fourth race was a 5-to-1 shot, a flashy three-year-old colt named Davey Do Good who had demonstrated early speed in previous races and who tended to win when he took an early lead. Davey Do Good, however, had not broken well in his most recent start, and the race appeared on paper to be a poor effort. The Handicapper had noticed, however, that this time Davey Do Good was to be ridden by Earlie Fires, whose name was well suited to his riding style. Fires was the best man in Florida at breaking a horse out of the gate quickly and stealing the lead. And, as predicted, Davey Do Good took an easy lead and never relinquished it. And the Handicapper was $12,000 richer.

On days like that, I felt that perhaps the Handicapper did have a clue to the way the world worked. When he got carried away, he would say that what he did was like Wordsworth seeing the world in a flower, Blake seeing the universe in a grain of sand. I thought of physicist Stephen Hawking in his quest to discover the unified field theory, the formula that would explain the workings of the disparate forces in the universe: gravity, electromagnetism, the strong and weak force fields. If you could predict the interactions of horses and humans, of earth and wind, maybe a broader vision would follow.

I still saw the track, however, as a world caught between the dark ages and the Enlightenment, where fatalism reigned over rational behavior. The track, it seemed to me, was a cosmos where events were determined by whimsical turns of the wheel of fortune, a wheel that was part Las Vegas roulette wheel, part fate. I saw the track as a place where one needed the consolations of philosophy as much as the analyses of science. Fortune, Boethius had said, is as much monster as friend: "I know the many disguises of that monster, Fortune, and the extent to which she seduces with friendship the very people she is striving to cheat, until she overwhelms them with unbearable grief at the suddenness of her desertion."

The morning after Foxy's victory, I was more convinced than ever. I had joined Bill Perry at the outside rail, where he was watching Sir Quasar gallop around the track. When I inquired about his horses, he winced. There wasn't a sound horse in the barn, he said. "Well, at least you've got Foxy," I said brightly.

"No," he said, "I don't have Foxy anymore." I thought he was referring to two offers he had gotten after the race to buy the colt. But it was Foxy's health he was referring to. The colt's breathing problems had gotten much worse; the flaps in his throat leading to his lungs had become paralyzed, and he was going to have to undergo surgery with only a minor chance of success. Perry seemed to sense that Foxy Greene, his only current hope for a big horse, would never win another race in Scorpio's colors.

"Well, I've always loved roller coasters," said Perry.

CHAPTER 7

Revenge of the Flamingo

> *. . . when I asserted that the yahoos were the only governing animals in my country . . . he desired to know, whether we had Houyhnhnms among us, and what was their employment: I told him, we had great numbers, that in summer they grazed in the fields, and in winter were kept in houses, with hay and oats, where yahoo servants were employed to rub their skins smooth, comb their manes, pick their feet, serve them with food, and make their beds. I understand you well, said my master, it is now very plain, from all you have spoken, that whatever share of reason the yahoos pretend to, the Houyhnhnms are your masters . . .*
>
> —Jonathan Swift, *Gulliver's Travels*

At THE END of January, the sun, as though to compensate for the freeze earlier in the month, began to broil Florida's dying citrus groves, and the temperatures began to hit near-record highs. Brushfires began to rage across the state, and southern Florida started to look like the target of a scorched-earth policy. Every time you went outdoors the air was smoky, and you had the impulse to run inside and see if you'd left the stove on.

Amid this strange cycle of fire and ice, the Chief had begun to make his recovery, and on February 2 he was scheduled for his first public workout since his illness. When I arrived at Roger's barn just after dawn, he quipped, "So you made it for the epic event." His spirits had picked up considerably, and he was now being cautiously optimistic about the Chief.

In a few moments, Andrew Rosen and his wife Adrian arrived, looking tousled and sleepy. As Roger and I climbed in the back seat of Andrew's Mercedes 450 SEL, he warned me about

Andrew's driving. After navigating an oddly circuitous route through the parking lot, Andrew pulled up to the clubhouse, and we took the elevator to the second level and occupied a set of box seats near the Gulfstream clockers, who were using their customary bag of tricks to figure out the identity of the horses working out on the track.

Looking through his binoculars, Roger watched as the Chief began his slow, preparatory gallop, commenting, "Already he's running different than yesterday. We put rundown bandages on, and he knows he's going to breeze." At the three-eighths pole, Cigar sat down on the Chief, and the little colt plunged his head down and began to streak around the turn. "He's going too fast," said Roger, but Cigar got the Chief under control, and he began to move at a steadier pace. "That's about perfect," said Roger, as the Chief passed the wire. "He went the first furlong in 11 4/5, and the next two in 12. Perfect would have been 12, 12, and 12. I had him at 36 for three." Roger glanced over at clocker Jim Milner. "What'd you get?" he asked. Milner had clocked him at a little over 35 seconds.

"Roger's such a perfectionist," said Andrew. "Last night we went to dinner and he orders a Caesar salad. They bring it to the table, and it has tomatoes in it. He tells the waiter, 'I didn't order this—a Caesar salad doesn't have tomatoes.' The waiter explains, 'It's on the menu, sir,' and he brings him the menu to show him. It says, "Like a Caesar salad.' So Roger says that's the last time he's eating there."

Adrian, who had found the latest issue of *Post Time USA* lying on a chair, began flipping through the pages and found a picture of Roger and his wife. "Hey, Roger, you're famous," she said.

Roger grimaced. "It's no honor to get your picture in there," he said. "I don't like to have my picture taken before a race."

After we drove back to the barn, Steve Jordan was holding the Chief by a shank, as Eddie Sweat began to wash the colt down with warm water and liniment-scented soap. As Roger was remarking at how well-mannered the colt was, the Chief reached out to nip Steve. It wasn't a particularly playful nip, but it wasn't meant to hurt; just the Chief's way of asserting himself. The Chief had grown a little since I first saw him, and he had begun to put on a little more weight, but he didn't have his customary energetic gleam. "The Chief looks bigger," said Andrew, "just like Adrian," who was five months pregnant.

"Are you going to the races this afternoon?" I asked Andrew.

"No, I think I'll play a little golf."

"Are you worried about the Chief?" I asked.

"I haven't been worried," he said. "Roger told me everything would be okay, and so far, it has."

So far, the fire and ice hadn't touched Andrew's optimism. Like the Great Handicapper, he seemed to have a constitutional immunity to dark thoughts.

Miss Hardwick's surprise

The Great Handicapper's optimism, however, was being sorely tested. So far, his quest to beat the Pick 6 had been stymied by bad luck. Just three days before the Chief's first breeze, the pot for the Pick 6 had built up to $143,000, and he and Luke had made approximately $1,500 worth of bets. In the third race—the first race included in the Pick 6—they had selected only one horse, a 4-to-1 shot named Hasty Tex. Hasty Tex got into a speed duel with two horses and then dropped back, convincing the crowd he was out of the running, but surprisingly he began to come on again in the stretch and won by a length.

The fourth race was no easier on the nerves. Again, the partners had picked only one horse, a filly named Smartenta who had not yet broken her maiden. I went down to look at her in the paddock, and she was covered with nervous sweat. She was as lathered as a bathing beauty in a soap commercial. What's worse, she broke quickly and went out in a speed duel. Like Hasty Tex, however, she miraculously held on to win.

In the fifth race, the partners had spread their bets generously, including Roger Laurin's Damascus Sam and a colt named Clock Tower, to be ridden by Eddie Maple, on their main ticket. On a backup ticket, they had put a long shot named Hatchet Dancer. As expected, Damascus Sam and Clock Tower went out in a speed duel, and Maple rode his colt like a vengeful driver caught on the freeway at rush hour. He hung on to win, but he was disqualified by the stewards for interfering with Damascus Sam, and the second-place finisher Hatchet Dancer was moved up as the winner. The partners were still alive, but because they were now on the backup ticket, they had only one choice in each of the following two races.

On the main ticket, the Handicapper had selected two horses for the sixth race—a first-time starter trained by Leroy Jolley named Miss Hardwick and a filly named Nancy English who would be running on Lasix for the first time. Since Lasix often improved a horse's performance by the equivalent of several lengths the first time the drug was administered, he had put Nancy English rather than Miss Hardwick on the backup ticket. Nancy English did, in fact, improve by a few lengths, but Miss Hardwick proved to be a very fast filly, and her victory killed the Handicapper's chances. To make things worse, his only choice in the seventh race, a colt named Right and Regal, won easily. And so all that stood between him and $143,000 was that foolhardy ride by Eddie Maple in the fifth race.

Gallagher's gelding

A number of such close calls had depleted the Handicapper's cash reserves, and even my token contributions began to take a toll on my own resources. I had been thinking about getting a job at the track, and now it seemed a better idea than ever.

Two days before Valentine's Day, I asked Jim Dowd, a young vet who had done some work for Bill Perry, if he knew anyone who needed a hot-walker. Dowd had left his private practice in Michigan to join a Miami clinic headed by the legendary Robert Birch, and this was his first season on the track. He had been appalled by the primitive beliefs and practices he had encountered on the track—it was as though he had set up his shingle in Mongolia, he said—and he had decided to return to Michigan at the end of the season. "Richard Gallagher needs somebody," said Dowd. "You'll notice that he usually hires only blacks—it's an aristocratic Kentucky thing. But I think he'd give you a shot —just tell him I sent you."

Gallagher was a young trainer from a wealthy Indiana family who spent the warm months in Kentucky with his horses and then shipped them down for the winter to Miami, which was his wife's home town. Georgia Gallagher, who had gone to school at the exclusive Everglades School for girls and then to Wellesley, frequently helped her husband out in the mornings. Her uncle owned Stanley Penn, Inc., the big feed company down the road from Hialeah that supplied most of the trainers in the area. The Gallaghers, in fact, were the only preppie couple I was to encounter on the backstretch.

Gallagher's barn was one down from Perry's, and he shared it with a small-time operator named Harold Brown and a taciturn, successful veteran named Harvey Vanier. He ran a small stable, with fifteen horses, four grooms, and two hot-walkers under his supervision.

Late in the morning, as the sun was beginning to burn off the cool mists, I found Gallagher sitting with a cup of coffee in his outdoor office, which consisted of a padded leather chair drawn up next to a couple of lawn chairs and a wrought-iron table. All of his horses, it appeared, had already been cooled down except one, who was walking very slowly beside his groom in the walking ring.

With his tinted aviator glasses, neatly trimmed hair and plaid Ivy League shirt, Gallagher might have been a lawyer taking coffee on his suburban patio. I introduced myself, mentioning that Jim Dowd had recommended me, and without a howdy-do Gallagher shouted out to the groom in the walking ring, "Hey, Gene, give her Snoltite." The hiring process at the track, I was learning, seldom involved extensive interviewing, and namedropping came in as handy on the backstretch as anywhere else.

Snoltite struck me as a lazy bum. He was a big bay gelding with a "goose butt," as they call it on the track. His rump stuck up in the air—a characteristic of his sire, Blade, himself a son of Bold Ruler. When Gene, his groom, handed me the shank, Snoltite didn't even look up; he continued plodding around the circle. I learned from Gallagher that he was owned by a partnership headed by Warner Jones, chairman of the board of Churchill Downs, and which included Carl Pollard, a bigwig at Humana Hospitals, the profit-motive hospital chain currently making headlines with its artificial heart implants.

"He won't give you no trouble," said Gene. Snoltite, Gene

informed me, was a three-year-old who hadn't seen action since the previous summer. He had raced twice then, apparently bucking his shins in his second start. He had gone to the farm for a rest, been gelded to control a nasty temper, and sent to Gallagher two months before. He must have been a terror, I speculated, since his breeding would have made him a good stallion prospect. I could see the scars on his nose made from repeated jerkings of the shank.

So far, the prospect of working for Richard Gallagher for $120 a week didn't seem inviting; I didn't see any horses I liked. All of his fillies seemed to have those pretentious, undemocratic names so commonly given to thoroughbreds. There was Royal Prestige, a royally temperamental filly who tried to bite and kick whenever she got you in range, and there was Royal Setting, a small, feisty filly whose teeth and hooves could also take you by surprise. And then there was Majestic Madonna, still a maiden at five, who was about to be sent to the breeding farm.

Nevertheless, I thought I'd at least give it a try, and I headed for the stable office to get a license. It was a simple process if you had a driver's license and you didn't have a Spanish accent. While I was getting fingerprinted, the FBI man in charge of fingerprinting said that he had managed recently to cut down on illegal aliens who got jobs on the track. "I'm lucky to have a secretary who speaks Spanish and spent some time in Latin America," he said. "So when they tell her they're from Puerto Rico, she can tell they're really from Mexico, and they're illegals."

Later that afternoon, I headed for Gulfstream to watch Sir Quasar make his first start since Saratoga. Perry had entered him in a $25,000 claiming race, gambling that other trainers would be reluctant to claim him after such a long layup.

The favorite for the race, ironically, was Roger Laurin's Thalassocrat, who once had been an early Derby hope but who never lived up to his potential.

When Quasar arrived at the paddock, he was sweating and quaking as he had done at Saratoga. One of the bettors standing beside me at the rail cracked, "He's doing an Elvis imitation." Worse still, the hot-walker in charge of bringing the equipment for Perry had forgotten Quasar's tongue tie, a strip of cloth commonly used for horses who tried to swallow their tongues when they ran. Quasar had never run without one.

When the gates opened, Quasar was only a step behind the leader, a colt named Rehearsing, but after a quarter mile he had fallen back to third. Then he seemed to lose speed rapidly, and he continued to drop back, finishing ninth, twelve lengths behind the winner. When Vernon Bush dismounted, he told Perry that the horse had started to gasp for air only a few yards from the starting gate, and he had been running on heart alone. At least, however, he had made it back. Another horse, a colt named Sugar Tex, who had been right behind Quasar at the quarter pole, had snapped a leg and staggered to a stop on the backstretch. As the other horses had crossed the finish line, the horse ambulance had reached Sugar Tex, and the vet was injecting his lethal painkiller.

As I looked over at Quasar, covered with dirt and sweat, his sides heaving, I got a sinking feeling. A track official had walked over and snapped a claiming tag on his halter. Perry had lost him. He had been claimed by Dave Vivian, an old rival of Perry's, from whom Perry had claimed his star Snowgun. Vivian was getting his revenge.

According to track regulations, Quasar had to be led back to the paddock, where his new owner would take possession. His groom, Lynette, was close to tears as she removed the halter and Dave Vivian's stable foreman pulled another over Quasar's ears. I walked up to the stall and gave the little horse a last hug, but I wasn't sure he even knew me. He was still flying on adrenaline, his eyes wild and his nostrils flaring.

I sensed that Quasar would never again have a moment like that one in Saratoga, when he had followed Slew o' Gold to the winner's circle. Dave Vivian would be moving to Robert Brennan's new track in New Jersey, where no one would know about that special day, nor about all the races when he had dusted other horses with his speed. In New Jersey, Sir Quasar would be just another cheap claiming horse, and to Dave Vivian he would be just another horse with a problem.

He had entered the downward spiral of the claiming game, and he would change hands again and again, each time further removed from his glory at Saratoga, each time closer to the final injury that would end his career.

How many warnings did I need about getting attached to a racehorse? I thought there would be little chance of making that mistake at Richard Gallagher's barn.

The next morning I arrived at 5:45, a good half an hour before dawn and fifteen minutes before Gallagher himself usually arrived. Mattie Brown, the exercise "boy," a short, wiry, deeply tanned man of fifty or so, had already made the coffee in the tack room, and he had fed the small tiger cat that had made itself the barn pet by hanging around persistently, purring and rubbing against the legs of anyone who came along, including the horses. I had been warned not to find myself alone in a stall with Mattie, but so far he was all talk. My fellow hot-walkers, Ramon, a Cuban emigré, and Cornell, a jazz musician from Ohio, had not yet arrived, and Jerry Terry, a rail-thin young black man who had come with the Gallaghers from Kentucky, told me I was to take out Pet on the Couch, a huge colt who had not been to the track for a few days. "He might be a little rough," said Jerry, looking at me with a faint smile.

I wasn't keen on starting out the morning with a strange colt the size of King Kong who had been cooped up, fretting, in his stall; the walking ring looked dark and ominous, the barn lights casting only a faint glow on the edge of the path. This was to be my initiation, I supposed. I had told Richard Gallagher I was a hot-walker in the same spirit I had told my friend Andrea years ago that I was a rider; the desire was there, if not the actual experience.

And so I walked into the stall, slipping the chain of the shank through the loops in the halter, talking all the while to the colt whose eyes were rolling suspiciously. As soon as we got out of the barn and headed onto the path, Pet neighed loudly, rearing up like Heigh-ho Silver, and I figured it was all over. "Give me a break, Goofy!" I asked him loudly, and to my surprise he did, settling down to a walk. "He's just a big chicken," said Jerry, who was watching with wry amusement. "He was acting up 'cause of the cat up in the tree." He pointed to the tiger-striped cat who had climbed up on a lower branch of the oak tree at the edge of the walking ring. In the colt's brain, which had suddenly reverted to the dim mists of the prehistoric past, the kitten could have been a cougar, waiting to pounce on his back.

I put Goofy, as I came to call him, in his stall, and as I was walking down the shedrow, Snoltite popped his head out of his stall and nickered softly, his eyes shining brightly. He looked glad to see me. Grudgingly, I stopped to pat him, and after a moment he put his head on my shoulder. "Hey, looks like he's your hoss now," said Gene. Reluctantly, I found myself with another friend.

The next afternoon, which was Valentine's Day, I was to accompany Royal Prestige and Jerry Terry over to Gulfstream, where the ill-tempered filly was entered in an allowance race. After loading up a tack box with equipment, Jerry led the filly down the long, pine-lined dirt boulevard to the eight-horse van that was to take us and three other competitors in the same race across town to Gulfstream. Although two of the fillies screamed and wheeled in nervousness as they were led up the ramp, then secured in the claustrophobic stalls inside the van, Royal Prestige merely pinned her ears back in disdain. Once inside her stall, though, she tried half-heartedly to kick Jerry as he argued with Gil, one of Woody Stephens's grooms, over the placement of the feed buckets that he had brought for us to sit on. "She's just common," he sputtered angrily, and I was reminded again of how atavistic the track was when it came to class distinctions.

In medieval times, the horse had been the heart of chivalry, the very name of the knightly code drawn from the beast who bore the warriors with their heavy armor and creaking honor. And in the track's feudal system, the horses themselves were the knights, the chevaliers, who competed in the mock combat of races. The grooms were both serfs, bound to the backstretch as to the land, and squires, who attended their chevaliers in the lists. The owners, of course, were the lords, who sent out their coursers to carry their silks as banners, and the trainers were the marshals, or "serjeants," who oversaw the work of the serfs and ran the stables.

On the track, horses like Royal Prestige who had no manners, particularly horses who didn't have a winning attitude, were called "common," as though they had betrayed their royal blood. A "kind" horse, on the other hand, was a courteous horse, a mannerly horse, almost as in the medieval sense. "Courtoisie," in chivalric times, had meant an adherence to noble values, an upholding of the social order.

The very word "kind," too, I felt, was also being used in the medieval as well as the modern sense. In the middle ages, "kind" referred not to generosity of spirit but to certain kinships inherent in the world order. In medieval science, everything was said to have its rightful place, its own niche in the order of things, toward which it would move by a kind of homing instinct.

Chaucer's description in *Hous of Fame* of the way the world works was also a description of that sort of "kindness":

Every kindly thing that is
Hath a kindly stede there he
may best in hit conserved be
Unto which place everything
Through his kindly enclyning
Moveth for to come to.

And so on the track, when a horse behaved kindly, he was observing his proper place in the order of things, subjecting his wild nature in a "kindly enclyning" to the humans whom he was obliged to tolerate.

As the van lumbered slowly across Hialeah, on its way toward the shore, one of the grooms chose to observe another kind of kindness. After lighting a huge joint, he passed it around to the other grooms, and soon the air was thick with the smell of burning weed. It was another of those familiar track smells that lingered in the air in the long, hot afternoons, blending not unpleasantly with the aromas of manure and liniment. Certainly the smoke seemed to soothe the frayed nerves of the grooms, but I wondered how it affected the horses, who continued to shift their weight restlessly, tossing their heads like the Prophet's war mares in anticipation of the forthcoming battle. I sat down on my feed bucket and watched the tops of the palm trees through the window, imagining that we were traversing a dense jungle, full of wild orchids and jaguars, and that we would disembark from the van in a strange new world.

We arrived at the receiving barn on the Gulfstream backstretch just as the losers from the first race were returning. The winners had been taken to the "spit box," where samples of their urine and saliva would be taken to be tested for illegal drugs. I felt as though I had arrived at a M.A.S.H. unit on the Korean battlefront, with horses limping in painfully, their flanks covered with sweat and their faces with dirt. I looked at Royal Prestige, in her fastidious hauteur, and wondered how she would deal with the grit and pain of combat. I gave her an encouraging pat, but she ignored me. Most horses know when they are about to race—they've been deprived of their ordinary ration of food and water—and in her own way Royal Prestige was girding herself up for battle.

I bought a canned drink from an elderly black man known as the Pie Man, because of the sweet-potato pies he dispensed along with the lukewarm colas. As he walked away, shouting his wares, there was something mournful in his voice: "Get 'em while they're hot, 'cause when they're gone, they're gone." He seemed to be talking about horses as well as pies.

As it turned out, Royal Prestige had a good moment or two, breaking well under the guidance of Earlie Fires and running within hailing distance of the leaders for a mile; but as the notation in the *Racing Form* chart described it the next day, she had been "no threat" to the winner. When Fires dismounted, he shrugged and told Richard Gallagher, "No excuse." When I looped the shank around her nose, I could tell she was tired.

On the trip back in the van, Gil upbraided his nervous filly, who had finished fifth in the race. "Cut it out, you nothin'. You're just too common to run." But Jerry Terry didn't seem angry at Royal Prestige, even though, he said, he had bet $20 on her to win and $20 to place. "The Gallaghers don't have to win," he said. "His father got a big farm and a shopping mall and her family got all those feed stores."

By the time we got back to Hialeah it was dusk, and the track was dark and deserted, except for the occasional flicker of light and sound from the TV sets tuned in to the news in tack rooms around the backstretch. A big bus loaded with racetrackers had just left for the Billy Graham crusade in Fort Lauderdale. "Hey, you goin' to that Billy Graham concert?" Jerry asked me.

Billy Graham's message

I might have found Graham's sermon edifying, since the evangelist's theme that night was rootlessness. Graham's theme was well taken in a divided community composed of so many of the deposed, the deported, the dispossessed, the displaced, and the deranged from other regions and other lands, who had arrived by yacht, by plane, by flotilla, or who had washed up on shore like driftwood. The racetrack itself was a refuge for many of them—the Jamaican rastas with their dreadlocks coiled like Medusa's snakes inside knitted caps, the Cuban marielistas, dreaming of a triumphant return to Guantanamo, the northern jobless who had headed south for the warmth and the tropical visions, the nice girls from horse country who had learned how to tough it out on the track.

It was a theme well taken in a community where police had recently created a Bumbuster squad to discourage garbage picking and sleeping in parks by increasingly visible numbers of the homeless and the adrift, whose presence was an affront to the prosperous and the beach-fronted. And it was a theme well taken in a region whose toniest enclave, Palm Beach, required its waiters, bartenders, clerks, janitors, servants and other workers to be fingerprinted and photographed at the police station and carry their ID cards at all times. Doonesbury cartoonist Garry Trudeau later picked up the theme by having a black motorist stopped by a policeman. "Pass card, officer?" the motorist inquires. "This isn't Pretoria." The officer replies, "No, sir, it's Palm Beach."

Rootlessness was a theme well taken in a city that often seemed divided by paranoia and adrift in dust—in cocaine dust, that is. In January, a toxicologist testifying as a defense witness in the federal money-laundering trial of the scion of a prominent Colombian family had analyzed money collected randomly from seven different Miami banks and had found microscopic traces of cocaine on each bill. And in February, reporters from the Miami *Herald* had done their own tainted-money investigation. Having collected bills from a former Miss America, the chairman of the Dade County Republican Party, the archbishop of the archdiocese of Miami, and other impeccably credentialed individuals, the *Herald* then sent the money to the Toxicology Testing Service. Of eleven bills submitted for testing, all but one showed traces of the narcotic.

This, after all, was the season of *Miami Vice*, when the entire nation was tuning in on Friday nights to tales of a city where crime had suddenly become hot and detectives had become cool. In the real city, as in the TV Miami, bodies were always turning up, folded in automobile trunks, floating in canals, eddying in tide pools.

One afternoon, after I got back to Westland Manor from the track, I had changed into my jogging clothes for my daily run around Miami Lakes. As I locked my front door and headed for my car, I heard a sound that was familiar only because I had watched a lot of cop shows on TV. It was the sound of a S.W.A.T. team removing the safeties on their weapons. A group of uniformed officers proceeded to fan out around the apartment building, while another squad made their way up the stairs to an apartment on the second floor. One man remained at the van with a walkie-talkie. After a loud hammering, a sound of scuffling and the exchange of shouts, two very chastened-looking young men emerged from the apartment in handcuffs.

Without the soundtrack and the slick montage of *Miami Vice*, the bathing beauties superimposed over the dark alleys and the neon and the broken mirrors, it had all seemed rather mundane and unexciting. But the message was still the same.

John Leonard had observed in his analysis of *Miami Vice* that the city comes across a bit like Vietnam, at least like the Vietnam we carry around in our heads. As Todd Gitlin, the Berkeley sociologist, put it, Miami evokes the same sensation of drugs and rock and the green places of the world in flames.

It was as though the city so long envisioned as a refuge, as a false paradise, had itself become the combat zone.

Jim Milner's rumor

The track, with all its wild horses and tack room drugs and shady characters and shedrow brawls, began to seem more than ever a walled oasis, and, oddly enough, I felt a certain safety in the mornings when I drove through the entrance gate. I had begun to feel safe, too, about the Chief, that he was going to make it.

The day after Valentine's Day, the Chief had gotten a stiff five-furlong workout, even as Spend a Buck was breezing at Calder for the first time since his operation.

This was the season of racetrack rumors, however, and most of them concerned Chief's Crown. A columnist for the New York *Post*, John Piesen, had implied in a recent dispatch that the Chief was lame, speculating that he was suffering from a bone chip. Piesen, however, was noted for such insinuations. The previous year his target had been Swale, who had then gone on to win the Derby and the Belmont.

Piesen, however, had not been toiling alone in the rumor mill. Dave Feldman, a well-known Chicago trainer, turf writer and handicapper, had also been reporting that the Chief was in bad shape and could be counted out of the Derby race.

One afternoon in the press box, the Great Handicapper took me aside, with the manner of a doctor giving a relative the bad news about a loved one. "The clockers haven't been impressed by the way Chief's Crown has been working," he told me. "They say that when he comes out to the track his neck is lathered, as though from the stress in anticipating the pain he's going to have to endure. And as soon as he gets to the wire, he quits immediately, as though it's a relief to stop." Lowering his voice still further, he declared, "By the time of the Derby, no one's going to remember Chief's Crown." There was a peculiar tone in his voice, and he looked at me expectantly. "Rhoman Rule," he said, "is going to win the Derby." He had already put down a substantial bet on the horse, he said, who was owned by a Brownell Combs syndicate, in the Las Vegas winter book.

I should have felt a frisson of dread, as though my ship had begun to sink in the middle of the voyage, but instead, I felt baffled. After walking horses around and around every morning, trudging in endless circles behind sore horses, tired horses, lazy horses, lame horses, razor-sharp horses, pigeon-toed horses, duck-waddling horses, I was beginning to get an idea about how horses looked when they were hurting. I certainly knew how their rear ends looked when things weren't going well.

One afternoon, I got permission from Stephen Selway, the Hialeah vet known as Dr. Demento because of his wild temper and flyaway hair, to watch him remove bone chips from a horse's knee, using arthroscopic surgery. Selway, who had also worked on circus animals, was one of the leading arthroscopic surgeons in the country, and he was going to be operating on a three-year-old colt named Triple Verdict, owned by Robert Clay. Using a magnifying device that projected and magnified the area of injury onto a television screen, Selway was able to use a suction device to remove the chips and a burr to polish the jagged edges of the bone without creating a large open wound. It was the same kind of operation that Smile, Script Ohio, and Spend a Buck had undergone in recent months. And similar operations had returned human athletes to action with a very brief recovery time. But as Selway finished polishing, he said angrily, "This is like removing shrapnel. God just didn't make these creatures for what we're doing to 'em."

That was what I thought every afternoon at the races, when I would stand by the paddock fence with Bill Perry while he pointed out bad knees, sore stifles, rough ankles. Once you knew what to look for, sore limbs leaped out at you.

Yet when I watched the Chief, I couldn't see any hitch in his stride, any favoring of a knee or ankle, any evidence of a problem. If there were something wrong with the Chief, he—or Roger—was doing a good job of hiding it.

The rumors also made me wonder about my judgment of people. Maybe I needed more cynicism. Roger Laurin had been acting downright chipper since the Chief's first workout, and he was certainly no Academy-award contender. When I asked Roger about the rumors, he shrugged. "It happens every winter to the favorite," he said. "It happened to Secretariat. Everybody was saying he was having problems, too." Roger, I knew, had also told a close golfing buddy, one who had no connection to the track, that the Chief was improving. "He'll just keep getting better," he told his friend.

The Chief's real problem, as far as I could determine, was not his legs, but his lungs. If he had been pushed too soon and too hard after his illness, he could have developed permanent scarring in his lungs, and he could still develop the same paralysis that Foxy Greene had suffered. The Chief's breathing sounded labored when he galloped, and I wondered if he were getting enough air.

One of the backstretch myths that had so annoyed Jim Dowd was that a horse could run an entire race on one breath; trainers would claim that their horses ran poorly because they had taken a breath and then held it until they reached the wire. But as Dowd had put it, "They've got their guts slamming into their lungs with every stride, and they have to breathe whether they want to or not." A thoroughbred, in fact, is an extraordinary model of aerobic efficiency. He takes a breath with every complete stride, and at full speed his heart beats four times a second. After a quarter mile he has used all the oxygen in his body, and the sustaining of his speed depends on his body's capacity to pump massive amounts of oxygen to his muscles.

If the Chief's breathing were impaired, he obviously had no shot at the Derby. But when I asked a vet familiar with the Chief's case about that troubling noise, as though the Chief were blowing raspberries at the ground when he ran, he indicated that all the Chief needed was time; the sound probably came, he said, from loose cartilage rather than an obstruction in the breathing passage. As for the fact that the Chief stopped running when he reached the finish line, I drew my own conclusions. From what I remembered, he had always done that, whether in a race or a workout; he got the job done, and he considered that sufficient. He simply looked to me like a horse who was not yet fit, who was still laboring to build up the stamina he would need to catch up with his healthy competitors.

I decided to track down the source of the rumors, and discovered that the main perpetrator was Jim Milner, the *Racing Form*'s clocker at Gulfstream. I knew Milner as the tall, red-faced man in the baseball cap who, when he first saw me reading the *Racing Form,* had advised me to get a cookbook instead.

Most clockers had a cynical outlook on the world, derived from their daily attempts to outwit trainers who were constantly devising new strategies to disguise either the identity or the fitness of their horses. Like air-traffic controllers, clockers sat high up in the stands trying to make sense of the chaotic action on the track, trying to identify horses breezing through the morning mists, sometimes a half dozen at a time, by their color, saddle cloths, or exercise riders. A good clocker was the bettor's best friend, since accurate workout times could point up older horses who were rounding into form or pointing out first-time starters who were likely to win at first asking.

Clockers, however, were notoriously stingy with their secrets, and when they actually volunteered information, handicappers and turf writers alike were liable to take them at their word. Milner was regarded as a particularly valuable source. He prided himself on his ability to judge the fitness of horses, and he passed out his opinions to certain favored writers with the conspiratorial air of a spy passing on classified information. He had managed to convince a goodly number of the occupants in the press box that the Chief was in serious trouble. It occurred to me, however, that Milner hadn't seen the Chief run during the fall, when the colt had been healthy, and he had no way of judging the difference. The Chief had an odd way of going, and if you'd never seen him run before you might think he was hurting.

In fact, I concluded, if the Chief's illness hadn't existed, it would have been necessary to invent it. What I had encountered was the annual epidemic of backstretch paranoia, when successful trainers come under suspicion of drug use and good horses come under suspicion of fatal flaws. Racetrackers, of course, had more reason than most for their cynicism, given the tendency of promising horses to fade. Last year's disappointing performance by Devil's Bag, followed by the belated discovery of a bone chip in his knee, had simply aggravated the ordinary suspiciousness that periodically swept the backstretch along with the flu.

The rumor problem was compounded by the half-assed reporting and airing of suspicions that sometimes passed for race-track journalism. Most turf writers were gamblers, and the ultimate achievement for many of them was picking winners rather than tracking down stories. This, it seemed to me, was "binocular journalism," since some turf writers never came closer to a horse than binocular range. Binocular journalists got so busy running to the betting windows during the races that they scarcely had time to check out the physical condition of horses before and after each race. And since they couldn't tell a bowed tendon from a bowstring anyway, they depended on "inside" sources for their information. Probably the most famous exception to that rule involved a champion who was said to have performed badly in a race because of an accident with a safety pin. One cynical turf writer, who knew his frogs and his coronas, then proceeded to sneak into the horse's stall to judge the horse's condition for himself.

De Kwiatkowski's odyssey

So much attention had been focused on Chief's Crown, it seemed, because there were so few other contenders. At the moment, Proud Truth and Stephan's Odyssey appeared to be the only serious threats to the Chief. Mighty Appealing, who had stirred up considerable interest after winning the Laurel Futurity and the Remsen Stakes in the fall, had been defeated soundly in the Hutcheson Stakes, the first Derby prep of the winter at Gulfstream, and all the T-shirts and bumper stickers that had been seen around Gulfstream, proclaiming "Get that Mighty Appealing Feeling," were suddenly no more popular than Dolphin paraphernalia.

On the Saturday before the Fountain of Youth stakes, in which Proud Truth would take on Stephan's Odyssey for the first time, I went to talk to Woody Stephens about his colt and about Danzig, whom he had trained five years earlier. Woody had finished training for the morning, and we went to his makeshift office, which consisted of the front seat of his new Mercedes. Accompanying us was his little Yorkshire terrier.

Woody had bought Danzig on behalf of Henryk de Kwiatkowski at the 1979 Saratoga yearling auction for $310,000. "He

would have brought more," he said, "except he had a splinter."
That summer, Henryk K., as Woody called him, had come to
Woody with his first horse, a filly named Kennelot, whom he had
bought from the estate of the late John Olin, a longtime friend
of Woody's. And, as Woody put it in his autobiography, "When
Henryk and I reached agreement about who was boss around
the barn, he wanted me to buy him more horses." Danzig was
one of those first purchases.

Although de Kwiatkowski, as one of his friends put it, "didn't
know which end of the horse eats," he seemed, like Carl Rosen,
to have been born with a lucky touch, as well as an urge to keep
parlaying his winnings into something bigger. De Kwiatkowski,
in fact, was to wind up the single most successful owner in the
racing/breeding business.

Born in Poland, de Kwiatkowski claimed to have led a life as
adventurous as his dashing good looks suggested. As he told it,
he had been one of three sons of a Polish Army officer who had
been killed in 1939 leading a cavalry charge against German
tanks. Escaping to the east, de Kwiatkowski had been captured
by the Russians and put to work in the kitchen of a Siberian
labor camp. But he was able to get away, he said, and make his
way to Iran, where he boarded a British ship headed for England. The ship was torpedoed off Sierra Leone, and de
Kwiatkowski swam ashore. Eventually, he said, he and his
brothers joined a Polish squadron of Royal Air Force Spitfire
pilots, and both his brothers were killed in action. When the war
was over, he took up aeronautical engineering at Cambridge.
Then, after a brief sojourn as a sculptor in Italy, he joined the
firm of Pratt & Whitney as an airplane salesman, and within a
few years he was ready to go out on his own as a broker.

Shortly before de Kwiatkowski walked into Woody's barn for
the first time, he had made his first big deal by selling nine
Boeing 747s to the Shah of Iran. De Kwiatkowski, $15 million
the richer, was ready to play the horses in a big way. But, unlike
a number of wealthy men who leap blindly into the game, he let
his trainer do the talking. He left most of his decisions to Woody,
and when he had complained once, Woody simply told him to
get his horses out of the barn—a ploy that Woody had been able

to use with considerable success with his owners once he was established as a top trainer.

And so far, de Kwiatkowski could hardly argue with Woody's judgment. Woody had picked out both Danzig and Conquistador Cielo at Saratoga auctions, Danzig named for the city on the Vistula River that the Poles and the Germans had fought over, and Conquistador Cielo named for an aviation club called Los Conquistadores del Cielo.

It was the rise of Conquistador Cielo, who had won the Metropolitan Mile and the Belmont Stakes within a week of each other in 1982, and was then syndicated for a record $36 million, that made de Kwiatkowski famous and established Woody as a kind of wizard. After Conquistador's syndication, it was being said that Woody Stephens was the trainer who could "make" a stallion, both by hyping the horse and by winning the crucial races. As the Great Handicapper put it, "Woody knows how to get the money."

Woody, who had grown up poor, could remember every payoff in his career, the long shots as well as the favorites, and he could tell you the value of the silver in his trophies as well as the shares in his stallions. And at this stage in his career, Woody was concerned only with the cream of the crop. He drilled his horses hard, pushing them to get those steady "twelves" in the morning, and the ones who survived often turned out to be the "big" ones. "Right now," he said, "I don't have the time or patience for bad horses." As jockey Roger Velez had told me, "They're gonna find a way to get Woody's money to heaven in a Mercedes Benz."

Woody knew not only how to get the money, but how to get the fame. Said de Kwiatkowski after Conquistador's Belmont: "Before I had a great horse the only racing people I knew were those who wanted to play gin rummy with me or those who told me how and when to bet. I guess that I always lost at gin made me popular with that set, and I know I never seemed to cash a winning ticket. Now I'm a celebrity, and for that I thank Conquistador Cielo and Woody Stephens."

Now, however, it was Danzig, who had run only three times, who had become de Kwiatkowski's claim to fame. But from the moment the horse was led from the auction ring, he had suffered problems. After Woody had sent him to Aiken over the winter, he came back with a chip in his knee. "I only ran him one time that year," said Woody, "but it was the fastest two-year-old race that year. We took the chip out and swam him for a couple of months. And the first time back, he went three quarters in 1:09, but he was still hurting in that knee. The next time he did seven eighths in 1:22. He never had another horse to put his nose in front of him." However, the next set of X rays showed further problems. "Dr. Copelan in Kentucky told me, 'You're going to destroy this horse if you go on with him,' " said Woody.

Woody convinced Seth Hancock to syndicate the horse, and the shares went for $80,000. De Kwiatkowski's doorman, who was about to retire, scraped together some money, along with other employees in de Kwiatkowski's building, and they bought two shares. Ten shares, however, didn't sell, and de Kwiatkow-ski kept them for himself. Two shares went to Woody. As a result, Woody had a barn full of Danzig colts and fillies, including Contredance, a stakes-winning filly, and Stephan's Odyssey, whose dam was Kennelot, Kwiatkowski's first racehorse. Shares in Danzig were virtually priceless—the doorman and his part-ners had sold one of their shares for $1 million—and single breeding seasons were already going for over $200,000. Roger Laurin, in fact, had owned a share in the young stallion, but, in Woody's opinion, he had sold it too soon. "He sold too cheap," said Woody.

Stephan's Odyssey, said Woody, was a "level-headed colt, a classy-acting colt." Around the barn, however, I knew that the stable hands regarded him as a holy terror. Some colts were considered "studdish"; that is, they acted like horny adolescents who had their minds on girls rather than school. And Stephan's Odyssey seemed to be obsessed with sex. On January 29, after Stephan had come back to the barn after a workout, his hot-walker, Jack, a rather frail man in his fifties, had stopped the colt behind another horse who was drinking from his water bucket. Stephan proceeded to rear up over Jack, as though trying to mate him, and one of his hooves crashed down on top of the man's head, opening a big gash. As another of Woody's hot-walkers told me, "You have to keep moving with Stephan. He sticks out his tongue and tries to play, and if you don't watch out he tries to breed you."

The next day, Jack reported for work in a metal rider's helmet, and Stephan struck fear into the hearts of every hotwalker. "Now when he comes back from the track," said one young woman, "all the hot-walkers scatter, saying, 'There's the killer.' "

On the track, however, Stephan, like the Chief, did not look like much of a killer, and it was easy to underestimate him. On Monday, when he was led to the paddock for the Fountain of Youth, he was completely overshadowed by John Galbreath's Proud Truth, a big, rangy, prancing chestnut who looked more like a classic racehorse than any other colt of his generation. "He looks like a rich man's horse," John Veitch had said. As a joke, someone had made a computer printout of a dollar sign, and John Veitch had tacked it up next to Proud Truth's stall.

Neither of the two horses, however, had much early speed, and both tended to drop far back in the field before making a big run. And so it was in the Fountain of Youth. A half mile from the finish, Proud Truth was ninth in the fourteen-horse field, and Stephan was eleventh. When the field began to bunch up around the quarter pole, both horses appeared blocked, with nowhere to run. Both, however, swung very wide, only a head apart, and they blew past the field. Proud Truth failed to change leads, but he got his head in front and kept it there, with Stephan shadowing him doggedly to the wire. As the horses passed the wire, Roger Laurin told an acquaintance, "Two really nice colts. The rest you can forget."

Bill Perry remarked admiringly of Proud Truth: "I don't think we've seen the best of that horse. When he came out of the pack, his ears perked up, and he dug in."

Said the Great Handicapper, glaring at Proud Truth in the winner's circle: "It was the same mediocre figure that all the horses of this generation have been running. I hate that horse."

Female equiphilia

The time for the race, 1:43³/₅, certainly wasn't spectacular. Nevertheless, Proud Truth and Stephan's Odyssey, for whom this had been only the fifth start, were making easy progress, while the Chief was having to scramble to catch up. He was working every four days, but he was not going to be ready, as Roger had hoped, for the Florida Derby on March 2. "They'll write a race for him," predicted the Great Handicapper, "get him hyped up so he'll win by ten, then declare they've discovered a bone chip and retire him."

I felt as though both the Chief and I were in limbo, waiting for something to happen, and I was beginning to melt into my morning routine, waking up every morning at five, stumbling around in the dark, trying to gulp down a sweet roll, then driving to the track down deserted streets, listening to the country-western station wake-up routine on the car radio. I never seemed to get enough sleep, even when I had dropped into bed, exhausted, at nine o'clock the night before. Sometimes I would find that I had already walked two horses, as though in my sleep, before I was actually able to put a sentence together.

By the time the sun was up, streaking the fronds of the palm trees and the manes of the horses, warming my cold hands, I would be in a kind of pleasant daze, the thudding rhythms of hoofbeats putting me in a trance, until the radios around the backside had begun to blare in different languages and beats. Sometimes I felt as though I were circling a barn of musical Babel, with salsa and heavy metal on one side and reggae and soul on the other. Sometimes the Jamaican grooms would make up their own songs as I walked beside the stalls where they were mucking dung into a bucket. Usually the songs were about freedom.

My running shoes had gotten torn and dirty, and I liked to imagine I was sinking into my job inconspicuously. "Hey, are you a stewardess?" one of the Jamaican grooms asked one morning, shattering my illusion.

Women, however, were no longer conspicuous on the backstretch; in fact, as one trainer told me, they had "saved" the backstretch. Over the years, as blacks and other minority groups showed more and more reluctance to work the long hours for low pay that the track required, trainers began to hire young women who had grown up with horses and who were eager to make any sort of living from their passion. As a result, the backstretch was a strange social mix of down-and-out white men living from drink to drink or bet to bet; immigrants, legal and otherwise, breaking into the economy at the bottom; black men without the education required for more lucrative jobs; ambitious whites and blacks trying to work their way up; and women from all backgrounds who loved horses. On the whole, women stablehands were on the track because they wanted to be; men were there because they had few choices.

Jenny Orensteen, a strong-looking blond woman who worked as an outrider at Hialeah in the mornings, catching runaway horses, and who hosted a question-and-answer show for tourists from the back of her pony, had shocked her parents when she had dropped out of college to work at the track twelve years earlier. "Nice Jewish girls from Philadelphia didn't do that," she told me one morning. The male stablehands weren't too crazy about the idea either, apparently; "it was always assumed that if you got a job, you were sleeping with the trainer." But over the years, she said, she had watched prejudices disappear. "At first, girl jocks and grooms had to talk tough, like cowgirls, but girls who've been around realize now that people don't appreciate you more if you talk tough."

Oddly enough, I heard more sexist remarks made on the track about horses themselves than about female stablehands. One morning I heard a frustrated vet tell a trainer, when neither of them could figure out what was troubling a reluctant filly, "Just train the bitch and see what happens." And one afternoon, when a filly ran poorly, the owner remarked to her trainer, "She just didn't seem in the mood to run," and the trainer snapped, "Yeah, just like a frigid bitch."

The worst problem for a woman on the track was actually her social life off the track. "Most of us have rough hands, and it's hard to feel feminine with a guy who sits behind a desk all day," said Jenny. "A guy with scars looks macho, but I've broken my collarbone three times, and when I put on a sundress I look like I was hit by a truck."

Not all women on the track, however, looked tough or able. Every morning, I watched incredulously as a short, plump woman of fifty or so emerged from the barn across the way and teetered around the walking ring in high heels, leading a young colt belonging to her husband. She clutched the shank gingerly, as though the colt had some communicable disease, but he plodded calmly behind her. And then there was Marsha, the mysterious glamor girl who wore long, dangling rhinestone earrings with a fringed buckskin jacket, and who sometimes had to lean companionably against her horses to recover her balance on the mornings when she arrived with the smell of whiskey overwhelming her perfume.

My friend Laurie, however, who had come down from New Hampshire to work for Bill Perry, didn't seem to need a crutch. She had been rubbing horses on the track for nearly a decade, and she had never tired of it. She had the kind of magical rapport with her animals that I aspired to, and the horses she worked with seemed to have a brighter outlook on life after being in her care. "I love to hear them eat," she would say after filling the feed tubs of her horses and sitting down on a bucket at the end of the barn, listening to a symphony of munching.

Women on the track tended to keep their passion for the horses to themselves, since to make a big thing of it would have made them seem unprofessional, somehow. I knew that men frequently succumbed to the malady—I had often seen male grooms surreptitiously kissing their horses—but most women wanted to avoid what turf writers called the Elizabeth Arden syndrome. The cosmetics doyenne, a longtime client of Leslie Combs, had changed trainers with the frequency that she changed lipstick shades, often calling them in the middle of the night with bizarre questions and visions of disaster. She sent buckets of eight-hour cream to the stable to be rubbed into their skin, and her trademark was the smear of lipstick she left on her horses' noses after the big smooches she lavished on them.

I suppose that I, too, could have been accused of excessive attachment to horses, a kind of acute equiphilia. I had gotten fond of all of Gallagher's horses, even Royal Prestige, who had become my buddy after I impulsively brought the little tiger cat to her stall one morning as a peace offering. She had nuzzled the cat tenderly, her customary hauteur softening, and now when I came around she would look eagerly for the cat, then look quizzically at me if I came empty-handed. Once, when I was standing absentmindedly in front of her stall, Jerry Terry shouted out a warning as her head darted out toward me. Before I could move, I felt hot breath and a muzzle on my neck, but instead of going for the jugular she carefully washed my ear with her tongue.

Snoltite, however, was my pet, and I would show off, leading him around the barn by his chin whiskers. As he got fitter, though, he began to get tough and arrogant, and it was more difficult to reach him with sweet talk. When horses got sharp, I was discovering, they got impatient with ordinary routines, as though they were already mentally in the starting gate. On the morning before Snoltite was to compete in a maiden race, I could hardly recognize him. Although he had run only twice before, more than six months earlier, he seemed to know what was coming. His ears were perked forward, and he swung his head around toward the slightest noise, shifting his weight restlessly. When I took him out for a walk, he tried to kick Ramon, who was leading Royal Prestige behind him. Once back in his stall, he bobbed his head up and down impatiently, a sign of warning and aggression. And on the way to the van, he bucked, cowkicked and squealed. As Gene put it later, "He took me to the limit."

At the Gulfstream receiving barn, Gene and I watched in amazement when he arched his neck and sniffed the air, as though in challenge to other horses who came near. It was as though something had stirred in his blood, something deeper than memory, something he had been born for. Suddenly he looked a lot bigger. "I never knew he was such a big hoss," said Gene. Snoltite began to strut proudly as we walked him to the paddock, and when Gene put him in the saddling stall it took three of us to hold him while Gallagher got the tack on him.

As I watched him prancing and playing on the way to the track, the muscles rippling powerfully across his chest, I felt like a parent who has come to a school play to watch her child perform and suddenly realizes not only that the child has grown up, but that there is a side to him that she has never known. I also realized that Snoltite was behaving in the way that I had come to recognize as a prelude to winning a race, and I ran for the betting window. Snoltite was going off at the same odds Foxy Greene had: 13 to 1.

Earlie Fires was aboard, and he had not won a come-from-behind victory during the entire meet. However, when the gates opened, Snoltite did not make the characteristic early Fires charge, and he found himself behind the field. Snoltite made steady but unspectacular progress around the backstretch, checking once as he almost clipped the heels of another horse, then somehow finding room to burst through at the top of the stretch. I saw his big head emerge from the pack, and then the rest of him. Fires was whipping him so hard he was bobbing up from the saddle, and the horse began to open up daylight on the rest of the field, crossing the wire three lengths in front.

Sometimes horses could really surprise you. I saw Georgia and Richard Gallagher grinning madly. "You don't know how much Richard wanted to win this one," Georgia whispered to me.

I thought about the Van Morrison song I kept hearing on the radio in the mornings: "Oh didn't I come to bring you a sense of wonder." Sometimes horses stirred feelings about winning and losing you didn't know you had. This was even more than a high school team winning a game, the Red Sox scoring a run. "That's my baby!" I found myself shrieking and sobbing, as I streaked toward the winner's circle. I threw my arms around Snoltite, getting covered with mud and sweat, and in the official winner's circle photo I'm standing between Gallagher and Gene, nearly hidden, looking over at Snoltite, the battered warrior, whose eyes are nearly swollen shut from the dirt clods kicked into his face during the race. "Oh didn't I come to bring you a sense of wonder."

I thought it ironic, somehow, that Carl Pollard, Snoltite's owner, hadn't made it to the race because Humana had just hosted its second artificial heart implant.

I remembered an owner saying once that you had to store up the wins for the long dry stretches, and I figured Snoltite would get me at least through the Chief's first race of the season. On the day of the Florida Derby, in which Proud Truth would meet Stephan's Odyssey again, the Chief would be running in a seven-furlong race, named the Swale Stakes, which had been written especially for him. The first part of the Great Handicapper's scenario of doom, then, had come true.

Gulfstream had gone all out for Florida Derby day, March 2, with a slate of entertainment that included a highwire act, a preliminary camel race, and allowance races featuring Rhoman Rule, the Great Handicapper's Derby favorite, and Roger Laurin's Damascus Sam.

After Dunes Berry, the lone female in the camel race, sprinted to a convincing victory, Rhoman Rule triumphed easily in the first equine race, at seven furlongs, taking the lead on the turn and romping home ten lengths ahead of the field. I looked over at the Great Handicapper, who was trying hard not to look smug.

In the fifth race, Damascus Sam, the colt of Herculean musculature and happy disposition, sprinted quickly to the lead and galloped home an easy winner. His time for the seven furlongs, however, was 1:23 3/5, nearly two seconds slower than Rhoman Rule's time for the same distance.

Later, as I went down to the paddock to watch the Chief get saddled for the Swale Stakes, the tenth race on the card, I found that my hands were trembling. I turned to Douglas Rosen and asked if he thought the Chief would win. Said Rosen, somewhat grimly, "He'd better." The Chief's main opponent was Creme Fraiche, a gelding trained by Woody Stephens, about whom Woody had been uncharacteristically silent, perhaps because there was no need to hype the horse for stallion syndication. Nina Laurin, Roger's wife, was asking one of the Rosens, "How can we stand this? So much self-inflicted pain." The Chief, as usual, seemed calmly unaware of the emotional disturbances he was causing, but I thought I could see some of the old hidden gleam in his eye.

Creme Fraiche, in fact, took the lead when the gates opened and set fast fractions of 22:3 and 45:1. The Chief was shadowing him, only a head behind, and he began to draw away easily around the turn, winning by almost four lengths. His final time was 1:22 2/5, which was two fifths of a second slower than

Rhoman Rule's time. His victory, however, had been just as effortless.

Roger said after the race: "I had told Don, if he comes out of the gate good, let him run on his own, and when the time comes, ask him. Don only tapped him once, and bing, away he went. The last eighth he had nothing to run at and he just glided home."

The Chief's victory looked good to both the "class" and the "time" handicappers. Both his time and the way he had won had been impressive. But the Florida Derby which followed caused a big split among the two camps.

From the start of the race to the top of the stretch, it looked as though burly Banner Bob, a strong front-runner who had won the Hutcheson Stakes, was going to maintain an easy two-length lead. Proud Truth seemed to be climbing—as his jockey Jorge Velasquez put it later, "He was jumping up and down like a kangaroo." However, at the top of the stretch, Proud Truth and the other closers in the field made their move simultaneously, in series of bumps and brushes. Proud Truth, who was following Stephan's Odyssey on the inside, came out around Banner Bob and nudged Covert Operation, while Irish Sur was rallying strongly on the outside, then bore in to brush the already beleaguered Covert Operation. Do It Again Dan, who had followed Proud Truth along the inside at the head of the stretch, brushed with Attribute in mid-stretch, then began to make up ground. Proud Truth, however, with his ears perked up eagerly, was just beginning to get in gear, and he moved away easily from Stephan's Odyssey, who began to fade badly. The big chestnut, however, finished only a neck in front of Irish Sur, who had continued his outside rally while Proud Truth was weaving his way down the stretch.

The time for the Derby was 1:50, the slowest for the race in years, on a very fast track. And so the speed boys remained unconvinced of Proud Truth's ability, while the "class" boys raved about his determination. According to Joe Hirsch, Proud Truth had demonstrated "courage under fire." But according to Steve Crist, Chief's Crown's time for seven furlongs "translates to a far superior performance."

Galbreath's noblesse oblige

Proud Truth, then, not only looked the part of a rich man's horse, but he had begun to act it. John Veitch had begun calling the horse his "little Alydar," after the colt who had dueled Affirmed so dramatically for the Triple Crown in 1978.

Veitch had always been something of a "society" trainer and defender of the old social and sporting order; his father Sylvester, who had been elected to the Hall of Fame in 1971, had trained for millionaire sportsmen C. V. Whitney and George D. Widener; though he did not particularly encourage his son to follow him in the trade, John worked for his dad part of the year during high school, and after graduating from Bradley University, where he played halfback for three years, he went to work for Elliott Burch, who was then training for Paul Mellon's Rokeby Stable. A witty, handsome man who took to shaving his head à la Yul Brynner, Veitch fit in easily with the younger members of the horsey set, once finding himself, along with the black-sheep scion of an old New York family, in an expensive New York "club," since closed, where members enjoyed the company of scantily clad women. At age twenty-five, he managed to total his Jaguar XJ-6 against the Belmont grandstand.

In 1976, Sylvester Veitch was offered the job of training for Calumet, but he was feeling somewhat burned out, and he advised Calumet, headed by Lucille Markey, Warren Wright's widow, to hire his son instead. It was a situation, ironically, that seemed exactly the reverse of what had happened with Lucien and Roger Laurin.

John Veitch had paid his dues, and he took Calumet back to the heights it had enjoyed with Ben and Jimmy Jones. In 1977, when Alydar was a two-year-old, the duel with Affirmed began, and the three-year-old filly Our Mims won the filly championship. In 1978, Alydar, named for Mrs. Markey's friend, the Aly Khan, shadowed Affirmed in the Triple Crown, and in 1979 the filly Davona Dale won the filly Triple Crown. In 1981, Veitch and Mrs. Markey won another Eclipse award with the two-year-old filly Before Dawn.

After Lucille Markey's death in 1982, however, her heir, J. T.

Lundy, a son-in-law of her late adopted son Warren Wright, Jr., seemed determined to wipe out the traces of Mrs. Markey's reign over Calumet. It was reported that he had ordered the color scheme of white-and-devil's-red, so favored by Mrs. Markey, to be toned down in the Calumet mansion to blue-and-white, and he brought in Frank Whiteley as farm manager before demoting Veitch, who then resigned. Lundy even renamed a Veitch namesake, a colt named John the Bald, ordering that the colt be called Foyt, after the racecar driver's son who would become the new Calumet trainer. In a final slight, Lundy cancelled Veitch's breeding right to Alydar, but eventually restored it, following widespread adverse reaction to his gesture.

After a year as public trainer, during which Dr. Carter had loomed as a Derby contender until his bout with the flu, Veitch was hired by John Galbreath to train for Darby Dan. Now in his eighties, Galbreath, a self-made man who had gotten his start by selling real estate in Ohio, had become one of the great elder statesmen of the sport, one of the foundation patriarchs that Veitch felt had built the sport. Galbreath, who also owned the Pittsburgh Pirates, was said to be puzzled by the ingratitude of the Pittsburgh fans. But he must have been puzzled as well by the racing public, who seemed to pay little mind to the old-line owners and breeders who had poured their money into thoroughbreds, more for glory than for gain, for so many years.

I had gone to see Veitch on a warm, humid morning shortly after the Derby, and his presence in the barn was heralded by a scurrying mass of cats who preceded him down the shedrow toward the empty food bowls next to the tack room. When we settled down on a bench in the sun, where we talked our way into the afternoon, a succession of cats and kittens made their way onto Veitch's lap, and he lavished compliments and endearments on each.

"This sport," said Veitch, tickling the belly of a small black cat, "evolved by wealthy people maintaining it as their own private game, when race meetings were five days a week, and racing seasons were shorter. People were in it not to make money but to compete with their friends. But now it's a business. People are in it to make money.

"The people who brought the horse to its best, who built the breed, never did make money. It's not a game designed for people to make money—except for the shysters putting syndicates together. They make their money up front.

"Our tax system has made racing more difficult. Fewer families have kept their wealth. I guess we do need the new money, but it's changed the game, and I don't think for the best. I think we've seen the zenith of the racehorse bred for soundness and durability. I don't think the commercial breeder will improve the breed. They breed fashionably, not for soundness."

Expanding on his theme, Veitch saw the glut of horses being compounded by a dearth of good trainers and grooms. "You don't get the good blacks now because they can make more money elsewhere. The pay isn't encouraging for people to come back here and learn it—it's not attractive for a family man." And as for trainers, "In the old days, you had to be pretty old by the time you came up through the ranks. The best way to learn about horses is to start at the very bottom. I don't mean working six months as a hot-walker. It takes ten years of working as a groom, assistant trainer, stable foreman to learn the trade, so if you do get your hands on a good horse, you'll know what to do with him.

"A lot of good horses get ruined because of people who are inept. One guy told me, 'It's like flying an airplane—it's easy.' I should have said, 'The way you're doing it is easy.' Working with horses is like flying an airplane—it's not hard if you don't mind crashing."

I was beginning to understand why Veitch had acquired a reputation for arrogance. As his friend had put it, "He has an aggressive, egotistical streak, but I don't mean it to sound as bad as those words usually do. You can't really dislike him for it because he's so forthright about things."

Veitch seemed to long for the old feudal system, when owners were more lords than entrepreneurs, when grooms were loyal family retainers, and when you had to learn the trade during a long apprenticeship.

J.R.'s lecture

Even for a trainer like Richard Gallagher, however, with his makeshift patio and his imported Kentucky stablehands and his inclination for gentility, things sometimes got out of hand. One morning, Ramon announced that he was quitting, and he disappeared from the track for a few days. Jerry Terry told me, however, that Ramon was on the lam. He had been involved in an automobile accident, and it was discovered that his borrowed car, which he had been driving proudly for several weeks, had been stolen. A few days later, I spotted Ramon at the races, leaning against the paddock fence, and the next week I saw him walking a horse two barns down from Gallagher.

Inevitably, some of the violence that was the underside of Miami's enticing vitality managed to filter its way on the track. According to the Miami *Herald*, marielistas with criminal records and mental problems had heard rumors that the federal government was planning to deport them, and some of them had stopped going to their counselors, doctors, or health centers. As a result, the mentally ill who were cut off from their medication began to do some strange, occasionally violent things. One man cut off his girl friend's head and hurled it at a policeman like a bowling ball.

It was difficult to sleep easily at night in certain neighborhoods. The Jamaican grooms who shared an apartment near the track would come to work complaining of the shootouts that had kept them awake during the night, and frazzled nerves led to bitter arguments over nothing more than the ownership of a water bucket. In the Gallagher barn, things were heating up between Gene and J.R., a slender, wiry groom whose hero was the gangster Calvin Stone. "My mama wanted me to be a lawyer," he told me one morning, "but I'm a simple man. All I want is to be left alone, like Calvin Stone." He was constantly looking for an opportunity to practice Wing Chung, his martial arts specialty. "People think they're going to try to mess with me," he said, "but they see something in my eyes and they stop." His horses, however, seemed unimpressed by his tough-guy pose.

One morning, a filly named Silk Splitter butted him playfully in the back with her head, and he collapsed with a moan.

J.R. constantly taunted Gene about his resemblance to his horses, referring to him as Mr. Ed, and one morning I reached the boiling point on Gene's behalf. "Shut up," I yelled at him.

I had crossed some invisible barrier, broken an unspoken rule, and J.R. swung around, looking at me with a mixture of anger and incredulity. "This is my home. I live here. How can you say anything to me in my own home? This is just a playground for you." I was already feeling bad about my outburst, but things were only getting worse. "This is a penitentiary without walls," he said, as though beginning a familiar lecture. "This place is an institution. People are here for the same reason they're in prison. They can't deal with 'out there.' They don't want to deal with things outside the walls." He was just getting started, and a small group of grooms gathered around to listen. "You don't know what it's like to smell horse shit twenty-four hours a day. People think we should be like horses—they just stay in the stalls all the time except when they come out to work. We're supposed to do the same thing—stay in our rooms all day and come out just to work. The guards aren't here to guard the horses—they're here to watch us, to protect the trainers and owners."

He had finished the lecture, and disappeared into a stall to finish mucking. Jerry Terry looked at me with a sympathetic smile. "Well, I guess you're a real racetracker now," he said. It was as though I had passed another initiation test, however unwittingly, into some secret backstretch order. Kim, a short, husky black woman who had been hired to replace Ramon, patted me on the back. Gene, however, retorted, "I don't want to be a racetracker myself. I just work on the track, that's all." When Gene left, Kim mused softly, "I wish trainers and owners would try living here for a week. They're always telling us to hurry up, but they don't know what it's like here. The track can take a clean person and corrupt the shit out of 'em. This place has an undertow to it.

"Most people don't have cars, so they're stuck here. Or even if you do have a car, you're too tired to go anywhere. You just have to wash your clothes the best way you can. You're not supposed to cook in your room. You can cook oats for the horses, but not for yourself. They treat us like children."

I realized that in some strange way, since I had come to the track, I had been focusing only on the problems of horses, and not on the problems of people. I had been like Gulliver among the Houyhnhmns, treating horses as the reasonable creatures and humans as the unreasonable Yahoos.

I had been idealizing track life, trying to block out, like the racetrackers themselves, the things outside the walls that bothered me, the "white noise," as Don Delillo called it, of contemporary life, the meaningless buzz that could blunt the senses and cloud the mind. The horses seemed so real, so demanding, so heroic in their limited way that they could fill your consciousness with their immediacy if you let them.

What I hadn't seen was the way the track could take away your dignity. Like the horses, you were more or less stranded on the track, and the dirt began to creep into your dormitory room, into your clothes, under your fingernails, and after a while you might forget to brush your teeth; you might not bother to take off your boots when you collapsed on the bed in weariness. You would begin to cave in.

Once I had been initiated, it was as if some kind of magic spell woven by the horses had been broken, and I began to see things differently. To work on the track was a precarious, sometimes degrading way to make a living. If you didn't love horses, if you didn't find their flaws a fascinating puzzle, or if you weren't caught up in the thrill of the races, it wasn't much of a life.

Sometimes the horses themselves didn't help things much. Some, like the pit bulls that had been attacking joggers and children with some regularity during my stay in Miami, were rogues. A few were simply born with a mean streak, but most had become so because of mistreatment by humans. Thoroughbreds, like pit bulls, had been bred for a function other than companionship, and if they weren't treated with a mixture of criticism and kindness they could get too tough to handle.

During the time I was working for Gallagher, there was one horse in particular, a colt trained by Harold Brown, who seemed determined to make life difficult for everyone around him. The only person who could handle the colt was a young Seminole Indian who customarily wore a bandanna and a Grateful Dead T-shirt; when he didn't show up for work one day, the colt stomped on Brown's foot, so that the wise-talking trainer had to get around the backstretch on a golf cart, his foot swathed in cotton bandages and a clear plastic wrapper.

Brown had difficulty keeping hot-walkers, and he would bring in one green Cuban after another, who would give things a valiant try until they were handed the problem colt. The colt would rear up, and they would simply drop the shank and make a run for it. One morning, while I was walking a fidgety filly named Miss Angie, the colt came back from the track and managed to get loose, with the unbuckled saddle dangling over his side. The colt then made a kamikaze run around the walking ring, charging at every horse he saw. First, he took aim at Pet on the Couch, who reared up in fear, and then he headed toward Miss Angie and me. I yanked her into the center of the ring, and he whizzed by, missing her by inches. He turned around to make another run at us, and we both just stood there, frozen. I was braced for Miss Angie's own reversion to her most basic fight-or-flight instincts. Fortunately, however, the runaway colt changed his mind, dashed straight into the barn and headed for his stall.

Now it was up to Brown's new hot-walker, an ancient wino named Jimmy, to get things under control. He brought the colt back out to the walking ring, and the first time the colt reared up, Jimmy lashed him with the end of the shank. The colt kept rearing, and Jimmy kept lashing, the colt squealing in anger, and no one was going to stop it. The two kept fighting each other, as though they were reenacting some ancient cycle of misery, like the indigent cabman beating the horse in Conrad's *Secret Agent*. "Poor brute! Poor people!" shouts the simpleton Stevie, in "his indignation and horror at one sort of wretchedness having to feed upon the anguish of the other."

The next morning, when I stopped by the track cafeteria for a cup of coffee, I saw Jimmy sitting there in his dusty jeans and tattered western shirt, talking with another wizened old man. Then suddenly Jimmy clutched his chest, writhing in pain, and fell to the floor. Within moments the ambulance, always parked by the track in case of training accidents, had arrived, and Jimmy was taken off to the hospital on a stretcher. "Well, that colt has finally managed to kill somebody," I thought. Two days later, however, when I drove through the stable gate, there was Jimmy, chatting companionably with the Pinkerton guard. "I thought you had a heart attack," I said incredulously. "Ah, it was just heartburn or somethin'," shrugged Jimmy the survivor, putting another odd spin on the wheel.

Once some of the magic had gone, so had some of my own immunity to pain. I had already given notice that I would be departing my hot-walking job that week, but Gallagher had not yet found a replacement, and I agreed to stay an extra day.

Things did not begin well that last morning. When I walked by Miss Angie's stall and said hello, her head snaked out, and her teeth missed my face by inches. Then Jerry Terry called me to get Pet on the Couch, and I walked into the stall as Jerry was putting a new blanket over the colt's back. I slipped the shank through the colt's halter and stood in the inner corner of the stall while Jerry reached down to pull the surcingle around the colt's belly and buckle it. The buckle, however, was cold, and when it touched the colt's belly, something snapped in his mind. Simply put, he went crazy. He screamed furiously and reared up. "Get out of here," Jerry shouted, as he edged out of the stall. But I was trapped between the flailing hooves and freedom. Things began to move in slow motion, and the stall seemed to fill up with smoke.

The next thing I knew, I was outside the stall, and I still can't remember how I got there. I turned to look into the stall, and I watched Pet's hooves repeatedly crash down on the spot where I had been standing. J.R. rushed into the stall, perhaps to try his Wing Chung on the colt, but in a moment he came sailing out of the stall and lay crumpled on the ground. In a moment, however, he got up and pulled up his shirt, looking down at a spot where a big bruise was beginning to spread. Jerry Terry was examining a big welt that was building on his leg. I reached up to my lip, where blood from a scratch was beginning to trickle. Solemnly, the three of us shook hands, simply because we were alive, and I felt as though I had passed my final initiation rite.

Warhol's fifteen-minute fame

As I said my goodbys around the barn later that morning, my hands still sweaty from fear, I wondered whether Jerry Terry or J.R. would ever get the one big payoff, the one big horse, that would compensate for all the hours of mucking stalls and the tense moments of dodging hooves. I realized, though, that no horse is a hero to his valet. Not even a great horse could possibly compensate for a life so stripped of roots, so bare of comforts. One had to choose such a life willingly, out of obsession or out of love.

As I began to watch Roger Laurin and the Chief more closely, as the countdown for the Derby began to get closer, I realized the initiation rites, the trials by fire, never really ceased. Perhaps the big horse just increased the ante and brought a different set of pressures and penalties. And petty annoyances.

One morning, after the Chief had settled down in his stall after his workout, bath, and walking session, a photographer from *Interview* magazine ambled into the barn. Back in New York, it seems, Andy Warhol had learned that Andrew Rosen, a young man of fashion, charm and money, a son of Seventh Avenue, owned a horse that was favored to win the Derby. And that made Andrew Rosen celebrity material.

The photographer inquired whether the Chief could be brought from his stall to pose for a photo, perhaps sporting a hat. Roger promptly kicked the man out of the barn, sputtering, "Who does he think the horse is? Mr. Ed?"

Turf writers, however, were not swarming around the barn in the way they ordinarily did around a Derby favorite. Racing for the season had moved to Hialeah, and the reporters were drawn there to their old mainstays, Woody Stephens and John Veitch, always good for a quote, if not a boast. The Chief had yet to make believers of the press, and the rumors about his fitness continued. John Veitch was claiming that the Chief could not possibly be ready to meet Proud Truth in the Flamingo Stakes on March 30. "I'm not worried about Chief's Crown," he told one reporter flatly.

Roger, of course, didn't help matters by his reticence. Although he was telling the Rosens not to worry, he was not exactly Norman Vincent Peale when the press did come around, and he did not make of the Chief's training the kind of major public campaign that a public-relations genius like Woody Stephens would have sustained.

Consequently, on March 25, when the Chief was loaded into a van to travel to Hialeah for a workout over that surface in preparation for the Flamingo, the only reporter around was a persistent stringer for the Hollywood (Fla.) *Sun-Tattler*. Roger, however, had not told the young man his plans, and when we piled into our cars, Don MacBeth into his black Mercedes 190E, the Rosens following in their 450 SEL, the reporter tailed us through Opa-Locka. When I was stopped at a light, the reporter held up a Hialeah program and pointed at it, questioningly. I nodded yes.

When the Chief arrived at Hialeah, word of the workout had spread on the backstretch, and when we climbed into the clubhouse seats there were trainers scattered everywhere. Woody Stephens and John Veitch waved casually. "Did you have to have a passport to get over here?" Leroy Jolley asked Roger. Joe Hirsch of the *Racing Form*, however, was the only turf writer on hand, and he joined the Rosens, his elegant, stately presence adding a further note of seriousness to the proceedings.

When the Chief made his way onto the track for his first leisurely gallop around the track, accompanied by the pony Hawkeye, there was dead silence in the stands, and when the colt broke off at the six-eighths pole for the work, you could hear the click of stopwatches coming from all directions. And you could hear the Chief huffing and puffing loudly, while his head pumped up and down like a piston. The Chief looked and sounded more than ever like a machine, an equine choo-choo chuffing around the track. One trainer was overheard to say, "He sounds like he's dying." Joe Hirsch rose and bid adieu to the Rosens with the grave manner of an undertaker. Nevertheless, although the Chief had not appeared the model of effortless grace, he had gone very fast—1:11 3/5 for six furlongs—a fact that was to remain virtually ignored until the conclusion of the Flamingo.

Back at the receiving barn, Don MacBeth was looking almost

cheerful. His continuing success with the Chief seemed to be melting some of his icy reserve. Like Roger and the Chief, however, his low-key manner tended to make you underestimate him. Perhaps he was describing all three of them— trainer, horse and jockey—when I asked him about the Chief's notorious reluctance to give more than the situation called for. "He's simply learned not to overdo it," said MacBeth. "He conserves himself for the times when it's important."

MacBeth had always considered the Chief to be highly intelligent. "He's very sensitive to his environment," said MacBeth, "but at the same time he accepts it. He's aware of everything, but at the same time, it doesn't bother him."

I discovered we had both just finished reading a Dick Francis novel, and I asked him if he agreed with Francis's description of skillful riding: "The trick of race-riding . . . was to awaken a horse's natural panic fear and then control it." Said MacBeth: "That's not far from the truth. The urge to run—it's developed as a herd instinct, to get to the front of the pack. Some horses have it to a greater extent than others. If you put a manger full of feed out, they'll display different characteristics in getting to it. You watch them in the field, the way they run there. They display some of the same characteristics on the track. Some are just more competitive than others.

"Some horses are complacent; they have too much herd instinct, and they just want to gallop along with the crowd. You have to shake them up. So the fear instinct does come into play. If something jumped out at them from the woods, they would run to escape. And when the bell rings, it's a signal. They learn to react. Their survival is based on reaction."

And the Chief? "He just has a lot of ability. It's a combination of different things. He doesn't just run wild; he responds to signals, and sometimes *he* gives the signals."

At the official Flamingo breakfast, held on the Wednesday before the race, Roger failed to appear, saying he preferred not to listen to the rumors about his horse. It was just as well. As we were walking up to the generous buffet display of lox and bagels and eggs, Joe Hirsch was telling one of his colleagues from the *Form*, "I think the story is going to be Proud Truth." Later, at one table, the Great Handicapper was saying, "I look at the Flamingo not as a race that will select the star of this generation, but as a race that will discredit a lot of horses." At another table, Jim Milner was joking, "There's no way Chief's Crown can win except with an injection, in the style of ————," mentioning a trainer who had been suspected of using mysterious drugs on his horses. "Do you know if ———— is a friend of Roger's? Maybe he'll be under the shedrow tomorrow." When someone objected to Milner's tone, he said, "I'm not denying the horse's accomplishments. But he's in no shape to win tomorrow."

Later that morning, when a Hialeah P.R. man took an informal survey of turf writers' favorites for the race, only two writers had selected Chief's Crown: the man from the *Sun-Tattler* and a writer for the Palm Beach *Post*.

The day of the Flamingo, however, was not a day for scoffers and cynics. It was one of those perfect Florida days, one that began with cool morning mists and cleared into bright, balmy sunshine. Hialeah looked like the magical never-never land I had seen that first morning, the bougainvilleas abloom, the fountains splashing, the grounds and stands dotted with fans wearing pink or purple in honor of the big race, and a man dressed up like a Disney flamingo fluttering about in a manner more befitting a dodo.

Royal Prestige was running in the sixth race, and I went out to the paddock before the race to see her. I leaned against the fence, enjoying the sun and the luxury of being an observer, rather than participant. I glanced into the paddock, and there was Royal Prestige walking toward me, her eyes shining with recognition. She pulled Jerry Terry toward the fence so that she could say hello. I reached out to give her a pat, and I suddenly felt tears in my eyes. Perhaps being an observer wasn't so terrific after all.

She went out at 54 to 1, and I wasn't surprised when she didn't win, although she did manage to finish sixth, out of a field of eleven. I had learned that for all her seeming thorniness, she really was something of a softy.

Royal Prestige had given me a gift of sorts, a sense of recognition, a bond that was both female-to-female and animal-to-human. I could feel that gift, still lingering in the air like a mist, when I went out to the paddock before the next race. It was a turf race for fillies, featuring the star, Persian Tiara, who was looking fierce. Circling the paddock was a French-bred filly named Marie d'Argonne, who had never raced in America and who had won only one race in France. She had a proud, confident look about her, though, and I suddenly felt that she was going to win the race. I ran to the betting window and asked for a perfecta box, linking her with Persian Tiara. Later, as I found my seat in the press box, I noticed that Marie d'Argonne was going out at 100 to 1. "So much for impulses," I thought. A European turf writer who had seen the filly race in Europe was telling the Great Handicapper, "Marie d'Argonne? She's a dog."

When the buzzer sounded, both Marie d'Argonne and Persian Tiara broke in the middle of the pack. April Sixteen and Petite Diable, the two fillies expected to give Persian Tiara the most trouble, were running on the lead. As they came around the second turn, Persian Tiara powered her way to the front, but there was another horse right beside her. It was Marie d'Argonne. Suddenly, the two horses seemed to be running together in slow motion, until one of them surged effortlessly to the lead. Marie d'Argonne finished nearly three lengths in front. I could hardly bear to look toward the tote board. But there it was. She was the longest shot to win for the season, and the perfecta paid $501.00. "Oh didn't I come to bring you a sense of wonder."

It was one of those days. When the horses were brought out to the paddock for the Flamingo, they gleamed like coins in the sun. Proud Truth looked magnificent, prancing as usual, and even Stephan's Odyssey—ordinarily, like the Chief, a somber sort—began to dance a bit. The Chief looked around alertly, then put his head down and plodded. Still, the crowd ignored the handicappers and the flashy dancing and made the Chief the favorite.

There wasn't much early speed in the race, and, as was expected, the Chief did the honors. He took the lead and set a moderate pace, going in his standard twelves: 241/5, 484/5. Surprisingly, however, Proud Truth, with Jorge Velasquez aboard, kept close to the pace, as did long shots Important Business and Mr. Happy. Around the turn, Important Business tried to pull up beside the Chief on the inside, and Proud Truth made a move on the outside. Stephan's Odyssey had come up a length behind Proud Truth. The Chief, however, edged away easily, and he began to open up ground on his pursuers. At the top of the stretch, he was two lengths ahead, and at the eighth pole had increased the distance another half length. Stephan's Odyssey had come up beside Proud Truth, and the two took aim at the Chief, who had begun to drift out a bit into the middle of the track, away from the whip, as MacBeth hit him left-handedly. Proud Truth, however, bore out into Stephan's Odyssey, as Stephan appeared to lug in toward the big chestnut, and the two appeared to bump repeatedly about thirty yards from the wire. The Chief maintained a clear lead as the three horses swept across the finish line. In the photo of the finish, the Chief is thundering ahead, with one ear cocked back toward Proud Truth, as though keeping an ear on the competition.

The little colt looked tired as Don MacBeth brought him back to the winner's circle, but he looked excited, in his own understated way, his ears flicking around toward Eddie Sweat, who was waiting, and then toward the crowd, which was roaring in approval. Then, as he often did, the Chief looked over at the tote board, perhaps attracted by the lights, where his number was on top. My Hopeful was now the best young horse in America, the leading Derby contender in the country.

Roger Laurin had begun to hurry toward the winner's circle when the red INQUIRY sign went up and the Chief's number began to flash. His face lost its ruddy color. "That's the only way they'll beat him," he said grimly. "Take his number down. You never win easy. The horse wins but there is always something. I just can't believe this!"

Don MacBeth dismounted, and Eddie Sweat led the Chief out of the winner's circle. In a moment, MacBeth was on the weighing-room phone to the stewards upstairs. "I was wide around the turn, and I stayed wide. I outrun 'em and I drifted out," he said, "but I was in front. Jorge congratulated me, and told me I ran a hell of a race. He didn't claim foul."

The Chief's number appeared to flash for an eternity. Actually, it was fifteen minutes, an agonizing interlude.

The jockeys were already in the shower when the Chief's number finally came down, and he was placed second, behind Proud Truth. A tight-lipped Don MacBeth came up to Jorge Velasquez and muttered, "Congratulations." Replied Velasquez, "I'm sorry. I didn't even claim a foul."

Velasquez, however, didn't have to. Declared steward Joe Anderson, who had temporarily taken charge that day while chief steward Walter Blum was absent: "Chief's Crown drifted out and impeded Proud Truth. Proud Truth had to avoid running up on his heels. We disqualified him for not keeping a straight course and for impeding Proud Truth."

Meanwhile, the crowd, particularly those who had bet on the Chief, was getting ugly. After a sustained chorus of boos, the more angry of them began to overturn trashcans. And when elderly John Galbreath walked out to the winner's circle, he heard remarks that were far worse than anything he had ever heard from angry Pirates fans.

John Veitch, gracious in victory, remarked, "It's certainly not the way you want to win a race. I thought Chief's Crown ran a brilliant race, and he was dead fit."

Henryk de Kwiatkowski was not quite so gracious in defeat. In the elevator going up to the stewards' office, he was telling Woody Stephens: "If they don't give me a logical explanation, I'm never going to race here again. I never interfere. I love this game. But this is an outrage."

Both he and Stephens were maintaining that Proud Truth had interfered with Stephan's Odyssey, but, surprisingly, that the Chief had done no wrong. Stephens wanted to see Proud Truth's number taken down to third and Stephan's moved into second.

De Kwiatkowski was still arguing when the last race of the day was run, and the turf writers were still buzzing when the janitors began to work on the torn tickets and overturned trashcans. Finally, the Chief had found some believers, and, surprisingly, almost all the turf writers had taken the Chief's side in the controversy. Wrote Bob Rubin of the Miami *Herald:* "To everyone in the crowded press box and jockeys' room, the decision was anything but clear-cut. A clear majority in both places seemed to feel that while perhaps technically defensible, the decision was a mistake in judgment." Bill Nack called the decision "an act of surprising folly." Said the Great Handicapper, "The stewards' decision to make Proud Truth the official winner was absolutely unjustifiable." The Chief, he said, had taken command of the race and "never seemed to be in any danger until the red 'Inquiry' sign appeared on the tote board."

The following day, however, the Great Handicapper, after reviewing his speed figures, wanted to clarify his support of the Chief. Said the Handicapper of the Chief and Proud Truth: "I think they are both grossly overrated mediocrities, and if either goes on to greater glory I might have to burn my speed figures." And who, in his opinion, was the best three-year-old in the country? Rhoman Rule, who had won the mile-and-an-eighth Everglades Stakes two weeks earlier in 1:47⁴/5, almost a full second faster than the Chief had run the same distance in the Flamingo.

After a day to think about it all, the folks back at Roger Laurin's barn were still feeling burned. "Proud Truth was running all over the track like a snake, like he always does," said Steve Jordan. And hot-walker Jerry Booth recalled an earlier encounter Roger had had with steward Joe Anderson, at a time when Anderson was working as a horse-identifier in the paddock. "Before the race, Anderson comes up to Band Practice," said Booth, referring to a stakes-winning colt by Stop the Music who was then being trained by Laurin, "and he says he has no record of the horse wearing a shadow roll. 'Take it off,' he says. Then Roger says, 'This horse has been wearing a shadow roll since he was born.' Almost all Roger's horses wear shadow rolls. But Anderson doesn't believe him. So Roger has to go to the office and ask them to pull the negative of Band Practice winning his last race. And there he was, wearing this huge shadow roll, not just one of those small ones. So Roger gets on the phone with Anderson and asks, 'Now are you satisfied?' I don't think they've gotten along real well since then."

Roger, however, didn't seem to bear a grudge. He felt that the Chief's performance was more important in the long run than the stewards' decision, and he was looking almost relaxed and sounding almost philosophical. "Of all the things that have happened to me in this business," he said, then let the sentence trail off. "You can't make up for other people's mistakes."

Was he bitter about all the criticism he had received over the winter about the way he was training the horse? "I think the horse has answered all the doubts and questions by himself. You either train the horse to satisfy yourself or to satisfy the other people. I'm going to train the horse to satisfy *me.*"

His plans, he said, were to ship the Chief to Keeneland in a few days for the Blue Grass Stakes in late April. He turned to me with a reassuring smile. I had never seen him so confident. "Don't worry about this horse," he said; "he's going to make it."

CHAPTER 8

Splendor in the Bluegrass

> *. . . nothing can bring back the hour*
> *Of splendor in the grass, of glory in the flower.*
>
> —William Wordsworth

AFTER the heat and flash of Miami, the white fences and columned mansions of bluegrass country seemed a cool, quiet sanctuary, a private park where people came to horse traders rather than cocaine dealers to buy their highs. Most of the electronics firms and housing developments that had spurred Lexington's growth from a small town to a small city lay to the south and the east of town, and once you drove north or west for a few minutes it seemed that nearly everything you saw had to do with horses. Every inch of ground seemed to be covered by the grass known to botanists as *poa pratensis,* which originated on the Caspian steppes and whose seed was first transported to Kentucky in waterproof kegs by Amish-Mennonite farmers from the Conestoga Creek region of Pennsylvania.

In April, the bluegrass of Kentucky is at its bluest, when tiny purple blooms cast a bluish tint among the green blades. The broodmares laze in the fields, their bellies ripe as late plums.

The bare branches start to bud, and the smell of spring is overwhelming. You smell not only the grass, but the clay beneath, and you get a feeling of life stirring in its most elemental forms. It becomes easy to believe a recent scientific theory that life began not in some primeval soup, but in clay, as the biblical scribes had it all along.

I had arrived in Lexington on the afternoon of April 12 and checked into the Eldorado Motel, which lay directly across Versailles Road from Calumet Farm. The two institutions, I thought, provided a perfect double image of the racetrack life: the temporary shelter of the rootless and transitory posed against the weathervaned gables of the landed and rooted American gentry.

Lured by the smells of spring, I took a long drive, past field after field burgeoning with new life, past hills and valleys replete with grass, pregnant mares and budding trees. That line by Dylan Thomas about life-force kept running through my mind: "The force that through the green fuse drives the flower." Feeling the general connectedness of things, I thought about the Romantics' notion of a universal force that flows through all things, and I thought about what it is that makes horses so beautiful.

More than any other creature, I thought, they appeared to be the embodiment of that universal force, an animating spirit that showed forth when they pranced or ran or arched their necks in a certain way. No horse with a broken spirit could be beautiful, and any horse with spirit can become beautiful, in the flash of his eye or the grace of his movement. I realized, too, that on those few occasions when I sensed from the way a horse looked and moved that he was going to be a winner, what I was picking up on was something of that animating spirit, that energy that Tesio had so firmly believed in as the source of life and victory. It seemed appropriate that racetrackers referred to finding a good horse or winning the Derby as catching lightning in a bottle. It took skill, accident and miracle. That's what great horses were, in a way; flashes of energy contained in the flesh.

Mr. Keene's pleasure palace

The next morning I woke at dawn and drove the short distance down the highway from the Eldorado to Keeneland. I was surprised when I encountered no guards or gates stopping my access to the barns, but I remembered that Kentuckians regarded Keeneland as their own public park as well as a racetrack, and, as part of the illusion, the barns were open to visitors. Keeneland's motto was "racing as it was meant to be," and that meant racing as Kentucky's bluegrass barons meant it to be. Keeneland was an extension of the bluegrass breeding farms, a showcase and testing ground for the local product.

Although Keeneland, with its gracious stone clubhouse and its pin oak arborway, radiated the same genteel aura of pastoral tradition as Saratoga, racing had begun there only in 1936, on the site of what one Kentuckian referred to as "Jack Keene's pleasure palace."

Racing in Lexington itself had been recorded as early as 1787. Mixed breeds had raced on Main Street, on the Commons, at Henry Clay's Ashland, or at any improvised course where a challenge might be issued. From 1828 through 1933, however, racing was conducted by the Kentucky Association for the Improvement of the Breeds of the Stock at a track at the end of Fifth Street, now a public housing project. When that track was closed, the Association agreed to buy a portion of the Keene estate, including the small track and clubhouse built by Jack Keene for his own amusement.

Since then, Keeneland had been run by a nonprofit organization who turned the track into what one official there called "the museum of racing." Keeneland's meets were even briefer than Saratoga's: three weeks in the spring and three in the fall. As one turf writer put it, Keeneland is either the "purest or most peculiar race track in America." Queen Elizabeth herself had chosen Keeneland for a royal visit in 1984 when she arrived in Kentucky for an inspection tour of the famous stallions to whom she had been sending her broodmares for so many years.

The Great Handicapper detested Keeneland, not so much for its genteel pretensions as for its indifference to horseplayers.

Except for the daily double, there were no exotic bets—no perfectas, no trifectas. Worse still, the state of Kentucky did not consider it important to inform the betting public either about workout times or about horses who were racing with medication. "The idea," said Steven Crist, "is to squint a little and pretend you're at Ashland, where horses raced to settle private arguments and not to yield pari-mutuel payoffs."

Keeneland was able to maintain the luxury of that illusion because its primary source of revenue was not racing, but sales. The track's commission on wagering amounted to only about five percent of Keeneland's revenues, and the rest came from the summer yearling sales and the November breeding stock sale. Although Keeneland had only recently begun paying taxes on its sales, profits were more than generous enough to keep the plant in fresh paint and the help in new uniforms. This year, construction had begun on an extension of the clubhouse, and the finishing touches were being put on a new turf course.

Keeneland's backstretch was so well kept that it looked like a country club for horses. As I walked toward the "Stakes" barn, where the Chief was stabled, I could see horses already grazing outside bright, roomy barns on the fabled bluegrass that was said to be like nectar and mom's home cooking to thoroughbreds. Roger Laurin would have the big barn almost to himself, since most of the other Derby contenders had chosen different prep routes to the big race. Proud Truth and Rhoman Rule were in New York, and Spend a Buck was in New Jersey.

The Chief had arrived in Lexington the previous day, about the same time I was driving around in my bluegrass daze. He had flown in on the same plane as Stephan's Odyssey, and as luck would have it they had been placed next to each other. Despite their shared Danzig blood and despite all those months of being stabled next to each other at Claiborne as babies, they seemed to know they were competitors. "Stephan was hollerin' at him the whole time," said Eddie Sweat, who had accompanied the Chief on the plane. Eddie mimicked the angry trumpeting Stephan had sent toward the Chief. "And the Chief just laid his ears back like he wasn't goin' to put up with it. I was lucky they didn't tear up the plane."

When Roger arrived back at the barn, which was located next

to the busy backstretch entrance to the track, trainers on the way to watch their horses work yelled out congratulations. Roger, looking pleased, responded with a kind of "aw shucks" routine. "He's a good horse—that's the key," he would say. But the trainers were also congratulating Roger on another twist of the wheel that had given the Chief back his victory.

For several days after the stewards had taken away the Chief's triumph, turf writers had been editorializing, and pressure had been mounting. And Henryk de Kwiatkowski had been getting angrier and angrier. It was de Kwiatkowski, in fact, who had first decided to file an appeal with Florida's Division of Pari-Mutuel Wagering, which had the final say on such matters. Don MacBeth heard about de Kwiatkowski's plan and informed the Rosens, who then decided that in order to protect their own interests, they, too, should file an appeal.

On the morning of April 9, a special hearing was conducted by Robert Rosenberg, head of the Pari-Mutuel Division, aided by a panel of three retired racing officials. Also present were Joe Anderson and the three jockeys involved, as well as the owners of the three horses and their attorneys.

Each jockey presented his own case, with the use of videotaped reruns of the race taken from different angles. It was Don MacBeth, however, who was the star of the show. He had watched the tapes over and over the previous week, and he was able to point out several times during the race when Proud Truth could be observed bearing out, long before the Chief was said to have impeded him. As the tape rolled, MacBeth gave the running commentary: "Proud Truth ducks out from the left-handed stick. He does it at the head of the stretch. Every time he [Velasquez] hits Proud Truth left-handed or shows him the stick, left-handed, he ducks out. The only time my horse drifts out was when I hit him for the fourth time, and that's right at the wire."

The panel agreed with MacBeth. Said panel member Cal Rainey, a former New York steward: "Any interference there might have been was right as they passed the wire. Prior to that, Chief's Crown drifted out, but he was well clear at that point." The panel reinstated the Chief and overturned the stewards' suspension of MacBeth. Proud Truth, it was ruled, did not impede Stephan's Odyssey. Later, Ed Morano, another panel member, commented: "MacBeth must have watched the films over and over; he really did his homework. He was organized and presented himself extremely well."

When it was all over, what everyone agreed on was the sportsmanship of John Galbreath, who agreed to the hearing even though he had nothing to gain and more than a purse to lose.

And as for the Chief, the blessings still seemed to outweigh the curses.

Meanwhile, I had decided to resume my hot-walking career, temporarily, for the duration of the Keeneland meet. The Gallaghers had recommended that I try Steve Penrod, who trained Claiborne Farm's second string—the horses that Woody Stephens had rejected. As it happened, Penrod's horses were stabled just across the way from the "Stakes" barn, so that I would be able to keep an eye on the Chief, and at one end of his barn both Stephan's Odyssey and Creme Fraiche were stabled, so that I would be even closer to the Chief's competitors.

At the other end of the barn were two horses who had just arrived from California, the filly Fran's Valentine and the colt Floating Reserve, whose sad-eyed, gravel-voiced trainer, Joe Manzi, could tell even Roger Laurin a thing or two about the cruelty of fortune. At the beginning of the winter of 1983, Manzi, who had undergone triple-bypass heart surgery a decade before, was training three of the top Derby contenders, and by the end of the winter all three had suffered broken legs. Roving Boy, who had been two-year-old champion the previous year, recovered from his fracture, and in the fall of 1983 he won a comeback sprint with ease. In his next and final race, the Alibhai Handicap, Roving Boy took the lead, only to start crumbling a furlong from the wire as long shot Hula Blaze made a run at him. Refusing to give up, Roving Boy won the race with a final lunge at the finish, then collapsed just beyond the wire, both his hind legs broken. The horse was buried in the Santa Anita infield.

The following year was also both blessed and cursed for Manzi. His promising two-year-old colt Ten Grand had impressed Manzi even more than Roving Boy had at that stage of his career. The colt finished a strong second to Saratoga Six in the Hollywood juvenile championship. He came out of the race, however, with a cannon-bone fracture, the same injury that had felled the three colts the year before. Ten Grand died before he could make it to the operating table. And then, in November, there had been the triumph and the debacle of the Breeders' Cup, when the disqualification of Fran's Valentine from first place cost Manzi and Earl Scheib the most expensive ruling in the history of thoroughbred racing.

Like the all-suffering Job, Manzi might have looked toward the heavens in bafflement: "I was at ease, but he hath broken me asunder: he hath also taken me by my neck, and shaken me to pieces, and set me up for his mark." Or perhaps he might have wondered if someone were trying to tell him something about the way young horses were trained in America.

I saw Steve Penrod standing outside his barn holding a pretty chestnut filly by the shank, and I introduced myself. Before I had even finished my first sentence, he handed me the shank, and I was in business again. I felt like a veteran, an old hand, and I wanted to show off. I wheeled the filly around confidently, and we were on our way. A few moments later, however, when Paul, Steve's foreman, mentioned that the pretty little filly I was walking was by Mr. Prospector and was probably worth a million dollars or so, my palms got sweaty. Things got worse when Fran's Valentine, herself worth a stallion's ransom, decided to guard the shedrow from invaders. Every time I walked past her stall with my million-dollar filly, she would reach out playfully and try to nip the filly or to bop me with her head. Frannie clearly was used to being the center of attention, and when she wasn't being treated as the star of the show she would find a way to assert herself. Escaping Frannie, we would approach the other end of the shedrow, where sex-crazy Stephan's Odyssey would smell the filly approaching and let out the equine equivalent of a wolf whistle; it started deep in his throat and came out as a kind of snorting chuckle, huh-huh-huh, like an old man laughing at a dirty joke. The colt sounded as though he needed a cold shower.

When I took the young filly outside the barn to the outdoor walking ring, I faced yet another obstacle—the gelding Creme Fraiche, who kept squealing and rearing as his hot-walker, a young woman named Mary, tried to cool him out. Woody had frequently referred to the slender-chested bay as his "frail little gelding," but there was clearly more to Creme Fraiche than met the eye.

I got a further comeuppance from a highstrung gray filly named Steps, a daughter of Spectacular Bid whom Woody Stephens had cut from his string after she lost a couple of races at Saratoga. She was one of those nervous thoroughbreds who seem too strung out on their own adrenaline ever to relax. According to Paul, she was notorious for her flakiness. Woody had simply given up on her. Steve Penrod, however, was famous for his skill with problem horses. Sometimes all a horse like Steps needed was a little time and a little patience in order to regain her confidence.

Although Steps habitually swung her head around like a battering ram while in her stall, oblivious to the humans around her, she seemed quite docile when I took her out to a patch of grass beside the barn to graze, and as the sun began to relax my reflexes I began to daydream. The track chaplain cleared his throat over the loudspeaker and began reading a verse from the book of Revelation: "And I saw a new heaven and a new earth: for the first heaven and the first earth were passed away; and there were no more seasons."

Suddenly, someone zoomed by the barn on a motorcycle, and Steps jerked her head up, quick as a shot. Wham! The top of her head jammed my glasses into the bridge of my nose, and I yelped in pain. I forgot about Steps as I reached up to assess the damage and then began to grope on the ground for my glasses. Then I noticed that Steps was standing there very quietly, and I could have sworn that there was a puzzled, solicitous expression on her face. Who had hurt me, she wondered innocently. She nuzzled my hand softly, as though to console me. In some strange way, this incident had broken a barrier between us, and subsequently we got along quite well. But I knew I was going to be adding a black eye to the thin little scar on my upper lip as a souvenir of the backstretch.

Ted Bassett's bailiwick

Later that day, I wore my dark glasses to the races. Grudgingly, I also dressed up more than usual, since the Great Handicapper had warned me that at Keeneland they expect women to dress like ladies and men to dress like gentlemen. Gallagher, too, had warned me, "If they don't like the way your shoes are shined, they don't let you in."

Keeneland, I learned, was an odd mix of openness and exclusivity. One could wander around the barns at will, watching the trainers in action or paying a visit to potential Derby stars. Parking was free, and admission to the grandstand was only $1.25. However, admission to the clubhouse was ten dollars, and one had to be a member to dine in the private club on the second and third floors of the clubhouse. Keeneland had kept the membership to around one thousand, and there was a long waiting list.

Keeneland's president, Ted Bassett, former head of the Kentucky state police, was said to run a very tight ship, and as I walked through the grandstand to get to the press box I noticed that the uniforms of the ushers and the guards seemed to reflect Bassett's dual identity. The guards resembled deputy sheriffs, with their brown hats, beige shirts and big badges. The ushers, by contrast, seemed to be dressed for a shooting party in the English countryside, with green Tyrolean hats, green jackets and beige pants.

In the stewards' office, adjacent to the press box, I met Howard Battle, Keeneland's affable racing secretary, who was also an accomplished equine artist. Battle's father had been a trainer in Kentucky, and he himself was as comfortable with trainers as he was with the owners and breeders that made up Lexington's equine society. Nevertheless, even Battle considered himself a bit of an outsider when it came to Keeneland's inner circle. "I've been here for thirteen years," he said, "and I've only been invited to the private dining room four times."

Still, Battle loved the track, and he loved to point out its peculiarities. "This is the only racetrack where you're directly facing the sun," he said, as we squinted out toward the flowering dogwoods that edged the track. "That's why you see all the parasols." Across the way was the farm, now owned by Keeneland, where Forego once grazed on display. Farther in the distance were the tobacco fields owned by Keeneland. "This place is a character factory," said Battle.

Keeneland's leading character, according to Battle, was steward Keene Daingerfield, who had written that pithy little book on training horses that I so admired. Daingerfield, he said, was planning to retire at the end of the season. When Battle introduced us, however, I realized that Daingerfield hadn't lost any of the irony that had peppered his advice to would-be trainers so many years ago. When I asked him about the book, he said that he had tried to update it a few years ago, but fate had intervened. He had taken the manuscript with him in his station wagon on a trip up from Florida, but when he stopped for lunch along the way the car had been ransacked, and the manuscript had disappeared. "They took everything but two jars of pickled okra," he said. "So I knew it had to be a Yankee."

Gazing down at all the parasols, I asked how the Queen's visit the previous fall had affected the track. "It was really quite pleasant," said Daingerfield. "It didn't put anybody out too much. In the winner's circle, though, where she was to present a trophy, was where the trouble came. The first point of protocol with the Queen is that no one touches her person. But here's old Foxy, who's been working here since the track opened in the thirties, getting everyone set for the photo. And he starts pushing her, taking her by the elbow, like he was saying, 'Here, Queenie.' I'm surprised her secretary didn't run him through with a poniard. So when they showed the special tape of her visit, here she was getting pushed and pulled. So finally they cut that piece out of the tape."

We were all laughing, when I saw Daingerfield stiffen imperceptibly. Ted Bassett had entered the room, and everyone seemed to stand at attention. He gave us a cool, polite smile and walked over to the window to watch the horses being led out onto the track for the first race. The women riding the lead ponies all wore bright green jackets and caps. Bassett's face darkened in disapproval. "I believe these pony girls are getting too informal," he said. "I know it's warm today. But they've been rolling the sleeves of their jackets up to their biceps." He gave us another polite smile and left.

Although the Derby was less than three weeks away, the backstretch remained relaxed, except for a little good-natured ribbing between Woody and Roger when they crossed paths in the morning. One morning, Woody told Roger: "People tell me I work too hard. But that's all there is, work and money." He seemed to be implying that Roger had other priorities. And on the morning of the Lexington Stakes, which Woody was using as Stephan's prep race for the Derby instead of the Blue Grass, Woody was exclaiming about Roger's early-morning appearances at the track that week. "I said to myself, Roger must be getting nervous; he's not getting any sleep."

Roger, however, was looking as cool and calm as the Chief. A few minutes earlier, the Chief had been walking behind Jerry Booth in the shedrow while Stephan was being walked just outside the barn. Stephan's feet were "toed out"—that is, his hooves seemed to point outward rather than straight ahead— and he looked a bit Chaplinesque when he walked. At one point, the Chief had come around the corner just as Stephan was coming around the bend outside, and the two were almost face to face. The Chief stopped and looked at Stephan, then yawned very deliberately as Stephan pinned his ears back and rolled his eyes.

Later that afternoon, Stephan had regained his composure, and when he was led to the paddock to be saddled for the Lexington he seemed bored by the proceedings. He seemed to know he was the overwhelming favorite, and that he wouldn't be meeting any colts of consequence. As usual, he broke rather slowly and dawdled, as two speed horses, Tajawa and Northern Bid, dueled for the lead. The opening fractions, however, were very slow, and Stephan's jockey Laffit Pincay seemed to have misjudged the pace. Keeneland had two finish lines, and for the mile-and-a-sixteenth race the line nearer the top of the stretch was in use. Pincay, however, was riding as though he had another sixteenth of a mile in which to catch the leaders. When he realized his mistake, however, he urged Stephan through on the inside, and the colt responded with an impressive burst of tactical speed, moving from fifth at the top of the stretch to first by midstretch. The final time was 1:423/5, which was a full four seconds faster than an earlier race conducted that day at the same distance. After the race I saw Keene Daingerfield, who remarked: "I wasn't impressed with his race at first, but the more I thought about it the more I liked it. The time was good, and he did what he had to do to win it." Perhaps the Chief shouldn't be yawning, after all, at his sex-crazy, splay-footed rival.

After Saturday, the Chief had even less reason to yawn. Four major prep races for the Derby were conducted across the country, and the results had both clarified and complicated the Derby picture.

In California, long shot Hajji's Treasure upset several top Western horses in the California Derby, knocking Turkoman and Right Con out of Kentucky Derby contention. And in the Arkansas Derby, Wayne Lukas had worked more of his traveling magic. Tank's Prospect, who had finished last in the Santa Anita Derby two weeks earlier, had undergone an operation to release a paralyzed flap in his throat, and after only a day or two of recuperation Lukas had sent him to Oaklawn Park. The big colt made a big move in the stretch and won easily, defeating the previously unbeaten Clever Allemont and knocking him out of the Derby.

After the race, owner Eugene Klein was asked by a reporter to compare ownership of racehorses to ownership of a football team like the San Diego Chargers. Said Klein: "I prefer horses. Tank's agent is not going to call me and tell me he's only going to run on Tuesday and Thursday."

In New York, the outcome of the Wood Memorial had been considerably more ambiguous. Most turf writers had considered the Wood the most important prep race of all, since it would bring together Proud Truth and Rhoman Rule against two speed horses that had emerged late in the season: Pancho Villa, a colt by Secretariat who had beaten Spend a Buck in the Bay Shore Stakes, and Eternal Prince, who had scored a big upset in the Gotham Stakes two weeks earlier.

Eternal Prince had been bred by Yankees owner George

Steinbrenner and sold as a two-year-old for $17,000 to Brian Hurst, a thirty-six-year-old former car salesman from Virginia. The horse had gone winless at two, including a defeat by Doubly Clear in the Tyro at Monmouth. Over the winter, the colt improved dramatically, although he had been beaten badly by Pancho Villa in the Bay Shore Stakes. In that race, however, the colt had been kept off the lead, and he simply didn't run well unless he was allowed to "roll" from the gate. In the Gotham, the jockey let him "roll," and he had simply fried two other speed horses, Nordance and Pancho Villa, with sizzling early fractions.

After that race, George Steinbrenner decided he wanted a piece of the action, and he bought back 37$1/2$ percent of the horse for $1 million. Asked by a reporter to compare ownership of racehorses to ownership of a baseball team like the New York Yankees, Steinbrenner replied, "I like my horses better than my ballplayers because they can't talk to sportswriters."

The Great Handicapper had predicted, in his usual dramatic way, that in the Wood, Proud Truth would meet his Waterloo: "Proud Truth comes into the Wood Memorial Stakes with glittery credentials. He has classic breeding, a powerful stretch-kick, and competitive spirit and a consistent record. He is the cofavorite in Las Vegas' future-book wagering on the Kentucky Derby, and he will be the solid favorite at Aqueduct. He doesn't have a prayer." He predicted that Eternal Prince would take the race, with his beloved Rhoman Rule second and Pancho Villa third.

As it happened, he was correct about Eternal Prince. The horse led the race wire to wire, finishing nearly three lengths ahead of the field. However, because the horse had gotten "loose on the lead," and was not challenged while setting very slow early fractions, most handicappers felt that Eternal Prince's victory was deceptive in its apparent ease. Said Steven Crist, "The style of his victory was unimpressive and the runners-up may have showed more Derby potential in defeat." Only Proud Truth, however, who finished second, three lengths ahead of Rhoman Rule, had made a good stretch run, after giving Jorge Velasquez a hard time during the early going. Rhoman Rule faded after seven furlongs—probably, according to the Great Handicapper, because he didn't like the condition of the track (which was still drying out from a torrential rain) and because he had been off for five weeks.

Far more impressive than Eternal Prince's victory had been Spend a Buck's win in the Garden State Stakes. Two weeks earlier the colt had won the Cherry Hill Mile at Robert Brennan's new track, thus becoming eligible for a bonus Brennan was offering to lure top Derby contenders to New Jersey. Spend a Buck's prospects sounded like something out of *Let's Make a Deal*. After winning the Cherry Hill Mile, if he then won the Garden State Stakes, the Kentucky Derby and the Jersey Derby, he would collect a $2 million bonus. If he should win only one of the first two in addition to the Jersey Derby, the bonus would amount to $1 million.

Spend a Buck seemed to love Garden State's hard, fast surface, and he had little trouble with his opponents in the Garden State, which included Irish Sur and a Maryland colt named I Am the Game, who had finished second in the Cherry Hill Mile. His time for the mile-and-an-eighth was 1:45⁴/5, a clocking that had the speed boys shaking their heads in disbelief. According to the Great Handicapper, Spend a Buck's speed rating for the race was the fastest *ever* for a Derby prep race. And Spend a Buck had missed Secretariat's world record for the distance by only two fifths of a second.

Before the race, trainer Cam Gambolati and owner Dennis Diaz had been debating whether or not to send the colt to the Derby. Early in his career, Spend a Buck had appeared to be a speed horse, a sprinter whose maximum distance was a mile. But in the Garden State the colt had not slowed down after a mile, nor after a mile and a sixteenth. After such a performance, the two men could hardly avoid sending their speedster to the Derby. Given a hard, speed-favoring track, Spend a Buck was at the moment the fastest horse in America.

Von Osten's folly

Meanwhile, back at Keeneland, Roger and the Chief seemed to be savoring the last few days before the storm. On a quiet Sunday morning, Eddie was getting the Chief ready to go out to the track for a gallop. As Eddie held up the bridle, with its simple snaffle bit, the Chief yawned broadly before taking the bit into his mouth. And then, after Eddie buckled the girth on the exercise saddle, the Chief did something that startled me. He leaned backward on his haunches, stretching out his fore-legs. And then he picked up each foreleg, stretching his knees forward. He looked like nothing so much as a human runner doing his prescribed stretching exercises before heading out to the cinder track.

In the paddock, a trainer will take a horse's knees and stretch them forward, in order to loosen them up in preparation for a race. But I had never seen a horse do it on his own. And after I surveyed a number of trainers, it seemed that they had never seen a horse take the initiative either. "The Chief does that all the time," said Jerry Booth proudly.

I was ready to conclude that the Chief was even smarter than I had realized, but I remembered another apparent genius among horses—the famous Clever Hans, who had startled Vic-torian-era scientists with his apparent ability to solve mathe-matical problems.

Toward the end of the nineteenth century, Darwin's theories about the links between men and animals had encouraged experimental psychologists to employ animals in experiments involving human learning. There were a number of remarkable beasts—dancing bears, talking dogs—that seemed to offer proof that animals could learn simple tasks in the way that humans did. In 1888, Wilhelm Von Osten, a Prussian aristocrat, under-took a series of such experiments with a stallion named Kluge (Clever) Hans. For two years, Von Osten drilled the horse in math, rewarding him when he answered correctly and railing at him when he missed. Clever Hans obliged by learning how to tap out the answers to Von Osten's problems with his hoof.

Von Osten, who sought scientific corroboration of his work, was visited by a commission from the Berlin Psychological Insti-tute, headed by Professor Carl Stumpf. The commission in-cluded a circus trainer, a zoologist, a veterinarian and a politi-cian, each of whom theoretically would be able to detect certain kinds of ruses. For days, Clever Hans performed like a model student, tapping out answers and receiving tidbits of carrot as a reward, and the commission could detect no signs of fraud. But when Stumpf put a student named Oskar Pfungst on the case, the young man discovered that Hans was not able to give the correct answers if the questioner himself did not know the answers. Pfungst then confirmed that Hans could not answer correctly when Von Osten was out of his sight.

Clever Hans had been responding to body language so subtle that even the human observers had not been able to perceive it. Pfungst found that Von Osten could stop the horse's tapping hoof merely by raising his eyebrows. Von Osten's reputation was destroyed, and he sold Clever Hans, believing that the horse had failed him.

It seemed to me, however, that Von Osten as well as his questioners had missed the point about Clever Hans's intelligence. The horse could not add or subtract like a human being. But he had demonstrated a different kind of intelligence—the ability, as zoologist John Sparks put it, "to recognize patterns in apparent chaos." He had the ability to recognize and adapt to human demands.

Animals, said Sparks, are not preprogrammed machines; they have the ability to adapt as individuals to their environment. They can change their habits and enlarge their vocabularies of behavior; they can "make connections, seize upon cues, however trivial, provided that they are relevant to something important: food, a mate or an enemy."

Anyone who has ridden a good horse knows how remarkable that ability to adapt and to respond can be—and how much it can vary from horse to horse. A horse can respond to the slightest shift in your weight, the slightest tensing of your leg, the subtlest change in the timbre of your voice. He can sense fear, insecurity or confidence, and he responds accordingly. If he senses weakness or indecision, he'll take advantage of it. But if you communicate clearly, he can respond willingly before you even realize you've sent him a signal, and you feel something like a centaur.

Jack Mann had once suggested to me that a truly intelligent horse would have the good sense to refuse to cooperate, particularly on the racetrack; it was human hubris, he insisted, to associate animal intelligence with the ability to obey human commands. I wanted to agree with him, given my tendency to romanticize rogues and misfits. But after I had been around a few thoroughbred rogues, I had begun to think it was Mann who was making the Von Osten mistake of confusing the nature of human and animal intelligence. In the wild, the function of intelligence was survival and adaptation to the environment, and for a horse that environment was now controlled by humans. And so, unless he lived in the wild, a horse's survival depended on his ability to read the cues supplied by humans.

According to a psychic who had "communed" with John Henry at the behest of *Equus* magazine, the ornery gelding had fought his handlers as a young horse until one of his friends who couldn't win was put to death in the stall next to him. According to the psychic, John Henry told her, presumably in equine language, what he had learned: "We have no real choices but only one path to follow—pleasing humans. The only real win we have is our own survival."

Whether or not John Henry was actually capable of such reasoning, it was true that a horse's choices were obviously limited, and that a horse who cooperated was ultimately better off than one who didn't.

The Chief, it seemed to me, possessed considerably more than his share of that particular kind of animal intelligence— the ability to pick up cues, to adapt to his surroundings, to learn a task, to perform willingly. He didn't particularly like human beings, and he didn't particularly respond to love or praise. He didn't seem to take as much joy in running as some horses did. But his sense of survival was as strong as his sense of pride and superiority. I think that he perceived in some way that his job was to run when asked, and he did so in as efficient a way as possible. Had other tasks been required of him, he would have performed those, too, with poise and pride.

Penny Chenery, who eventually came to admire the Chief, would remark a few months later: "He has that unique way of moving. He dives out of the starting gate and he drives with his head, as though he is using it as a lever, and he reaches with his shoulders. I think he has worked out for himself how to carry himself most efficiently."

But were intelligence and efficiency enough to win the Derby?

Robert Al Clay's seraglio

In any case, the Chief had already earned himself a sinecure as a pampered stud, whose duties, once he retired from racing, would be limited to "covering" strange mares of noble bloodlines. Later that Sunday I drove over to Three Chimneys, his prospective seraglio, where Robert Clay had promised a tour and an introduction to Slew o' Gold, who had taken up residence at the farm a few days after his valiant defeat in the Breeders' Cup the previous November.

Clay was seated in his office behind a shiny new nameplate that a friend had sent as a joke after Clay's recent trip to Dubai. It said Sheik Robert Al Clay.

Clay, it seems, had been invited by Sheikh Maktoum al Maktoum to his desert kingdom after Clay had sold him some yearlings and had helped the sheikh purchase part of the bluegrass farm that he had bought as an extension of Three Chimneys acreage. "I've become kind of a middleman for them here," said Clay. "When they trust you, they become very loyal."

The new stallion barn was very quiet that afternoon, since Slew was the only stallion so far ensconced there, and he was out grazing in a pasture. However, standing in the stall next to Slew's was Triple Verdict, the big colt whom I had watched being operated on in Florida. "I put him there while he recuperates to keep Slew company," said Clay.

The barn had been designed in the shape of a hexagon, with six large stalls arranged around an airy central court where the stallions could be paraded for prospective clients. At the rear of the barn was the circular breeding shed with state-of-the-art technology for the teasing and preparation of mares for the brief, expensive act of actual penetration. Clay said he planned to put the Chief in a stall directly across the way from Slew so that the two could see each other. I looked at the big barn and tried to imagine Slew at one end and the Chief at the other. The scenario reminded me of one of those cartoons of a wealthy couple seated at either end of a long banquet table.

"We designed the barn so that it can't be expanded. My original plan was to stay small and selective. If you analyze the last ten years, the oversupply of stallions became so overdramatic, I felt there was a market for someone with a good stallion that was not part of a big factory. I thought it would take a lifetime to get six good horses. I never expected to get the first two so fast."

What a life, I thought as we walked out to Slew's two-acre paddock. Slew, who looked a bit shaggy in his winter coat, stopped grazing as we approached, and stood there calmly as Clay grasped him by the mane. He seemed rather tame for a stallion who had taken so eagerly to his two mountings a day. When I patted him, however, he began to get an interested look in his eye, and when he began to circle me we decided to make a retreat.

I asked Clay how he was getting along with Roger and Andrew. "Sometimes Roger will call me, or I'll call him, if there's a problem with the Rosens, and if both of us tell them something, they'll listen. You know, Roger, Andrew and I have a lot in common. I think of us as three lucky guys. Andrew expects things to go right, and they usually do. And when Roger makes a good shot in golf, he always says, 'Just lucky.' And I consider myself a lucky guy. I know I was lucky to get Slew o' Gold.

"We all grew up with that father-son thing, too," said Clay, whose father Albert, head of the Clay Tobacco Company, was a prominent man in Kentucky business and social circles. He had served as chairman of the Federal Reserve Bank of Cleveland as well as vice-chairman of the University of Kentucky board of trustees. The younger Clay had been a partner with his father in the Burley Belt Fertilizer Company. The company had developed into Top Yield Industries, which Robert Clay had sold for a very healthy profit in March 1984, enabling him to devote all his time to the horse business.

"I can really sympathize with Roger," said Clay. "The first thing people want to know about is his father."

Clay, however, was troubled by Roger's lack of assertiveness with the media. "It's interesting to see the contrast between Woody and Roger. When the TV cameras are there, Woody's out there. He can add 25 percent to the value of a horse advertised on the back page of the *Racing Form*. But Roger's not like that. I think that's why there were so many doubts over the winter. Roger just won't brag about the horse. If he had told the press what he told us—'I don't think we've seen the best of this horse'—that might not have happened." Clay shook his head. "Roger was a speaker at the Thoroughbred Club of America the other night, and he just didn't have anything to say. He just said, 'I'll be happy to answer any questions.'"

At Keeneland, however, even the turf writers had been remarking on how relaxed and confident Roger had become. On Tuesday afternoon, two days before the Blue Grass, he had pulled up a lawn chair next to the shedrow door, directly across from the Chief, and he was leaning back in the chair, contemplating his wonder horse. A group of sightseers bearing cameras came by looking for the Chief, and they stopped in front of Damascus Sam's stall. The big red colt, whose head was nearly twice the size of the Chief's, was standing there in a glamor-boy pose, practically flexing his muscles. One man, wearing a red gimme cap, glanced over at the little Chief dismissively, then pointed at Damascus Sam, saying, "This must be him." Another man, however, corrected him, and they clustered in front of the Chief's stall. "Hey, baby, come say hello," said a woman in a bright pastel dress, aiming her camera at the little colt. The Chief looked over at Roger, as if to ask what was going on. This part hadn't been written into the contract. "It's okay," said Roger reassuringly. But the Chief had disappeared to the back of his stall.

I asked Roger how he felt about having to answer to so many different owners now. "One person that interfered would be too many," said Roger. "But twenty that don't—it doesn't matter. They're looking out for the best interest of the horse; they're not going to do anything foolish. They don't even ask to have their picture taken with the horse."

And how about the pressure? "If you had a lot of problems and you just felt you had an outside chance to win, it would be worse. Borderline cases are much worse."

One of Roger's friends had told me that before the Chief

came along he had been thinking of retiring. I asked Roger if he thought he might retire when the Chief did. "It's a possibility," he said. "I think anybody who can see what the future will bring . . ." He let the sentence trail off. "I'm afraid I'll be spoiled after this colt retires. I'll never get another one like him. But it's such an interesting game, and the time goes by so quickly. I'm not into discos."

Had anything prepared him for a horse like the Chief? "Training is a cumulative thing," said Roger. "You learn something every day. There are things you can fall back upon. But there's no set pattern to what you do. You have to treat every horse as an individual."

Roger, I thought, had been drawing on his experience with hundreds of horses, including his frustrating experiences with his two previous Derby candidates, Current Hope in 1983 and Bear Hunt in 1984. But in some ways the Chief, who was to be his last good horse, was his first. He had been feeling his way along from day to day, sometimes letting the Chief show the way, trying not to squeeze the lemon. He would do this until the Chief showed him what his limits were.

And then I asked Roger about something that I had been thinking for a while, but that I hadn't really been able to articulate. "I've begun to think," I said, "that a good horse is like a gift of grace." He looked at me, a bit startled, but with a nod of recognition. "Yeah," he said, "it is." He thought for a moment. "It's not something that you can earn. When you get it, you just try to make the most of it."

As it turned out, the Chief would be facing only four rivals in the Blue Grass, and it was likely that after the race Roger still would not know his horse's limits. A number of turf writers, however, felt that they already knew those limits. At the Blue Grass dinner held the night before the big race, the writers seated at my table were taking turns roasting the Chief, enjoying my discomfort. The Great Handicapper was saying, "The horse has never surprised anyone, run any better than anyone expected." A New York handicapper disagreed: "I think he surprised everyone in the Flamingo. He won off two works, and he was trained worse than the other horses." Said the handicapper's woman companion: "He doesn't look like much. Some people say he looks like a filly." Replied the Great Handicapper, "He's a scruffy . . . ," then faltered. "Old crow," said a writer from *Sports Illustrated,* completing the sentence.

Meanwhile, some of the principals involved in the Blue Grass were taking the platform. One of the Chief's rivals was a Louisiana horse named Under Orders, owned and trained by Louis Roussel III, a genuine New Orleans character. Roussel's father, a real estate developer, had won a certain amount of notoriety in New Orleans by tearing down the historic St. Charles Hotel and other landmarks. Young Louis himself now owned and operated the Fair Grounds racetrack, yet he enjoyed training his own horses.

"I flew in a little late Friday after a poker game in New Orleans," said Roussel, who was making no pretenses about his chances to win the next day. "When we got here there was a copy of 'The Charge of the Light Brigade,' except it said: 'Into the valley of death rode Under Orders.' We know we're just up here filling the race," said Roussel. "Joe Manzi and I bet each other on who's going to come in third."

When Ted Bassett took the podium, the turf writers tensed in anticipation. The Great Handicapper was always bemoaning the ironclad nature of Keeneland's traditions. Every year, he said, Ted Bassett concluded the proceedings the same way: "And now the bar, gentlemen." In recent years, Bassett had omitted the males-only directive, but that had been the only change. And so one of the Great Handicapper's friends had challenged him to put his money where his mouth was, offering a friendly little bet that Bassett would conclude the dinner with his traditional words. Unbeknownst to the Great Handicapper, however, his friend had let Bassett in on the joke. And as Bassett wound down his speech, he uttered the famous words, "And now to the bar . . ." Then, as the Handicapper turned to his friend in triumph, Bassett said, "And that includes you," looking at the Great Handicapper, and calling him by name. The room erupted in laughter.

Later, as the proceedings had adjourned to the bar, I heard the Great Handicapper telling an interviewer, "Chief's Crown is the most overrated horse in history."

It was fortunate the Chief did not have to read his reviews. The next day, as he was brought to the paddock before the race, he yawned with his usual demonstration of calm. This time, he was surrounded by a large crowd of people, all of whom had a proprietary interest in him. Said Robert Clay, "It's all family." Said Douglas Rosen, pointing to his brother Andrew and the array of Rosens talking under the trees, "This horse has brought our family closer together." The Chief, I realized, had become the center of two different forms of community—that of financial interest and that of blood ties.

The Chief was led from the paddock into the walking ring, where a silver-haired gentleman with a Teutonic accent was telling Ted Bassett, as he pointed to the dark bay Under Orders, "I think ze four horse is ze most impressive in terms of harmony." Said Mrs. Bassett, "I understand all the Danzigs are rather unattractive."

The rather unattractive Chief broke quickly, as usual, and when the speedster Banner Bob, who had equaled the track record at Latonia in his last start, seemed reluctant to take the lead, the Chief pumped his head vigorously and took command after the first few strides from the gate. Banner Bob followed, a length and a half behind, with Floating Reserve a few steps back and Under Orders trailing by ten lengths. The Chief ran his steady twelves, and after six furlongs in 1:12 he maintained his length-and-a-half lead. When Banner Bob tried to make a move at the top of the stretch, the Chief moved away effortlessly, and MacBeth showed him the whip. The Chief began to chase the ghost horse, and he drew off by five lengths, finishing only a fifth of a second off the track record held jointly by Round Table and Roger's filly Numbered Account.

Buddy Sarner, Banner Bob's trainer, was stunned. He announced that Banner Bob was not going to be running in the Derby. "I don't care who Chief's Crown is going to go against, he's going to whip them. He just played with those horses today."

Back at the barn, Eddie Sweat, wearing a bright yellow shirt, was jubilant. "He's like me when I was playing baseball," he said, as he removed the run-down bandages from the Chief's hind legs. "When I got wound up, I was really hot. You know, he give me a fit all this week."

A group of young black grooms passed by the barn. One pointed to Eddie, saying, in a hushed voice, "He's going to be the only groom to win the Triple Crown three times." (Eddie had actually won it only once before, since Riva Ridge had lost the Preakness before going on to win the Belmont.)

All week, Eddie had been thinking back about those earlier days, about Riva Ridge in particular. The stallion had died suddenly at Claiborne a few days ago, only a day before Eddie had planned to join Lucien Laurin at the farm for a visit with their two great Meadow Stable horses. The morning of the horse's death, in fact, Roger and Lucien had been talking about the old rivalry between Riva Ridge and Roger's filly Numbered Account. Said Eddie, "Roger still thinks his filly could have beat Riva Ridge."

Now, however, Roger was on his own. He returned to the barn, making his way through a crowd of well-wishers. He patted the Chief, saying, "Well, boy, it's over for today." The Chief reached out to nip at him, missing his hand by inches.

Douglas Rosen was saying, "If this were my full-time business, I couldn't sleep at night. It's scary to be at the top, to realize how temporal it all is. In this business, it really is short-lived." We discussed America's need for disposable heroes, and I mentioned that, according to a recent Roper Poll survey, the current heroes of America's youth included both Michael Jackson and Mother Teresa.

Meanwhile Andrew Rosen was at the middle of a circle of turf writers, and he seemed to be enjoying himself. His wife Adrian was joking: "Hey, look at him. He's developed a public personality." Looking at the front page of the *Racing Form*, she said, "How come he's on the cover, and not the horse?"

The next morning, I had taken my friend Steps out to graze on the rapidly dwindling patches of bluegrass, as Roger prepared his horses for the journey to Louisville and Churchill Downs. The glow of victory had vanished, and Roger looked tense. Jerry Booth came over to say hello, and he patted the filly, looking worriedly over at Roger. "He keeps it all inside, but if you know him like I do, you can see that it's starting to get to him."

After the van had been loaded with Roger's equipment and Eddie Sweat's portable tack room bed, Eddie led the Chief to the van, followed by Jerry and Damascus Sam, Cigar and the veteran Lord Darnley, and Roger and the pony Popeye.

The loudspeaker crackled with the voice of the chaplain, who had selected one of those admonitory passages from the book of James, a warning about the transitory nature of wealth and power. It struck a chilling note on that bright bluegrass morning, when the Chief seemed to be on his way to glory.

Let the brother of low degree rejoice in that he is exalted: But the rich, in that he is made low: because as the flower of the grass he shall pass away.

CHAPTER 9

The Jewels in the Crown

A dark horse, which had never been thought, and which the careless St. James had never even observed in the list, rushed past the grandstand in sweeping triumph.

—Disraeli, *The Young Duke*

I

ONCE the Chief headed for Louisville, he had left the relatively cloistered world of a minor sport in America to enter the spotlight and the Big Time, the world of TV commentators and ornamental celebrities. He was now in the running for one of the most prestigious, highly visible trophies in America, the ultimate status symbol, a trophy that wealthy and prominent men had been coveting for over a century.

The Derby, it was said, was the most thrilling two minutes in sports. If you won the Derby, what else was there to achieve? You had reached the peak, the pennant, the gold medal, the happy-ever-after, the climax of the Horatio Alger story. You had defeated your peers, beaten the odds and conquered your fate. In 1973, the year of Secretariat, Kentucky Governor Wendell Ford had stood up at a Derby Week dinner and proclaimed that the ninety-ninth Kentucky Derby would be "the greatest thing that ever happened on the face of the United States."

The Colonel's coup

The first Kentucky Derby, held in 1875, was named for the Epsom Derby, the prestigious English race that itself had been named for the twelfth Earl of Derby. In 1771, Lord Derby, a devotee of cockfighting as well as horse racing, had won a coin toss with Sir Charles Bunbury, president of the Jockey Club, for the honor of having a race for three-year-olds named after him.

As it happened, that first run for the roses, held at a new track built on the stud farm of a family named Churchill, just outside Louisville, caught on quickly, and a resourceful newspaper reporter christened the new track Churchill Downs, after Epsom Downs, where the English Derby was held. The winner of that first contest, Aristides, was owned by Price McGrath, one of those hardboot-to-mansion Kentucky successes who maintained the illusion of horse racing as a wide-open sport where luck ran neck and neck with money. McGrath, who had been born to poor parents in Woodford County, had gone west during the Gold Rush, then returned to New York, where he opened a gambling house. After winning $105,000 in a single night, he returned to Kentucky to establish a stud farm. The master of McGrathiana Stud, however, continued his eccentric ways, choosing to drive a team of mules rather than a matched pair of horses.

Despite an abundance of such self-made characters, however, by the turn of the century Churchill Downs and the Derby had begun to languish. In 1902, when Matt J. Winn, one of Kentucky's seemingly endless supply of colorful colonels, took over, the track was losing money, and the Derby had lost prestige. Within a dozen years, however, the iron-willed Winn managed to turn the provincial track around and began to build the Derby mystique. The race needed only a superstar to firmly establish the run for the roses as one of the great all-American events. And oddly enough it was a filly—Harry Whitney's Regret—who was to give the race its oomph. As Colonel Winn put it, "The race needed only a victory by Regret to create some more coast-to-coast publicity and really put it over. She did not fail us. Regret made the Kentucky Derby an American institution."

Over the years, a number of other horses succeeded Regret as Derby legends. My favorite had always been Exterminator, the homely gelding known by his fans as Old Bones, who had won the Derby in 1918 after his stablemate, the flashy Sun Briar, had been injured before the race. Bones had been purchased by Sun Briar's trainer Henry McDaniel, as a pace horse for the star, but the gelding, by a fluke, had been nominated for the Derby. McDaniel had been impressed by Exterminator's determination in morning workouts, and when Sun Briar was unable to compete he sent the gelding, still unraced as a three-year-old, to post. Old Bones paid $61.20 to win that day, and he went on to become one of the great handicap horses of all time, winning races through his ninth year.

The silly season

Like the Super Bowl, the Kentucky Derby was a media event that attracted swarms of reporters, customarily some sixteen hundred or so, and trainers had to brace themselves for a week-long onslaught of questions, silly and otherwise. Jack Mann once called the Derby the "silly season, when almost everybody who ever found a Turf Writers button in a box of Cracker-Jacks makes the pilgrimage to Louisville to second-guess the care and feeding of the most likely 3-year-olds of the cosmos."

Mann observed that approximately one half of the media who showed up every year for the first Saturday in May never covered any other horse race, and three quarters never covered any but the Triple Crown races. Said Mann, "The Kentucky Derby is covered by experts: experts on baseball, football, hockey, basketball." The result was pack journalism, in which each of the dozen or so trainers found himself surrounded at dawn by jostling innocents to whom he had to tell his life story all over again.

On Sunday morning, six days before the big day, Woody Stephens was standing outside Barn 42, with his hat cocked to one side, winding up into his quote-a-minute delivery that never failed to charm. The previous day, Creme Fraiche had narrowly beaten a California horse, Fast Account, in the Derby Trial on a muddy track, and he had soundly beaten potential Derby contender Tiffany Ice, the Chief's old rival. Woody had decided to bypass the Derby with the reliable gelding, whom he still referred to as a "frail little horse," but Fast Account's trainer, Patty Johnson, had decided to keep her horse in the Derby.

Woody was telling a reporter that Stephan's Odyssey wasn't going to meet much competition on Saturday. "There's no Swale or Devil's Bag in this field," he said. "Outside of Roger's horse, you could kick 'em twice." When asked about Wayne Lukas's horse Pancho Villa, who was still a possible entrant on Saturday, Woody replied, "Pancho Villa—isn't he back in Mexico?"

Patty Johnson, the only woman trainer in the Derby barns, was surrounded by a considerably smaller crowd, since Fast Account, a grandson of Roger's champion filly Numbered Account, was considered a talented long shot who lacked the will to win. Johnson was saying that her favorite Derby had been five years ago, when the filly Genuine Risk had been the first filly since Regret to win. A quiet, strong-looking woman with short blond hair and sunburned skin, she seemed surprisingly confident about her horse's chances. She exercised the horse herself, and she felt he was ready. "I expect him to be on the board Saturday. With Chris McCarron, I've got the leading rider in the country, and he picked the horse to ride on Saturday."

This year, there were fewer horses than usual entered in the Derby who were given no shot by handicappers to win. The maximum number of entries allowed in the field was twenty, with track earnings to be used as a cut-off point if more than twenty were entered. This year only thirteen horses would be running, with seven of them considered solid contenders: Chief's Crown, Proud Truth, Stephan's Odyssey, Tank's Prospect, Rhoman Rule, Eternal Prince and Spend a Buck. It was considered one of the most contentious Derby fields ever.

In most years, however, the field would be filled out with long shots. Every year, owners and trainers across the country were afflicted with what the Great Handicapper called the Derby

Fever Syndrome, a malady that clouded one's judgment about the ability and readiness of one's favorite three-year-old. Horses whose owners or trainers were afflicted with the disease were entered in the Derby despite illness, despite soreness, despite inexperience, despite a demonstrated inability to go a distance.

Perhaps the most famous case of Triple Crown fever had been suffered by trainer Pancho Martin, who in 1973 kept insisting that his horse Sham could beat Secretariat. Before the Preakness, Martin had told Bill Nack, "If I don't win, I'll be very, very, very, very disappointed. Not disappointed—very, very, very, very disappointed. Sham is going to win easy, believe me!" Martin indeed was to be very, very, very, very disappointed. But it didn't seem to blunt his optimism. The next year, during Derby week, he was telling sportswriters, "I have a horse who's better than Secretariat, and his name is Rube the Great." Rube finished tenth in the Derby that year.

These Derby-fever horses, who entered the race without the fitness, talent or experience necessary for such a grueling contest, often paid a heavy price. A good horse would keep trying, long after his body had lost its capacity to absorb the punishment. If such a horse didn't actually break down, he often required months of recuperation to recover from the stress of the race.

In last year's Derby, the casualties had been particularly high. Althea, the filly who had been favored to win, had never won again, nor had the long shot Bear Hunt, who suffered a bowed tendon. Both Vanlandingham and Taylor's Special, who had competed despite recent bouts with fever, took nearly a year to recuperate.

I had once asked John Veitch why so many trainers overestimated the ability of their horses. "It clouds your judgment, the hype and excitement of being able to say you ran a horse in the Derby," he said. "Every year about half the horses shouldn't be there. There's no sense destroying a useful horse by running him before he's ready. You've got to have seasoning. It's not like a boxer who's fought nothing but pugs but who doesn't know what it is to fight a real man.

"People get high on a horse. They say, 'I've got a world beater.' The problem is, they've never been around a good horse before. If you've never drunk champagne, you might think Ripple tastes just as good."

This year, most of the Derby-fever horses had been knocked out by the stars who had won their prep races so definitively. A crop of colts that had looked so mediocre early in the year had begun to look very tough. Speed horses like Lukas's Pancho Villa and Image of Greatness were faced with two superior speed horses—Eternal Prince and Spend a Buck—who had shown they could sustain their speed beyond a mile. And come-from-behind horses like Do It Again Dan were faced with horses like Proud Truth and Stephan's Odyssey, who could make big runs from a long way back.

The handicappers were already predicting the probable scenario of the race. Eternal Prince and Spend a Buck, they said, would go out in a speed duel, with the Chief not far behind them. Rhoman Rule would probably be next, while Proud Truth, Tank's Prospect and Stephan's Odyssey would drop back toward the back of the field. The scenario then split into three possible finishes. The first was that the two speed horses would maintain a pace that would not kill each other off, and one or the other would hang on to win. The second was that the speed horses would tire, and the Chief would take over the lead to win. The third was that the Chief as well as the speed horses would tire, and the stretch runners would begin a cavalry charge.

The Great Handicapper continued to deny the chances of Proud Truth, predicting the horse's "demise." Accordingly, one morning, Charlie Rose, the colt's fifty-year-old exercise "boy," concluded an interview session by saying, "Well, I've got to go look after old Mark Twain." The reporter looked puzzled. "Mark Twain," repeated Rose. "You know, 'Rumors of my death are greatly exaggerated.' "

Other handicappers were waiting to see how the contenders worked out during the week before making their final predictions. Roger, however, was sending the Chief out so early every morning that virtually no one had seen him gallop. On Wednesday morning, the heavy rain from the night before had barely slowed to a drizzle, but Roger had the Chief out before the sun had even begun to rise over Churchill's twin spires. He had led the way out to the track on the pony Popeye, while the Rosens and I took refuge in the clockers' stand near the entrance to the backstretch. When the Chief broke off for his work, Roger, still marooned out in the rain on his pony, found his glasses too cloudy to read his stopwatch, and the track was still too dark for anyone else to catch the time precisely. "I didn't catch him," said one clocker. "That mother's sailing," said another. Said an old man named Charlie, a retired clocker who worked on a freelance basis, "He beat forty-eight a little." Turning to one of the Rosens, he said, "You can tell Roger that he likes the track."

Steve Davidowitz, the famous handicapper who specialized in morning workouts, had been watching the Chief intently. "I don't trust my time," he said, "but I can tell you that he went real slick. I trust Roger's seat-of-the-pants horsemanship. I think he's ready."

Later, back at the barn, Roger was faced with a sea of microphones. An interviewer from ABC-TV asked him about the time he gave Secretariat to his father. "Well, I'm not giving *this* horse to anyone," Roger said. "When this horse gets the lead," he said, as though he had been rehearsing the line all week, "he doesn't pass the dice." Then, inevitably, he was asked what he had learned about horse racing from his father. "Never to give interviews," said Roger with a grim smile.

Living up to the legends

Thursday morning brought the official draw for post positions, to be held at the new Kentucky Derby Museum, just outside the grandstand gates.

I arrived early and headed for the instant-replay exhibit, where you could watch tapes of some of the great Derbies of yesteryear on a huge TV screen. Someone had already selected Secretariat's Derby, and the race was on. Shecky Greene, Foxy Greene's sire, had sprinted to an early lead, while Secretariat had dropped back to eleventh out of a field of thirteen. After six furlongs, Sham had cut Shecky's lead to a length and a half, while the great Forego had moved from ninth to sixth. But Secretariat: he had passed six horses in one tremendous surge that made your heart pound. After a mile, Shecky Greene had started to fade, and Sham took over the lead. Forego moved up to fourth. In almost any other year, Sham would have kept that lead and won the race. But Secretariat continued like a juggernaut, his blinkers now at Sham's flank. By the top of the stretch, Big Red had gotten his nose in front, and although Sham responded gamely, Secretariat's long, pounding stride made Sham's motion look choppy and inefficient. The small crowd assembled near the screen cheered as though the outcome had been in doubt.

The next race I chose was Northern Dancer's 1964 Derby. The Dancer's chief opponent had been the big chestnut Hill Rise, who had seemed a likelier candidate that year to get the distance. Bill Shoemaker had thought so, and he chose Hill Rise as his mount, leaving Northern Dancer to Bill Hartack. Northern Dancer, according to Hartack, had been hard to rate. "If you got him wound up," Hartack had told me one morning, "he was overly willing. If you asked him to run, he'd fire with everything he had, and you had to try to save a little of it." Still, in that astonishing Derby performance, he had laid back in the middle of the pack, along with Hill Rise, the two of them running sixth and seventh for six furlongs. It was at that point that Hartack had asked the Dancer, and the little colt had exploded, and within two furlongs he had the lead.

At that moment, I got a very strong feeling of déjà vu. There was something very familiar about the way Northern Dancer was running, with that big, swimmer's reach and pounding stride. Suddenly I realized that he was running like the Chief, making the most of his small stature, his head moving up and down like a piston. At the top of the stretch the Dancer was two lengths ahead of Hill Rise, who had also begun his move. Inch by inch, Hill Rise began to overtake the Dancer, until he loomed up beside him. "It was like an eclipse," one observer of the race had told me, with the big chestnut blocking out the small dark colt from view. The Dancer, however, had held on to win by a neck, setting the track record that would be beaten only by the Chief's other grandsire.

I was feeling overwhelmed by the notion of bloodlines and destiny, and as I studied the results of the next twenty Derbies after Northern Dancer's I realized that thirteen of them had been won by descendants of either Bold Ruler, Secretariat's sire, who himself had lost the race by six lengths, or Native Dancer, Northern Dancer's sire, who had lost the Derby by an unfortunate nose. Perhaps the Chief, who carried the genes of both lines, was destined to win. Andrew Rosen had begun to talk as though the little colt were fated to win. I think Roger, too, felt that the Chief was going to win. The little colt was his second chance, his long-delayed consolation prize for losing Secretariat.

Carl Rosen, I thought, would make a fitting entry in this exhibit of colorful owners and breeders, the various honorary colonels and capitalist lords who had made Derby history. Rosen, who had not been particularly well received by the current generation of Kentuckians, would have been better appreciated, I thought, by Colonel E. R. Bradley of Idle Hour Farm. Bradley, the son of an Irish immigrant, had gambled his way from obscurity to the top of the horse world. Beginning as a steel mill laborer, Bradley had worked as gold miner, cowboy, and even a scout against the Apache Indians. When called to testify by the U.S. Senate, Bradley was asked by Huey Long to describe his occupation. "I'm a speculator, racehorse breeder, and gambler," said Bradley. And what did he gamble on? "Almost anything," retorted Bradley.

Rosen, like Bradley, a gambler and entrepreneur, had combined intuition and calculation in his forays into the breeding business. Rosen had stumbled, seemingly by chance, onto the Secretariat/Northern Dancer nick that was to prove so effective. Unfortunately, however, the Chief's extraordinary bloodlines, which had brought him this far, could very well be his undoing in the Derby, if the dosage experts were correct. Too many of the Chief's ancestors, it seemed, had outrun their pedigrees. Chris Evert's stamina, like that of Northern Dancer and Secretariat, had been in doubt.

The Chief's was a family tree of high achievers, of very fast horses who had overcome genetic limitations. The problem was that there were no strong plodders lodged in the tree to give the Chief the extra stamina to draw on when he hit the wall after a mile and an eighth. He would be going up against four good horses who had been genetically gifted with that extra stamina: Spend a Buck, Stephan's Odyssey, Fast Account and Proud Truth.

At the drawing, the Chief drew the second post position, with Irish Fighter, a Derby-fever horse, to break inside him on the rail. Rhoman Rule had drawn the third hole, but he would be labeled number one in the program and coupled in the betting with Eternal Prince, whose ownership was now split between George Steinbrenner, Brian Hurst, Spendthrift Farm, and Spendthrift partners John and Pauletta Post.

So many horse-trading deals had been proposed and closed during Derby week that the action resembled a cross between Keeneland and the floor of a commodities trading center. The breeders had been placing their own wagers on their favorites a few days before the general public got a chance at the betting windows. Everyone seemed to want a piece of a Derby horse. "It's been like a marketplace this week," said turf writer Dan Farley. The stakes were high, but the returns for the winner would be even higher.

Will Farish, the genteel Texan who had hosted Queen Elizabeth during her visit to Kentucky the previous fall, had been trying all week to talk Dennis Diaz into selling him a half-interest in Spend a Buck, while Steinbrenner and Hurst had sold a quarter-interest in Eternal Prince to Spendthrift, with the understanding that the colt would stand there at stud once he was retired. Brownell Combs had little trouble convincing Dallas millionaire John Post and his wife Pauletta to buy a piece of the action. The Posts had recently bought their own stud farm outside Versailles, which they invited the editors of *Architectural Digest* to inspect, and with Eternal Prince they were buying a very expensive ticket to the Derby to go along with it.

After the drawing, most of the trainers and turf writers lingered in the hall to watch a multimedia show called the "Derby Spectacular," which was to be projected onto a screen that wrapped around the four walls of the hall. The show's producers had taped the preparations for last year's Derby, focusing on the victorious but ill-fated Swale, and then had interwoven that footage with snippets of tape and memorabilia from previous runnings of the race.

The show, which was to become a regular part of the museum's offerings, might have been titled "The Dream." It begins with the peaceful chirping of birds on the dawn of the big day, a familiar backstretch sound that gets lost in all the bustle of preparations for the track. A blacksmith mutters to a horse, "Whoa, big boy," and you hear the tap of a hammer on an aluminum shoe.

The routine activities of the backstretch take on an added intensity. Laffit Pincay, who is donning Claiborne's golden silks in the jockeys' room, explains that although he has never before asked God to help him win a race, he has prayed this time for help. You hear Claiborne Farm's manager John Sosby talking about what it takes to breed a horse and raise him and train him to get this far. "The heart and determination is bred into them," says Sosby. "But you're trying to catch lightning in a bottle." And finally, in an explosion of light and color, you are surrounded by the Derby Day crowd that has filled Churchill's enormous grandstand and spilled over into the infield.

The gates open, and the horses begin their charge. But as they run, the race becomes every Derby, it becomes the Dream, and you are rooting again for Secretariat, for Carry Back, for every horse that carried part of the Dream. "Carry Back is too far back to make it," shouts the announcer. "Can't unless he hurries." And then you hear "It's Swale," as the black colt draws off from his pursuers and Pincay stands up in the irons, as though lifted by the roar of the crowd, waving his stick in triumph.

At the conclusion of the show, with the hall surrounded by a screen full of glistening roses, there was not a dry eye in the house. Hardbitten turf writers were searching for handkerchiefs, owners were snuffling, trainers were clearing throats, trying to pretend there were no lumps of emotion there. As trainer Angel Penna, Jr., had once told me, "When someone tells you they don't care about the Derby, don't believe them."

Jack Price's star

A few moments later, the crowd moved outdoors to the courtyard for a ceremony commemorating the horse whose owner had once dared to claim that the Derby was just another race. As the bugler played a mournful call to post that served as taps, a metal box containing the ashes of Carry Back was buried in a grave marked by a stone that read "The People's Choice."

Through their tears, sportswriters recalled the irony of that Derby week, twenty-four years ago, when Jack Price, Carry Back's breeder, owner and trainer, had been telling everyone that the Derby was nothing more than the feature race on the first Saturday in May. A former bookmaker and small-time trainer, Price had acquired Carry Back's dam Joppy as repayment for a longtime debt, and he had bred her to the unlikely stallion Saggy as a matter of convenience.

After the low-born Carry Back won the Derby, however, in a stirring come-from-behind finish, Price revised his opinion about the big race. As Price told Louisville journalist Billy Reed, that fateful Derby not only changed his mind, but it changed his life. "We'd won the Florida Derby and the Flamingo and the Garden State," Price said, "but when we'd go out in the world, people would say, 'What the hell's the Garden State?' But after we won the Kentucky Derby, it was like you were a god or something."

Carry Back had made the Prices the toast not only of America but of Europe. After the ceremony in the courtyard, Katharine Price, a frail, stylish woman wearing a turban to cover the baldness caused by recent chemotherapy treatments, was reminiscing about the time she and her husband took the horse to France for the Prix de l'Arc-de-Triomphe and found themselves the hottest attraction in Paris. "We came back to the hotel one afternoon," she said, "and someone had just put an invitation into our box. Jack said, 'Who is this guy?' and he was standing right behind us. It was Edmund Wilson. He wanted to have a luncheon for us. DeGaulle was supposed to be there, but it was the Algerian war, and he couldn't come.

"None of that would have happened to us without Carry Back. He changed everything. Some people resented us because they thought we were being too flip about the whole thing, but the public loved us because we were poor people who were bucking the big shots."

The adulation had continued long after the horse had retired. "When he was sick, people sent crates of apples. This year, on April 6, I still got cards for his birthday. They didn't know he had passed away."

How had she felt about Carry Back being buried at Churchill Downs? "I felt the most gratitude today. Finally he's taken care of. You see, we didn't know what to do with him. And I've given my trophies too. After the first shock, my kids understood. When you have a horse like that, he doesn't just belong to you." She looked at me with a sad smile. "No one in my family has ever gotten cancer before," she said. "I have to think that losing him had something to do with my getting sick."

Dennis Diaz's hobby

That night, at the Trainers' Dinner, the ballroom of the Louisville Hyatt was full of people who were looking for a bit of the brief godliness that the Prices had experienced. I must have been a little misty-eyed about it all myself; I vaguely remember Seth Hancock telling me, after I had finished listing the Chief's accomplishments, "I think you've lost your objectivity."

Some contenders who were mingling that night, however, had undertaken the search more casually than others. There was King T. Leatherbury, for example, the Maryland claiming trainer whose colt I Am the Game was to be his first Derby horse. Said King, a brisk, soft-spoken man who had just flown in for the dinner from Maryland, "I just put in a claim today for a five-thousand-dollar horse, and I felt a little ashamed, this being Derby week."

Ordinarily, King T. trained his horses from the ordered calm of his office, with the help of his computer and a crew of assistants. King T. seldom ventured out to the paddock either to saddle his own horses or to look over those of his opponents. Training, he felt, was mostly a game of business management, and he was handling the Derby the same way. King T. had remained in Maryland most of Derby week, leaving his assistant to take care of his Derby colt. On Sunday morning, however, his absentee style had left the colt saddled up in his stall for hours, with nowhere to go and no one to ride him. "Everyone's at church," said one of the stable boys that morning. Eventually, Woody Stephens's exercise boy had volunteered his services.

Dennis Diaz, by contrast, had already discovered that a good horse could change your life, and he was taking the ride on the wheel of fortune in a big way. He had come into Louisville this week as the ultimate outsider, the grandson of a Spanish immigrant who had made cigars in Tampa.

Diaz, however, could claim that he came from a landed family. His father Sacramento, an avid gambler who played the horses as well as the dogs and jai alai, had started a small dairy on his father's land. "Back then you could tie a cow in your backyard and peddle the milk to your neighbors," said Diaz. "I milked cows for my daddy, but he said if I wanted to farm I had to get the hell off the farm. So I left the farm when I was twenty and got into the insurance business. The name Diaz went well in Tampa, but not in Clearwater, where I had moved, and I branched out into real estate and construction. By the time I was in my mid-thirties, I was burned out. I had made enough money to retire on, as long as I invested it well."

Diaz had soon gotten bored with retirement, however, with swimming and boating and wandering around his grandfather's farm with a glass of Johnny Walker Red in his hand. He and his wife had set new goals: adopting a child and getting into the horse business.

"The first time I came to Kentucky," said Diaz, "I was nobody, and I was treated like nobody. Lexington is a hard town to break into unless you have a million dollars to spend." Unless, like the Posts, you have the wherewithal to buy the whole package—farm, stallion syndicate and all. Diaz had hardly come to town in 1983 as a big spender. He bought the mare Belle de Jour from breeder Rowe Harper, whose farm near Owensboro lay outside prime bluegrass country, for $60,000, and he had bought Spend a Buck for $12,500 after watching the colt in a field. Diaz, in his 4-H and FFA days, had been an excellent judge of cattle—he had won a national judging prize as a teenager—and he liked the way Spend a Buck was put together. He had also liked the way the colt used another, bigger colt, as a kind of shield, a bodyguard. It indicated to Diaz a precocious intelligence.

This time around, however, Diaz had gotten a different reception in Kentucky. With his blond wife Linda, their adopted Puerto Rican child Elliott, and his novice Italian trainer, he headed the sort of motley entourage that ordinarily would have found a cold reception in the heart of hardboot country. But with a calling card like Spend a Buck and a suitor like Will Farish, who rivaled Robert Clay as the most popular new stallion syndicator, Diaz had one of the hottest Derby tickets around.

"Having a horse like this opens a lot of doors, some of them that you don't want to go through," said Diaz. "There's all this talk of syndication, but I don't want to sell a hair on his head. Still, we've been treated well. We got a good box seat for the Blue Grass, and we got invited to lunch out on all the big farms. I had dinner the other night with Bunker Hunt. But it was the horse that's responsible, not us. I wouldn't have been treated like that unless I had come to the farms with a lot of money to spend."

Diaz was still a bit dazed about the improbability of it all. "In the insurance business, you can make your own luck, but in this one, you can't. This was a lightning bolt. I told Will Farish: 'I don't know why I have this horse. I don't have any right to this horse. You have a right to this horse—you've got the great mares, you've got the investment in the business. I haven't earned this.'"

Later that evening, when Diaz joined Andrew Rosen and Brian Hurst at the dinner table, the three had begun to boast about their horses, and Hurst proposed a $1,000 personal bet among the three concerning the outcome on Saturday. This was like the old times, when horse races settled disputes among wealthy owners. But then again it wasn't really like the old days. Only Dennis Diaz, of the three, still owned his horse outright. Hurst had already hedged his bets and split his risks; he was gambling on OPM—other people's money. He had already won the horse-trading contest, and he would be a winner whether his horse won or lost on Saturday.

The ownership of Eternal Prince had been sliced up like a pie, and I wondered if there would be enough magic as well as enough money to go around if Eternal Prince won. And how would the disappointment be split up among the partners and syndicate members if he lost? At least the Chief was still a "family" horse, even though his future had been divided up among wealthy strangers.

Later that night Diaz began to get cold feet and resolved to find Hurst the next morning to call off the bet.

Carl Rosen's odds

By dawn on Friday morning, however, as trainers and turf writers gathered in the coffee room on the backstretch, near the gap leading to the track, Brian Hurst's enthusiasm had not abated, and his boasts were beginning to sound like the ravings of a Derby-fever victim. "Eternal Prince is going to break Secretariat's record," said Hurst.

Wayne Lukas, still wearing the chaps he donned when riding his pony out on the track, had taken Tank's Prospect out to graze and offered some of his secrets for getting along with wealthy and powerful owners. "I think the reason George Steinbrenner and I get along is that I'm a former coach, and he understands the coaching philosophy. I find that sports people make excellent clients because they understand it's not an exact science; they understand winning and losing."

Tom Tatham, the young red-haired Texan who ran the small syndicate that owned the California horse Skywalker, had climbed the trainers' observation platform with his two sons to watch his horse work out. They were joined by a group of three locals who were discussing how much all the Derby horses were worth. "That horse Skywalker," said one of the men, "he's already worth $2 million, and if he wins the Derby, he'll be worth $25 million." Tatham smiled happily.

Meanwhile, the Chief had returned from his morning gallop to Barn 42, while Stephan's Odyssey headed for Barn 41. I didn't like the way the Chief looked—nor the way Roger looked, for that matter—but I attributed the perception to nerves. Earlier that week, Stephan's Odyssey had seemed to be favoring his right front leg, and I knew the vets had been working on him, but this morning his customary waddle seemed back to normal.

Andrew Rosen was waiting for the Chief, as was Freddie Bond, the "gambling advisor" who had been helping him with his bets the previous summer at Saratoga. "I've been following this horse since Saratoga," said Freddie. This time, however, there was a cool distance between the two men. Freddie, it seems, was currently involved in litigation with the Rosens over some alleged promises made by Carl that Freddie felt hadn't been kept. Freddie had found himself wishing that Andrew was a little bit more like his father.

Bond had met Rosen in Florida in 1969 at the dog races, and they had become friends. As Bond told it, "I liked golf, horses and women, and we liked a lot of the same things." Three years later, when Rosen was starting his new stable, he had asked Bond to come to New York as his "leg man." Said Bond, "I'd do anything for him—get him cigarettes, make bets."

In 1976, Bond had been in charge of a busload of people that Carl had invited to the Derby. Carl had decided to come down to look at Six Crowns, his new filly, and he had decided to make a Derby party of it. When the Rosen party arrived at Churchill Downs on the bus, Freddie got off and began to hand tickets to people as they came down the steps. However, a cop who was watching the proceedings arrested Bond as a ticket scalper, and Bond pleaded guilty and paid the fine on the spot rather than miss the Derby.

"Don't let anybody kid you," said Freddie. "What motivated Carl was getting to the betting windows. He'd get to know trainers, use his charm so they'd give him tips on the races.

"Carl was the kind of guy that liked to be abused. If you were nice to him, he'd run all over you. I remember when he played gin rummy with a guy that used the old peek-in-the-sky trick to beat him. The guy had a partner telling him what cards to lay down and pick up. Carl lost $60,000, and when he found out about the trick he loved it. He said, 'That's the first time any-body beat me out of anything.'

"I've never seen anybody as lucky as Carl was. He buys a couple of horses and he gets Chris Evert. You know, he used to buy $100 chances for a boy scout raffle, and he won it three times out of five. He won a Cadillac one year.

"We had the game beat all to hell. We used to make six-figure payoffs all the time. The day Secretariat ran in the Belmont, Carl had $8,000 in his pocket. We were down to $1,500 after the third race. But by the end of the day we had run it up to $125,000.

"The last bet Carl made was a month before he died. It was on a horse named Boom Soon. We got the double, the triple, and the horse won by eight lengths. I came to the hospital and laid $150,000 on the bed. Carl sat up and raised his fists in victory. I said, 'That's the last time we're going to be doing that together, Carl. You gotta take care of me.' And he did."

Bond looked over at Andrew ruefully. "If this had been Carl Rosen instead of this bunch," he said, "you'd see a lot more hype and excitement. People would be thinking this horse was the greatest thing since sliced bread."

Andrew, however, if he wasn't seeking out the limelight, was not exactly dodging it either. A UPI photographer had asked him to pose beside the Chief, and Andrew agreed. The Chief was in his stall, vigorously attacking his haynet, and seemed to be ignoring Andrew, who was trying to edge up beside him. "He's scared to death of the horse," joked Adrian Rosen. And at that moment the Chief lunged at Andrew, the camera catching him with his teeth bared. The resulting photo looked as though the Chief were giving Andrew a piece of his mind. It reminded me of Sam Rubin, John Henry's owner, who also enjoyed a rather tentative relationship with his cantankerous horse. John Henry had bitten his owner on more than one occasion. "You can't ever really know a horse like that," Rubin once said. "He won't let you near him."

Andrew, it seemed to me, was very much aware of his father's legacy. His own style, however, was very different. In the weeks preceding the Derby, he had quietly requested mountains of information and statistics from agent John Stuart, whom he had put on retainer. Andrew had asked Stuart to send him a complete computer analysis of previous Derby winners, including the frequency and duration of their workouts prior to the race.

What's more, the Rosens had been building an entourage this week that would have made Carl proud. Andrew had asked Robert Clay to get him more than two dozen Derby tickets to accommodate family and friends. And later that morning the whole gang would be making a trip by limo to Claiborne Farm to view Six Crowns and her new foal by Mr. Prospector, a half-sister to the Chief. Andrew wasn't entirely comfortable with the idea of the limo procession, however. "Just this once," he said.

Nevertheless, as the limos rolled through Claiborne's gates, the receptionist at the farm office remarked, "This reminds me of the Queen's visit last fall."

While the Rosens went off to lunch, I went to see Danzig. I walked out to his paddock with his groom, Ben Whaley, who was saying: "Dan is superintelligent. And he's as strong as he looks." The stallion walked willingly up to Whaley, who slipped a shank through his halter, but Whaley was careful to keep out of range of his teeth. "He likes to grab at you, like all the Northern Dancers," said Whaley. I was startled to see that one of the stallion's eyes was completely white. "He got something in his eye over the winter," said Whaley. "The vet sewed it shut to let it heal, but when he took the stitches out the sight was gone." With his massive chest, his pot belly, and his wild-looking blind eye, the arrogant stallion made a frightening image that did not suggest, but despotic power.

I tried to imagine the lithe, delicate Chief's Crown a few years hence, grown like his sire into a ponderous, muscled hulk, a kind of fat equine sultan whose only cares were servicing his harem and filling his belly. Whether or not he won the Derby, he would take his place among these lords of the pasture, to beget sons and daughters who would do his competing for him.

That afternoon I returned to the backstretch to see an old friend. I had learned that Snoltite had been sent up to Kentucky to Shug McGaughey's barn by syndicate manager Warner L. Jones, who also happened to be board chairman of Churchill

Downs. Jones had actually nominated the gelding for the Derby Trial the day after he broke his maiden in Florida, in order to give his partner Carl Pollard the thrill of having a Derby contender. But Snoltite, apparently, had run poorly after I left Florida, and Pollard would have to be content with watching the horse run in an allowance race on Kentucky Oaks Day, the day preceding the Derby.

Snoltite, McGaughey's stable foreman told me, had been recovering from a hoof infection, and he might not be in the best of moods. I found him sulking in the back of his stall, and at first he refused to lift his head. But suddenly he rushed up and popped his head over the stall webbing, and he put his head down to be scratched. In a moment, after ruffling my hair with his nose, he rested his head on my shoulder with a contented sigh. It was difficult to believe that my sweet-natured pal belonged to two of the most powerful men in Louisville.

Humana Institute, where Carl Pollard was vice-president, had built a new headquarters building downtown, designed by Michael Graves, that sparkled in postmodern splendor over the rest of a city whose depressed economy depended heavily on the annual boost of the Derby. Pollard, sensing that horses were the other big game in town, had bought season box seats in the Churchill Downs clubhouse right on the finish line.

Peter Fuller's Pyrrhic victory

Snoltite's race was to precede the Kentucky Oaks, the filly equivalent of the Derby. The Oaks had been shaping up as a showdown between Fran's Valentine, the best of the West, and Mom's Command, the best of the East. It had also been shaping up as a foreshadowing of the Derby, since Mom, like Spend a Buck, was a speed horse who intimidated her competition by sprinting to huge early leads, and she, too, had recently run a sensational race at Garden State.

The race would also have marked a dramatic return to Kentucky by Mom's owner and breeder, Peter Fuller, whose last trip here, in 1968, had involved the most controversial Derby in history.

Peter Fuller had begun flouting conventional Kentucky wisdom from the very beginning of his involvement with thoroughbreds back in 1951. Instead of breeding "the best to the best," he mated fillies he purchased in claiming races to stallions who were unproven on the racetrack. In 1965, however, he bred a claiming mare named Noor's Image to the great Native Dancer, and the result was a colt who was to make Fuller, in the words of one sportswriter, "the most famous Boston horseman since Paul Revere."

A month before the 1968 Derby, Dancer's Image had been scheduled to run in the Governor's Gold Cup at Pimlico. When Dr. Martin Luther King, Jr., was assassinated, two days before the race, Fuller—a longtime conservative Republican—was so disturbed by the murder and subsequent riots that he pledged to himself to donate his share of the Gold Cup purse to King's widow. Dancer's Image won impressively, and Fuller delivered a check for $62,000 to Coretta Scott King. He had intended, he said, "to show that a member of the Establishment cared about the murder of such a great man."

When word of the gift reached Kentucky, however, Fuller received a number of threats, including warnings against entering his horse in the Derby. A number of Kentuckians did not remember Dr. King with fondness; they remembered instead a King-led protest that had threatened to disrupt the running of a previous Derby. Nevertheless Fuller, a former Golden Gloves boxer, came to town with all his impulsive Yankee brashness, spoiling for a fight. He told reporters: "The Derby is what it's all about. I could be like some first-timers and say it'd sure be nice to finish fourth. But I'm in business. I'm going to tell it the way it is, pal, and the way it is is this: I know the Derby is made for this horse. I'm here to win."

Dancer's Image was going up against Forward Pass, Calumet's first Derby hope in ten years, and against Gleaming Sword, Sonny Whitney's hope to break a fourteen-Derby losing streak.

But Fuller's horse seemed destined to win that day. He was bumped at the start by Forward Pass, and he dropped back to last place. After a mile, when he began his move, the colt had eight horses ahead of him. In his fervor, jockey Bobby Ussery lost his stick at the three-sixteenths pole. Nevertheless, the big gray colt surged to the lead at the top of the stretch, and he held off Forward Pass by a length and a half.

In the photo taken of Fuller holding Dancer's Image in the winner's circle, his daughter Abigail is peering up in wonder at jockey Bobby Ussery, who is making a victory sign as he sits atop the horse. Tiny and blond, she caught the attention that day of a reporter for the Louisville *Courier-Journal:* "clutching a red rose to her bosom, looking as bewildered as she was happy, the little girl dodged and skipped to keep from being trampled. One of these days, when Abby Fuller is older, she will understand why all those grownups were making such a big fuss around her father, Peter . . ."

Fuller's jubilation, however, was cut short by an announcement three days later by track officials that a test of the horse's urine had revealed traces of Butazolidin, the anti-inflammatory drug now used almost routinely in Kentucky and other states. At the time, however, the drug was prohibited for pre-race use. Fuller flatly denied that either he or his trainer had authorized the use of the drug, and he volunteered to take a lie detector test.

Kentucky racing officials, however, ruled that the horse be disqualified from the race and that the purse be awarded to Forward Pass. In the Churchill Downs courtyard, where the names of the winners down through the years were painted in gold, the name of Dancer's Image was wiped out and the name Forward Pass inserted. Fuller, however, took the officials to court, and the Derby trophy stayed in storage for ten years, until Fuller had exhausted his legal recourses.

People who knew Fuller were convinced that he had done nothing wrong, and that somehow he had been framed. Derby historian Jim Bolus painted his lawn jockey in Fuller's colors in protest of the unfair treatment he felt Fuller had received in Kentucky, and the colors remain to this day. In the entry for 1968 in the Derby museum is a statement by turf writer Bill Reed that summarized the bafflement surrounding the affair. "Before I die," said Reed, "I'd like to know what really happened."

Fuller himself remained bitter, and he still carries around documents concerning the incident in his pocket. When he persisted in fighting the stewards' decision, collaring people with the fervor of the Ancient Mariner to tell them of the injustice wrought upon his horse, he developed a reputation as a stubborn New England eccentric who had failed to observe the proprieties and traditions of a sport whose ruling class is mostly New York blueblood and Kentucky bluegrass. Fuller received a number of messages through the grapevine, saying that he had done enough to disrupt racing and to cease and desist.

Fuller once told me, "They say time heals all wounds, but there are some that it doesn't."

Nevertheless, there was one thing that could assuage the wounds: another great horse. And since her debut, a small stakes race that she won by nineteen lengths, Mom's Command looked destined to be that horse. After a promising but uneven season in 1984, she had begun her three-year-old campaign with a series of races that pointed her out as a strong contender in the filly triple crown. Fuller, however, had made a decision concerning Mom's campaign that stirred up the embers of controversy again. He had chosen his daughter Abby to ride the filly. As he put it, his homebred daughter would be riding his homebred filly. "I don't mean to be presumptuous about it," said Fuller, "but if you want to get hearts and flowers about it, this is the kind of story that makes Liz Taylor and *National Velvet* take second fiddle."

Sportswriters had even speculated that Fuller might enter the filly in the Derby as the ultimate hearts-and-flowers scenario. Fuller, however, had decided to let the filly keep running against her own kind, and he had finally decided not to run her in the Oaks, choosing instead to prepare her for the filly triple-crown races.

And so it was that Fran's Valentine, the hard-luck filly, would be facing a field that seemed a cross section of the new world of racing: Folk Art, Will Farish's highly regarded filly; Wising Up, a Wayne Lukas charge; Rascal Lass, a stakes-winning filly owned by Motown's impresario Berry Gordy; and Savannah Slew, the daughter of Seattle Slew whom Allen Paulson had bought at Keeneland for the then-record auction price of two and a half million dollars. The longest shot in the field would be Foxy Deene, an erratic filly trained by maverick Ronnie Warren who had won Keeneland's Alcibiades Stakes at odds of 100 to 1 when the Queen had been present; she hadn't won a race since.

But first there was Snoltite's race, the Old Rosebud, in which, as usual, the big gelding was given little chance to win. "He's going to run big," I told the Great Handicapper, who had ignored Snoltite in his wagering. The favorite, Something Cool, had only run twice, but in his previous race he had beaten the promising Danzig colt Government Corner in very fast time. Snoltite was 10 to 1 in the morning line, and he went off at even longer odds, 20 to 1. This time, as he had in his big race at Gulfstream, he broke slowly, and he seemed to get lost in traffic. I had given up on him, but around the middle of the turn he started to make a big move. He swung very wide, coming out nearly halfway to the fence to get around a half dozen horses stretched out across the track. The favorite, Something Cool, was some ten lengths ahead of him. Snoltite took aim, and he began to eat up the ground between them. He kept gaining, gaining, but he ran out of ground. Something Cool crossed the wire a neck ahead of him. I was as proud as if he had won, as if he had been my horse instead of Carl Pollard's.

Frannie, too, ran as though she were evening some old score, although Foxy Deene, who had gone off at 40 to 1, almost caught her at the wire. I had bet on Frannie to win, and on Foxy Deene to place, and I was feeling smug until I ran into Andrew Rosen, who had had the sense to couple the two horses in an exacta. The exacta paid $291.20, and Andrew had made nearly $3,000.

I was beginning to think that Andrew was getting more like his father every day. However, that night, when he could have been the guest of honor at either of the two big Derby Eve parties, he and Adrian had Chinese food and retired to their rooms at Brown's Hotel.

It was his brother Douglas who took up the celebrity mantle. The older Rosen decided to attend Anita and Preston Madden's Jungle Fever party and arrived just as the volcano was erupting.

Preston Madden, owner of Hamburg Place Farm, was of the

bluest of bluegrass blueblood, but his wife Anita had established a reputation for flamboyance that made her the rival of that other assertive hostess, Marylou Whitney. At the Maddens', one was expected to dress in wild costumes and join in the madness. As Marylou Whitney described her rival, "She has things like nude girls coming up out of fountains painted gold."

At this year's party, with its jungle theme and punk leitmotif, leopardskin Spandex mingled with tuxedos and decolletage, while a hired Tarzan cavorted in a treehouse high above the fifteen hundred partygoers. As the stage-set volcano erupted, an alleged virgin wearing tennis shoes and a gold lamé gown was held up as a sacrifice. From the "mouth" of the volcano emerged a King-Kong-like hand that lifted the sacrificial victim toward the ceiling, as the band played "Devil with the Blue Dress On."

At the Whitneys', the theme was a more genteel "Rhapsody in Blue," with a giant wicker birdcage for Sonny and Marylou to greet the celebrities that they had captured as their guests. This year they included Bunker Hunt, Pat Wayne, Esther Williams, Rock Hudson and Kitty Carlisle. Mrs. Whitney had hired fortune tellers to entertain the guests, but no one was making any canny prognostications for the outcome the next day.

The party animals

On Saturday morning at dawn, as I drove to the track, a huge full moon was looming in the western sky. As I parked my car near the Derby barns, a small gray cat in heat was meowing plaintively, and I could hear the twangs of a Hank Williams, Jr., song coming from one of the small houses located across from the Derby section of the backstretch, where an all-night party was just winding down. The lawn was jammed with motorcycles, and an occasional tattooed biker would wander out, mount his machine and zoom off loudly. "I hope the horses like Hank Williams," said one of the night watchmen. "They were going at it all night over there."

As the morning wore on, the residents of the depressed little neighborhood of South Louisville prepared to ply their wares in the annual spree of creative commerce that surrounded Churchill Downs. Some sold barbecued ribs and beer, others battery-lit headbands or T-shirts with such mottoes as "To heck with the races! I came to party!" Some used their yards as parking lots, for which they charged five to ten dollars a car. Others set up tables for three-card monte. This year's favorite party hat appeared to be a kind of batting helmet equipped with a rack carrying two mint julep glasses, from which a drinking tube hung down to the lips.

By 10 A.M., the Derby-goers known as party animals began to arrive, those who had come to the Derby in the same spirit with which they would have gone to Ft. Lauderdale for spring break —to get drunk and obnoxious and ogle women, as though in tribute to the late John Belushi. They seemed oblivious to a young man just outside the gates who was holding up a large wooden cross. "God doesn't care who's gonna win the race," said the young man from Jacob's Well Full Gospel Church. "You should bet on the white horse—the one Jesus will be riding when he comes again."

A number of celebrants tried to smuggle their own booze into the track infield, including a woman who claimed to be carrying a wedding gift in her cooler, another woman pretending to be pregnant, and a man who had placed a bottle of Jim Beam into the middle of a molded salad. This year, however, because new track president Ralph Meeker had doubled ticket prices, the crowd was smaller and more sedate than in previous years. "When I saw all the preppies," said one security guard, "I knew we were going to have an easier time this year."

Early in the afternoon, the Great Handicapper and I left the grandstand to make a foray into the infield, and I was grateful for an escort. A group of rowdies had gathered around the group of port-o-cans that had been designated for women, and they were rating the looks of each woman as she emerged from the toilet. One of them began leading a cheer. "Give me a T!" he yelled. "Give me an I! Give me a T!" One of the toilet voyeurs held up a sign reading "S.U.Y.T.—Show us your tits!"

The action in the clubhouse, of course, took on a much different tone. On the sixth-floor Skye Terrace and scattered among private parties and box seats were Kentucky V.I.P.s and their celebrity klatches. Governor Martha Layne Collins had Gary

Hart in tow, while John Galbreath had brought former president Jerry Ford. Malcolm Hernan, chairman of Snyder's Department Store, had claimed the hottest guest: Mary Lou Retton.

I searched out Warner Jones, who was sitting in his private box perched over the finish line. "I just wanted to tell you how much I like your horse," I told him. "Which one?" he asked. "Snoltite," I said. "Oh, yes, Snoltite," said Jones. "You know, he's the only one left from that bunch of colts we bought together for the partnership," said Jones. "He was the cheapest one. There was a Nijinsky colt who died who was worth much more than he was. You never know how things are going to work out."

Meanwhile, back at the Derby barns, Roger was sitting in a folding chair outside the tack room, watching the biker party across the way that had begun to heat up again. "They haven't missed a beat all afternoon," he said. "And the guys in the infield. If they put cars in the race instead of horses, they wouldn't know the difference." Rhoman Rule's trainer, Angel Penna, Jr., had come around the shedrow to chat. "I hope you don't mind," he told Roger, "but when they asked me over there in the grandstand if there's anything I'd like to do at the last minute, I said it was put a padlock on Chief's Crown's stall."

Penna, like a number of other trainers, was concerned about the condition of the track. In anticipation of rain, the track had been rolled the night before, to seal it and prevent the absorption of moisture. But Penna was worried that the track maintenance crews had overdone it. "Last night they were harrowing and rolling, harrowing and rolling. And now the track is so hard and fast—it's like the interstate. I think they want a new track record today. The maidens were running in 1:09 and change and the little babies run 52 for 4 1/2 furlongs. It's crazy. The speed horses are going to have it their own way."

And then came the announcement over the loudspeaker. "Get your horses ready for the eighth race."

Eddie was already in the Chief's stall, giving the Chief a final rubdown that made him gleam. He seemed to relish the motion of the brush against the Chief's skin, giving him a chance to release his nervousness in activity.

At this point, I was so nervous myself that I was thankful I had no official tasks to perform. It was all I could do to keep the pen from falling out of my shaking fingers.

This was it. Eddie was leading the Chief out of his stall, with Roger and Andrew Rosen right behind him. I followed, scrambling to keep up, as Eddie led the way through the gap onto the track, toward the paddock located behind the grandstand. As we turned toward the grandstand, the noise of the crowd hit us in the face like a wave. Ahead of us, I could see horses rearing and dancing away from the noise. But the Chief, his ears perked, kept his head down, plunging ahead, as though into a strong wind. As the spectators saw him, the Derby favorite, the noise swelled, and we could hear individual cheers and taunts. "Get 'em, Eddie! Get 'em, Chief! Hey, he's lookin' at us! He's so small! He'll never make it!" The noise felt like an assault, and the crowd of 108,000 seemed to be bearing down on us.

The track was hard, as Penna had said; my shoes were hardly making a dent in the surface. Ordinarily, your feet can sink up to the ankle in the deep loam of a track.

Ahead of us, Proud Truth entered the paddock, and the crowd roared. He was prancing and dancing, his chestnut coat glimmering. A real crowd-pleaser. And then came Skywalker, whose name aroused a roar from *Star Wars* fans. Then Spend a Buck, who got away from his groom for a moment and started to dive into the crowd of owners in the center of the paddock. And then the Chief, who had more backers than any of them.

As the horses walked out onto the track for the parade to post, to the plaintive strains of "My Old Kentucky Home," I thought about the way the Derby, like certain other spectacles, had become part of the American psyche, part of the American dream of success: the Olympics, the Super Bowl, the World Series, the Miss America pageant. This event, however, more than any of the others was tied to a region, to a place full of paradoxes and contradictions.

This was a conservative, church-going state where, until this year, you couldn't gamble on the horses or buy liquor on Sundays. Yet it was a state whose very identity was intertwined with racehorses, tobacco and whiskey, and whose economy had long been dependent on the kind of "sins" that might be denounced from the pulpit: horseplaying, smoking and drinking. Anywhere else, that might be called hypocrisy, but here it was simply the way of the world.

The Derby, with its million-dollar deals, its Cinderella horses, and its julep-drinking dignitaries, embodied the fractured ideals of the bluegrass—of old-time chivalry and hardboot opportunism—the kinds of things that on this day, at least, when the horses pranced to post, faded into a blur of sentiment and brought a tear to the eye of tycoon and groom alike.

And so the horses headed for the starting gate, not knowing they had become part of American mythology. Into the gate went Irish Fighter and then the Chief, then Rhoman Rule and Tank's Prospect. Stephan's Odyssey made a lunge at Eternal Prince, attempting to savage him, and Pincay had to restrain his colt as the two horses were loaded. Then Encolure, I Am the Game, Floating Reserve, Spend a Buck, Proud Truth, Skywalker and Fast Account.

And then the one scenario that no one had considered. The gates buzzed open, and the Chief dived out first, leading for a few strides. Spend a Buck had broken second, and MacBeth let him surge by. It would have been suicide to try to run with him, and the Chief was not getting a good grip on the hard track. But where, where, where in the name of heaven was Eternal Prince? Where was the speed horse who was to challenge Spend a Buck for the lead? When the gates had opened, he had been turned sideways, distracted by the crowd and probably by Stephan's Odyssey. His jockey, Richard Migliore, did not try to hustle him to the front, but conceded the lead to Spend a Buck. It was a bad decision.

The race took a mere two minutes and one-fifth second, but the time stretched out like an eon. After that first five seconds, I knew it was over. Standing there in the clubhouse amid all those julep-sippers who had nothing but a betting ticket at stake, I felt strangely stoic. The horses thundered away from me, my dreams for a Derby winner thundering away with them.

At the first turn, Angel Cordero, atop the dark bay colt, was a blue blur in his Hunter Farm silks, five lengths ahead of the Chief. He had gotten Spend a Buck loose on the lead—a situation, I well knew, after the Great Handicapper's tutoring, that led to victory for speed horses on fast tracks. This was Spend a Buck's day of destiny, not the Chief's. After a moderate first quarter in 23 seconds, he had streaked six furlongs in 1:09 3/5. At the quarter pole he was six lengths ahead, and he had racked up the fastest mile in the history of the Derby: 1:34 4/5.

Don MacBeth realized, as Spend a Buck sped past him, un-challenged, that his only shot to win was to stay within close range, and he sent the Chief chasing after Spend a Buck, all the way around the track. But he had chosen the most stressful possible route for a horse like the Chief, who had to maintain the same killing fractions as the leader, but with no chance to relax, to settle into his stride, as the stretch-runners had. He had the discouraging prospect of Spend a Buck's flying heels in front of him, and the sound of thundering closers behind him.

In the middle of the far turn, MacBeth asked the Chief, who was already going flat-out, for more, and painfully, slowly, the Chief cut the lead down a length. Tank's Prospect had tried to pull even with the Chief, but began to drop back.

Stephan's Odyssey began to make his move along the rail at the top of the second turn, and he passed a crowd of tiring horses—Skywalker, Eternal Prince, Irish Fighter and Encolure. He came out at the bottom of the turn, bumping both Fast Account and Tank's Prospect. Proud Truth had begun a move on the outside, but he was not making up any ground on the leaders.

The Chief, with that determined, pounding stride, was not going to give up, even though the game was lost. But Stephan's Odyssey, with his perfect ride along the rail and his greater powers of endurance, took aim at the Chief, and he began to close the gap between them, as Fast Account, another endur-ance horse, began to close as well. This was what the Derby distance was all about—this extra, telling furlong. In the closing strides, Stephan's nose and then his neck and then his chest passed the Chief, and Fast Account had come up on his flank.

The Chief dug in for those last strides and held on for third.

Patty Johnson's horse, as she had predicted, had made the board. Proud Truth had moved up for fifth, Skywalker sixth, Tank's Prospect seventh. Eternal Prince, the package-deal horse, was next to last. The only horse he beat was I Am the Game.

Spend a Buck had run the third-fastest Derby in history, a time that had been beaten only by the Chief's grandsires, Secretariat and Northern Dancer. Dennis Diaz would join the owners of Black Gold, Carry Back and Canonero II as the outsiders with the Cinderella stories.

For the Chief, the dream was over. As I pushed my way through the crowd on the way back to the barn, the replay of the race appeared on TV screens, and I heard an inebriated young man say, "Chief's Crown is a piece of shit."

Back at the barn, Charlie Rose, who had believed so strongly in Proud Truth, who had ridden him with such patience for so many mornings, for so many months, was in tears. "I haven't felt like this since Alydar," he said. "It's not like another race that you win or lose. There's something so final about this. The horse never gets another chance, and you feel like you'll never be back again either. It's so hard just to get here." I knew what he meant.

Charlie tried to manage a smile. "I bought a bottle of champagne," he said, "that I was going to put up on the rail with a sign saying, 'Cheap—unused.' But it doesn't seem so funny now."

I saw Angel Penna, who just shook his head when I asked what had happened to Rhoman Rule. "He just wasn't good enough," he said sadly.

Roger didn't look as bad as I had expected, perhaps because he was so used to rehearsing those nightmare scenarios in his mind. "The way Spend a Buck ran today," he said, "there was nothing we could have done."

Robert Clay said that he felt the Chief hadn't been able to get hold of the track. Some horses, as John Veitch had been saying all week, just didn't like the Derby surface, and you had no way of knowing until the race.

Roger shook his head. "Every horse had to run on the same track," he said. He looked over at the Chief. "This horse was supposed to win."

The Rosens felt that the Chief, for the first time, had not "run his race," that their consistent little colt had let them down. But I knew that Roger was right, that there was little the Chief could have done to beat Spend a Buck that day. He would have had to run considerably faster than Affirmed, Seattle Slew, Spectacular Bid, faster than any Derby horse in history but two, in order to beat Spend a Buck. He had not run badly, in fact, and his time for the race was consistent with the speed figures he had been running all year. His time would have been good enough to beat Seattle Slew, the Bid, or even last year's winner, Swale. The Chief was a good horse. It just happened that Spend a Buck had been better on that day, and on that track. On the day that counted.

I had learned from the Great Handicapper that the outcome of a race was not a matter of random chance, that everything could be explained. But no handicapper could have predicted that Eternal Prince would break badly, nor that Spend a Buck would give one of the great athletic performances of the year. Nor could a handicapper have predicted how badly I would feel when the Chief lost.

I walked over the Shug McGaughey's barn and found Snoltite standing calmly in his stall, and I flung my arms around his neck and buried my face in his neck. He stood there, solid and real, accepting, in his "kindly enclyning," and I thought about the young trainer who had told me about the time his marriage was breaking up, how he would go out to his barn in the middle of the night, when the pain was strongest, and just stand next to his horses in their stalls, stand there in the dark, hearing them breathe, feeling their hearts beating. It did give you a kind of comfort.

II

The next morning the sun did come up, affirming yet again Woody Stephens's rule of racetrack recovery. At trainer Butch Lenzini's barn, George Steinbrenner was standing in front of Eternal Prince's stall, demonstrating the kind of patience he had never shown Reggie Jackson. Letting the colt nibble on his cuff, he said: "Poor little fella. You don't have many friends today."

At Barn 42, Dennis Diaz and Cam Gambolati were talking to reporters on one side of the shedrow, while the Chief's Crown contingent was continuing on the other side with business as usual. Eddie was talking quietly to the Chief. "You've got to lose sometime," he told him softly, brushing out his mane with a little extra tenderness. "You know," he told me, "he knows he lost. He's mad. He been wanting to kick somebody."

There were a number of humans who might also have wanted to kick somebody when Cam Gambolati revealed that morning that his horse had raced the day before on lasix, the diuretic that so often improved performance the first time it was used. Spend a Buck had bled a bit after a workout earlier in the week, and Gambolati had used the medication, he said, as a precaution. The information came as a surprise to trainers, turf writers and handicappers alike.

If this had been 1968, Spend a Buck, like Dancer's Image, would have been disqualified. But this was 1985, in the era of chemical tolerance, of drug-boosted Olympics and steroid athletes. I found myself counting the five lengths by which Spend a Buck had won, the margin by which some horses were said to improve in their first race using the medication. Probably it hadn't made a difference, since Spend a Buck hadn't needed to improve on his previous race, his blazing-fast Garden State. But then again, that was something that no one would ever know for sure.

Roger came out of the tack room, looking better than he had in the middle of Derby week. He gave the Chief an affectionate pat, and the Chief accepted the caress quietly. On the racetrack, waiting for disaster was somehow worse than the disaster itself. A moment later, when Roger walked by the Chief's stall, the Chief reached out to grab him. Roger laughed, and then I knew he was all right. "Well, we've got to start another day," Roger said cheerfully.

As we walked out to the track to watch Damascus Sam work out, he said, "The game has to go on." I asked him if he thought the Chief knew he lost. "Yeah, I think he did. But he's been beat before. He just gets more aggressive. He tries harder. This isn't over."

Later on, in the track kitchen, we joined Andrew Rosen for breakfast. "This has been a different kind of experience for us, losing," said Andrew ruefully. After the race, he had been pale with shock and disappointment, but he seemd to be learning the rudiments of the racetrack rebound, and now, like Roger, he was taking stock.

Before the Derby, the Chief had been "any kind of horse," a horse whose limits were not yet known. He had never been passed in the stretch. But now that he had shown that he was fallible, that under adverse conditions he could lose, it was time to think about strategy.

Woody Stephens had spotted Roger and he came over to the table. "Well, my exacta got messed up yesterday," he said. "I had the two Danzigs back to back. Spend a Buck got in the way."

Next it was Dennis Diaz and Cam Gambolati who walked in with a happy entourage. Roger got up from his table and greeted them with a handshake. "Congratulations," he said, and you could see that it hurt.

But Roger was already thinking about the future, about the second and third jewels in the Triple Crown. He had let the Derby go. As we walked back over toward the track, a reporter stopped him to ask about his plans for the Preakness, two weeks hence. "We shall meet again," he said with mock solemnity. "Time to reload. It's not going to be a walk-over."

It had begun to look, however, as though Dennis Diaz was not going to give Roger the satisfaction of a rematch. Winning the Derby had made Spend a Buck eligible for the big bucks in New Jersey, the $2 million bonus, and it had placed Diaz in an unprecedented quandary.

Ordinarily a Derby winner shipped directly to Baltimore and the Preakness, unless his handlers figured he had no shot at winning. That had been the case with Gato del Sol, a stretch-runner who would have had difficulty negotiating the sharp turns and hard, fast track at Pimlico.

Spend a Buck, however, was a speed horse who should love

the Pimlico surface. But Spend a Buck also loved the surface at Garden State, and if he won the Jersey Derby there on May 27 he would win $600,000, as well as the $2 million bonus Brennan was offering. Such a historic, record-setting payoff would move him up to second on the list of all-time thoroughbred money-winners, just behind the legendary John Henry, who had required seven years of racing to amass his record earnings.

The choice, obviously, wasn't simply between the $350,000 the colt could earn in the Preakness versus the $2.6 million at Garden State. Nor was it simply a choice between tradition and big bucks, between the Triple Crown and Robert Brennan's extravaganza.

The Triple Crown itself, the linkage between the Derby, the Preakness and the Belmont, had begun as a coincidence, when Sir Barton won all three races in 1919. Until then, the races had in common only the fact that they were limited to three-year-olds. Pimlico and Churchill Downs began to regard each as competitors for top horses, and each began to raise purses in order to draw the stars on the circuit. The Derby offered $20,000, while Pimlico offered $25,000. In 1920, Man o' War bypassed the Derby in favor of the Preakness because Samuel D. Riddle, his owner, had long harbored a phobia about entering his horses in the Derby, contending that the race was an interloper in the Eastern racing circuit. He considered Churchill Downs to be part of racing in the "West," which he despised because it was so far from the hallowed haunts of high society.

Nevertheless, despite these regional and social differences, the Triple Crown had become a sacred tradition, one of the few sources of unity in the racing world as well as a proving ground for the breeding shed. But in recent years, winning those races had also meant a syndication bonanza. That was where the money was, in the multimillion-dollar syndications, not in the purses for the big races.

And so it was that Diaz found himself with a potential syndicate superstar, whose future value could be computed in several different ways. This was bluegrass economics at its most complicated.

Chick Lang, the general manager of Pimlico racetrack, a

husky, blunt-spoken man with a military crewcut, had come by the Derby barns to offer Diaz his own set of blandishments to counter those of Brennan. Lang talked less about tradition than he did about dollars. Diaz would lose most of the $2 million in taxes, he said, while a victory in the Preakness would increase the colt's value by at least $2 million.

Ironically, it was Will Farish, Jockey Club official and host to Queen Elizabeth, who began to swing Diaz away from tradition and toward Garden State glitz.

Will Farish had made one of the quickest and most successful entries ever into the bluegrass ruling class. His grandfather, William Farish, a founder of Humble Oil, had raced horses, and his aunt, Martha Gerry, had raced the great Forego. Farish, however, a native of Houston, had started out as a polo baron and only incidentally became interested in racing through friends and through his father-in-law, Bayard Sharp. In 1972 he had caught some of that elusive racing lightning himself when his mud-loving colt Bee Bee Bee had taken the Preakness from Riva Ridge on a muddy track.

Farish told Diaz that if he were to become involved with the horse, he would want him to run in the Jersey Derby, reasoning that the record-setting earnings would mean more in the long run than a victory in the Preakness.

For Gambolati and Diaz, of course, there were other considerations as well. Better a bonus in the hand than a Belmont in the bush. Chances were that, even if the colt won the Preakness, he would not be able to go the mile and a half of the Belmont, especially without the use of lasix, which was prohibited in New York. And it was the Belmont, of all the Triple Crown races, that breeders respected most. Moreover, the colt had come back from the Derby exhausted, and he was not cleaning up his feed bucket the way he should. The Preakness left him less than two weeks to recover, while the Jersey Derby would give him an extra nine days.

Chick Lang knew the game was up when Robert Brennan sent his private jet to Kentucky for Diaz, and on Monday morning, Spend a Buck headed for his stall at Garden State. "Sure, I'd love to have Spend a Buck," Lang told a reporter, "but I can't compete with Brennan. I drive a Ford, cut my own grass, and bring a sandwich to work in a paper bag. But when I go to sleep, I rest, and when I look into the mirror to shave, I don't have to apologize to anybody. I don't feel guilty."

On Tuesday, Diaz made it official. Spend a Buck would be bypassing tradition and going straight to the gate at Garden State.

CHAPTER 10

The Hollow Crown

. . . what foul dust floated in the wake of his dreams . . .

—F. Scott Fitzgerald, *The Great Gatsby*

I

IT HAD BEEN a bad spring in Baltimore, with the Orioles on a losing streak and the local savings and loan institutions in a state of crisis. The absence of Spend a Buck had been the latest blow in a cycle of defections and defaults in a city struggling with urban renewal and at a track struggling with faltering attendance.

The Maryland Jockey Club, which founded Pimlico in 1870, was the oldest sporting organization in America. It dated back two hundred forty-two years, back to the colonial cavaliers, and its traditions were both elite and populist. George Washington was known to have frequented Jockey Club races at Annapolis, and Andrew Jackson was a member of the Club when its headquarters were first moved to Baltimore. Fans, however, knew that tradition would not save them, not after the Colts had deserted their city for Indianapolis without so much as a salute.

One of the most popular Pimlico posters featured a view of the track with the motto: "You Can Still See Baltimore Colts."

In the days following the Derby, Chick Lang had taken up the mantle of another sharp-spoken Baltimore native, H. L. Mencken. Bitter at Spend a Buck's defection, he told the Baltimore *Sun* that Robert Brennan reminded him of "a snake oil salesman who comes into town selling you something that will take the spots off your dalmatian. He winds up years later in a saloon in Dry Gulch, New Mexico, doing something else."

When I arrived in Baltimore for Preakness week, the skies were gray and leaden, and the mood at the track was quiet. With the absence of Spend a Buck, the atmosphere was that of Los Angeles after the Russians announced their boycott of the Olympics. Of the horses who had run in the Derby, only the Chief, Eternal Prince, Tank's Prospect and I Am the Game were to attempt the speed-demanding Pimlico surface.

Some reporters were echoing Lang, decrying the death of tradition, forecasting the death of the Triple Crown. It all seemed tied in somehow with the advent of the free agent, the use of the designated hitter in baseball, the disappearance of the non-giant in basketball. Others were pointing out that the oldest tradition in racing, as in other sports, was not the Triple Crown or team loyalty, but winning. Traditions in sports often began and ended fortuitously, to be replaced by other instant verities.

Stan Hodge's treasure

Thursday morning, at the long, rambling, salmon-pink Preakness barn, where competitors for both the Preakness and the Black-Eyed Susan Stakes for fillies were stabled, the stalls were full of Preakness-fever horses, horses whose owners had been afflicted with a dreaminess akin to Derby fever. There was Tajawa, the colt who had cost his three Kentucky owners something over three thousand dollars at auction. Tajawa was to be ridden by Patricia Cooksey, the first female rider in the history of the Preakness. She had earned the mount by discovering, as no male rider had, that the horse despised the whip, and that he ran better without the prodding of the leather and fiberglass stick. And then there was the northern California horse, Hajji's Treasure, who had been the first local horse ever to win the California Derby at Golden Gate Fields, near San Francisco.

Hajji's owner, Stan Hodge, was a New Jersey native who had always dreamed of moving to California and owning racehorses. In recent years he had succeeded in both ventures, moving his insulated-glass business to Pleasanton, California, and beginning a small farm nearby. Hodge, whose childhood, street-tough nickname had been Hajji, incorporated the name into those of all his horses. Hajji's Treasure, which had cost him $9,200, had been his first big horse. In the California Derby, Hajji had gone off at odds of 25 to 1, and Hodge and his family felt that they had been ignored by the bigwigs at Golden Gate. They had been assigned the worst table in the owners' section of the clubhouse, and after the horse won, no one came over to congratulate them. Finally, a waiter had come over to offer his best wishes, saying, "Crummy table, but the best horse won."

Hodge had then decided to go for it all—to enter his horse in a classic race. Hodge would have to pay a twenty-thousand-dollar supplementary entry fee to get Hajji into the Preakness, as well as another twenty thousand or so to transport the horse to Baltimore, but he had decided it was worth the gamble. So far, however, things were not coming up Black-Eyed Susans. The previous week, the horse was vanned the four hundred miles from San Francisco to Los Angeles, then placed on a plane to New York. The plane, however, had made stops at Portland, Salt Lake City and Louisville before arriving in New York. The horse was then vanned the two hundred miles down to Baltimore, arriving at nearly midnight, more than twenty-four hours after he had first set out on his journey.

Compared to the last-minute entries and wish-and-a-prayer horses, the Chief seemed a privileged veteran. He had been stabled in the stall customarily reserved for Derby winners who had come to town to continue their Triple Crown campaign. Tacked over the stall was a list of previous legendary occupants: Carry Back, Northern Dancer, Forward Pass, Secretariat, Seattle Slew.

When I arrived at the barn, Eddie had just finished applying poultices and bandages to the Chief's front legs. Roger was in

New York seeing to the new two-year-olds that arrived at his barn. "This horse been bad all week," said Eddie as he worked on the Chief. "Bit me right here and here," he said, showing the black-and-blue marks on his arms. I asked Eddie if the Chief had shown any remorse. "No," said Eddie. "He mean everything he do. He don't play."

As he had during Derby week, Eddie had stayed near the Chief night and day, not even leaving to go to the track kitchen. "I haven't slept since I been here," he said. "If you're a groom," he said—"if you're a groom," he said again, emphasizing the noun—"and the boss leave you in charge, you have to be alert all the time."

Eddie had been feeling downcast since the Derby. It had been a sad time in those days after the Chief lost the big race. First he had lost Lord Darnley and then Damascus Sam. Lord Darnley, the veteran stakes-winning gelding and Eddie's special pet, had finally been retired. He had livened up the barn with his passion for doughnuts and other assorted snacks, including, once, Eddie's ham-and-cheese sandwich. "I miss him," said Eddie. "I'll never forget the time he grabbed that sandwich. He had mustard smeared all over his mouth. Roger looked at him and says, 'Jesus Christ! What'd he get into this time?'"

Lord Darnley, at least, had retired sound and healthy. Damascus Sam, however, the strapping, handsome chestnut colt, was dead. After a bone chip had been discovered in one of his knees, he had been scheduled for the same kind of operation that Spend a Buck, Smile, and so many other colts of his generation had undergone. But he had never woken up from the anesthesia; he had died on the operating table.

It was painful to think back about that happy procession at Keeneland, when the Chief, fresh from victory, was leading the way to the van for the trip to Louisville, with Damascus Sam and Lord Darnley following. Everything had seemed possible on that day, and yet there had been that undercurrent of melancholy. *Because as the flower of the grass he shall pass away.*

Eddie was cheering himself up by thinking about those new colts that had arrived in New York. "I have two new colts," said Eddie. "Both handsome. Both strong. One by Seattle Slew and one by Halo." His eyes lit up as he described them. The whole cycle was beginning again, the cycle of hope and anticipation, even before this one had run its course.

Later that morning, at the drawing for post positions, the absence of Spend a Buck seemed more cause for talk than the presence of the Chief or his competitors. Guest celebrity Mickey Rooney, who was introduced as a former jockey (in fact, he did exercise the legendary Seabiscuit in his younger, trimmer days), took the microphone and said gravely, "No one can take away the thrill and solemnity of the Preakness, not even Spend a Buck." Rooney then proceeded to tell a few bad jokes, succeeding only in increasing the mood of melancholy. Boston sportswriter Mike Madden later wrote, "It was painful . . . Mickey seemed off rhythm, out of synch, many in the audience uncomfortable as Rooney chattered onward, groping for laughs. It is no longer Mickey Rooney's day, just as it is no longer Pimlico's."

The next morning Roger had returned from New York, and a rooster was crowing as I joined the Rosens at the Preakness barn. This rooster, unlike many on the backstretch, was still in possession of the feathers on its legs, signifying that it did not lead a double life as a cockfighter.

Lisa Rosen was telling Roger about a psychic that her mother Shirley had consulted about the Chief. "They took this big, eight-by-ten glossy of the Chief," she said, "and cut it up. The psychic said that the Chief had been sick and that he had almost died during the Derby, but that he would win the next two races."

Roger mounted the stiff-legged pony Popeye and led the way to the track, with Cigar and the Chief following. The Chief trotted dutifully behind Roger once around the track the wrong way, then turned around for his regular gallop. He opened his mouth, as if to protest the restraint of the bit, and he seemed full of pent-up energy.

As we were watching in the stands, Andrew's cousin David was recalling the Preaknesses he had attended with Carl in the old days. In 1974, David had bet eight thousand dollars on Little Current, who had gone out at 13 to 1 and won by seven lengths.

Andrew, however, was following his father's example of look-ing for tips. He asked a distinguished-looking black man stand-ing next to us if he had any winners for the races that afternoon. The man took Andrew's *Racing Form,* turned to the feature race, the Black-Eyed Susan, and circled the name of Micki Bracken, the Cinderella filly who had made her way up from the claiming ranks to stakes-race status. She was owned by a group of investors who called themselves Thoroughbred Breed-ers, Inc. I had seen her run in Florida, and she was a very game, likeable filly. Andrew, however, already had his picks for the race. "We're throwing out Contredance. It's going to be Denver Express and Koluctoo's Jill, cold."

The Chief's defeat had shocked the Rosens, who had begun to take winning for granted, but it had not dampened Andrew Rosen's new-found fascination for the game. Nor had it so far dampened the ongoing family reunion that the Chief's suc-cesses had caused. Their racing claque was growing to Carl Rosen proportions—tomorrow there would be fifty-four people in their party, cheering the Chief.

Later that morning, at the Alibi Breakfast for owners, trainers and press, the annual event took on greater solemnity than usual. Thomas Bancroft, New York blueblood and Jockey Club official, had come down to Baltimore to lend his support for the Preakness. "I wanted to come down here to express my faith in the Triple Crown," said Bancroft. "I think it's too premature to weigh the events of one year versus the tradition of fifty years. We stand for a strong Triple Crown." Bancroft also admitted that racing officials of the Triple Crown tracks were also consid-ering a bonus, à la Brennan, for winning the three races.

It was Howard Cosell, however, who put things in their proper light. In his most pompous tones, Cosell announced: "It will not resolve the conflict in Lebanon. Apartheid will still reign in South Africa. Western civilization will not crumble by the absence of Spend a Buck."

When the owners and trainers were queried for quotes, Brian Hurst volunteered. "There are some things I'd like to tell An-drew Rosen and Roger Laurin. But I can't right now." Appar-ently George Steinbrenner had told him to button his lip—no boasting. Said one turf writer, sitting next to me, "If Steinbrenner is the most responsible adult in the room, you know you're in trouble."

Later that morning, when a local sheriff tacked on a lien next to Eternal Prince's stall, Hurst was more subdued. Trainer Butch Lenzini allegedly owed some money to the auction firm of Fasig-Tipton, and one of their lawyers had gotten overzealous, deciding to keep Eternal Prince from running until the debt was paid. After considerable hubbub that afternoon, a livid George Steinbrenner made a few phone calls, and the lien was removed.

Later that day I decided to go to the track for the Black-Eyed Susan, to see if Micki Bracken could continue her success story, or if Andrew Rosen would score with his big perfecta. Before the race, I walked down to the indoor paddock with Dell Hancock. As we watched the fillies being walked around the ring, we both noticed that Micki Bracken was favoring her left front leg, putting it down gingerly on the springy paddock surface. I thought at the time that if she were my filly I would have scratched her from the race.

As it happened, Andrew did win his big perfecta. But Micki Bracken didn't make it. About midway down the backstretch she was running with the leaders, but she faltered, terribly, her ankle so shattered that the hoof was hanging on by the skin alone. As the horse ambulance made its way around the track to pick her up, I ran out of the press box, full of rage.

I headed for the Preakness barn, where the ambulance was headed, hoping somehow that Micki Bracken could be saved. When I reached the barn, the vets were tending the filly in her stall, debating whether to put her down to end her pain or to send her to the New Bolton medical center, over an hour away by van, for an operation that had a ten percent chance of success. The filly had been insured, and one of the vets represented the interests of the insurance company. Her trainer Enrique Lopez was standing outside, his face ashen.

I walked away, and as I burst into tears I ran into Bill Mooney, a writer and editor for the *Thoroughbred Record*, whom I had gotten to know in Kentucky.

Mooney looked at me calmly and took me aside for a lecture. "If you go around crying on the backstretch," he said, "you'll lose your credibility. You've worked hard, and the guys in the press box accept you. But if you get emotional about this, they'll dismiss you as just a girl. You have to be dispassionate about these things."

Mooney tried to put things in perspective. "My folks come from the circus," he said, "and I used to see terrible things happen, animals being abused. I saw a woman fall from a trapeze who should never have gone up. It's that way in all sports. Athletes don't seem to know when to stop. Look at Muhammad Ali now. Almost all athletes abuse themselves."

Mooney was also angry at the implication that other writers didn't care. "You're wrong if you think we don't care. But this is a tough and dirty business."

Mooney was implying, I think, that Leroy Jolley was right all along about the nature of the game, and I was one of those in short pants not willing to accept the pain that inevitably accompanied the payoffs in racing.

But as I saw more and more casualties on the track, both human and equine—the damaged humans who anesthetized their pain with alcohol, bets and clichés; the horses who kept running despite their bum ankles or negligent handlers—the terms of the pain/payoff quotient kept shifting. In these new terms, just surviving seemed to be a victory of sorts.

The next afternoon, in the hours before the Preakness, I saw Stan Hodge in the V.I.P. room, where he was standing at the bar, trading stories with Jack Mann. I asked him how his horse was doing, and he joked: "I didn't see him this morning. I've been spending my time drinking and partying and talking to reporters. I don't have time for horses." He knew that I was working on a book about racing, and he asked me if I had a working title. "The Hopeful," I said. "Ah," he said, "as in daydreams. I know all about that."

In a moment, TV sportscaster Jim MacKay came over to greet Hodge, whom he had met earlier. "Stan," he said, "why don't you join me? I'd like you to meet some of my friends."

Back at the barn, the contenders appeared to be in preparation for a boxing match rather than a race. Cutlass Reality was standing with ice bags wrapped around his legs, while I Am the Game was poised in a huge tub of ice. Eternal Prince's legs were attached by hoses to a refrigerating machine.

As the horses were led from the backstretch to the special outdoor paddock located in the track infield, the Chief was acting uncharacteristically rambunctious. He kicked up his heels in front of the crowd of eighty thousand or so, and as the horses were led around in a circle he did it again, sending spectators flying for safety. Tajawa was also feeling his oats, and he almost got away from his groom, heading into a small group of well-dressed women. One woman jumped away fearfully, then turned to her tall male companion angrily. "You promised you'd protect me," she said accusingly. "That horse almost got me." She looked very familiar, and with a start I realized it was Ethel Kennedy.

As the starting gate buzzed open, the scenario unfolded as most handicappers had said it would. This time, Eternal Prince, ridden by the great Chris McCarron, broke well and dashed to the lead. But this was where Roger and Don MacBeth had planned a surprise. The Chief hung back and let the other speed horses rush past him: Tajawa, Sport Jet and Hajji's Treasure. Those three horses chased Eternal Prince around the first turn, with Hajji's Treasure forced to the outside but trying desperately to keep pace. As he entered the backstretch he was even with Tajawa, but then things seemed to slow down, and I thought I was having a flashback from the day before. Not far from the spot where Micki Bracken had faltered, Hajji seemed to stumble, but he kept trying to run, and then I realized that his ankle was shattered. The Chief, who had been a few strides behind him, faltered for a split second in reaction to Hajji's breakdown, but then swept by, and then the rest of the field.

Eternal Prince had set an extremely fast pace, going the first quarter in $22^2/5$, the half in $45^1/5$. It was a pace that had destroyed Hajji's Treasure, who had tried so gamely to keep up. He was going even faster than Spend a Buck had in the Derby, and the Chief seemed to be chasing the ghost of Angel Cordero and the bay colt that had beaten him. This time, however, MacBeth had started pushing the Chief at the top of the far turn, and the Chief was making a very big move, sweeping around the speed horses at the bottom of the turn. He dug in as he tried to stay on course around the hairpin curve. And he was doing all this as Eternal Prince continued to set a blazing pace, going the mile in 1:34$^{1/5}$. The Chief had run the fastest quarter of his career, and he had caught Eternal Prince, blowing by him at the top of the stretch. There he was, all alone in the stretch, and Roger Laurin raised his fist in triumph. He had beaten the ghost horse.

But again, there was the dark horse that had never been thought. Pat Day was giving Tank's Prospect an astonishing ride. Wayne Lukas had told Day to hit the horse liberally, that he could take a lot of "punishment," and the usually restrained Day was whacking Tank as though the colt were made of steel. The colt responded with a burst of speed that began to eat up the ground between him and the Chief. MacBeth had put his whip away, and he was giving the Chief a hand ride to the finish. At the last moment, when he saw Tank's nose at his boot, he raised the whip. But it was too late. The Chief began to come back, but it was Tank's nose in front when the horses crossed the wire.

Both horses had beaten the official track record of 1:53$^{3/5}$ and tied Secretariat's unofficial record of 1:53$^{2/5}$. A stride after the horses passed the wire, the Chief had regained the lead. But it was too late.

The Chief had given the greatest performance of his life. A truly great race that measured up to both his grandsires who had won this race. And yet he had lost.

Back at the barn, a team of vets were putting Hajji's leg in a splint. The decision had been made, as it had been that morning with Micki Bracken, to send the horse to New Bolton for an operation to save the leg. And as with Micki Bracken, the prognosis for success was only ten percent. Micki Bracken had lived through the night, and it was decided that she could endure the trauma of the operation. And so far she had. The word from New Bolton was that the operating team that had spent the day working successfully on the filly was taking a dinner break before preparing for the arrival of Hajji.

As Hajji was loaded into the van for the journey to Pennsylvania, Stan Hodge wrapped his arms around his daughter Jean, who was crying inconsolably. "I'm going to lose him," said Hodge, breaking into tears himself. "He was so sound, so fucking sound. I didn't care if he won the race. I don't care if he never races again. All I wanted to do was get him back safe. I just want to take him home."

This time, Roger was not ducking the press, but remained outside the shedrow, leaning on the fence, as though talking to reporters might act as a kind of catharsis, a way of making sense of what had happened.

As usual, Roger was not going to make excuses nor assess blame. The Rosens were unhappy with MacBeth's ride, certain that if he had kept hitting the colt with the whip, he would have won. Reporters were already using a nickname to describe MacBeth: MacDeath. But Roger refused to blame MacBeth. "This stings," he said. "It is discouraging. The horse ran the race I wanted . . . except for the finish. But we have no excuses today. None at all. Our horse ran all the way to the wire."

The Chief was back in his stall, and I could hear Eddie talking to him. "You're still my big horse," said Eddie firmly.

II

A week later, the focus was on Robert Brennan, Garden State Park and Spend a Buck. Would the horse who had forsaken tradition for bucks win the big cash payoff? Brennan had hoped that his bonus would lead to the kind of publicity his track was getting, but he could never have envisioned the sequence of events that had transpired this spring. Spend a Buck had been a phenomenal stroke of luck, the lightning in the bottle.

On Sunday night, Jersey Derby eve, as I was driving down to Brennan's "Track of the Twenty-first Century" on the Jersey Turnpike, idling past the exits to Newark, the exhaust fumes of holiday traffic merging with the pink haze atomized from shoreline chemical plants, Bruce Springsteen's "Jungleland" was playing on the radio. It was a strange place for two New Jersey visionaries to coincide, Springsteen the savior of rock and roll and Brennan the prophet of racing future.

Brennan's fast track

Brennan had been born in a place close to this juncture of poverty, chemicals and traffic. The son of a salesman, he had been raised with his eight brothers and sisters in a five-room apartment in Newark's North Ward. Brennan's father, Henry, had been a resourceful sort who never made it big. He sold neckties; he peddled turkeys around the neighborhood at Thanksgiving. After a son, aged twenty-two, was murdered, and Henry's wife, just fifty-three, died the night of the funeral, the elder Brennan unexpectedly entered a monastery and was ordained, living out the last ten years of his life as a Roman Catholic priest.

Meanwhile young Robert, who revered his father, was demonstrating his own sort of resourcefulness. The day after his graduation in 1962 from St. Benedict's Prep in inner-city Newark, he began classes at Seton Hall University in South Orange, arranging his classes so that he could work a seven-hour shift taking classified ads for the Newark *Evening News*. By the time he graduated, two years later, he was managing the classified ads department. Less than ten years later, he was to hit his first million-dollar score and turn his life into one of those American-dream stories similar to the dare-to-be-great commercials with which he was to flood the nation during televised sporting events.

Along the way, however, Brennan encountered his first problems with pedigree and elite traditions. As a teenager he had gotten interested in racing, and he would ride the bus or take the subway into New York to watch the races at Aqueduct, Belmont, or the now defunct Jamaica Park. He began to dream, not so much of making the big betting coup, but of becoming one of the fashionable owners who mingled in the paddock before the races. In his accounting work, he became intrigued with another bastion of old money and tradition: Wall Street. As Brennan told a reporter, the Wall Street of those days "was dominated by great-grandsons. They all went to Harvard or Yale, and the attitude was, 'Let's start drinking together at four o'clock and, oh, if you see anyone on the horizon trying to break into our club, squash him.' "

Brennan became the quintessential Gatsbyesque outsider, a man driven by the desire to find his own way to the top, to build his own mansion by the water, to challenge the clubs and cliques that denied him entry. And like Gatsby, a pragmatic dreamer, he proceeded deliberately, step by step. If Jay Gatsby, however, had been motivated by hope, by "romantic readiness," Brennan was spurred on by positive thinking.

Brennan developed his own personal code of conduct, a kind of morale-boosting cheer, of which Norman Vincent Peale and Robert "Hour of Power" Schuller would have approved. This was how it went:

S is self confidence.

C is courage.

H is honesty.

R is responsibility.

I is impatience (with yourself, not others).

D is determination.

E is enthusiasm.

Brennan named his first horse Newkidontheblock, and his second, Schride. Brennan's dream, however, was soon tainted with controversy. Like Gatsby, he had chosen an unorthodox way to success. In 1969, he joined Mayflower Securities, a small, troubled New Jersey firm; within three years, he was president.

Jersey Securities was born the day that Mayflower was suspended for selling shares in a bankrupt electronics company. Brennan, who was not held responsible for the firm's transactions, bought Mayflower's office in Red Bank, and set out with five brokers to find a new market of stock-buyers—the little guys looking for high returns who would invest in what Brennan liked to call "emerging companies." Sometimes, however, Brennan himself had already bought the stock, so that he benefited both by the commission on the sales transactions and by the inflation of the value of the stock. In 1979, Brennan came under scrutiny of the SEC, and in 1984, *Forbes* magazine charged in a lengthy profile of Brennan that his company's success was due to "a marriage of greed and gullibility" on the part of his customers.

Meanwhile, Brennan had learned that he could apply his brokering techniques to the horse business: raise capital by selling bargain-basement shares, preferably shares that you already owned yourself. By 1985 he was claiming that shares in his International Thoroughbred Breeders, in which he was principal stockholder, had grown in value from one to thirty-five dollars. Through ITB, he was able to indulge in all the big-money, high-risk aspects of horse racing: broodmares, stallion shares, racing partnerships. But ITB had also allowed him the ultimate racing indulgence: his own racetrack. And with Spend a Buck, he had his own racing star.

Like Gatsby, he could stand on the veranda of his palatial home and look across the lawn, down to the dock, to the lights glimmering across the water. If Daisy with the voice that sounded like money finally eluded him, he would have the satisfaction of throwing glittering parties.

As I continued down the Jersey Turnpike, the traffic finally began to thin, and spuming towers and storage tanks gave way to housing developments and farms and then to the single-story malls of suburbia. I was approaching the town of Cherry Hill and Robert Brennan's vision of racing future. Past a series of sprawling, convention-sized restaurants and a billboard sign that inquired, "Will Spend a Buck win $2,600,000?" the outlines of Garden State glowed like a gamblers' oasis, a cross between a casino and a theme park. The "crystal paddock," so named for its translucent roof, shimmered in the night like a lost wing of the Reverend Robert Schuller's see-through Crystal Cathedral, the ultimate monument to positive thinking.

In Schuller's sunlit cathedral, one felt that there were no dark nights of the soul, no ancient hierarchies of holiness haunting the pulpit, and in Brennan's Plexiglas paddock one felt that the ancient hierarchies of pedigree and privilege had been banished, including the unkempt losers who made up the bottom of those hierarchies at the track.

My hotel, the Cherry Hill Inn, located just across the way from the old gatehouse entrance to Garden State, appeared to have been infected by Brennan's schizoid approach to equine tradition. In the Jockey's Club lounge, where an impassioned crooner was singing "Girl from Ipanema" to piano and bass accompaniment, racing silks were framed and spotlighted on the green baize walls like relics. Elsewhere were oversize horse-and-hound paintings of the solemn hunt-club school, painted by one Reginald Baxter. In the lobby was a hand-lettered sign directing horseplayers to a "Professional Handicapping and Money Management/Hi Teck Computer Handicapping Seminar," directed by a Mr. Armond Cannella.

The next morning I walked over to the backstretch to watch Spend a Buck gallop in preparation for the race that afternoon. He was considered a shoo-in for the trophy and the bonus, given his affinity to the Garden State surface and the track record of his opponents. The quality of his competition was considered far inferior to the Kentucky Derby horses he had beaten. Only one of them, I Am the Game, had actually competed in the Derby, and only one, Skip Trial, had run in the Preakness. There were only two real possibilities for an upset: Woody Stephens's steady second-stringer Creme Fraiche, whom Woody had kept out of the Derby, and the stretch-running El Basco, who had recently won the Withers with a late burst of speed. The odd horse in the field was Huddle Up, a Wayne Lukas sprinter who had only run six times before.

When Spend a Buck emerged from the barn with his blue shadow roll and blue polo bandages, it was as though Robert Redford had emerged from a limo. He was greeted by a buzzing crowd of reporters and paparazzi flashes. Everywhere I looked were people wearing blue satin jackets sporting the Hunter Farm logo with the name Spend a Buck arched over it.

I looked over at the adjacent barn, and there was Wayne Lukas, standing by Huddle Up as the colt grazed on a sparse patch of grass, and the intense look he gave Spend a Buck did not reveal admiration. Only a week before, Lukas had been at the center of all the commotion with Tank's Prospect, and he seemed to begrudge the displacement.

Although he denied the charge, most turf writers felt that Lukas had entered Huddle Up merely in a kamikaze mission, to push Spend a Buck early in the race so another horse, any other horse, would win the race. If he succeeded, Spend a Buck's prestige would drop, while that of Tank would rise, and chances were a tired Spend a Buck would not even be entered in the Belmont.

As Spend a Buck walked onto the track, a young man in the clockers' stand yelled out to Dennis Diaz, "Hey, Mr. Diaz, can I get one of those jackets?" A moment later, as Spend a Buck began to head slowly around the track the wrong way, a horse who had thrown his rider came hurtling in his direction, but passed Buck safely.

Back at the barn, Diaz was trying to stay calm as he reflected on the way his life had been turned upside down. "I don't mean to complain, but the Derby changed things, for good and bad. We've been criticized right and left, offered this and that. Since we've only been in this thing less than two years, we haven't had a chance for a trial run, to try things out." He broke off, as a horse from the adjacent barn that was being bathed broke loose from his hot-walker and made a beeline for the shedrow, where Spend a Buck was walking quietly. He ducked his head, then charged into the barn. He passed Buck once, miraculously without collision, then was headed off by a groom. "That's two loose horses," said Diaz grimly.

Later that day, Garden State welcomed a crowd of more than thirty-five thousand who were greeted at the gates by a Dixieland band. Inside, after they had confronted a huge bank of escalators, they could hear a marimba version of "All Night Long." Drifting across the way from the crystal paddock were the strains of "Rhapsody in Blue." To complete the musical cacophony was a local marching band marking time on the track.

In the infield was a row of huge billboards blocking one's view of the far side of the track. One was from the New Jersey Lottery, the other from Resorts International Casinos. Everywhere were souvenir stands loaded with Spend a Buck mementoes, including T-shirts that read "Spend a Buck/Make a

Buck." I heard one memento-seeker tell a friend, "It's like people are coming to see Frank Sinatra. The other horses are just the band."

The race itself, however, did not unfold as a fanfare of lone greatness for Spend a Buck. As expected, Huddle Up was sent to run head-and-head with the star, who had stumbled at the start but soon was setting his usual fractions: 22$4/5$, 45$2/5$. Then, after six furlongs in 1:09, Huddle Up gave way. But before Spend a Buck could relax, Creme Fraiche had come up on the rail, and at the top of the turn he had actually gotten his head in front. The crowd was very silent. The two horses dueled head-and-head all the way, with Spend a Buck getting his nose in front again and keeping it there. As they neared the finish, El Basco made his rush from the outside, and the three horses swept under the wire, with only a neck and a head separating them. After a moment of shock at the closeness of Spend a Buck's victory, the theme from *Rocky* started blaring from the loudspeakers.

Spend a Buck's time was 2:02$3/5$, a far cry from his time in the Derby, and it made you wonder again what would have happened three weeks earlier if Eternal Prince had run with him. But Dennis Diaz's colt had shown great courage and determination, and it had been a thrilling race. I felt that he had somehow managed to shine through all the cheap glitz with which Brennan had surrounded him.

As I left the grandstand, the final tawdry straw was a huge tinsel figure of Uncle Sam fluttering in the breeze. Was Brennan trying to tell us that Garden State was America's track?

On the drive back home the transmission of my car failed, and I had plenty of time, as I sat in the breakdown lane of the Jersey Turnpike, to sort out what it all meant.

I had felt disturbed by Brennan's track and Brennan's vision of success, but it was not because he was upsetting the sacrosanct traditions of racing. Those traditions, I felt, had been born of an ongoing hypocrisy, the sport-of-kings pretense that when one owned and raced horses one behaved like a gentleman; one was a good sport. Many of the tycoons of racing had been ruthless competitors, rapacious in business and cruel in their personal lives. A sporting attitude on the track was hardly the sort of virtue that belonged at the top of the list when it came to ultimate morals or values.

Brennan posed, in the place of elitism, the classless society of the casino, the meritocracy of the marketplace. He had simply approached racing as a businessman, with the notion that competition was the way of the world. As he told Joe Hirsch, "In my business, the securities field, I've always brought in periodic infusions of new blood. The young people come up with fresh ideas that force me to change my way of thinking. If you don't change, you grow moribund and eventually you die."

Given the decline of attendance in racing across the nation, and the financial troubles of many of the existing tracks, it was hard to deny the need for new blood, new ideas, and new tracks like Garden State. Brennan's view, as he often described it, was that seeking a slice of the existing pie was a losing proposition; the solution was simply to bake more pies.

What disturbed me, finally, I think, was those billboards in the infield. The great tracks of America, like Saratoga and Hialeah, created a pastoral illusion, with trees, flowers and lakes in the infield. You felt that you were in a garden, a refuge from the pressures of the urban world. Without that illusion, the no-frills tracks like Aqueduct or Suffolk that were merely functional had a soulless, sterile quality about them.

At Brennan's track, however, you felt that he was always selling you something. Everywhere you turned, you were surrounded by marketing strategy.

III

When I arrived at Belmont Park for the last leg of the Triple Crown, turf writers were headlining their columns CHIEF'S CROWN'S LAST CHANCE. If the Chief, who was favored to win, lost the Belmont, he would earn the dubious distinction of becoming the third horse in history to lose all three Triple Crown races as the betting favorite. What an end for my Hopeful.

Turf writer Stan Hochman, reaching for a parallel in golf, had asked Roger, "When you're down two strokes, and you have one hole to play, do you press?" Roger answered, "You press automatically, to cut down on your opponents' options."

It appeared, however, to be Spend a Buck who had done all the pressing. Diaz and Gambolati had decided not to run him in the Belmont, and if the Chief were ever to get a rematch with their colt he was going to have to go to New Jersey. As Woody Stephens put it, "When you cross the Hudson River, you can say the Buck stops here."

Woody himself was going to be sending in a double entry: Stephan's Odyssey and Creme Fraiche. Woody had won the Belmont the past three years in a row, and he wanted this one very badly. He wanted a record that no one else in history would have a prayer of duplicating. One morning, as we were walking by the Trustees' Dining Room, he looked over toward the row of pictures of Belmont winners, and he pointed to the blank space left for this year's winner. "There's room there for a fourth picture," he said.

He was sending in his temperamental gelding, who had become known around the barn as Little John Henry, or Henry for short, almost as a fluke. Originally Creme Fraiche had been entered in the Ohio Derby instead, but his owner, Elizabeth Moran, couldn't go to Cleveland. "She's never had a horse in the Belmont, so we thought it would be nice to let him run on Saturday," said Woody. "We never thought he'd be this kind of horse. We're just shooting for the moon with him."

Tank's Prospect, too, would be running on Saturday. After the Preakness, he had hardly been able to walk up the ramp into the van, but Wayne Lukas claimed that he had solved a minor foot problem with a protective bar shoe. Lukas, however, was currently in California, and his son Jeff, who ran his New York stable, was in charge of Tank.

Jeff, like his father, ran a tight ship. The elder Lukas had banished both radios and a coffee machine from his barns in California because they detracted from work, and there was a similar regimental feel at his Belmont barn. Grooms did not simply rake and sweep to keep the shedrow clean. One groom would perch on top of the rake while the other dragged it along the floor of the shedrow, thus insuring deep, herringbone grooves. Another groom would then head outside the barn with a two-by-four attached to a piece of chain-link fence to erase any hoof or tire marks from the ground. Then all the grooms would pick the loose straws out of the tuffets of hay that were placed at the bottom of each stall door. Said Jeff, when asked his philosophy of training: "I just do what my father tells me to do. In this operation, there's one president, and everybody else is below."

Both Lukases seemed confident. There would be no Spend a Buck to steal the lead, and there would be no Proud Truth to surprise them in the stretch.

After Proud Truth had beaten Stephan's Odyssey in the Peter Pan Stakes on May 26, John Veitch had discovered a saucer fracture in the horse's ankle, and he had decided to keep him out of the Belmont. It had been a difficult decision. The Belmont was the one race Veitch had thought all along that his big, headstrong colt, with his extraordinary stamina, would win.

When I saw Veitch on the Belmont backstretch, he was trying to make light of the situation, but I could tell he was extremely disappointed. "It took me longer than I thought to break him down," he joked. "We could have made the Belmont with this horse," he said, "but how he would come out of it is a questionable thing. I told Mr. Galbreath the alternatives. If we ran in the Belmont, we might not be able to compete in the fall. But we could pass the Belmont and come back in the fall and be three-year-old champion. Somebody else might have said, 'I've got three hundred people coming, we've got to go in the Belmont.' But Mr. Galbreath was willing to wait."

The Chief's advocates

As I continued around the backstretch, I discovered that the Chief had become a sentimental favorite, much as Veitch's Alydar had when he kept losing valiantly. Security guards, exercise boys and trainers alike felt that the Chief hadn't gotten the recognition he deserved. I ran into Mack Miller, Paul Mellon's trainer, who said he thought the Chief would win on Saturday. "At first I didn't think he'd like a distance, but I think he'll win." Miller recalled our conversation almost a year ago at Saratoga and said ruefully, "My colts didn't turn out so well, did they?"

The guard who was stationed at the backstretch entrance near the clubhouse told me, as he tossed some grain out to a couple of pet chickens, "I hope Chief's Crown wins on Saturday. He deserves it."

Angel Penna, Jr., too, was going to be rooting for the Chief, since Rhoman Rule was out with a shoulder problem. "I think Chief's Crown is the best three-year-old," he said. "He's just unlucky. The Derby was a silly race. But the Preakness—he was very unlucky. He deserves to win a classic."

The Rosens, however, were not currently the backstretch favorites. After the Preakness, the family had decided to fire Don MacBeth. Initially, Andrew tried to put it as diplomatically as possible. "We felt that we, as a team, had failed in the Preakness," he said. But then he got more specific. "It wasn't up to the horse to look back to see if there was another horse coming. That was up to the jockey."

According to John Veitch, that decision had put the Rosens in the camp of the new, nonsporting owners. "You have two kinds of owners," he said: "the old-guard and the new. With the old owners, you wouldn't have had a situation like this, with the trainer saying he is satisfied with the jockey's ride and then you hear that the owners have decided to fire the jockey. The old-guard owners hire the trainers to make those kinds of decisions. They rely on their trainer because that's what they hire him for. They understand the business."

And one of the old-guard owners, Alfred Gwynne Vanderbilt, whom I ran into on the backstretch, took me aside to stress his displeasure. "They didn't handle that situation very well," he said of the Rosens. "Donnie has been a perfect gentleman through it all."

The backstretch security guard agreed. "Don MacBeth has a lot of class," he said. "He has a nice way of talking. He still loves that horse. But you better believe he's going to try to beat him on Saturday."

I saw MacBeth himself atop one of Roger's horses on the way to the training track. He was still riding regularly for Roger, and he was trying to stay philosophical about it all. He looked down at me and wiped away an imaginary tear.

Later, MacBeth told me that he had felt insecure all along

about his relationship with the Chief. "I always felt that they would take me off at the slightest excuse," he said. "I was always on edge."

With MacBeth taken off the Chief, it appeared that Saturday was going to become a jockey jumble, with Angel Cordero and Laffit Pincay in the middle.

It had all started with Cordero's commitment to ride Leroy Jolley's Track Barron. Track Barron's owner, Peter Brant, had offered Cordero a breeding share in the colt on the condition that Cordero keep the mount until the colt retired. On the day of the Jersey Derby, when Cordero was to ride Spend a Buck, Track Barron had been entered in the Metropolitan Mile at Belmont, and there was no way for Cordero to make both races. He had waffled until the last minute, then chosen Track Barron.

Diaz and Gambolati had then secured the services of Laffit Pincay, and after the colt won they announced that Cordero would get no percentage of the two-million-dollar bonus, even though he had ridden Spend a Buck in the three previous races that had allowed him to qualify for the money.

Cordero responded in his usual macho fashion, declaring that he knew how Spend a Buck could be beaten, and that he would share his information with the trainer who offered him a mount on a competing horse. Since he knew that MacBeth had lost the mount on Chief's Crown, the offer seemed to point directly to the Rosens and Roger Laurin.

By the beginning of Belmont week, however, Roger still had not announced a decision on a jockey. Cordero was not known as a master at the mile-and-a-half Belmont distance. He had only won the event once, out of sixteen tries. Consequently, Roger was leaning initially toward Laffit Pincay, since Pincay had not yet made a commitment to ride Stephan's Odyssey. But Pincay now had the permanent assignment on Spend a Buck, and if the Chief were to meet Spend a Buck again, Pincay would have to desert the Chief.

Finally, Roger announced that Cordero would be riding the Chief in the Belmont. Pincay, who had won the Belmont the previous year on Swale, would be riding Stephan's Odyssey, and Eddie Maple, Stephens's hard-luck jockey, would be riding

Creme Fraiche. And Don MacBeth would be riding the fast but uneven Cutlass Reality.

On Saturday morning, the clouds began to gather early. The mood was gloomy as I stood with the Rosens drinking coffee beside Roger's barn. You could feel the rain on the way, and a muddy track would mean yet another of those turns of the wheel that had made winning more elusive for the Chief.

Andrew had been feeling defensive about the criticism he had received for firing Don MacBeth. Until then, the Rosens had been making all the right, sporting, old-guard decisions— upholding tradition. But losing the Preakness, he felt, had called for a different approach. "I think we got a little frustrated," he said, "because we weren't used to losing."

There were two things Andrew was learning as a true horseman, and the first was how to lose gracefully. The second was to appreciate what a marvel it was to win. "Roger told us early on that we'd never see another horse like this one," he said, "and we didn't really know then what he meant."

Ironically, it wasn't until the Chief started losing that the Rosens could really appreciate his true worth. "Sure we've been disappointed, but he's become part of the family. He's done so many great things," said Andrew, "that you can reach back and see how fortunate we've been to have a horse that's done what he has. There is so much to look back on and be proud of. You look back and see those horses that he was running against at Saratoga—where are they?"

Perhaps Andrew's question would be answered, in part, later that day. The Chief's destiny as a classic horse had diverged from that of the other early Hopefuls I had seen last summer— Tiffany Ice, Ziggy's Boy and Doubly Clear. He had followed the fast track to the Derby, while the horses for whom the classic distances were unobtainable had fallen into another level of competition as "useful" horses. In a fitting irony, those three horses, the Chief's early rivals, would be running against each other in a small stakes race, while the Chief went for the last jewel in the Triple Crown.

I wondered how Judy Bujnicki, with her nervous stomach,

was faring now that Doubly Clear was not running as a wunder-kind, but as an ordinary horse.

I found her standing beside Doubly Clear's stall in Belmont's bright, flower-laden receiving barn. She had gained a little weight since I had seen her last, and she was looking relaxed and cheerful. "Since he started running badly," she said, "I haven't had any pressure." He hadn't done badly, however, by ordinary standards. He had won a small stakes race a month after the Hopeful, and Bujnicki had given him the winter off. In his first start of the year, at Garden State, he had finished seventh, but in his next start he had won a small stake at Monmouth.

"We're here today," she said, "to do what we can. At this point, we have nothing to lose." She patted the horse, who had reached over to nuzzle her hair. "I know it's not going to last forever. People say you only have one chance to have a good horse—I just happened to have mine with the second horse I got. I guess I'll have to go back to junk horses after this one. But you know, I'd hate to be in the position of the Chief's Crown people, to be the beaten favorite. If I lose, I'll just take my fifteen-hundred-dollar horse and go home. He's not going to be a top racehorse, but he was never meant to be."

Bujnicki pulled a carrot out of her pocket. "Hey, Wimpy," she said to the horse. "Say yes." The big gelding nodded obediently. "He's going to make one hell of a show horse," she said happily.

Rain on the Chief's parade

The rain had started by 9 A.M., and the day seemed to get darker by the minute.

The Great Handicapper, who was serving as guest expert at the Paddock Club, was advising the fans at the Paddock Club, "Chief's Crown can't lose." He had told me after the Preakness that he thought the Chief would win the Belmont. The Chief, he felt, was the kind of horse whose running style suited the Belmont. The race was not won by speed horses, he said, nor by horses with big closing kicks. It was won by horses who could set a steady pace and maintain it. Swale had won it the year before with his steady twelves, and the Handicapper felt the Chief would win it the same way.

I wondered, however, if the Chief would get a chance to keep a steady pace. Eternal Prince had been entered in the race at the last minute, and surely he would either set a fast pace or push the leader into a suicidal duel. This was Eternal Prince's last chance, too, to become a classic horse—to justify the millions that had been spent on him in the past two months.

By the time of the fifth race, the Riva Ridge Stakes, the rains had stopped and the track had begun to dry out. The race should have been called The Reality, with entries limited to Hopeful also-rans who were making a comeback. It was a very fast race, with Tiffany Ice setting a fast pace and Ziggy's Boy taking over the lead midway on the turn, then drawing off to win by eight lengths. Tiffany Ice was second, and Wayne Lukas's Huddle Up third. Doubly Clear, however, had finished less than a length behind Huddle Up. At the top of the stretch, he had been next to last, but he finished energetically, showing that he did belong, after all, in fast company.

The track continued to dry out, and by the time the horses were being saddled for the Belmont it was just muddy enough to be tiring. The only person happy about the track condition was Woody Stephens, who knew that Creme Fraiche loved the mud.

Roger had been sitting in the tack room as he waited, watching an ESPN-TV special on injured horses, on the life-saving techniques vets had developed to repair broken limbs. "I've sent six or seven horses to that place," he said, referring to a certain medical center, "and all I got back was the halter."

The show had brought sad associations for all of us, and as the Chief headed toward the underground passage to the paddock, Steve Jordan patted him, saying, misty-eyed, "This one is for Sam and the Faquer."

The horses reached the paddock and began circling, some in front of the saddling stalls, some behind. Tank's Prospect, covered with nervous sweat, suddenly neighed shrilly and reared, almost getting away from his groom. He was exhibiting all the most obvious signs, in horse language, of fear and anxiety. Clearly he didn't want to run today. And when his groom led him into the saddling stall, he reared again. I was reminded of a grotesque accident I had witnessed at Belmont two weeks earlier, when a colt named Sarcophagus had fulfilled the doom implicit in his name. While being saddled, he had reared up, hit his head, and fallen over dead.

In the adjacent stall, the Chief kicked the wall angrily in response to Tank. He lost his cool for the first time ever in the paddock, rearing up when Roger placed the saddle pad on his back. Roger looked frightened; he had never seen the Chief like this.

Finally, all the horses were saddled, and the Chief had calmed down. The jockeys walked out in their bright silks, Angel Cordero looking bizarre, I thought, in the pink-and-green Rosen colors. He bounded up to Roger for his instructions with the avid expression of a kid asking for candy. This is all wrong, I thought. I just didn't believe that Angel's aggressive, macho style would be suited to the calm, deliberate Chief. As Roger boosted him up onto the Chief's back and the horses began to make their way out to the track, the fans serenaded Cordero with their usual collection of insults and catcalls. He was getting more attention than the Chief.

As the horses walked out onto the track for the parade to post, most of the jockeys were looking ahead or adjusting the reins. Don MacBeth was looking over at the Chief with the bittersweet intensity of a scorned lover.

Everyone had known that the last-minute entry of Eternal Prince would insure a fast early pace, but no one could have predicted that El Basco's stablemate, Purple Mountain, would outsprint him to the lead. The Chief was right behind them at the break, and Don MacBeth raced up beside him on Cutlass Reality, pinning him on the rail. The Chief had to check his stride, and as Cutlass Reality moved ahead, Angel took the Chief out to the middle of the track. Purple Mountain was setting one of the fastest paces in Belmont history, with Eternal Prince right behind him and Cutlass Reality just a half length behind. Angel was trying to keep the Chief off the killing pace, in fourth place. Gone was the notion of trying to control the pace. Meanwhile, both Stephan's Odyssey and Creme Fraiche were trailing the field.

At the top of the second turn, Cutlass Reality took over, and both Creme Fraiche and Stephan's Odyssey began to move. In the middle of the turn, the Chief began to go after Cutlass Reality, and the two Stephens horses began to go after the Chief. At the top of the stretch, at a mile and a quarter, the Derby distance, the Chief took the lead from Cutlass Reality. The time was 2:01$^{2/5}$ on a very tiring track, one of the fastest Belmont paces ever. Now there could be little doubt that he could go that distance. But the effort had exhausted him. When Stephan's Odyssey challenged him from the inside and Creme Fraiche from the outside, he tried to respond, but Stephan's Odyssey took over the lead. Creme Fraiche, however, seemed to be enjoying himself. He was bounding along in the mud like an antelope, his ears perked forward, and he passed Stephan's Odyssey with a furlong to go. The Chief held on for third. The final time for the race was 2:27, the fourth fastest Belmont ever. Only Gallant Man, Secretariat, and Affirmed had run the distance faster.

One horse didn't finish the race. Tank's Prospect, who had fallen back steadily from fifth position after a quarter mile, broke down in the stretch. Lukas had squeezed the lemon dry this time. Eugene Klein announced that his colt, who had suffered an injury to a suspensory ligament, would be retired from racing.

As I walked over to the backstretch after the race, I saw Don MacBeth. He had done his best, as the security guard had predicted, to beat the Chief, but he was sorry that the little colt had lost. "Another sad tale in the saga of Chief's Crown," he said. "I thought he could go the distance. I'm really sorry he didn't make it."

Back at Roger's barn, you could hear the corks popping at Woody Stephens's barn next door. You had to give Woody credit. He had won it, one-two, and he had won it for the fourth year in a row.

The Rosens had gathered out in the grass in front of Roger's barn, the Chief out in the yard grazing quietly. The family was talking quietly under the trees. Douglas Rosen was saying, "I don't know what's going on at Woody's barn, but I don't think they could care any more about their horse than we do about the Chief."

From a distance, it looked like a cheerful scene, like the end of a Renaissance comedy, where all the disguises are dropped, all the disputes resolved, and the community comes together in harmony.

I found myself thinking about what a remarkable gift Carl Rosen had left his family. With the Chief, Carl Rosen had given his family a means of understanding him, indeed of experiencing for themselves the passions that had driven him so many years ago to the track. The Chief had brought the family together in a way that he himself had found so difficult to do during his lifetime.

The Chief had brought them together first in prosperity, then in loss. And perhaps that was the most precious gift of all.

Conclusion

My crown is in my heart, not on my head;
Not deck'd with diamonds and Indian stones,
Nor to be seen: my crown is called content;
A crown it is that seldom kings enjoy.

—William Shakespeare, *Henry VI*, Part III

I

AFTER the Chief's loss in the Belmont, Roger was still talking like MacArthur: "We shall return," he kept saying. He had not yet squeezed the lemon dry. As long as there was another race, there was hope, and he felt that the Chief still had a chance at glory. The three-year-old championship would be won, he felt, in the summer at Saratoga and in the fall, when the Chief, Spend a Buck and the other contenders took on older horses for the first time.

Roger worked the Chief very hard during the month of July, in order to prepare him for Saratoga. Dennis Diaz had taken a house in Saratoga, and he had talked about sending Spend a Buck to the Travers, and Roger wanted to be ready for the rematch. Spend a Buck had lost the Haskell Handicap at Monmouth on July 27 to Skip Trial, whom the Chief had beaten easily in the Preakness, and he was beginning to look vulnerable.

When I arrived in Saratoga at the beginning of August, the geraniums were just as red and the spires just as white as last year, but this time I was arriving at the end of the cycle of hope rather than the beginning.

Roger, however, the perennial pessimist, was sounding cheerful and optimistic. The Chief was that kind of horse; even when he lost, you felt that he would redeem himself. There was a core of determination in him that never softened. He had never stopped trying in a race, never dropped to the back of the field. Even in his morning workouts, he never slacked off, never got lazy. Roger was always amazed by how eager the Chief was, how sound and willing he remained, even after a long year of campaigning, with no respite except when he had been sick.

"I didn't let myself get down too far," said Roger, as we walked over to the track to watch the Chief gallop one morning, "because the horse always ran true. It came up muddy in the Belmont. It wasn't muddy the day before or the day after. There are things that are just beyond your control. But the Chief and I are both feeling good now," he said. "I think it's our turn this time."

Roger, however, had caused a buzz of controversy around the backstretch by his choice of prep races for the Chief. Instead of the Jim Dandy, the traditional prep for the Travers, he had entered the Chief in the Tell Stakes, a mile race on the turf, to be run on August 3, the same day as the Whitney. Turf writers seemed puzzled until Angel Cordero, self-appointed spokesman for the Chief, informed them that Chief's Crown would have nothing to lose in such a race. If he won, it would add to his value as a stud, demonstrating that he was capable of winning on the grass as well as the dirt.

Roger, however, told me that his main purpose in the race was a strategic one. He wanted to get the Chief more accustomed to relaxing behind speed horses, to learn to reserve himself for a big run at the bottom of the turn. In the Chief's earlier races, Roger had always given the same orders to Don MacBeth: either get an early lead or get the lead a quarter of a mile from the finish. He felt that the Chief would not relinquish the lead once he got in front. But Stephan's Odyssey had passed him in the Derby, Tank's Prospect had passed him in the Preakness, and both Stephan and Creme Fraiche had passed him in the Belmont.

The Chief was not invincible. So Roger felt he had to go back to the drawing board, to plan a strategy that would take advantage of the Chief's versatility. The Chief could give you speed anytime you asked for it; the question was, when to ask for that extra-fast quarter that would leave the rest of the field behind.

Roger's strategy was probably sound. But he never seemed to take into account the element of chance that seemed to follow the Chief like a cloud. In the Tell, the Chief's opponents would include Paul Mellon's Lightning Leap, one of Mack Miller's hopefuls the previous summer; Foundation Plan, a colt who had run impressively on the grass in Florida; and Exclusive Partner, a colt owned by Paul Cornman, the handicapper who had an extraordinary knack for buying horses who looked ordinary on the dirt but who became monsters on the grass. Cornman's horse, Win, was one of the top grass horses in the country, and Exclusive Partner appeared to be a grass star as well.

When the gates opened for the Tell, the Chief dived out, his head dipping down like a dousing rod. Angel tried to hold him back, but the Chief was fighting him, and he raced wide around the first turn, just outside Foundation Plan and Exclusive Partner, before Cordero got him to relax and drop back to fifth. Cordero began his move toward the bottom of the second turn, as another colt, Equalize, was making his move outside the Chief. Cordero felt that Equalize, with Robbie Davis aboard, was bearing in on him, so in customary macho fashion he swung the Chief extra wide around the top of the stretch, carrying Equalize even wider around the sharp inner-turf-course turn. It was a risky move at best, the kind of move that had almost cost him the Preakness on Codex, when he had intimidated Genuine Risk. But in so doing, Angel had saved the Chief's life.

Foundation Plan, who had been in front of the Chief near the inside rail, suddenly dived toward the hedge, and he fell, flipping over and over, rolling through the hedge, as his jockey, Eddie Maple, sailed over the hedge and landed with a thud. The Chief, whose momentum had already carried him wide, veered out even further as Foundation Plan went down, and he was clear of the accident. Had Angel kept him near the rail, he would have gone down too. As it was, once he was clear he dug in with his most determined stride, correcting his course, and by midstretch he was even with Exclusive Partner. He put his neck in front, flicked his ears back and forth, as though in challenge to Cornman's colt, and then drew away easily in the last few strides. Cordero was unable to stop him past the finish line, and the Chief continued to charge around the backstretch at full speed, his ears flicking back and forth. He seemed to enjoy showing Angel who was really in control.

By the time the Chief returned to take his place in the winner's circle, his number was blinking on the tote board, as though it were a Florida déjà vu, and the INQUIRY sign had lit up. And then his number disappeared from the top of the board and reappeared at the bottom. The stewards ruled that the Chief had interfered with Equalize, and they placed him fourth, behind the colt whom he had carried wide around the turn. At least, however, he was alive. Foundation Plan had crushed his skull in the spill, and although he had gotten up and walked away from the accident, the vets were unable to save him.

In the meantime, the show went on. Track Barron had gone on to avenge his loss in last year's Whitney against Slew o' Gold. In this year's Whitney he had beaten, among others, Carr de Naskra, the colt who had won the Travers the year before.

It was all part of the great Saratoga cycle, the progress from the Hopeful for juveniles to the Travers for three-year-olds and then the Whitney for older horses.

This legendary cycle had produced a number of upsets as well as a number of vindications. In 1930, the Travers had produced one of the greatest upsets in racing history when the lowly Jim Dandy, a 100-to-1 shot, had beaten Triple Crown winner Gallant Fox on a muddy track. Among other notables, Katherine Price's father had been there, and she claimed that he had put fifty dollars on the long shot's nose.

No horse had actually won all three of Saratoga's milestone races, since so few horses with enough early promise to win the Hopeful had competed past their third year. Often, horses who had done well in the Triple Crown were winding down by the time of the Travers, and the more lightly raced colts were just beginning to come into their own. Man o' War had won the Hopeful and the Travers and then had no one left to run against. Alydar had won both the Whitney and the Travers, finally beating his nemesis Affirmed in the latter, through a disqualification.

A total of seven horses had won the Hopeful and then gone on to win the Travers—including Triple Crown winner Whirlaway and the great Native Dancer. If the Chief became the eighth, he would rule Saratoga, if not Kentucky, and Carl Rosen's racing colors would be painted on the totemic canoe floating in the infield lake. Surely it was better to rule in Saratoga than to evade in New Jersey.

The next morning, the mood at Roger's barn was cheerful despite the Chief's brush with death. Said Jerry Booth, "We got ripped off again." But Roger's optimism hadn't been dented. "At least he felt like he won this one," he said. "He came back pleased with himself. When he loses, he comes back mad and frustrated."

The Chief did indeed look pleased, standing with his head poking alertly out of his stall. He even allowed a few pats of affection, as though accepting tribute.

He had gained a little weight over the summer, and there was more of a sense of mass and power in his body than before, a hint of heaviness about the jowls, neck and chest. He was looking less and less coltish and more and more like a stallion. He was starting to get that look of rugged arrogance I had seen in both his sire and his grandsires, as though blood were beginning to tell.

As Roger and I walked out to the track, I was saying, "The Chief is blessed and cursed." Said Roger, "Yeah, blessed with talent and cursed with bad racing luck." Had Carl Rosen's luck finally run out, I wondered? "There's no telling what would have happened if Carl was still alive," said Roger. "I think the Breeders' Cup party would still be going on. He was lucky, but not everybody would have been able to capitalize on it the way he did. He would keep parlaying and keep parlaying. He'd win and keep getting stronger."

As Roger reached the clockers' stand, he met a chorus of condolences from his fellow trainers. Said Shug McGaughey, whose horse Vanlandingham had just lost to Track Barron in the Whitney, "I think I'll stay away from you for a day or so." Quipped Roger, "Don't you want some of my good luck to rub off?"

Angel Penna said, "Your horse has such bad luck—what are you going to do now?"

Said Roger, "I think I'll send him over the jumps," referring to the weekly steeplechase races that Saratoga was sponsoring.

The following Saturday, another saga was concluded as Mom's Command and Abigail Fuller, who had gone on to win the filly triple crown and all the hearts and flowers, finally met Fran's Valentine, who had also won her share of hearts. Mom and Abby won the Alabama Stakes easily, leading from wire to wire, as they had done in the Acorn, the Mother Goose and the Oaks. And although Mom had inspired disparaging remarks among certain members of the press—she was a big, muscular filly, and one writer had described her as "masculine-looking"—her extraordinary speed and gameness had made her a champion.

Peter Fuller could finally begin to let go of that long-ago Derby defeat. The plaque honoring Mom at Belmont, after all, would be placed next to the one honoring the previous winner of the filly triple crown, owned by the late Lucille Markey and Calumet Farm. Fuller, at last, would be on an equal footing with the family that had taken the 1968 Derby trophy. And in a final poetic irony, after retiring his prize filly, Fuller would sell a half-interest in her to Jule Fink, the man who had first challenged the power of the Jockey Club.

By the time of Travers week, the clouds seemed to be descending again. New York jockeys had threatened to boycott the races, beginning Friday, in a dispute over pay scale, and at Roger's barn Steve Jordan joked they might have to send to Suffolk Downs for substitute riders.

Worse still, Spend a Buck had opted to run in New Jersey on the day of the Travers. While the Chief would be battling it out with Stephan's Odyssey at Saratoga, Spend a Buck, with the help of Lasix, would be going against a small field in the Monmouth Handicap. His only real competition would be provided by Carr de Naskra, who had been beaten by Track Barron in the Whitney.

Dennis Diaz, who had been hanging out at the polo matches in Saratoga with his new friend and syndicate partner Will Farish, was reputed to have told a reporter that the main feature would be at Monmouth, while the cartoon would be at Saratoga.

Robert Brennan, too, had brought his own brand of one-upmanship to Saratoga. On Travers eve, one of the old barns from Horse Haven, the oldest part of the Saratoga backstretch, was being sold at auction. Originally scheduled for demolition, the seventy-five-year-old structure was neither old enough nor distinguished enough to be rescued by the local preservation society. As Joe Hirsch put it, "It has no more value than a seventy-five-year-old cigar. It's just an old ramshackle barn that nobody uses."

Robert Brennan, however, immediately saw its symbolic value. He went to thirty thousand dollars in the bidding, and his competitors finally dropped out. The underbidder was Penny Chenery, who was distressed to discover who had outbid her. Brennan announced that the barn would be taken apart and then reconstructed at Garden State Park: a shrine to progress, erected in the ashes of tradition.

The Chief had become, by default, the upholder of tradition, the defender of the faith. But again, the gloomy theme in the press box was "Last chance, Chief." He had also become the underdog, the unlucky champion-turned-loser. If he didn't win the Travers, he would be written off as a miler, an also-ran who couldn't win at a classic distance. Paul Cornman, acting as guest handicapper, told a Paddock Club audience that he expected the Chief to win, and if he didn't, he'd never again pick him for a race over a mile and an eighth.

Back at Roger's barn, Andrew, the optimist, had changed roles with Roger the pessimist. "What if this whole year goes for nothing?" he asked Roger in a moment of despair. I asked him how much confidence he placed in Angel Cordero. "Well, he's zero for three on the horse. I mean, zero for two." Steve Jordan winced, as though Andrew had just walked under a ladder.

Later I ran into Don MacBeth, who, ironically, would be competing against the Chief on a colt named Don's Choice. "Personally, I think he can go a mile and a quarter," said Don of the Chief, "but if you took a poll of horsemen, I think it would still be a question mark. If he doesn't win the Travers, there will always be that question."

I asked Don how he felt now about the Chief's strengths and weaknesses. "He's a little finicky about his racetracks," he said. "He needs a glib track, a track that he can get some bounce from. But he was born with the right combination of genes, the biological makeup that goes into any great athlete, animal or human. He has whatever it is that makes a great human athlete, physically, and he has the right attitude for winning."

Stephan's Odyssey, however, had run such an impressive race in the Jim Dandy ten days earlier that most turf writers expected the Chief to have a tough time. Roger had managed to keep his Travers strategy a secret, and everyone assumed that the Chief would try to take the lead from Don's Choice, the only other horse in the race with good early speed, while Stephan's Odyssey would make his characteristic big run at the end.

On the day of the Travers, for which the second largest crowd in Saratoga history was gathering, Roger was feeling nervous about Angel Cordero. All week, he had been telling Cordero that he wanted the Chief to be held back in the early going. But Cordero was known to make his own decisions, and his forte was going to the lead and trying to steal the race on the front end.

Roger fretted and worried and finally made a trip to the jockey's room to make his point one more time. Cordero told him he thought he could win the race on the front end, but Roger insisted: "Take back, take back unless the rest of the field drops dead. Just do what I tell you, don't go to the lead." Cordero had been thinking about riding his own race, but he decided he'd better obey orders. "If I do what he says and the horse wins," Cordero reasoned to himself, "I still might ride him again. But if I ride him my way and get beat, well, then, I'm fired."

As the horses were led into the paddock, Charlsie Cantey, who was working as a commentator for ABC-TV, heard the results from New Jersey over her earphones, and she announced to the owners gathered in the center of the paddock that Spend a Buck had just won the Monmouth by a neck over Carr de Naskra, and he had set a new track record.

The Chief seemed unaware that he had just been upstaged, and that pressure on him to win had just quadrupled. He seemed calm and self-assured, quite unlike his angry defensiveness in the Belmont. Roger boosted Angel up on his back, and Cordero slapped the Chief's neck, hard, like a lineman greeting his quarterback on the field. The Chief responded with a grunt. Maybe Cordero would make a macho horse out of him after all.

When the gates opened for the one hundred and sixteenth running of the Travers, it was apparent from the start that Angel had decided to do it Roger's way. There was a surprised buzz in the press box when Cordero took a strong hold on the Chief, letting a startled Darrel McHargue on the California horse Turkoman surge to the front. Surprised to find himself in the lead, McHargue held Turkoman to a very slow first quarter, 24 1/5, usually a slow enough pace for a good front runner to hang on. But Don's Choice, with MacBeth aboard, took over the lead after half a mile, continuing the slow pace. Skip Trial had come on to be third, with the Chief back in fourth and Stephan's Odyssey back still farther. By the bottom of the turn the Chief began to move, his legs churning furiously. It was not graceful, but it was inexorable. The Chief looked angry. He churned around the top of the stretch, catching Skip Trial and then Turkoman. This time, he was all alone in the stretch, and Stephan's Odyssey was nowhere to be found.

In those last few strides before the Chief surged under the wire, I kept waiting for something terrible to happen, a big bird to swoop down and send him off course, a ghost horse to suddenly materialize in front of him. I was feeling dizzy and breathless, as though I were on a carnival ride, and I recognized the feeling as that moment of anticipation before the wheel of fortune brings you to the peak, like a child on a ferris wheel, where you will rock, breathlessly, for a moment, at the top of the world.

It was just as I had imagined, almost exactly a year earlier, the Chief sweeping under the wire all alone, the cycle that had begun with the Hopeful culminating in this victory.

What I hadn't foreseen was the series of setbacks and losses that would make this his most important race.

I ran down to the winner's circle, where the Rosens were cheering and embracing. Robert Clay was saying, "This should convince the Arabs. They kept telling me he was just a miler."

The Chief came back like a battered warrior, his face covered with dirt, looking very tired and very proud of himself. At that moment, it didn't matter that this win, in the long run, would mean no more than the throw of the dice one hot summer day. It didn't even matter that I was standing on a racetrack built by tycoons, surrounded by millionaires, by the children of fortune, and I barely had enough money in my pocket to get home after the race.

I had cast my lot with my Hopeful, let my fate ride on his back, and he had finally come through for me, made my dreams come true. I had ridden the wheel.

After the race, the Rosens were led to the Directors' Room for glasses of victory champagne, to be greeted by Penny Chenery and other lords and ladies of the horsey set. Sitting in a corner of the room was Liz Whitney Tippett, former wife of Jock Whitney and once the toast of Saratoga with her jewels and hounds and wild parties. She still owned racehorses, but she was gradually getting out of the game. "I was going to get out last year when Sonny did," she said, "but I couldn't get my act together." At one point, when the race was being replayed on the television monitor, she glowered at Andrew Rosen, who was blocking her view. "He doesn't know who I am," she said tartly. "Now I'm just an old lady with a cane." You could almost hear the clanking footfalls of the changing of the guard.

The next morning, at Roger's barn, his father Lucien came by. "Where's the horse?" he asked. Steve Jordan pointed to the Chief's stall. Lucien walked over and looked in. "Look at the size of him," he said incredulously, then repeated it. "Look at the size of him. So small." He turned to Roger. "He has something very big in here," he said, pointing at his chest. "He finally made a believer of me."

II

In the days that followed the Travers, before the fall championship series at Belmont began with the Woodward Stakes, I tried to discern a pattern in this strange year of racing.

A friend with an analytical turn of mind noticed that the Chief had won both the Hopeful and the Travers during a new moon. Just for fun, he then looked back to compare the Chief's other races with the phases of the moon, and he discovered that the Chief demonstrated a pattern of running well when the moon was young—during the first quarter of the lunar phase. The newer the moon, the better his performance. His defeats had occurred during the phase when the moon was waning. The Belmont Futurity, the Derby and the Belmont were all run when the moon was old, and the Derby, of course, had been run during a full moon.

My friend, who is far from a lunar determinist, began to get carried away. Even the anomalies, he said, fit the pattern. The Preakness, in which he had lost but beaten the track record, had been run a few hours short of a new moon. "This," my friend says, "explains his narrowest and most perplexing of defeats." The Tell, in which the Chief ran so well but nearly lost his life, was in a third-quarter phase. His winning efforts that were not so impressive, my friend pointed out—the Flamingo, Cowdin and Swale—were under moons in the second quarter.

If the pattern held, my friend suggested, the Chief would lose the Woodward, win a "smashing victory" in the Marlboro, and lose both the Jockey Club Gold Cup and the Breeders' Cup.

Although I'll never be convinced the moon had anything to do with it, the Chief did go on to lose the Woodward on a dreary, rainy day on a muddy track. Since Angel Cordero was committed to ride Track Barron in the race, the Chief got the services of Laffit Pincay, Jr., for the first time. But Cordero was able to play his best game, sending Track Barron to the lead and then stealing the race on the front end. The Chief finished third, a half length behind Vanlandingham.

The Chief was then almost forgotten in all the excitement over the Marlboro, which was shaping up as the most competitive race of the year. Said trainer Charlie Whittingham, who was sending in his California star Greinton, "This will be the best Marlboro in years." Greinton would be going against the rogue Gate Dancer, Carr de Naskra, Track Barron, Vanlandingham, Bounding Basque and the Chief. As the Great Handicapper said, the Marlboro would represent "the strongest field to contest a race in the United States this year."

Riding the Chief in this race would be . . . Don MacBeth. Since Laffit Pincay was previously committed to Greinton, and Cordero to Track Barron, Roger convinced the Rosens that MacBeth deserved another chance on the Chief. Said MacBeth before the race, "I always hoped I'd get him back. That's all I wanted."

It was the sweetest of ironies. The Chief went off at 10 to 1, sixth choice behind the top older horses, the first time that the bettors had neglected him.

Vanlandingham and Track Barron went out in an early duel for the lead, while Greinton stayed close on the rail behind them. The Chief dropped back to fifth. At the top of the turn, Gate Dancer accelerated outside him, and the Chief let him go by. But by the middle of the turn he started to move. At the bottom of the turn, Gate Dancer was moving strongly outside Vanlandingham and Track Barron, and the Chief, churning furiously, was just outside him, widest of all.

I could hardly bear it. The four horses went charging down the top of the stretch, and there was the little Chief, suddenly, with his nose in front. That was the way it went, Chris McCarron working on Gate Dancer, Pat Day trying to hold Vanlandingham together. Greinton had swung outside and had begun to move strongly. But the Chief was holding on, and I was screaming in incredulity. The Chief wouldn't give up. And he began, inch by inch, to edge away from Gate Dancer, as Track Barron faded and Greinton advanced outside him. As they crossed the wire, the Chief had his neck poked out in front, straining furiously with each stride.

It had been the most exciting race of the year, and the Chief had beaten the best older horses in the country at the classic mile-and-a-quarter distance, the distance at which his genes were supposed to let him down.

The wheel had not yet finished turning, however. The Chief bypassed the Jockey Club Gold Cup, the last race in the fall series, in order to prepare for the Breeders' Cup in November. Roger had announced that he would retire after the big race, along with the Chief. The Chief would be heading for the Kentucky bluegrass after that first week in November, while Roger would be heading for the putting greens in Florida. And before long, Don MacBeth's career, too, would be concluded, when it was discovered that he was seriously ill. I felt that the curtain was coming down before the final act had even begun.

Roger had just turned fifty in September—"No matter how you look at it, that's old," he said—and he was tired of all those pre-dawn awakenings, all those flawed horses. With wise investments over the years, and with the help of the Chief, he had become a millionaire, and he could now choose how to spend his time. "I spent thirty years waiting for a horse like this one," he said, "and I don't want to wait another thirty years to find another one."

This time, most of the turf writers had picked the Chief to win. After his surprising victory in the Marlboro, the Chief could wrap up the three-year-old championship as well as horse-of-the-year honors with a victory in the Breeders' Cup classic. Spend a Buck had never run again after the Monmouth Handicap, and he had been officially retired in September after suffering a minor ankle injury.

This time the underdog was another forgotten three-year-old, Proud Truth, who had won a comeback race in October and then squeaked by in the Discovery Handicap only a week before the Breeders' Cup. Most turf writers scoffed at Proud Truth's chances against older horses and against the Chief. But at the big publicity party two nights before the Breeders' Cup, I ran into Charlie Rose. "I never bet," he confided in me, "but this time I went to the bank and took it all out. My horse is going to win on Saturday." As a further omen, I opened a special Breeders' Cup fortune cookie, and the message said: "You're ahead in the stretch, but the field is closing fast."

The next day, on Halloween, it appeared that Robert Brennan was going to upstage the Chief again. The SEC announced that it was filing suit against Brennan and First Jersey Securities, charging him and his company with defrauding customers through manipulative stock recommendations. Brennan had replied that a witch hunt was appropriate on Halloween day. And the next day he would come to the races, and his face and his helicopter would again adorn the commercials scattered between the races on the television broadcast.

Saturday turned up cloudy, as nearly all the Chief's bad-luck days, and it had been raining off and on since dawn. By the time of the first race the drizzle had stopped, but the track was just wet enough to be dull and tiring. Every race was going to stretch runners, even the sprint that had been won wire to wire the year before.

The race began as a replay of the Marlboro, with Track Barron bolting to the lead and Vanlandingham pushing him. The Chief followed, running head to head with Imperial Choice, the top Canadian three-year-old. After a mile, toward the bottom of the turn, Imperial Choice swung wide around the two front runners, and the Chief came through on the inside. For a moment, the Chief had his head in front. But the field was closing fast. Both Gate Dancer and Proud Truth had begun big moves, and Gate Dancer surged up to the Chief, then passed him. Proud Truth, too, flew by, and then the California horse Turkoman; but it was Proud Truth and Gate Dancer dueling for the lead, until Proud Truth finally poked a head in front at the wire.

The Chief, who was to go out in a blaze of glory, had faded instead, a very tired fourth. The race that could have established the Chief in the Hall of Fame enshrined him instead in the memory of the public as a loser.

A disgruntled sportswriter, who had bet heavily on the Chief, clanked his binoculars down on his desk. "That horse has lost on the most important days of his life!"

Now there would be no more chances, no more rematches.

The Chief now belonged to the stallion-makers. If he were to have another chance to make racing history, it would have to be through his sons and daughters.

Perhaps if Carl Rosen had still been alive, or if the Chief had been born before the era of the breeding syndicates, he would have gotten a chance to come back the next year and redeem himself. To retire him before he had even finished growing meant that we'd never get to see what he might have done, what he might have become.

It all seemed so evanescent now and yet so final, the Chief's brief career on the track, those twenty-one two-minute trials interspersed over a year and a half.

III

Had the Chief finally beaten the pain/payoff quotient? Judging by the look on Roger Laurin's face that bleak November afternoon when his horse and his dreams began to fade in the stretch, he hadn't. After a year and a half of hard campaigning, Roger had finally squeezed the lemon dry.

The Chief had not been a superhorse. Often, he had not been able to overcome adversity. When racing luck began to go against him, he had not been able to win. But on the other hand, the Chief had been a marvel of consistency. The Great Handicapper admitted that he had rarely seen a horse with such consistent speed figures. The Chief was a horse who gave you everything he had every time he raced.

Looking back at the Chief's entire career, there was no doubt he had been a winner. He had been one of the best two-year-old champions ever, and he had won more than $2 million in less than two years of racing. And in twenty-one races, he had never been worse than fourth. Few horses in recent years had endured such a rigorous campaign. He had danced every dance, the traditional dances as well as the glitzy new Breeders' Cup waltz.

He was even more remarkable in the context of his own generation. Although, except for the Chief, it had been a late-blooming group, the Chief's generation had turned out to be one of the strongest ever. They had run: a Garden State Stakes two fifths of a second off the world record for a mile and an eighth (Spend a Buck); a Wood Memorial equal to the second fastest ever (Eternal Prince); the second fastest Blue Grass ever (Chief's Crown); the third fastest Kentucky Derby ever (Spend a Buck); the fastest and second fastest Preakness ever (Tank's Prospect and Chief's Crown); the fourth fastest Belmont (Creme Fraiche); and the fifth fastest Travers (Chief's Crown).

Within the top contenders of that generation, however, the casualties had been heavy. Saratoga Six had been the first to go, with a career-ending ankle injury. At the end of 1985, Smile, Spend a Buck and Script Ohio had undergone bone-chip operations and recovered; early in 1986 Nordance had also undergone a bone-chip operation and recovered. During the Triple Crown campaign, Skywalker had suffered a hairline fracture and Rhoman Rule had suffered a shoulder injury in the Derby; Hajji's Treasure had broken down in the Preakness; and Tank's Prospect had broken down in the Belmont. Proud Truth had suffered a saucer fracture in the Peter Pan Stakes and had recovered. And at the end of 1985, Stephan's Odyssey suffered a terrible fracture during a workout at Hialeah; six months later, on July 4, he had been put down, after fighting a series of infections. Only the Chief, Creme Fraiche, and Skip Trial survived unscathed.

The Chief, as it turned out, was the only horse of his generation to run with distinction in all three Triple Crown races.

What were we doing to our young horses, in the name of "improving the breed"? Not all of those injuries were a result of bad luck, the random turn of the wheel. Most, in fact, could have been prevented. But to do so would have required a thorough revamping in the way horses were trained and raced in America.

In the time I spent on the track, I came to the conclusion that the way horse racing was conducted in America, from the highest level to the lowest, was greatly in need of change, to benefit the horses as well as the sport. Ironically, the "democratization" of the sport of kings in recent generations has not improved the sport either for horses, horseplayers or owners.

Horse racing, like so many other sports, had become an activity of high expendability. Like the aging greyhounds gassed or sent to labs, the lesser boxers used as punching bags, the football players with permanent disabilities, the college basketball players who remain illiterate, thoroughbreds who broke down were considered a necessary if unfortunate cost in keeping the sport going.

First of all, most breeders in America were not interested in "improving the breed." They were interested in "making" stallions, in creating fashionable studs. There has been little discernible progress in the overall speed and soundness of thoroughbreds since the days of Whirlaway and Citation. If the interest were really there in improving the breed, unsound horses would not be bred in the hope that a certain percentage of their offspring would transcend the flaws of their parents. Even Danzig, who was producing such extraordinary sons and daughters, was also producing a number of flawed horses who shared his own proclivity for unsoundness. A Danzig foal was like a Fabergé egg with a microscopic crack in it; a thing of great value that would not stand much rigorous handling.

Second, the rigorous racing of two-year-olds in America was producing a generation of potential cripples. Horses did not finish maturing physically until the age of five, and yet often they were already competing before they were even two years old; often their careers were over by the time they were "grown up." Spend a Buck, for example, had won the Derby before his actual third birthday. There was a good reason why so many young horses were getting bucked shins, bone chips and suspensory injuries—their bones and joints were not yet strong enough to withstand the extreme stresses of training and racing.

Third, the administering of drugs, particularly Bute, that allowed horses to run sore was also producing permanent cripples. If one could not afford to give a horse the time off to rest, to recover from injury and stress, then one should not be in the sport at all. Moreover, in the long run, allowing horses time to recuperate was more financially rewarding anyway.

Fourth, track veterinarians were frequently not vigilant enough. They should be given far greater power and independence, with unquestioned authority to prevent horses from running who appear sore or unfit. And when a horse breaks down on the track, the vet should immediately follow up the case and determine the cause.

Fifth, track surfaces on a number of tracks were hazardous to a horse's health. The hard, fast tracks of California and elsewhere might produce glamorous times, but they also produced breakdowns. Adding more cushion and banking the tracks would cut down on injuries considerably. Even more important, it has been demonstrated that horses who train on a wood-chip rather than a dirt surface suffer fewer injuries. Most injuries result from the cumulative stress of training rather than the actual stress of a single race. Every racetrack should provide a wood-chip or similar stress-reducing training track.

Last, a number of horses were simply being raced until they broke down, regardless of their previous earnings. I saw horses running in the fairs who had earned their previous owners hundreds of thousands of dollars, and yet these animals were simply being run until they were too old or too lame to win, and then they were given to the "killers," to be hauled to a rendering factory. This was the result of the claiming system, in which horses continued to change hands until no one really felt any responsibility or loyalty to them.

My proposal is that a social security system for racehorses be set up, so that a horse who earns a certain amount of money will be assured a retirement in green pastures. New York's prison program, which, at the time of this writing, provides for the care of some two dozen retired horses, is only a beginning. A small percentage of purse money at every track could be set aside for this purpose, so that any horse who earns his way would be eligible for retirement. A retirement facility could also function as an adoption agency and a retraining center, so that some horses would find their way to riding academies and backyards. Given that humane option, most trainers, undoubtedly, would retire their veteran campaigners rather than run them into the ground.

The ultimate problem in racing, I think, is that horses mean something different to everyone who deals with them. To some they are "athletes," to some "investments," to some just numbers on the tote board. The racetrack is populated with people looking for a payoff, people who use horses to fill all sorts of needs and obsessions.

The racetrack is full of rockinghorse winners, who, like the little boy in D. H. Lawrence's story, remain dead to real emotions, to real commitment, even to real horses. The little boy frantically rides the artificial horse, a horse who can go nowhere, in his desire to beat the odds, to control fate, to control luck. He is the horseplayer, the trainer, the owner, who has lost sight of what the horses really do have to offer: the gift of wildness and wonder in a world where frontiers are gone, the lots divided, the ground paved, the lines drawn.

On the track, humans and horses are like the blind men and the elephant. No one really knows the whole beast, just bits and pieces. The owners know the pride and anxieties of ownership, the financial risks and rewards. Trainers know their horses as athletes, as hospital patients, as purses for which they get a ten percent cut. Grooms know their horses as temperamental creatures whom they must keep clean and bandaged. Only exercise riders and jockeys know what it feels like to ride such a creature, and jockeys know horses only minutes at a time, during the stress and excitement of a race.

Something I had been searching for at the racetrack still eluded me. Maybe I was still caught up in the National Velvet dream: "It was not the silver cup . . . that Velvet saw—but the perfection of accomplishment, the silken cooperation between two actors, the horse and the human, the sense of the lifting of the horse-soul into the sphere of human obedience, human effort, and the offering to it of the taste of human applause."

One day, I decided I had to go out on the track myself. I asked Bill Perry if I could take Frankie, his stable pony, out on the track. Frankie was part quarterhorse, and he was a powerfully built animal who could actually keep up with a thoroughbred for a few strides.

I borrowed a helmet from Paul Solomon, Perry's exercise rider, and Solomon gave me a few pointers. "You have to find the center of the horse," he said, "the eye of the storm. When a record is spinning around and you put your finger on the outside edge, it throws you off. But if you put it in the middle, you can keep it there. You have to find the center of the horse and in yourself."

I headed Frankie out to the track, and he seemed to know that the roles were reversed this time, that he was to be the racehorse and not the escort. He played along with the game, perking up his ears and prancing.

At first we galloped slowly in the middle of the track, and then I moved him over toward the rail. And Frankie started to fly. The track was strangely silent as Frankie's hooves sank into the deep layers of loam and clay and then pushed off. I felt as though I were in a dream, as we whizzed past horses who were galloping slowly on the outside of the track. We were caught up together in the fantasy, in this make-believe race, Frankie and I, and for those moments I knew what racing was all about, this mingling of human and animal wills, this mutual love of speed, of pushing to the edge, born of some inchoate desire that goes beyond mere survival.

A great racehorse might be bred by the most deliberate of genetic determinists; he might be trained by the most calculating of trainers; he might be owned by the silliest of jet-setters. But ultimately, he is something that eludes all of them.

IV

Since its heyday in the Man o' War era, horse racing has failed to become a popular national pastime, not only because racetrack operators initially resisted the broadcasting of the sport, but because racing resists the usual virtues we like to attribute to sports and athletics. Going to the races does not build character, nor does racing suggest that victory is born of hard work, perseverance or positive thinking. It is not a democratic sport; it was built on the wealth of robber barons and on the servitude of grooms from economically disadvantaged groups. Something about the sport of kings still, rightfully, stirs latent puritan antipathy.

Yet horse racing, of all sports, is perhaps the best mirror of human as well as animal nature, and therefore the most instructive. A horse race represents the naked striving to win, to be the best, to get the money, that we like to disguise in other pursuits.

The thoroughbred represents the desire of humans to mold nature in their own image, to control it. The thoroughbred, like the humans who bred him, is an overreacher, a flawed creature whose desire to win outstrips his instincts for survival.

In the months that followed the retirement of Chief's Crown, the wheel of fortune continued to turn, causing yet more fluctuations in the fortunes of the overreachers in the horse world.

In 1986, the bluegrass bubble began to burst, as yearling prices at the Keeneland and Fasig-Tipton auctions decreased by 15 to 20 percent. And as plans for the new federal tax bill tightened, it appeared that limited partnerships, as well as certain tax breaks for the owners and breeders of racehorses, were in jeopardy.

Spendthrift Farm, which lost Seattle Slew to Robert Clay's Three Chimneys, was beset by lawsuits, and Cousin Leslie began to divest himself of his holdings in the farm. Nelson Bunker Hunt declared bankruptcy. And Robert Brennan resigned suddenly, and with little explanation, from the chairmanship of First Jersey Securities.

Ultimately, a horse like Chief's Crown embodied hope, greed and ambition back through the generations. And yet he arrived in the lives of those around him like an accident, like an unexpected gift of grace. Like all good horses, he came as both a gift and a test.

The Chief had given everyone associated with him a dizzying spin on the wheel. But finally there was just too much riding on him, too much weight on his back, and he failed. As the old track story goes, a trainer tells an owner before a race, "The horse has the whole stable riding on him," and the owner says, "But won't that be too much weight?"

I found that both of those ancient scriptural prophecies about horses had held true. As the Muslim legend predicted, the horse does fly without wings, and great riches repose on his back. But as the Hebrew psalmist warned, a horse cannot offer safety. "Neither shall he deliver any by his great strength."

ACKNOWLEDGMENTS

Although I ventured into the world of horse racing as an apprehensive novice, I often found acceptance, and even kindness, on the backstretch.

I particularly want to thank Bill Perry for his patience in the face of endless questions, for letting me hang around the barn in bad times as well as good, and for actually entrusting his horses to me. Steve Penrod, Shug McGaughey, and Richard Gallagher, too, put their horses in my hands, and had much to teach me about the day-to-day routine of training thoroughbreds. And trainers John Veitch and Angel Penna, Jr., were not only helpful, but candid and witty.

I also wish to express my gratitude to Roger Laurin, to Eddie Sweat, to Don MacBeth, and to Andrew Rosen and the other partners of Star Crown Stable. At first bemused by my obsession with Chief's Crown, they, too, let me hang around in bad times as well as good, and they let me share the highs and lows in the brief, intense career of a remarkable racehorse.

The folks at Claiborne Farm, too, were most helpful, and I remember with particular fondness my tour of the farm with Dell Hancock, who introduced me to Six Crowns just a week before the mare gave birth to Chief Crown's half sister. And Robert Clay, in whose fields at Three Chimneys Farm the Chief now romps, was most hospitable.

And, of course, I couldn't have followed my Hopeful without complete access to tracks across the country, and I thank Steve Schwartz, Joe Tanenbaum, Jim Williams, Chick Lang, Jr., and Edgar Allen for their help in providing credentials and useful background information. Steve Schwartz also gave me my first good tip on a Hopeful when he told me about a little Danzig colt who he thought had a future.

I found considerable encouragement, help and companionship from a number of turf writers I met along the way. My special thanks to Andy Beyer, whose enthusiasm for playing the horses is most contagious and whose intelligence and generosity never cease to astonish. Thanks are also due to Bill Nack for his good company and for his book, *Big Red of Meadow Stable*, which remains an inspiration; to Stan Hochman, Dale Austin and Jack Mann for big-brotherly advice and wisdom; and to Joe Hirsch, Steve Crist, Sam McCracken, Ed Gray, Maryjean Wall, Jim Bolus, Bill Christine, Bill Mooney, Steve Thomas and Russ Harris, whose dispatches were invaluable and who made my time in the press box more interesting.

Lastly, my thanks to John Tirman, who came up with the idea for this quest for a Hopeful one day at the Great Barrington Fair. Without his encouragement, affection and support, I would never have made it out of the starting gate. I also want to thank my agent, Tim Seldes, as well as Phil Pochoda, my first editor, and Jim Moser, who took over the project, for encouraging my quixotic quest.

Finally, there is the Chief, who made the quest real and taught me a few lessons about what it means to ride on the wheel of fortune.

INDEX

Asterisks (*) indicate names of horses

Affirmed*, 12, 42, 43, 66, 67, 231, 342
Aga Khan, 59–60
Aga Khan IV, 171–72
Agee, James, 72
Aiken, S. C., 24
Ainslee, Tom, 197–98
Ainslee's Complete Guide to Thoroughbred Racing, 197
Alabama Stakes, 343
Alexander, David, 110
Alibhai*, 42
All Along*, 154
All Beautiful*, 65
Allen, Bill, 155, 156, 173
Althea*, 277
Alydar*, 44, 67, 194, 231, 342
Amberoid*, 109, 139
Amory, Cleveland, 79–80, 99
Anderson, Joe, 245, 246, 252
Ansara, Marge, 21
A Phenomenon*, 43, 45
Appeals of racing decisions, 252–53
Aqueduct racetrack, 125
Arabian horses, 5, 56–57
Arden, Elizabeth, 42, 226
Aristides*, 274
Arkansas Derby, 259
Arlington Million, 113, 115–16
Assault*, 66
Astaire, Fred, 162–63
Attribute*, 230

Bacharach, Burt, 46, 51
Ballade*, 54
Bance, Peter, 141
Bancroft, Thomas, 315
Band Practice*, 246
Banner Bob*, 230, 270
Barich, Bill, 160
Barrera, Oscar, 24, 119, 138
Baruch, Bernard, 75
Bassett, Ted, 256, 257–58, 269, 270
Bates Motel*, 97
Battle, Howard, 256–57
Beal, Terry, 155, 173
Bear Hunt*, 107, 268, 277
Beat Me Daddy*, 14
Beau Père*, 42
Beau Purple*, 123
Beauty of horses, 249
Bee Bee Bee*, 308
Before Dawn*, 231
Belle de Jour*, 286
Belmont, August, 120–21
Belmont, August, II, 17, 120, 121
Belmont, August, IV, 100
Belmont Juvenile race, 138, 139–40
Belmont Park, 118–20
Belmont Stakes, 327–37
Benat el-A'waj horses, 56
Bennett, James Gordon, 76
Bessarabian*, 169
Betts, Tony, 121
Big Burn*, 21
Bionic Light*, 137–38, 139–40, 141, 150, 166

Black-Eyed Susan Stakes, 315, 316
Black Gold*, 2, 15
Black Stallion series (Farley), 2
Black Toney*, 47
Blade*, 206
Blengs, Vinnie, 96
Blenheim*, 172
Blenheim II*, 61
Bluegrass, 248–49
Blue Grass Stakes, 268–71
Blue Norther*, 108
Bly, Nellie, 82
Boethius, 201
Bold Lad*, 114, 115
Bold Ruler*, 61–62, 63, 90, 172,
    184, 206, 281
Bolles, Richard, 180
Bolus, Jim, 294
Bond, Freddie, 111, 135, 289–90
Boom Soon*, 290
Booth, Jerry, 246, 258, 262, 271,
    342
Boswell, James, 120
Bradley, Col. E. R., 47, 281
Brant, Molly, 74
Brant, Peter, 331
Brede, Tom and Ann, 104
Breeders' Cup races, 122
    California selected for, 147
    the Classic (1984), 172–73
    the Classic (1985), 350–52
    hotel accommodations, 149–50
    the Juvenile (1984), 150–51, 153,
        163–64, 165–67
    the Juvenile for fillies (1984),
        168–69
    media coverage, 150, 163, 167,
        171
    Pavilion of the Stars, 149
    as Super Bowl of racing, 48–49,
        54–55
Breeding of thoroughbreds, 11
    American–European
        interbreeding, 60–61
    commercialization of, 43–44
    dosage system, 59–60

energy and, 66–67
flawed horses, use of, 44–45
foal-sharing system, 62
genetics of, 40, 59
improving the breed, 354
matings, 67–68
syndication, 42, 43, 140–41, 142–
    45
Breeding the Racehorse (Tesio), 67
Brennan, Henry, 321
Brennan, Robert, 87, 311, 344,
    351, 358
    Jersey Derby, 261, 308
    middle-class audience, focus on,
        169–71, 326–27
    profile of, 320–23
Bride*, The, 62
Bright, James, 182
Brooks, Clem, 46
Brown, Harold, 206, 236–37
Brown, Mattie, 209
Brunetti, Joseph, 184
Bryan, William Jennings, 182
Buckpasser*, 70, 115, 127
Bujnicki, Judy, 104–6, 113, 332–33
Bull Lea*, 46
Bush, Vernon, 194, 208
Bushel 'n' Peck*, 172
Butler, Judd, 172
Byerly Turk*, 57

Calcagni, Frank, 24
California Derby, 259, 312
California racing, 147–48
Calumet Farm, 39–40, 90, 231–32,
    343
Camel, Thomas, 78
Campbell, Cot, 101–2
Canadian Factor*, 158
Cantey, Charlsie, 346
Carr de Naskra*, 341, 344, 346
Carry Back*, 15, 284–85
Casseleria*, 51
Centennial Farms, 101
Center Court Star*, 128
Chaleureux*, 67–68

Charlie (clocker), 279
Chaucer, Geoffrey, 211
Cheering by horseplayers, 33
Chenery, Chris, 61–62, 63, 109
Chenery, Penny Tweedy, 62, 65, 69, 70, 109–10, 123, 127, 128, 166–67, 264, 344, 347
Cherry Hill Mile, 261
Chief's Crown*, 53
    appearance of, 88–89
    awards, 188, 194
    Belmont races (1984), 136–37, 138–40
    Belmont Stakes (1985), 327, 329–30, 333–37
    Blue Grass Stakes, 268–69, 270–71
    Breeders' Cup (the Classic), 350–52
    Breeders' Cup (the Juvenile), 150, 164–65, 166–67
    career, assessment of, 352–53, 358
    Cowdin Stakes, 141–42
    dosage index, 195–96, 281
    Flake's selection of, 89–92, 107
    Flamingo Stakes, 238–41, 242, 243–46, 252–53
    in Florida, 176–78, 191, 194, 202–4, 215–18, 224
    the Hopeful, 113–15
    injuries, rumors of, 215–18
    intelligence of, 262, 264
    at Keeneland, 251–52, 258, 261–62, 267
    Kentucky Derby, 278–79, 281, 282, 288–89, 299–304, 305
    Kentucky Derby win, odds against, 92, 114–15
    Laurin's training of, 134–36, 247
    lunar phases, influence of, 348
    lung problems, 217
    the Marlboro, 349–50
    naming of, 128–29
    pedigree, 69–70, 71, 128, 173
    the Preakness, 311, 312, 314, 318–19
    retirement, 350, 352
    Saratoga Special, 88–90
    specialness of, 158
    Swale Stakes, 229–30
    syndication of, 140–41, 142–45
    Tell Stakes, 339–41
    Travers Cup, 338, 342, 343–48
    virus attack, 177, 178
    Woodward Stakes, 348–49
Childhood experiences with horses, 2–4
Chosen Crown*, 128
Chris Evert*, 19–20, 112, 126, 134, 165, 281
    Secretariat*, mating with, 69, 127–28
Churchill Downs, 274
Cicada*, 62
Cigar (exercise rider), 135–36, 177, 203, 314
Citation*, 40, 66, 93, 184
Claiborne Farm, 60–61, 63, 69
Claiming races, 19–20, 33–34
"Class" of a horse, 197–98
Clay, Albert, 266
Clay, John, 77
Clay, Robert, 101, 143–45, 216, 265–67, 270, 291, 303, 347
Cleason, Joe "The Orator," 82
Clever Allemont*, 259
Clever Hans*, 262–63
Clockers, 218
Clock Tower*, 204
Cocaine trade, 213–14
Coke, Edward, 58
Coleridge, Samuel Taylor, 8
Coll, John, 28
Combs, Brownell, 43–44, 45, 46, 52, 282
Combs, Dorothy, 41
Combs, Leslie, II, 41–42, 46, 163, 358
"Common" horses, 210–11
Condition books, 24

Conquistador Cielo*, 221
Contredance*, 222
Cooksey, Patricia, 311
Cordero, Angel, 97, 152, 301, 348
  as Chief's Crown's* jockey, 136,
    331, 335, 339, 340–41, 345–46
Cornman, Paul, 340, 344
Cosell, Howard, 315
Count Fleet*, 21, 37
Cousté, Col. H., 93
Covert Operation*, 230
Cowdin Stakes, 141–42
Creme Fraiche*, 229, 255, 275–76,
  324, 326, 328, 332, 334, 336,
  353
Crist, Steven, 137, 141, 230, 251,
  260
Crumpets*, 139
Current Hope*, 268
Curtiss, Glenn, 182
Cutlass Reality*, 318, 332, 335,
  336

Daingerfield, Keene, 22–23, 27,
  257, 259
Dama II*, 172
Damascus Sam*, 135–36, 204–5,
  229, 267, 313
Dancer's Image*, 293–94
Danger's Hour*, 102
Danzig*, 53, 69, 71, 92, 100, 219–
  20, 221–22, 291, 354
Darby Dan*, 232
Dark Star*, 123
Darley, Thomas, 57
Darley Arabian*, 57
Davey Do Good*, 200
Davidowitz, Steve, 279
Davis, Robbie, 340
Davona Dale*, 231
Day, Pat, 172, 319, 349
Debrett*, 64, 65, 66
Deering, James, 186–87
Degenerate John*, 133
De Kwiatkowski, Henryk, 196,
  219–21, 245, 252

Delillo, Don, 236
Deputy Minister*, 89
Derby, Lord, 6, 274
Desert War*, 102–3, 104, 137
Desert Wine*, 154
Designer jeans, 19–20, 112, 130–31
Devil's Bag*, 12, 14, 36, 140, 195,
  218
Diaz, Dennis, 325, 328, 331, 338,
  344
  Kentucky Derby, 261, 286–88,
    303, 305
  the Preakness, bypassing of,
    306–9
  purchase of Spend a Buck*, 152,
    286–87
Diaz, Linda, 287
Diaz, Sacramento, 286
Dickson, Loy, 137–38
Disraeli, Benjamin, 53
D.K.'s Pleasure*, 28, 29
Dr. Carter*, 177, 178, 232
Do It Again Dan*, 89, 114, 230
Donn, James, Jr., 185
Don's Choice*, 345, 346
·Don't Fool With Me*, 89, 141
Dosage index, 59–60, 195–96, 281
Doubly Clear*, 104–7, 113, 114,
  260, 332–33, 334
Dowd, Jim, 205, 217
Dowst, Robert Saunders, 198
Dreyfus, Jack, 123
Drugging of thoroughbreds, 32,
  35, 48, 205, 294–95, 305, 354
Du Pont, Allaire, 123, 144
Du Pont, William, Jr., 87

Eastern Racing Association, 17
Eclipse*, 58, 120
Eclipse Awards, 188
Eillo*, 173, 188
El Basco*, 324
El Gran Señor*, 53
Elizabeth II, Queen, 250, 257
Ellsworth, Rex, 172
Encolure*, 301, 302

Engberg, Dick, 167, 171
Engelhard, Charlie, 103
Equalize*, 340
Equine virus, 177-78
Equipoise*, 84
Eternal Prince*, 259-60, 278, 288, 301, 302, 304-5, 311, 318-19, 334, 335, 353
Eurythmics (rock band), 95, 98
Everett, Marje, 148-49, 163, 173
Everett, Webb, 148
Evert, Chris, 112, 165
Exclusive Native*, 44, 67
Exclusive Partner*, 340-41
Exterminator*, 2, 275

Fair circuit, 9-10
Faquer*, 107, 177-78
Farish, Will, 144, 282, 287, 295, 308, 344
Farish, William, 308
Farley, Don, 282
Farley, Walter, 2, 4
Fast Account*, 276, 301, 302
Fast Lane Gal*, 96
Faulkner, William, 5
Feldman, Dave, 215
Felipe (groom), 96
Feminism and racing, 7-8
Fink, Jule, 121, 343
Finney, Albert, 100
Finney, John, 52
Fires, Earlie, 200, 212, 228
Firestone, Bert, 144
Fisher, Carl, 181-82
Fit to Fight*, 138
Fitzgerald, Robert, 105
Flagler, Henry, 180-81
Flamingo Stakes, 184, 239-43
    appeal of decision, 252-53
    the race, 243-46
Floating Reserve*, 253, 270, 301
Florida, development of, 180-82
Florida Derby, 229, 230
Florida racing, 176
Foal races, 38

Folk Art*, 295
Foolish Pleasure*, 7
Ford, Wendell, 273
Forego*, 6, 123, 279, 280, 308
Forli*, 128
Forsythe, John, 163
Forward Pass*, 293-94
Foundation Plan*, 340-41
Fountain of Youth race, 223
Foxy Deene*, 296
Foxy Greene*, 23, 31-32, 186, 194, 199, 201
Francis, Dick, 241
Frankie*, 356-57
Fran's Valentine*, 168-69, 253, 254, 292, 295, 296, 343
Freak accidents, 193
Front Pew*, 125
Fuller, Abigail, 294, 295, 343
Fuller, Peter, 20, 72, 292-95, 343
Fulton, John, 151

Gaines, John, 47-50, 86, 163
Gainesway Farm, 47-48
Gait efficiency, 95
Galbreath, Dan, 141
Galbreath, John, 141, 164, 232, 245, 253, 299, 329
Gallagher, Georgia, 206, 228
Gallagher, Richard, 205-7, 212, 228
Gallant Fox*, 61, 341
Gallant Man*, 90
Gambolati, Cam, 152-53, 261, 305, 306, 308, 328, 331
Garcia, Joe, 105
Garden quality of racetracks, 187-88, 327
Garden State Park, 170, 323, 325, 327
Garden State Stakes, 261
Garson, Greer, 163
Gate Dancer*, 156, 157, 161, 172-73, 349, 351
Gates, John "Bet a Million," 17
Gato del Sol*, 306

Gene (groom), 206–7, 227, 234–35
General Assembly*, 66
General Buck*, 194
General Duke*, 90
Gentry, Tom, 51–52
Genuine Risk*, 7, 67, 133, 276
Gerry, Martha, 123, 308
Ghost horse, 127
Gil (groom), 210, 212
Gilchrest, Alvert W., 180
Ginistrelli, Cavaliere, 67–68
Gitlin, Todd, 214
Godolphin, Lord, 58
Godolphin Arabian*, 57
Goldsmith*, 82
Gordy, Berry, 295
Gould, Stephen Jay, 93
Graham, Billy, 213
Grant, Cary, 148, 163
Great Barrington Fair, 9–10
Great Handicapper, the, 160–62,
    171, 173, 174, 190–91, 194,
    195, 204–5, 215, 221, 223, 224,
    229, 242, 246, 250, 260–61,
    268–69, 276, 278, 296, 298,
    333–34, 349, 352
  handicapping system, 161, 197,
    198–200
Greentree Stable, 144–45
Greinton*, 349
Griffin, Mike, 63–64, 71
Guggenheim, Harry, 109, 123
Gulfstream Park, 176, 185, 188–90,
    229–30

Haggin, James B., 47
Hail Bold King*, 85, 87, 171
Hajji's Treasure*, 259, 312, 318,
    319–20, 353
Hancock, Arthur B., Sr., 60–61
Hancock, Arthur B. "Bull," Jr., 60,
    63, 67, 172
Hancock, Dell, 316
Hancock, Seth, 65, 66, 69, 127,
    128, 134, 140, 141, 143, 222,
    285

Hancock, Waddell, 103
Handicapping systems, 19, 161,
    197–200
Hannon, Jim, 34
Harness racing, 16
Harper, Rowe, 286
Harris, Russ, 140
Hartack, Bill, 90, 280
Hasty Matilda*, 62
Hasty Tex*, 204
Hatchet Dancer*, 204, 205
Hatton, Charlie, 88
Herat*, 103
Hertz, John D., 37
Hialeah community, 179, 180, 182
Hialeah Park, 176, 183–85, 187–88
Hill, Jim and Sally, 45–46, 144
Hill Rise*, 280
Hirsch, Joe, 165, 177, 230, 240,
    241, 327, 344
Hirsh, Warren, 130–31, 132
Hochman, Stan, 327–28
Hodge, Stan, 312, 317, 320
Hollywood Park, 147, 148, 162–63
Hopeful (race), the, 12, 82, 112–15
Horses. See Thoroughbreds
Hot-walking, 24, 27–29, 209–10,
    254–55
Huddle Up*, 324–25, 326, 334
Hunt, Nelson Bunker, 38, 51, 149,
    287, 358
Hurst, Brian, 260, 282, 287–88,
    315

I Am the Game*, 261, 285, 301,
    302, 311, 318, 324
Icaza, Manuel, 108, 125
Image of Greatness*, 151, 278
Imperial Choice*, 351
Inca King*, 85, 87
Indian Chief II*, 126
Intelligence in horses, 30, 262–64
International Thoroughbred
    Breeders (ITB), 87, 169–70,
    323
Irish Fighter*, 282, 301, 302

Irish Lad*, 82
Irish Sur*, 230, 261
Iron Liege*, 90
Ishmael, 56
ITB. *See* International
   Thoroughbred Breeders
Izza Valentine*, 168

Jackson, Andrew, 310
James, Will, 2
Jeff (groom), 27, 29
Jerkins, Allen, 101, 102
Jerkins, Steve, 102
Jersey Derby, 261, 307–9, 320–21,
   324–26
Jim Dandy*, 341
Jimmy (hot-walker), 237–38
Jockey Club (England), 120
Jockey Club (U.S.), 120–23
Jockey Club Gold Cup, 123
Jockey Club's Experimental
   Handicap, 194–95
John Henry*, 6, 31, 95, 153, 188,
   290
   Arlington Million, 112, 115–16
   psychic conversation with, 264
Johnson, Don, 54
Johnson, Patty, 276
Johnson, Phil, 126
Johnson, William, 73–74
Jolley, Leroy, 7, 66, 97, 114, 118,
   194, 205, 240
Jolley, Moody, 7
Jones, Aaron, 165
Jones, Johnny, 143
Jones, Warner L., 206, 291–92, 299
Joppy*, 284
Jordan, Steve, 177–78, 203, 246,
   334, 343, 345, 347
J.R. (groom), 234–35, 238
Jumel, Madame (Elizabeth
   Bowen), 78–79

Kathy (hot-walker), 29
Keene, James R., 82, 120, 250

Keeneland
   Blue Grass Stakes, 268–71
   exclusivity of, 256
   horse sales, 38, 51–52, 53, 126,
      251
   Lexington Stakes, 258–59
   Queen Elizabeth's visit, 250, 257
   racing at, 250–51
Keepayourmouthshut*, 102
Kelley, Walter, 105
Kelso*, 6, 123
Kennedy, Ethel, 318
Kennelot*, 220, 222
Kentucky*, 77
Kentucky Association for the
   Improvement of the Breeds of
   the Stock, 250
Kentucky Derby
   casualties of, 277
   Dancer's Image's* race, 293–95
   Derby Fever Syndrome, 277–78
   history of, 274–75
   Northern Dancer's* win, 280
   record times, 93
   Secretariat's* win, 279–80
   as ultimate goal in racing, 273
Kentucky Derby (1985)
   Derby Eve parties, 296–97
   Derby Spectacular show, 282–83
   drugging of horses, 294–95, 305
   field of horses, 276
   handicappers' predictions, 278
   horse trading at, 282
   media coverage, 275
   party animals, 298
   post positions, draw for, 279, 282
   prep races, 258–61, 268–71
   the race, 299–303
   track condition, 299, 300
   vendors, 297–98
Kentucky Oaks race, 292, 295–96
Khaled*, 172
Kilroe, Jimmy, 165
Kim (groom), 235–36
"Kind" horses, 29, 211
King, Ed, 18

King, Martin Luther, Jr., 293
Klein, Calvin, 20, 112, 130, 131, 133
Klein, Eugene, 51, 88, 151, 259, 336
Kram, Mark, 53–54
Kumin, Maxine, 4

Lady Foxcroft*, 23
Lady Godiva Handicap, 17
Lady's Secret*, 69
Lambton, George, 59
Landaluce*, 46
Lang, Chick, 307–9, 311
Lashkari*, 171, 174
Laurie (stablehand), 226
Laurin, Lucien, 70, 108-10, 347–48
Laurin, Nina, 167, 229
Laurin, Roger
  Belmont races (1984), 138, 139
  Belmont Stakes (1985), 327–28, 331, 334–35
  Blue Grass Stakes, 268, 271
  Breeders' Cup (the Juvenile), 150, 167
  Chief's Crown's* syndication, 143
  Chief's Crown's* training, 134–36, 247
  Clay and, 266
  Cowdin Stakes, 141–42
  equine virus episode, 177
  Flamingo Stakes, 239–40, 241, 244, 246
  in Florida, 185, 191, 202–3, 216-17, 223
  the Hopeful, 113
  at Keeneland, 251–52, 258, 267
  Kentucky Derby, 271–72, 278–79, 289, 299–300, 303–4, 305–6
  MacBeth, selection of, 89
  pessimism of, 107–8
  Phipps family and, 70–71, 110
  the Preakness, 312–13, 314, 318, 320
  racing strategy, 339–40, 345
  reticence of, 108, 266–67
  retirement, 268, 350
  Secretariat* and, 20
  Swale Stakes, 230
  Tell Stakes, 339–40
  training background, 108–9
  Travers Cup, 338, 342–43, 345, 348
Lawrence, D. H., 4, 356
Lear Fan*, 153
Leatherbury, King T., 285–86
Lennox, Annie, 98
Lenzini, Butch, 316
Leonard, John, 214
LeRoy, Mervyn, 148, 163
Let Burn*, 21, 26, 118
Lexington*, 76
Lexington, Ky., 248–50
Lexington Stakes, 258–59
Lightning Leap*, 340
Lilian (groom), 26
Little, Don, 101
Livingston, Bernard, 120
Long, Huey, 281
Longden, Johnny, 163
Lopez, Enrique, 316
Lord Darnley*, 313
Lukas, D. Wayne, 50–51, 66, 88, 137, 142, 151, 259, 288, 295, 319, 324–25, 328, 336
Lukas, Jeff, 328–29
Lunar phases, 348
Lundy, J. T., 231–32
Luro, Horatio, 32, 100
Lyphard*, 53
Lypheor*, 173

MacBeth, Don, 113, 136, 230, 270, 332, 335, 336, 349
  Breeders' Cup (the Juvenile), 164, 166, 167
  as Don's Choice's* jockey, 345, 346
  firing of, 320, 330–31
  Flamingo Stakes, 244–45, 252–53

hired by Laurin, 89
the Preakness, 318, 319, 320
retirement, 350
riding technique, 240–41
McCarron, Chris, 115, 276, 318, 349
McCarron, Gregg, 98
McDaniel, Henry, 275
McGaughey, Shrug, 343
McGrath, Price, 274
McHargue, Darrel, 346
MacKay, Jim, 317
McKnight, William, 65
Madden, Anita and Preston, 296–97
Madden, Mike, 314
"Made" horses, 118
Majestic Madonna*, 207
Majestic Prince*, 44, 67
Majestic Wine*, 96
Majesty's Prince*, 154
Maktoum, Sheikh Maktoum al, 144, 265
Maktoum, Sheikh Mohammed bin Rashid al, 53
Mann, Jack, 8, 108, 263–64, 275, 317
Manning, Dennis, 135
Man o' War*, 12, 47, 307, 342
Manzi, Joe, 168, 253, 269
Maple, Eddie, 204–5, 331, 340
Marie d'Argonne*, 243
Marino, Dan, 191–92
Markey, Lucille, 231, 343
Marlboro, the, 349–50
Marsha (stablehand), 226
Martel, Charles, 5
Martin, Frank "Pancho," 100, 118, 277
Martin, José, 100
Martin, Nina, 155
Mary (hot-walker), 255
Maryland Jockey Club, 310
Maud Muller*, 127
Mayer, Louis B., 42, 163
Meadow Stable, 63, 64, 65

Medieval Secret*, 105
Meeker, Ralph, 298
Mellon, Paul, 65–66, 102, 104, 138
Memorials to thoroughbreds, 46-47
Mena, José, 88, 138
Merrick, George, 181, 182
Merritt, Bobby, 121
Miami, Fla., 213–14
Miami Lakes, Fla., 178–79
Micki Bracken*, 315, 316, 319
Middle class, racing's appeal for, 170–71
Mighty Appealing*, 219
Migliore, Richard, 301
Miller, Mackenzie, 102, 103–4, 329
Mill Reef*, 61, 172
Milner, Jim, 203, 217–18, 242
Minstrel*, The, 52, 53
Miss Angie*, 237, 238
Miss Cavandish*, 108
Miss Disco*, 61
Miss Hardwick*, 205
Miss Musket*, 127, 165
Mr. Prospector*, 44, 134, 151, 291
Mohammed, 56
Molter, William, 163
Mom's Command*, 20, 21, 292, 295, 343
Mooney, Bill, 316–17
Moon Prospector*, 14
Moran, Elizabeth, 328
Morano, Ed, 253
Morris, Anita, 99
Morris, John A., 99
Morrissey, John, 76–77
Muybridge, Eadweard, 146–47
My Bupers*, 53
My Sierra Leone*, 173

Nack, Bill, 88, 246, 277
Namath, Joe, 189
Nancy English*, 205
Nashua*, 12, 42, 45, 46, 61, 115, 184
Nasrullah*, 60–61, 172, 173–74

Native Dancer*, 6–7, 12, 20, 115, 123, 281, 293
Nearco*, 173
Nearctic*, 174
Neloy, Eddie, 62, 110–11
Neoclassical*, 200
Never Bend*, 61
Newkidontheblock*, 322
New York Racing Association, 122
Niarchos, Stavros, 53, 144
Nickel Back*, 88, 89
Nijinsky II*, 53
Nijinsky's Secret*, 115
Noor's Image*, 20
Nordance*, 100–2, 260, 353
Northern Bid*, 258
Northern Dancer*, 11, 32, 52–53, 54, 68–69, 93, 173, 184, 280
Numbered Account*, 70

Oakward*, 95, 96
O'Brien, Vincent, 52
O'Connell, Charlie, 124–25, 126
Old Rosebud*, 93
Old Rosebud race, 296
Olin, John, 220
Onion*, 123
Orensteen, Jenny, 225
Ortega y Gasset, José, 86
Our Mims*, 231
Outstandingly*, 168, 169, 173

Palmer, Joe, 73, 75, 82
Pancho Villa*, 259, 260, 276, 278
Parisella, John, 118
Paul (foreman), 254, 255
Paulson, Allen, 54, 295
Pavilion of the Stars, 149
Penna, Angel, Jr., 283, 299, 303, 330, 343
Penna, Eleanor, 100
Penrod, Steve, 253, 254, 255
Perry, Bill, 21–22, 23–25, 26–27, 32, 95, 96, 97, 98, 154, 157, 159, 185, 186, 201, 207, 208, 223

Persian Tiara*, 153, 243
Pet on the Couch*, 209–10, 237, 238
Pfungst, Oskar, 263
Phipps, Gladys Mills, 61–62, 63
Phipps, Ogden, 62, 65, 70, 110–11
Phipps, Ogden Mills, 70
Pick 6 bets, 161–62, 174, 204–5
Picou, Jimmy, 135
Pie Man*, 212
Piesen, John, 215
Pimlico racetrack, 310
Pincay, Laffit, 147, 258, 283, 301, 331, 348
Pirate's Glow*, 169
Plymouth Hotel, Miami Beach, 186
Politics and racing, 159–60
Pollard, Carl, 206, 228, 292
Post, John and Pauletta, 282
Pratt, George, 95
Preakness, the
    Alibi Breakfast, 315–16
    post positions, 314
    Preakness fever, 311
    the race, 318–20
    Spend a Buck's* absence, 306–9, 310–11
Price, Jack, 284
Price, Katherine, 284–85
Prince Andrew*, 128
Prince Jac O*, 10
Princess Rooney*, 171, 173
Proudest Hour*, 166
Proud Truth*, 151, 219, 223, 230–31, 243–44, 245, 246, 250, 252, 260, 278, 300, 301, 329, 350–51, 353
Prove Out*, 123
Psychic conversations with horses, 264
Pulitzer, Joseph, 82
Purple Mountain*, 335
Putnam, Gideon, 76

Quill*, 109

Racetracks
  class system, 15
  garden quality of, 187–88, 327
  surfaces of, 355
Racing
  appeals of decisions, 252–53
  as business, 11, 44
  changes needed in, 353–55
  class system of, 15
  feminism and, 7–8
  laws against, 16–17
  middle class, appeal for, 170–71
  odds, respect for, 14–15
  politics and, 159–60
  promotional gimmicks, 17 18
  public interest in, 6
  regulation of, 120–23
  rumors in, 215–19
  secrecy in, 13–14
  spiral of problems, 55
  televising of races, 48–49
  the wealthy, appeal for, 86–87
  year-round racing, 18
Racing commissions, 122
Rainey, Cal, 252
Raise a Native*, 44, 67
Rascal Lass*, 295
Rasmussen, Leon, 60, 153, 195–96
Reconditioning of thoroughbreds,
  119
Red (hot-walker), 29–30
Reed, Billy, 284, 294
Regret*, 7, 85, 274–75
Regulation of racing, 120–23
Rehearsing*, 208
Rhoman Rule*, 215, 229, 246, 259,
  260–61, 278, 282, 301, 303,
  353
Riddle, Samuel D., 307
Riding techniques, 241
Right and Regal*, 205
Right Con*, 259
Riva Ridge*, 21, 70, 271
Riva Ridge Stakes, 334
Riverman*, 61
Rockhill Native*, 12

Rockingham Park, 17
Roman, Steven, 195
Rooney, Mickey, 314
Roosevelt, Franklin D., 75
Rose, Charlie, 278, 303, 350–51
Rosen, Adrian, 164, 202, 203, 271,
  290
Rosen, Andrew, 107, 111, 115,
  125, 130, 144, 165, 202–4, 266,
  281, 344–45, 347
  education in racing, 134
  Kentucky Derby, 287, 289, 290–
  91, 300, 306
  MacBeth, firing of, 330, 332
  publicity for, 239, 271
  Puritan Fashions, 112, 132–33
  wagering by, 168, 169, 296, 315
Rosen, Carl, 337
  champion, desire for, 126
  Chief's Crown* and, 128–29
  Chris Evert* and, 19–20, 126–28
  Chris Evert*–Miss Musket* race,
  165
  death of, 70, 132
  early interest in racing, 123–25
  horse breeding, 69–70, 127–28,
  281
  illness, 129
  Laurin, hiring of, 134–35
  luck of, 289, 342
  Puritan Fashions, 19–20, 112,
  123–24, 130–31
  Schwartz and, 131–32
Rosen, David, 111, 314
Rosen, Douglas, 111, 164, 229,
  270, 271, 296, 337
Rosen, Lisa, 111, 134, 314
Rosen, Michelle, 111
Rosen, Shirley, 111, 164
Rosenberg, Robert, 252
Round Table*, 90
Roussel, Louis, III, 269
Roving Boy*, 253
Roving Minstrel*, 113
Rowan, Steve, 105, 106–7, 113,
  114

Royal Heroine*, 115, 171, 173
Royal Prestige*, 207, 210, 212,
   226–27, 242
Royal Setting*, 207
Rube the Great*, 277
Rubin, Bob, 245
Rubin, Miles, 134, 141, 143, 144
Rubin, Sam, 115, 290
Ruffian*, 7–8, 13–14
Rumors in racing, 215–19

Sabarese, Ted, 118–19
Saggy*, 284
Sangster, Robert, 52, 53, 54, 171
Saratoga
   decline of, 81–82
   hot springs, 73–75
   introduction of racing, 76–77
   Madame Jumel, 78–79
   racing season, 72–73
   Saratoga cycle, 341–42
   Travers Stakes, 77
   Whitney family, influence of,
      79–83
Saratoga (1984 season)
   Dog Show, 99–100
   the Hopeful, 12, 82, 112–15
   Museum Ball, 99
   Saratoga Special, 82, 88–90
   Whitney Stakes, 80, 95–98
Saratoga (1985 season)
   Tell Stakes, 339–41
   Travers Cup, 338, 342, 343–48
Saratoga Association for the
   Improvement of the Breed of
   Horses, 77
Saratoga Six*, 137, 142, 152, 188,
   195, 254, 353
Saratoga Special (race), 82, 88–90
Sarner, Buddy, 270
Saros*, 168
Savannah Slew*, 295
Scheib, Earl, 168–69, 254
Schride*, 322
Schwartz, Barry, 87, 102, 112, 130,
   131–32, 133–34, 144

Scorpio Stable, 21, 23
Scott, Walter, 149
Script Ohio*, 141, 150, 165, 216,
   353
Seattle Slew*, 45–46, 97
Secrecy in racing, 13–14
Secretariat*, 7, 12, 20, 21, 88, 123,
   161, 195
   Chris Evert*, mating with, 69,
      127–28
   gait efficiency, 95
   Kentucky Derby win, 93, 279–
      80
   as national hero, 159–60
   offspring of, 65–66, 68–69
   pedigree, 61, 62–63, 173
   in retirement, 64
Secretary General*, 136, 150, 165,
   166
Secreto*, 53
Selling of horses
   bidding wars, 53–54
   international nature of, 52
Selway, Stephen, 216
Seminole Indians, 184
Sexuality of horses, 4
Shahian, Paul, 21, 98
Sham*, 277, 279, 280
Sharp, Bayard, 308
Shecky Greene*, 23, 279, 280
Shelton, Robert, 177–78
Shifty Sheik*, 138
Shoemaker, Willie, 90, 108, 163,
   280
Shooting Party, The (film), 34
Shuvee*, 101
Signorina*, 67–68
Signorinetta*, 68
Singleton, Brian, 92
Sir Barton*, 307
Sir Gallahad*, 61
Sir Quasar*, 21–22, 26–27, 95–96,
   98, 186, 207–9
Six Crowns*, 69, 128, 291
Sixty Minutes, 48
Skip Trial*, 324, 338, 346

Ski Resort*, 26
Sky Command*, 88, 89, 114
Skywalker*, 288, 300, 301, 353
Slew o' Gold*, 45–46, 97–98, 138, 153, 154, 155, 172–73, 265, 266
  syndication of, 143–44
Smartenta*, 204
Smile*, 137, 142, 152, 216, 353
Smith, John, 33
Smith, Lou, 17
Smith, Red, 40
Smith, Robyn, 162–63
Smoot, Joseph, 182
Snaafi Dancer*, 53, 54
Snoltite*, 206–7, 210, 227–28, 291–92, 296, 299, 304
Snowgun*, 26, 33, 208
Social security for thoroughbreds, 99, 355
Solomon, Paul, 356
Something Cool*, 296
Somethingroyal*, 61–62
Sommer, Sigmund, 118
Sosby, John, 47, 283
Sparks, John, 263
Spectacular Bid*, 7, 12
Spectacular Love*, 137, 138, 139–40, 141, 150, 165, 166
Speed charts, 161, 198–99
Spend a Buck*, 137, 195, 215, 216, 328, 338, 343, 346, 350
  Breeders' Cup (the Juvenile), 151, 152–53, 161, 165–66
  Diaz's purchase of, 152, 286–87
  Garden State Stakes, 261, 353
  Jersey Derby, 320, 324–26
  Kentucky Derby, 278, 300, 301–3, 304, 305, 308–9
Spendthrift Farm, 40–41, 42–46, 282, 358
Sport Jet*, 318
Stablehands
  lives of, 234–36
  women as, 224–26
Stallion barns, 265–66

Stanford, Leland, 47, 146–47
Steinbrenner, George, 151, 259–60, 282, 288, 304, 315–16
Stephan's Odyssey*, 196, 219, 222–23, 230, 243–44, 251, 254, 258–59, 276, 278, 301, 302, 328, 331, 336, 344, 345, 346, 353
Stephens, Woody, 13, 63, 107, 108, 109, 118, 121, 185, 193, 196, 219–22, 229, 245, 258, 275–76, 306, 324, 328, 334, 336
Steps*, 255, 271
Steve's Friend*, 151
Stevens, Gene, 190
Strawberry Road*, 153
Stuart, John, 141, 143, 144, 291
Stud Book, 6, 58
Stumpf, Carl, 262–63
Suffolk "Sufferin'" Downs, 16–19, 35–36
Sugar Tex*, 208
Sun Briar*, 275
Surgery on thoroughbreds, 216, 319–20
Suzest*, 13
Swale*, 35, 46, 47, 63, 188, 195–96, 215, 333
Swale Stakes, 229–30
Swaps*, 163, 172
Sweat, Eddie, 70, 138–39, 158, 203, 244, 251, 261–62, 270–71, 299–300, 305, 312–13, 320
Swigert, Daniel, 41
Swoon's Son*, 126
Syndication, 42, 43
  of Chief's Crown*, 140–41, 142–45
  of Slew o' Gold*, 143–44

Tajawa*, 258, 311, 318
Take Control*, 194
Tank's Prospect*, 151, 166, 259, 278, 288, 301, 302, 311, 319, 328, 334–35, 336, 353
"Tapped" horses, 32

Tarantara*, 31
Tatham, Tom, 288
Taylor, E. P., 53, 65
Taylor, Elizabeth, 171
Taylor, Karen and Mickey, 45–46
Taylor's Special*, 277
Teasers, 68
Televising of races, 48–49
Tell Stakes, 339–41
Ten Grand*, 253–54
Terlingua*, 66
Terry, Jerry, 209, 210, 212, 227,
    234, 235, 238
Terwick*, 33–34, 35
Tesio, Federico, 40, 59, 66–68
Thalassocrat*, 207
Thomas, Dylan, 249
Thomas, Karen, 135–36
Thoroughbred Retirement
    Foundation, 99, 355
Thoroughbreds
    abuse of, 7–8, 33–36, 277, 316–
        17, 354
    aggressiveness in, 156–57
    Arabian horses, 5, 56–57
    as athletes, 94–95
    beauty of, 249
    blood of, 59
    breathing in, 217
    "class" of, 197–98
    "common" horses, 210–11
    conditioning programs, 157–58
    confidence in, 157
    drugging of, 32, 35, 48, 205,
        294–95, 305, 354
    foundation lines, 58
    gait efficiency, 95
    genetic history, 92–93
    intelligence of, 30, 262–64
    as international currency, 153–
        54
    kamikaze element in, 30–31
    "kind" horses, 29, 211
    lameness in, 26
    legs of, 31–32
    "made" horses, 118

memorials to, 46–47
nervousness of, 29
origin of, 5–6, 57–58
reconditioning of, 119
run instinct, 30–31, 241
social security for, 99, 355
surgery on, 216, 319–20
"tapped" horses, 32
wildness of, 236–38
word, origin of, 58
See also Breeding of
    thoroughbreds
Three Chimneys Farm, 265
Tiffany Ice*, 113, 114, 136, 276,
    332, 334
Time for a Change*, 177, 178
Timely Writer*, 36
Timphony, Vincent, 155, 156, 172
Tippett, Liz Whitney, 347
Todd, Liza, 45, 46
Tournament Star*, 128, 134, 135
Tower, Whitney, 90
Track Barron*, 97, 331, 341, 348–
    49, 351
Traditions in sports, 311
Trainers
    at Belmont Park, 118–19
    conditioning programs, 157–58
    duties of, 23–24, 25–26, 32
    education of, 22–23
    secrecy among, 13–14
Training for Fun and Profit—
    Maybe! (Daingerfield), 22–23
Travers, William R., 76–77
Travers Cup, 338, 342, 343–48
Travers Stakes, 77
Trevathan, Charles E., 60
"Trip" handicapping, 199
Triple Crown, origin of, 307
Triple Crown winners, 6–7
Triple Verdict*, 216, 265
Trovato, Joe, 125–26, 127, 128,
    129, 131, 132
Trudeau, Garry, 213
Trumpeter Swan*, 10
Tuckerman, Bayard, 16, 17

Turkoman*, 259, 346, 351
Tweedy, Penny. *See* Chenery,
    Penny Tweedy
Two a Day*, 104

Umaticca*, 193
Under Orders*, 269, 270
Ussery, Bobby, 293–94

Valenzuela, Pat, 169
Van Berg, Jack, 157
Vanderbilt, Alfred Gwynne, 65,
    123, 162, 330
Vanier, Harvey, 206
Vanlandingham*, 277, 343, 349,
    351
Varola, Franco, 60
Veeck, Bill, 17–18
Veitch, John, 151, 185, 223, 231–
    33, 239, 245, 277–78, 329, 330
Velasquez, Jorge, 230, 244, 245,
    260
Velez, Roger, 221
Verbatim*, 173
Veterinarians, authority of, 354–55
Vice Regent*, 53
Vindaloo*, 114
Vivian, Dave, 208
Vizcaya (Florida estate), 186–87
Volkman, Ron, 155
Von Osten, Wilhelm, 262–63
Vreeland, Diana, 5
Vuillier, Col., 59–60

Wall, Maryjean, 47
Warhol, Andy, 239
Warner, Jack L., 148
Warren, Ronnie, 296
Washington, George, 76, 310
Weekend Delight*, 169
Werblin, Sonny, 51
Westchester Racing Association,
    120
Westland Manor, Fla., 179

Whaley, Ben, 291
Whirlaway*, 21, 40, 61, 66, 172
Whiteley, Frank, 13, 232
Whiting, Lynn, 24–25
Whitney, Cornelius Vanderbilt
    "Sonny," 47, 79, 83–87, 99,
    297
Whitney, Harry, 82–83
Whitney, Marylou, 79–81, 83, 87,
    100, 297
Whitney, William Collins, 80, 81,
    82, 120
Whitney Stakes, 80, 95–98
Whittingham, Charles, 147, 163,
    349
Widener, Joseph, 182–84
Widener, Peter, 183
Wild Again*, 155–56, 172–73, 174
Wildness of horses, 4–5
Wilmot, Mollie, 100
Wilson, Edmund, 284
Wimbledon Star*, 128, 135
Win*, 340
Winfrey, Bill, 110
Winn, Matt J., 274–75
Winning horses, selection of, 154–
    55, 156–57, 174–75
Wising Up*, 295
Wolf (groom), 31
Wolfgang, "Tiffany," 82
Women jockeys, 17
Women stablehands, 224–26
Wood Memorial Stakes, 259–61
Woodward, William, Jr., 42
Woodward Stakes, 138, 348–49
Wright, Warren, 40
Wright, William Monroe, 40

Yoshida, Zenya, 65

Zation*, 10
Ziggy's Boy*, 53, 88, 104, 105,
    140, 332, 334